DERRY DAY BY DAY

Sean McMahon is a native of Derry, where he has lived for most of his life. He has more than fifty titles to his credit as author and editor, most of them in the fields of Irish history, literature and biography. He is the author of *The Bloody North: Infamous Ulster Murder Cases*, *The Belfast Blitz: Luftwaffe Raids on Northern Ireland, 1941*, *A Brief History of Belfast*, *A Brief History of Northern Ireland*, and *'Wee Joe': The Life of Joseph Devlin* (all published by The Brehon Press), and his editorial credits include the highly-praised *Derry Anthology*.

Trevor Temple is a respected researcher and local historian who received his early education at Carlisle Road Primary School and Clondermott Secondary School in Londonderry. He was later a mature student, gaining a BA Honours Degree in Combined Humanities from the University of Ulster in Coleraine. Trevor has contributed many articles to local newspapers, completed a book, *Saint Columba: A Protestant Dilemma Revisited*, and compiled the Diamond War Memorial Project's *Commemorative Diary 2008*. In his spare time, he enjoys music, films, reading and walking.

DERRY DAY BY DAY

SEAN McMAHON
& TREVOR TEMPLE

THE BREHON PRESS
BELFAST

Published by
The Brehon Press Ltd,
19 Glen Crescent
Belfast BT11 8FB
Northern Ireland
www.brehonpress.co.uk

ISBN: 978 1 905474 38 7

For William Temple
With Love and Gratitude

Acknowledgements
We would like to thank the staff of the Central Library, Derry, especially Jane Nicholas for unfailing courtesy and helpfulness.

CONTENTS

JANUARY

1 JANUARY 1883

The D'Oyly Carte Company presented *Patience* by W.S. Gilbert and Arthur Sullivan in the Opera House in Carlisle Road on the first of only two nights, Monday and Tuesday. It was something of a coup for the owner-manager James F. Warden. He had built the theatre six years before and it opened on Friday, 10 August 1877 to general approval though one local minister attacked the Opera House and labelled its clientele as 'thieves, drunkards and profligates'. With his theatrical connections Warden was able to attract such London names as Henry Irving, Ellen Terry, Frank Benson, and the great Sarah Bernhardt, and it truly *was* an opera house with visiting companies presenting *Rigoletto*, *Il Trovatore* and *La Traviata* in season.

When it arrived in Derry, *Patience* was less than two years old, having opened at the Opéra Comique in London on 23 April 1881 and then transferring across the street to the theatre specially built by Richard D'Oyly Carte—real name Richard Doyle McCarthy—in the Strand. The Savoy, which gave its name to the canon, was the first British theatre to be lit by the new electric light. D'Oyly Carte, with typical showmanship, insisted on smashing an electric lamp to prove that no fire would be caused and when the thirty-eight incandescent lamps placed round the dress circle, upper circle and gallery were set in action, the gas was at once extinguished and a blaze of illumination proclaimed 'the light of the future'. As Warden's bill advised, there had been already 750 performances of *Patience* at the Savoy, making it Gilbert and Sullivan's greatest contemporary success.

Patience, unlike most of the other Savoy operas, satirised a contemporary literary movement, aestheticism. Its male chorus of red-coated dragoon guards were matched with a female chorus of 'rapturous maidens', and its two clashing male lead characters were Reginald Bunthorne, a 'fleshly poet', and Archibald Grosvenor, 'an idyllic poet'. The targets of the really genial satire were Oscar Wilde, A.C. Swinburne, John Ruskin, and James Whistler and their cultural struggles. D'Oyly Carte took care that Wilde's lecture tours, which he organised, should precede or come just after Savoy performances of *Patience*. Wilde appeared on the stage of the Derry Opera House exactly one year later, lecturing as ever with tongue-in-cheek on 'art for the sake of art'.

Warden proclaimed that he would charge only sixpence for seats in the pit and four shillings for balcony stalls. A private box 'to hold six' could be had for one pound and four shillings. The *Londonderry Sentinel* on the Tuesday gave twelve column inches to its report: 'Last night a house crowded in every part bespoke the firm hold which this light and pleasing opera still keeps in the popular imagination.' The reviewer was very pleased with Richard Purdom, who was successful as Bunthorne 'in a part that is often overacted'. The sight of the 'fleshly poet' bereft of his Patience with only a lily for company had the right blend of humour and wistfulness.

2 JANUARY 1918

The *Derry Journal* of 2 January 1918 carried on its second page a grim tale with the heavy black headline 'Squalid Derry Tragedy' and two sub-heads, 'Young Married Woman Killed' and 'Husband Charged with Murder'. 'Domestics', as the police call them, are always difficult to handle; they seem to be a contradiction of normality. Yet statistically, it seems that you are more likely to be murdered by a person known to you than a stranger. The *Journal* reporter pulled no punches—'terrible sordidness and brutality', 'shocking details'—and it does seem that the rather heated language was not inappropriate.

The facts were perfectly straightforward. Rebecca Bone had been married for two years to Frank MacNamee when, on the previous Saturday night at about ten o'clock, he stabbed her in the left breast near the heart. The police were soon on the scene; there were many patrols on Saturday nights in Foyle Street, close to 21 Sugarhouse Lane, where the couple lived. It was an area of wretched slums and they lived in a room in a sordid tenement owned by a woman named Doherty. The constables found Mrs MacNamee in an unconscious condition, 'showing signs of having been badly maltreated'. Her blouse was saturated with blood, her hair dishevelled, her clothes torn. She was taken to the hospital in Infirmary Road where Dr Cooke tried to save her life, but because of the nature of the injury his medical skill was unavailing. With the almost total exsanguination she lasted only two hours after admission. The police had taken possession of a pair of scissors with sharp points that they presumed was the murder weapon. MacNamee, arrested by Head Constable Ballintine, had been charged with 'grievous bodily harm', but on his wife's death the charge was changed to murder.

The pair had a reputation for public quarrelling. Early in December the wife had made a complaint of violence against MacNamee at Victoria Barracks, the Royal Irish Constabulary's headquarters in the city, in Waterloo Place. Typically she appeared as a witness on his behalf but he was still fined. She herself was brought before the Petty Sessions Court on a charge of 'loitering' and was given a prison sentence. This time the husband paid for her release. Earlier on the fatal Saturday evening MacNamee had seen his sister and Rebecca in the company of sailors. A challenge from him later led to a verbal row in the street outside the tenement. It broke out again, this time with physical violence, inside the house. There was a kind of free-for-all for the denizens of number 21. As the paper reported: 'Blows were exchanged and when the police arrived the house bore evidence of the desperate encounter.' MacNamee, at thirty-five—five years older than his wife—was revealed to have a shattered leg, the result of wounds sustained in the Second Boer War in South Africa.

3 JANUARY 1900

The first recorded showing of moving pictures to a paying audience was at the Grand Café, Boulevard de Capuchine, in Paris on 20 February 1896. It was then quite an occasion when, less than four years later, Derry had already experienced what the distributors called 'Living Pictures'. On 3 January 1900 a capacity audience in St Columb's Hall enjoyed an entertainment that combined local talent with two sessions of the new moving picture sensation. The event was a charity concert that 'owed its inception to a respected city priest and a number of thoughtful gentlemen, was for the object of a most deserving charity—the District Nurses—and to assist them the better to carry on their good work among the poor of Derry'. Newspaper language was rather more decorous and formal at that time than since.

The city had already a sound musical reputation and a *1798 Cantata* had been written two years earlier by two talented Derrymen to celebrate the centenary of the United Irishmen's rising in Wexford, Carlow, Antrim and elsewhere. Edward Conaghan, the composer, and Thomas Mullan, who wrote the lyrics, produced many patriotic ballads such as 'Tone is Coming Back Again' and 'There are Bonfires on the Hillside' that have persisted till today. These formed part of the entertainment. Incidentally the 'the respected city priest' was the charismatic Fr Willie Doherty, who, as curate and administrator of St Columba's Church, Long Tower, from 1890 until 1917, had rebuilt the church and established an intense devotion to the city's patron saint.

Most attention, however, was focused on the 'exhibition of living pictures'. They came in two sections with a further selection of songs and music in the interval to allow the 'cinematograph' to cool. As the local press reported: 'The views which were of the most varied character—comic, sentimental, historical and military—were splendid beyond praise, in fact the finest obtainable in the market, and drew forth from a delighted audience successive ... rounds of applause.'

It is hard for people of the twenty-first century to appreciate the excitement that moving pictures generated. There had been magic lantern shows from the middle of the nineteenth century, some even in three dimensions, after the invention of photography, but they were static. Now the people actually moved and an incredible new source of entertainment had been found. There were shots from the Cuban War; the launch of the *Oceanic*, the predecessor of the ill-fated White Star liner, the *Titanic*; fire-fighters at work; panoramas from trains in different countries; the marriage procession of the Princess Maud, Queen Victoria's granddaughter, who became Queen of Norway; street scenes from Dublin, London and Belfast—and Venice. A popular sequence showed trains arriving at terminuses, the original cameraman holding the oncoming engine in view until the last minute. The 'lantern' for some of the stills that accompanied the songs was worked by Frank Coghlan, a leading local photographer.

4 JANUARY 1884

On 4 January 1884 Oscar Fingal O'Flahertie Wills Wilde was three months into his thirtieth year and preparing to marry Constance Lloyd. He was famous—or infamous—as the public face of the aesthetic movement, sporting velvet breeches and silk stockings, and giving Gilbert and Sullivan a ripe object of satire for their comic opera, *Patience* (1881). His only source of income was reviewing for the plethora of magazines in that golden age of the periodical, including the scandalous *Yellow Book*, and he would in 1887 accept the editorship of *Women's World*. Now he needed money to begin his married life. Being in debt to the amount of £1,200—£90,100 in today's purchasing power—he found it necessary to try to pay it off and so engaged upon an exhausting lecture tour in the season 1883–4. He was aware that Constance's family allotment would be £5,000 but felt it necessary to demonstrate his own appropriate earning capacity. While in Ireland he received word that Jimmy, the marmoset he had given Constance as a gift, had died, and he did his best to console her by the highly efficient postal system obtaining then.

He gave two talks at the Derry Opera House, one on 'The House Beautiful' and another with the title 'Impressions of America', but did not flaunt his aestheticism in dress. He wore an evening wardrobe of full coat and tails but his tie was 'of curious cut' and from the front of his shirt there sprouted a silk handkerchief in 'Derry crimson'. The white cuffs of his shirt were turned back over the sleeves of his coat. During the delivery of his first lecture he toyed with a pair of white gloves; for the second the gloves were lavender coloured. He spoke without a written text or notes, slowly and deliberately, ever the performer, seeming to take himself very seriously.

This was long before the public popularity of his humorous plays or the disgrace of his trials, though he was well known for his wit in café society. Certainly the Derry audiences found him an object of extreme curiosity. The reporter for the *Londonderry Sentinel*, with exquisite tact, wrote: 'He has a fine figure, not by any means attenuated in form, and his face is slightly florid. His voice, though pleasant, is not what could be called musical and his tone is rather monotonous.' Unlike his erstwhile friend and nemesis, Edward Carson, he had long lost his Dublin accent and, as the son of two nationalists, did not share Carson's politics—in so far as he considered politics worth notice. His earnest style, as noted by the *Sentinel* reporter, was 'relieved here and there by dashes of humour, which are all the more effective from the fact that they appear to be let slip almost unconsciously'. His publicity posters carried earlier reviews: 'His anecdotes are told with abundant humour; his manner is graceful and easy.' The performances in Derry he regarded as very successful, and when he and Constance married on 29 May 1884 he was debt free.

5 JANUARY 1939

Bernard O'Kane, who served as Bishop of Derry from 1926 to 1939, was a man of remarkably varied talents. He was born in Garvagh on 3 January 1867 and died seventy-three years and two days later. He was the first bishop to be educated in the new diocesan junior seminary, St Columb's College, which had opened in November 1879. He had a distinguished career there, gaining a gold medal for taking first place in Ireland in the intermediate examination in 1882, and won a three-year scholarship to the Royal University from which he took his primary degree in 1887. Ordained priest on 18 May 1891 he did a year's post-graduate work at the Dunboyne Establishment at Maynooth and was then appointed to the staff of his old school, becoming its president in 1905.

His years in Bishop Street were taken up with teaching and administration but, though a noted classical scholar, he was also deeply interested in mathematics and science. He was a regular contributor to scientific journals on astronomy, light, radio waves and modern wireless, working in parallel with and sometimes anticipating the discoveries of the great Guglielmo Marconi. These articles came to the attention of the British War Office's own scientists and also of the contemporary equivalent of MI-5. A device invented by him that could select and isolate particulate radio waves was never developed commercially. His skills were not just theoretical; he could strip down and reassemble an automobile engine as quickly as a radio or a clock. While living in Bishop Street his expertise in horology was called upon by the city engineers to improve the workings of the Guildhall clock.

He became parish priest of Maghera in 1923 and was loath to leave it when called to return to Derry as bishop in 1926, where he was consecrated in St Eugene's Cathedral on 21 June. Both as president and bishop, he, like other Catholic leaders, had endless and largely unrewarded struggles with the Unionist administration in the matter of secondary education. On 21 April 1936 the cathedral, at last free of debt, was able solemnly to be consecrated in a service lasting five hours. Two years before, a new city church, St Patrick's, Pennyburn, was dedicated in May 1934. He regarded these two events as the highlights of his episcopacy. He was taken ill late in December 1938 and went to his sister's home in Kilrea, County Derry, where he died on 5 January 1939. When the body was brought home by car for burial in the cathedral the hearse was met by a guard of honour at the city limits, where Altnagelvin Hospital now stands, and was driven through streets so densely crowded that special traffic arrangements had to be made. His remains lie in the cathedral vault.

General Ulysses S[impson] Grant, ex-President of the United States of America, arrived in Derry on 6 January 1879 by the 2 p.m. mail train from Dublin. The train reached the terminus of the Great Northern Railway in Foyle Road at a quarter past two. Mr Graham, the stationmaster, placed two men to guard the various entrances and prevent crushing. A constable and two other policemen were on duty on the platform to keep order. On alighting the platform General Grant was received by Henry Darcus, Mayor, Bartholomew McCorkell, High Sheriff, and Arthur H. Livermore, Consul of the United States for Londonderry. The Mayor, taking his hand, said, 'General Grant, I am glad to see you, and welcome you to the Maiden City.' The general was then introduced to and shook hands with the High Sheriff and the American Consul, after which he passed down the platform on the Mayor's arm.

A great crowd which had assembled in the vicinity of the station greeted the general with cheers. He took his seat in the carriage of the High Sheriff, accompanied by the Mayor and the Sheriff, and drove to the Jury's Hotel, Foyle Street. Immediately on his arrival St Columb's Cathedral's joy bells were rung in honour of the visitor and were heard at intervals during the evening. The flag was hoisted on top of the Corporation Hall in the Diamond alongside the American Stars and Stripes.

Three o'clock was the hour appointed for meeting the general in the Corporation Hall, to present him with an address of welcome and freedom of the city. The address was read by Samuel McCurdy Greer, City Recorder, who began by tendering 'a hearty welcome on your arrival within the walls of our ancient and renowned city'.

In a speech that partly emphasised the links between the city and the United States, Greer continued: 'The citizens of Derry must always feel deeply interested in the well-being and prosperity of the country you represent. The principal foreign commerce of our port is with the United States. Many persons formerly resident amongst us have from time to time emigrated thither and numerous family relationships have been extended across the broad dividing water, making the people of each country one in heart, thought, and affection, and interchanging kindly intercourse one with the other…'

Responding, General Grant said: 'There is that kindly feeling existing between my countrymen and yours which has been spoken of here tonight. You have numerous relations with us, and we all of us have relations on this side of the water, although some of us would, unluckily enough, have to go back five or six generations to find them. But we are related, and the majority of our kindred come from this side of the water… We have a vast country, a productive country, a good climate, and a home for all who find themselves limited on this side of the water... We hope to see more of the people of Derry and Ireland there after a while...'

'The Night of the Big Wind', or *Oiche na Gaoithe Móire*, as it was known to the half of the population of Ireland for whom Irish was their first language, was probably the country's worst hurricane. Nothing of even close ferocity had ever been recorded and it passed from folk memory into legend. When the Old Age Pension Bill was introduced in 1909, because of an almost total lack of personal documentation, a memory of the night was taken as proof that the client was over seventy and thus eligible. The result of that interrogation was that those who had an exact memory of the event exceeded by 30 per cent the total expected by the authorities.

The wind had begun as a light westerly breeze at 9 p.m. on Sunday, 6 January, but it soon reached hurricane force. The weather had been ominous from early that day with a heavy morning snowfall which melted in the sun as the temperature rose to an unseasonal 10°C and caused flash flooding. The sky darkened with jet-black clouds and there was an unnatural stillness that made sound travel unusual distances. In West Donegal the people on shore could hear the crew of the ship *Silesia* talking to each other, though it was quite a distance off at sea. The tempest reached its height at 2 a.m. on the Monday morning, bringing death to both animals and humans on land and at sea. A figure of 219, including thirty-seven at sea, was suggested as the total of human fatalities with thousands of animals, especially sheep, elementally slaughtered, but more recent research suggests that the true figure for human fatality may be as low as ninety-five. Many houses were demolished and thousands lost their roofs, causing financial loss or gain as banknotes, safely anchored in the thatch instead of the mistrusted banks, went flying through the air, the contemporary equivalent to pennies from heaven for those deft enough to catch them.

Most of the destruction was done in Ulster, the west and north midlands, and by 5 a.m. it had gone. Accounts of city damage were given by the *Londonderry Journal*, as it was then called, which carried the story under the headline 'Great Storm' and opined:

So noisy was the elemental strife that it must have banished sleep from every eye.

In the morning there was not a lane or street in the city that did not exhibit proofs of its violence… The Court-House was much damaged, the glass in the windows of the Grand Jury Room having been shattered to pieces, and one of the scales in the hand of the figure of Justice in front of the building carried away.

The *Londonderry Sentinel*'s headline was 'Tremendous Storm' and both papers were relieved that though there were 'some providential escapes' there was no serious personal injury; both lamented the damage to 'Mr George Foster's rope-walk' that 'was blown into the sea'. Lightning, as the *Derry Standard* revealed, set alight the thatch on many of 'the huts of the peasantry'.

8 JANUARY 1934

The Long Tower churchyard, Derry, was the scene of a serious landslide on 8 January 1934, caused by the collapse of the eastern boundary wall. People living in the neighbourhood were startled and terrified by a crash when the wall opposite Stanley's Walk gave way and tons of earth, headstones, and a number of coffins came toppling down to the street with a great noise. Only two people, it was believed, witnessed the landslide, and neither of them was in close proximity at the time, and nobody was injured, though a youth was struck by a flying piece of stone. On going to investigate, the residents of the locality were met with a tragic and gruesome scene. They were shocked at the disaster which had occurred. Strewn amongst and protruding at places were the remains of human bodies, bones of arms and legs, and skulls, as well as bits of rotted coffins and broken headstones.

The wall, which was forty yards long and twenty feet high, was on the eastern side of the graveyard and was built in a semi-circular shape on the steep incline leading to Lecky Road. Practically the whole of this boundary wall cracked and collapsed and a landslide of the cemetery, for a distance of sixty yards, a breadth of twelve feet, and to a depth of about nine or ten feet, followed. The human remains, as far as possible, were gathered together and placed in a box.

A graphic story, typical of the experience of many people in the houses nearby, was given to press representatives by Mrs Maggie McNelis, of Foster's Terrace. She said she was sitting in the kitchen nursing a baby when she heard a terrible crash and noise like thunder, so loud was it. She had a terrifying time with the shock that she received. She rushed out with the child in her arms to witness the catastrophe. One of the eyewitnesses was George Dornan, who said he was coming from his home when he saw a big crack in the wall. Suddenly the wall gave way with a terrific crash, which could be heard over a wide area, and collapsed in a piece. A fragment of flying stone struck James McCloskey, a young man who was standing at a corner ten yards away. Young children were passing to school at the time. Some of them actually saw stones falling on the street and they ran up the church steps out of the way.

The roll was called in the schools and every child was accounted for, while in the houses in the district a check was made of all the residents. Police were later that day satisfied that nobody had been caught by the collapse of the wall, barring the slight chance of a stranger being there at the time. Later also the human remains found at the place were buried in the graveyard near the chapel.

9 JANUARY 1900

On Tuesday, 9 January 1900, Thomas Lindsay, coroner, held an inquest on the body of James Cogley. Cogley's remains had been found in the Foyle, adjacent to the shipyard, that morning. It appeared that the deceased, a young man of about seventeen years of age, who was apprenticed to learn the trade of ship's carpenter, was engaged at his occupation with fellow employees of the Derry Shipbuilding and Engineering Company when he came to his death by falling into the river.

The precise time when the occurrence took place was not clear, but was surmised to be between half past four and six p.m. on the Monday evening. Cogley, it appeared, was intended for a spell of night work, and he was not missed at the shipyard until near midnight when his brother arrived to make inquiries about him. No noise, nor splash in the water, had been heard by any comrade of the apprentice. At about ten o'clock on Tuesday morning the body of the deceased was recovered some distance away from the new vessel, SS *Parkside*, on which he had been working before the fatality took place. It had been commented upon that it was a very sad coincidence that the young man's father and grandfather had likewise met their deaths by drowning.

The inquest was held in the licensed premises of John Doherty, Waterloo Street. Sergeant Dobson and Sergeant Morrow appeared for the constabulary, and P. Maxwell, solicitor, watched the proceedings on behalf of the deceased's next of kin. Francis McGrath, an uncle to the deceased by marriage, identified the body as that of Cogley.

William McAdam, foreman carpenter at the shipyard, stated that the last time he'd seen Cogley alive was at three o'clock on the Monday afternoon when he had been assisting another workman in putting a paint-line on the *Parkdale*. McAdam expected Cogley to work all that night but not at that particular task. At half past five the witness went to look for the young man but could not find him; he guessed he had gone to the shipyard for tools or something. McAdam did not know how the accident had occurred or when.

Cuthbert Carr, a carpenter at the shipyard, said the last time he had seen Cogley alive was at half past four when he had asked him if he had finished his job; Cogley replied that he was going to work at some chains on a scow. Carr did not see him afterwards, and had heard no splash, even though he'd been working on the bridge of the ship till half past nine. Carr had worked with the young fellow for several months and when Cogley's brother came down to the yard looking for James, he was quite astonished for he thought he had gone home.

Dr James Craig said he had externally examined the body which bore no marks of violence. Its appearance led him to believe that death was due to drowning. The jury returned a verdict in accordance with the medical evidence.

10 JANUARY 1938

'The playing of jazz has been prohibited on the Derry Guildhall organ, as it is injurious to the instrument.' That was the decision of the Corporation General Purposes Committee on Monday, 10 January 1938. A report from the City Surveyor, A.S. Hamilton, stated:

> The men who lately cleaned the Guildhall organ informed me that the instrument is not in good order, due to it being insufficiently played. With a view to attracting more players I recommend that the charge for the use of the organ be reduced from 1s 6d to 6d per hour.

The committee adopted the report and decided to order that practices cease at ten o'clock.

The decision of the Corporation caused hilarity in Londonderry's musical circles. Musicians were unanimous and emphatic in their view that playing jazz on an organ, as with any other genre of music, pleasing or unpleasing according to the listener's preferences, could not affect its mechanisms and had not the least harmful effect upon the instrument.

'It is the biggest nonsense I ever heard of,' said J.T. Frankland, the Derry Cathedral organist, when told of the Corporation's decision. 'The whole thing is absurd, and the people across the water will be laughing at our Corporation tomorrow morning for this.' Frankland had been the first to play on the Guildhall organ when it was constructed twenty-three years before. He commented:

> I remember presiding at the Guildhall organ at a Twelfth of July Orange service in the Guildhall in 1914. The organ was officially opened in the January following. It does not matter what music you play on an organ; it will not harm it, so long, of course, as you don't wilfully damage it. Jazz does not appeal to me, but I know I could play jazz on any organ for a week without it having any injurious effects on the instrument. I know there are organs specially built for jazz and light music but you can play jazz on any organ. An organ is for producing sounds and it does not matter what the noise produced is like.

Mr Frankland's comments were given as he sat at his cathedral organ. 'Listen to this,' he continued, producing sounds resembling the rumble of thunder. 'That does not do the least harm. To say jazz music destroys an instrument is ridiculous. What about the organs all over the country on which they play every kind of music? Even thumping on the keys will do no harm.'

Two months later, on 15 March, the *Sentinel* announced that the Guildhall organ controversy had been resolved and that playing jazz on the instrument would resume. In addition, the proposal to reduce the playing charge to sixpence had been abandoned in favour of a levy of one shilling. The Corporation had apparently adopted a recommendation from the organ manufacturers which suggested that certain minor alterations be made to ensure that the instrument would not be 'injured' by jazz playing.

11 JANUARY 1912

Dr Douglas Hyde—the future first President of Ireland—was born in Frenchpark in County Roscommon in 1860. His father was a local Church of Ireland rector. He quickly became fascinated with the Irish language and entered Trinity College where he studied other languages including French, German, Greek, Latin and Hebrew. He was determined to thwart the continuing decline of the native language, however, and in 1893 he was one of the founders of the Gaelic League. It was as its president that he addressed a meeting held under the auspices of the League in St Columb's Hall, Derry, on the night of Thursday, 11 January 1912. Dr Hyde, who was given a very cordial reception, in the course of his speech said they wanted that night to strike a blow for the language that had left the most luminous and most consecutive track of all languages behind it—the language which in vernacular and in literature could be compared to that of ancient Greece alone.

In Derry they had been working for the good principles in a quiet and unobtrusive way. He knew that in this city they had close upon 2,000 children learning Irish in the national schools—and that they had seventeen or eighteen qualified teachers under the National Board engaged in this important branch of education. In short, Derry people were showing the lead to the whole of Ireland. This great national movement for the resurrection of the language of their forefathers during the last ten or fifteen years had swept over Ireland like a flood. It was a movement sacred to the city of Derry; in it provincialism was cut away, sectarianism wiped out. Mother Ireland stood as *their* Mother Ireland, and stood so in their hearts first and last.

Having mentioned that the Irish language was being taught in 3,000 schools and that 7,000 students the previous year—as compared with 473 in the year 1900—had taken up the study in Irish intermediate schools, Dr Hyde emphasised that all had been established at the League's own expense. Further, they had established eight splendid colleges of their own, in which the previous year 1,100 persons began receiving the advantages of university training.

Some said this movement was only a flash in the pan and wouldn't last. But there was no sign of that. It was, rather, becoming stronger every day, and they had the South, the West, the Midlands, and part of Ulster with them. The reason for this was twofold: it had been laid down by educationists that there was no more suitable, more flexible, or more useful language offering training to the mind than the Irish language; and, secondly, a change of feeling was coming over the people. The speaker, continuing, attributed the growth of the movement to an awakened spirit of patriotism. Ireland, in its undeniable right, stood as a nation and they would never consent to see it sink to the rank of a paltry province.

12 JANUARY 1877

On Friday, 12 January 1877, the *Londonderry Standard* reported that the well-known enterprising firm of Messrs. Welch, Margetson and Company had recently completed the erection of a factory in Carlisle Road. The building had cost nearly £8,000 (half a million pounds in today's purchasing power) and rose to a height of sixty feet. Due to its being in the shape of a trapezium, or trapezoid, to fit into the space on which it stood between Carlisle Road and

Horace Street, it stretched along the former about sixty feet, and along the latter 130 feet, whilst facing Ferryquay Gate, or Fountain Street, and its side measured 165 feet in length.

The firm carried on in one portion the manufacture of shirts and ladies' underclothing for foreign markets, whilst in another part Messrs. Alexander Grant & Co., Oat Lane, Wood Street, London, manufactured shirts for the foreign and wholesale trade only. The two firms together gave employment to about 2,000 persons including those who worked in the country as well as others who were engaged in the several departments of the factory itself.

The building was marked off in its divisions to accommodate the two firms, the workers in the employment of Alexander Grant entering by Carlisle Road, whilst the employees of Welch, Margetson occupied the upper half of the building. The new buildings, commented the *Standard*, presented 'very pleasing frontages to both streets'. The imposts, *voussoirs* alternating, with the brickwork in door and window opens, sill-courses, etc, were of Dungiven stone. The base-course main, cornice, and string courses were of white bricks (in the cornices shaped and moulded) which, with the stonework, presented 'a pleasing and well-modulated contrast with the red pressed brickwork in walls'.

The factories were divided centrally by a spacious gateway in Horace Street in which there was one grand lift for both departments. By this entrance goods were received and sent for shipment. On either side of the gateway were the factory entrances. Vestibules in each led to spacious counting rooms, handsomely furnished with varnished pitch pine fittings and well lighted. Off those were the examining rooms with the packing rooms in rear, beneath which were the heating cellars, etc. Wide and easy staircases formed of hard material, partially plated with metal, and enclosed between circular brick walls, plastered in cement, led to the several floors; besides which there were numerous inner stairs on the several flats for the convenience of the workers and management.

Close by the stairways, and conveniently placed, were spacious cloakrooms, WCs and lavatories fitted with the latest improvements. In addition to the cisterns above these apartments there were twelve galvanised iron cisterns capable of storing 7,200 gallons of water placed over the stairways which received the rainwater from the roof as well as the town supply. From these were conveyed to each landing iron-barrel pipes fitted with lever cocks and hose unions for attachments to be employed in case of fire.

George Formby, the entertainer, was born in Wigan, Greater Manchester, on 26 May 1904, the eldest of seven surviving children—four girls and three boys. The son of a music hall star of the same name, he developed an art in venues throughout England that was later transferred to film. In a series of low-budget, slapstick comedies he portrayed a simple Lancashire working lad with an irrepressible grin and ubiquitous ukulele, and popularised songs such as 'Mr Wu' and 'Cleaning Windows'. From *Boots! Boots!* (1934) to *George in Civvy Street* (1946), he was one of Britain's most popular film stars.

His wife and manager, Beryl, died of leukaemia on Christmas Eve 1960, and he followed her to the grave less than three months later after suffering a second heart attack (he suffered his first in 1952). An estimated 100,000 mourners lined the route as his coffin was driven to Warrington Cemetery where he was interred in the family grave.

Formby entertained an estimated three million Allied service men and women during WWII throughout Europe and the Middle East. Although he never performed in the United States, he did make personal appearances and was quite popular in Canada, Australia, New Zealand and South Africa.

Londonderry was included in his Second World War itinerary, and he arrived in the city on 13 January 1942, receiving a warm welcome from sizeable audiences at ENSA entertainments for the services. Accompanied by Beryl, he remained overnight in Derry, and left the following morning to continue his tour of Northern Ireland. Before coming to Londonderry, he took part in a show at Ballykelly.

The Mayor, Senator F.J. Simmons, called on Mr and Mrs Formby at the hall in the city in which the concerts were given and had a brief chat with them. The talk was chiefly about tea, of which, it appeared, George was very fond. The moment he arrived in the city he requested a cup of tea and there were plenty of willing hands to see that his needs were catered for.

'Tea is my beverage,' declared the comedian when a question was put to him on the subject, and Beryl augmented this statement by declaring, 'If anyone wants to get on the right side of George, the best thing is to give him a cup of tea.' Senator Simmons had a request to make, and that was that George should sign a number of autograph books. The comedian and Mrs Formby were happy to comply.

In the evening George gave two shows, and the men and women from the services had some grand fun as a consequence. Prior to his arrival in the Maiden City, George spent almost an hour helping to push his car up a hill on a Derry mountainside. The vehicle, in which he and Mrs Formby were returning after a day of three concerts, had stopped owing to a skidded lorry in front.

On Thursday, 14 January 1954, the *Londonderry Sentinel* told its readership that Jimmy Delaney, who had 'won every soccer honour possible', would arrive in Derry that morning, and the first stage of an all-out effort to revive Derry City Football Club's fortunes would begin when the ex-Scottish International took to the field on Saturday in the Irish League engagement with Ards. Delaney, at thirty-eight, was, like his English counterpart, Stanley Matthews, one of the fittest men playing in top-class football. He was at the peak of his physical condition and adhered faithfully to a rigorous training schedule which had been conceived at the start of his career twenty years before with Glasgow Celtic. Delaney had made it a condition of his agreement with Derry FC that he be allowed to keep to this schedule of three hours' training each morning for five days a week. Every facility at the Brandywell was to be made available to him in this respect.

'Tremendous satisfaction' was felt throughout Londonderry and the North-West, according to the *Sentinel*, when the news came from Glasgow that Delaney, who was a prized member of the Falkirk squad, had signed for Derry City. As had been stated in the previous Tuesday's edition of the newspaper, the negotiations for his transfer were practically completed on Monday, but until he had signed on the dotted line there was always a possibility of a hitch occurring at the last minute to upset plans. His signature was finally obtained by George Sidebottom, one of the club directors, who had flown to Scotland at the weekend to clinch the deal. Credit was due to him for the successful way in which he carried out the transfer negotiations, as well as to J. Allison Borland and Dr D. Sidebottom, directors, and the team management committee for their prompt action in acquiring Delaney once they had learnt of his willingness to sign to an Irish League club. Falkirk directors had informed Sidebottom that Delaney was the fittest and fastest man on their team.

Delaney was already showing keen interest in his new club and had ideas of his own with regard to his particular role as a forward, and team tactics in general. He had found that these had worked very successfully with Falkirk and hoped they would be useful for Derry City.

Delaney had begun his senior football career with Glasgow Celtic in 1934, and afterwards played for Manchester United and Aberdeen. He had eleven International caps and obtained inter-League honours on some twenty occasions. He ranked among the select few who had won English and Scottish Cup medals. Although the *Sentinel* had reported that his arrival would take place on 14 January, the Scotsman did not arrive until the following day. A reception committee greeted him at the UTA Station on the Waterside and there was a large group of interested people who witnessed his arrival; there were many others who waited near the Brandywell in the hope of seeing Delaney visit the ground.

15 JANUARY 1941

At Londonderry Petty Sessions on Wednesday, 15 January 1941, before the Resident Magistrate, Captain P.S. Bell, a certain Michael O'Kane Sr. of 4 Cedar Street was charged with harbouring fifteen ounces of cigarettes and nine and a quarter pounds of chocolate. The defendant's son, Michael O'Kane Jr., was likewise charged with being knowingly concerned in the fraudulent evasion of customs duty on the aforementioned goods. Mr John Young, Crown Solicitor, prosecuted.

Sergeant Boyle gave evidence that, on 13 November 1940, he visited the defendant's grocery shop and inquired if there were any Éire-made chocolates or cigarettes in stock on which duty had not been paid. O'Kane Jr. pointed to some chocolate and said that was all he had brought in. Boyle made a search and found some more chocolate bars and cigarettes in old wrappings, originating from south of the border. The younger O'Kane admitted he had taken the wrappings off the chocolate before leaving Éire. O'Kane Sr. insisted the cigarettes had been bought in the city. The sergeant also found in a drawer a quantity of cigarettes which had been purchased outside of the North. Constable Kane, who accompanied Boyle, also found some cigarettes which were in Éire slides. O'Kane Jr., in a statement, admitted he had gone into Éire on 11 November and brought back a quantity of chocolate valued at 13s 6d wholesale; he had paid no duty on the chocolate. On 12 November he'd gone to Bridgend and brought back three hundred cigarettes, which he did not report to the customs authorities. An officer of Customs and Excise stated that the duty on the cigarettes was 23s and the duty on the chocolate was 3s 2d.

Mr J.G. O'Kane, who defended, said there was an extraordinary demand for chocolates and cigarettes in the city at that present time and, as supplies were difficult to obtain, the defendants had taken the risk of procuring supplies from across the border. The Resident Magistrate subsequently imposed a fine of 25s on each of the defendants.

In a similar case, John and Margaret McClean from William Street were charged with knowingly harbouring 950 cigarettes and two and a half pounds of chocolate. The omnipresent Sergeant Boyle stated he had visited the defendants' shop on 19 November, having previously seen a bar of chocolate from Éire in the window. The sweets in the window were covered with papers, and when Mrs McClean was removing the papers she also removed the bar of 'foreign' chocolate, which Boyle recovered from the paper. The sergeant found a quantity of Éire-made cigarettes in the shop, and upstairs, on examination of a bed, he found more Dublin-made cigarettes concealed among the bedclothes. In the yard at the back of the premises he also found a number of tins which had contained Éire-made cigarettes.

A fine of £2 10s was imposed on John McClean. The case against Mrs McClean was struck out.

16 JANUARY 1936

Fritz Kreisler, the violinist and composer, was born in Vienna in Austria in 1875, and studied at the conservatoires there and in Paris. He made his first tour of America in 1888–9, then returned to Austria and applied for a position in the Vienna Philharmonic Orchestra. He was turned down, and left music to study medicine, then painting. He spent time in the army before returning to the violin in 1899, giving a concert with the Berlin Philharmonic Orchestra.

It was this concert and a series of American tours from 1901 to 1903 that brought him acclaim. In 1910 Kreisler gave the premiere of Edward Elgar's *Violin Concerto*, a work dedicated to him. He served in World War I before being discharged wounded. He spent the remaining years of the war in America and lived in Berlin from 1924. He moved to France in 1938 but thereafter settled in America, becoming a US citizen in 1943. He gave his last public concert in 1947 and broadcast performances for a few years after that. He died in New York City in 1962.

Kreisler gave a two-hour recital before a large audience in the Guildhall on Thursday, 16 January 1936. After opening with Beethoven's *Sonata in G major No. 3* he played from memory. His next group was *Preludio, Loure, Gavotte en Rondeau* from *Partita in E major* (for violin alone) by Bach, and *Poeme* by Chausson. After the interval Kreisler played three of his own compositions, *Recitative and Scherzo* (for violin alone), *Prelude and Allegro* (in the style of Pugnani), and *Chanson Louis XIII and Pavane* (in the style of Louis Couperin), which he followed by *Piece in forme de Habanera* (Ravel), *La Fille aux Cheveux de Lin* (Debussy), and *Three Caprices* (B flat major, B major, and A minor) by Paganini. In response to prolonged applause he played *The Londonderry Air*, *Rondino* (Beethoven-Kreisler), and *Fair Rose Marie*, a Viennese waltz.

Interviewed afterwards by a *Londonderry Sentinel* representative, Kreisler expressed his appreciation of the Assembly Hall, the acoustics of which, he remarked, were fine, although, he thought, the ceiling was a little too high. He had a good opinion of the audience which he described as 'charming'. It was a delight to play before them. Commenting on the effect of radio on music, Kreisler said in addition to throwing thousands of people out of work and spoiling the sale of musical instruments it also had a cheapening tendency.

'The man on the street,' he said, 'does not appreciate what is thrown at him every hour of the day. Of course, it is worse in America, where you have symphony concerts interrupted to say that they are coming by the courtesy of Jones' Motor Company, for instance. In the old days if you wanted music you had to be able to play an instrument, but now just turn a knob. It killed the incentive to learn.'

Kreisler added that he had not seen much of the city on account of the weather, and had spent the afternoon at the pictures where he had watched a Mae West feature.

17 JANUARY 1928

The Opera House was crowded for the opening night of the second visit to Derry of Charles Doran and his Shakespearean Company. He opened with *The Merchant of Venice* in which he was a memorable Shylock, and played the leads on subsequent nights in *Macbeth, Hamlet, Julius Caesar* (as Brutus) and Petruchio in *The Taming of the Shrew*. The houses were good for the Bard but they were *great* for the second week's offering of the stirring melodrama, *The Sign of the Cross*, written in 1890 by the actor-manager Wilson Barrett. He had devised it as a vehicle for his company with the heroic part of Marcus Superbus reserved for himself. As a Roman patrician he goes nobly with the Christian girl he loves to face death from the lions in the Rome of Nero; Barrett made a fortune by continuing to play it for years after. The melodrama's popularity lasted into the Hollywood era. It was filmed as an early Cecil B. de Mille spectacular in 1932 with Fredric March in the star part and Charles Laughton as a memorable Nero.

Marcus Superbus was also a great part for Charles Doran who did not in the least mind the melodramatic aspect of the play. Though over fifty, he still had the voice and the physique, and he knew that *The Sign* would help pay for the staging of the Shakespeare plays he loved so dearly. He had been a member of the famous Frank Benson company and would in turn nurture such talents as Ralph Richardson, who toured Ireland fearlessly with Doran during the War of Independence, and Donald Wolfit, who barnstormed much more bullyingly during and after World War II bringing Shakespeare, Jonson, Ibsen and Massinger to the provinces, even during the Blitz. Like Doran he was the star and once said to one of his company, 'The boomlights placed in the downstage wings are for me and me only. You must find what light you can.'

Doran was much nicer and was popular as an after-dinner speaker. While in Derry he was the lunch guest of the city's Rotary Circle. He admonished them that the artist 'has to hold the beacon high so that it can be seen by all'. He told the *Derry Journal* reporter: 'My memory of my last visit to the Maiden City is ineffaceable, for it is the memory of an intellectual and loveable people of a country I will never forget.' The *Journal* story casually reminded its readers that 'Mr Doran's Shakespearean repertoire includes most of the plays chosen for examination purposes, and students, by arrangement with the management, in groups of twelve or more, can witness the performances at specially reduced rates.'

Doran spent most of the 1930s as a 'Shakespeare Wallah' touring India and playing all of the Bard's parts on radio. He continued with his acting career back in Britain and appeared in the 1950 film *Seven Days to Noon.*

18 JANUARY 1924

On Friday, 18 January 1924, the *Londonderry Sentinel* reported that Sir James Craig, Prime Minister of Northern Ireland, was on the previous day made an honorary freeman of the City of Derry and the ceremony of presentation, which took place in the Guildhall, was witnessed by a 'fashionable and representative gathering of the citizens'. The Prime Minister, who, with Lady Craig and their family, had spent the night at Molenan as the guests of the Mayor—Alderman Maxwell Scott Moore—and Mrs Moore, arrived at the Guildhall shortly after three. The square in front of the building was occupied by a guard of honour of the 'A' Specials under Captain Abraham and these were inspected by Sir James, accompanied by H. Connor, City Commissioner.

A large crowd had thronged the square to witness the Prime Minister's arrival and when he reached the vestibule of the Guildhall he was received by the Mayor who introduced the members of the Corporation, dressed in their robes for the occasion. A procession was then formed, as follows: Sergeants-at-Mace; the City Sword-bearer and the Mace-bearer (William Hamilton and David S. Irvine); the Mayor and the Prime Minister; the Prime Minister's Private Secretary, the Town Clerk (Sir F. Henry Miller), and the City Surveyor (M.A.

Robinson); Sergeants-at-Mace; the members of the Corporation and Corporation officials.

As Sir James entered the hall he was greeted with cheers by the large company of guests, numbering upwards of a thousand. The Mayor occupied the chair, having on his right Lady Craig and on his left Sir James. The members of the Corporation also occupied seats on the platform. 'The Assembly Hall was artistically decorated for the historic occasion,' wrote the *Sentinel*. 'Behind the Mayoral Chair on the platform was an immense Union Jack, surmounted by a shield, with a trophy of flags while the City Flag, bearing the historic arms, also found a conspicuous place over the platform. The south wall was tastefully adorned with flags and garlands of evergreens, gracefully looped so as to give a pretty setting for a variety of shields and trophies of flags. The entire wall space was spanned by a broad crimson band, dotted with coloured bannerettes, surmounted by quite a variety of flags. The windows, front of the platform, and other vacant spaces were filled with evergreens and plants in pots. The front of the gallery was adorned with flags, and there was also a nice display of large Union Jacks and other flags in the background.'

The Mayor having welcomed Sir James to the Maiden City, Sir Henry Miller read the resolution of the Corporation conferring the freedom on the Prime Minister and then administered to him the Oath of Allegiance to the Throne and the Oath of a Freeman of Derry. The ticket of freedom in the muzzle of a solid silver replica of the canon 'Roaring Meg', mounted on oak, was then presented to Sir James amid applause. Having expressed his thanks for the honour, three cheers were given by the assembled company.

19 JANUARY 1927

On 19 January 1927, the *Derry Standard* reported that at the resumed inquest by Dr Thomas MacLaughlin, coroner, and a jury on the bodies of the three Quigley sisters, Sarah Ann (65), Rose (56), and Kate (53), the jury had before them the result of the analysis of the contents of the stomachs and intestines of the deceased and, in accordance with the views expressed by the analyst, a verdict of death from ptomaine poisoning was returned. The inquest was held at the residence of Hugh McCool, Culmore. One of the surviving sisters, Mary Eliza Quigley, who kept house for her uncle, and who was temporarily ill, gave evidence but Maggie Quigley, though reportedly out of danger, was not sufficiently recovered to be called as a witness. District Inspector Cahill conducted the inquest on behalf of the constabulary.

Mary Eliza Quigley was examined and was much affected when giving her evidence. She stated that on Sunday, 26 December 1926, she attended eleven o'clock Mass at Iskaheen Chapel and afterwards proceeded to her sisters at Ballynagard, arriving there about 1.45 p.m. They all had dinner together, consisting of duck, potatoes, and a cup of tea afterwards. For tea they had plain bread and butter, and for supper porridge and sweet milk. On the following morning for breakfast they had loaf bread, butter and tea, and for dinner mincemeat and potatoes was served followed by a cup of tea with loaf bread and butter.

Mary Eliza added that she left Ballynagard between one and two o'clock for her uncle's house at Birdstown. She retired that night about ten o'clock. At around one o'clock in the morning she felt unwell. She was sore about the body, vomited, and suffered from diarrhoea. This illness continued till seven in the morning when she got up but she had to return to bed again. On Friday she got a message that her sisters at Ballynagard were unwell, so she went there in a motor car, arriving at ten o'clock.

The coroner asked if Mary Eliza had sent for medical advice, to which she replied no. He supposed, in the form of a question, that she was not in the condition to do so, to which she also replied no. Dr H.M. Sproulle, medical officer for the district, said he was called to the house of the Quigleys about 4.30 p.m. on 31 December and found three of the sisters—Rose, Sarah Ann and Kate—very ill. Subsequently, in conjunction with Dr J.N. MacLaughlin, he held a post-mortem examination on their bodies.

An extract was read from the report of a Professor Wilson from Belfast on his analysis of the organs submitted to him. From all the organs he 'cultivated' the same micro-organism, a member of the salmonella or food-poisoning group, which he concluded had brought about the deaths of the sisters.

20 JANUARY 1947

John Harrigan, a forty-five-year-old boilerman of Isle Farm, Shantallow, was at Londonderry Petty Sessions on 20 January 1947, returned for trial at the Assizes on charges of breaking and entering the lock-up premises of Patrick Lynch, publican, Butcher Street, and stealing £7 in cash and two bottles of wine valued at £2, as well as breaking and entering the licensed premises of Con O'Doherty, 69 Bishop Street, on 14–15 December 1945, and stealing six dozen bottles of stout and beer with a value of £3. The defendant, an ex-soldier who had been engaged in bomb disposal work in London, was remanded on bail of £30 and two sureties of £15 each.

Patrick Lynch said ten or fifteen minutes after locking up his premises at 10.40 p.m. he returned and on opening the side door it was slammed back in his face. Lynch remained outside the door for ten minutes and heard a crash. He went to the front door and saw it had been opened and that there was a hole in the glass panel. He saw three people running across Butcher Street and another one running up the footpath. Lynch caught up with the man on the footpath—the defendant—who said, 'We'll go back to the shop again.' When Lynch and the accused went inside, Harrigan put some money on the counter and said he knew he was caught out. The money amounted to seven pounds, four shillings and four-and-a-half-pence.

Sergeant Durkan stated that on arriving at the premises, Harrigan declared, 'This is my first attempt and I was caught.' Durkan asked Harrigan about the money, who replied he got it in the office. When cautioned by Detective Constable Robb, the accused said: 'I am making no statement until I see a solicitor. I concealed myself inside the bar. When the chap came and I heard him putting the key in the door I made a race to get out; he pulled the door against me to keep me in and I was pulling to get out. This is how the top lock got broken. I would like to see a solicitor before I go any further.' Harrigan had refused to sign that statement.

Giving evidence on the second charge, Con O'Doherty said when he went to his premises at 1.30 a.m. on 15 December 1945, he found they had been broken into and there were a lot of stout and beer bottles lying about. Detective Constable McPhillips stated that he took possession of bottles and glasses and forwarded them for fingerprints.

Detective Constable Robb said that, when cautioned after arrest, the accused insisted, 'I was never in Con O'Doherty's in my life,' and gave permission for his fingerprints to be taken. Constable George Bradley, of the fingerprint department, said he found the prints on the bottles and the impressions taken by the police to be identical.

21 JANUARY 1950

Charles W. Gordon died at 7 Crawford Square, Derry, on 21 January 1950. A native of Coleraine, he was the son of Thomas Gordon, who came to Londonderry while Charles was still a child. His father founded the firm of Thomas Gordon & Son, The Diamond, and after several years with Alex Finlay

& Co., soap and candle-makers, in Orchard Street, and at their London office, Charles joined his father in business and became the principal of the firm following Thomas's death.

Charles had the distinction of founding the Slate Club movement in Ireland, and the City of Derry Slate Club, which he helped to establish in 1887, flourished for many years. (A Slate Club is a group of people who save money in a common fund for a specific purpose.) Gordon had been always interested in the Band of Hope movement (the name given to societies to promote total abstinence from intoxicating drink among children) and social and temperance propaganda, and carried on the work in the Methodist Church in East Wall.

In the year 1883 he went to London, where he made his first acquaintance with a Slate Club, the members of which met weekly in a public house in a room lent by the proprietor on the understanding that when the money contributed during the year was being distributed—generally in Christmas week—his establishment would benefit by extra trade. On returning to the Maiden City, Gordon conceived the idea of starting a club there and with the assistance of a London friend sowed the seeds of the first Slate Club in Derry. After very hard work they held their inaugural meeting in the People's Hall, then in Bishop Street.

One of the founders in Londonderry of the Society for the Prevention of Cruelty to Animals, Charles Gordon resigned after about a year to establish in 1895 a branch of the Society for the Prevention of Cruelty to Children. He remained as Hon. Secretary for fifty-two years, resigning in 1947. Throughout his life he was a strong temperance advocate, and was a valued member of Londonderry Temperance Council from 1909. When he retired from the chairmanship the Council marked their appreciation of his services by presenting him with a silver salver and sending a handsome donation to the National Society for the Prevention of Cruelty to Children.

One of the most prominent and faithful members of the Methodist Church, Charles Gordon was part of the Londonderry congregation when the Church was in East Wall. From the opening of the church at Carlisle Road in 1903, he continued to play a prominent part in the work of the laity. Filling every lay office in the congregation, he served as representative to the District Synod and to Conference. In 1932 he represented Irish Methodism at the British Conference. Later in the same year he represented the Methodist Church in Ireland at the Conference in the Albert Hall when, after years of negotiation, the three Methodist bodies in Britain were united in one Methodist Church. He was Circuit Steward for many years and frequently filled the pulpit in Carlisle Road Methodist Church.

On Thursday, 22 January 1942, the *Londonderry Sentinel* reported that the prompt action of a soldier had led to the appearance at the local Petty Sessions Court the previous day of a youth named Daniel Logue, stated to be from Carndonagh in County Donegal, on charges of failing to produce a document of identity and trespassing on HM property.

The soldier stated that while he was walking past the property at night he saw someone inside, tight against the wall, apparently not wanting to be seen. He climbed on to the railings, caught hold of the youth, and asked him what he was doing there. The youth, whom the squaddie identified as the defendant, replied that he was playing hide and seek. The soldier also asked him for his identity card, and when Logue replied that he had none, he was handed over by his captor to the police.

The defendant said he had come to the place in search of a man who had promised him a job, but the man did not turn up. He added that he'd arrived in Northern Ireland some time previously to look for work but had so far been unsuccessful in gaining employment. He was at present living with his mother who, in turn, was residing with her sister until she could get a room, as both she and her son had been put out of their house in County Donegal. The mother, who appeared in court, was asked by Captain Bell, RM, how she intended to support herself while in Northern Ireland; she replied that, while she was being supported by her sister at the moment, she hoped to obtain outdoor relief. Captain Bell asked, 'Is that the latest; that people are coming in from Donegal to look for poor law relief at the expense of the ratepayers here? It is very astonishing. Can you not get poor law relief in Donegal?' Logue's mother replied, 'I have no house there. The house was very bad and we were put out for the rent as well.'

Captain Bell, who adjudicated with Major McLean, RM, said he believed the defendant's story about falling in with a man who was to give him a job. However, he added that Logue had one hour to leave Northern Ireland and, if he wished to return, he would have to apply to the Civic Guards in Éire in order that he might re-enter in the proper manner.

In January 1879 a British force sent to deal with King Cetewayo of the Zulus met disaster when 20,000 Zulu warriors overwhelmed the advanced British base at Isandhlwana in southern Africa. The disaster was brought about both by a clever Zulu ruse which drew the British general, Lord Chelmsford, and his main force away from the camp, and by the clumsy positioning of the garrison—a mixed force of soldiers, colonists and native levies—who were scattered over a vast area.

The defenders fought until their ammunition ran out but were then slaughtered. The Zulus took no prisoners. Very few got away and some rode to alert the small garrison of 139 British soldiers left behind at Rorke's Drift, under the command of Lieutenant Chard of the Royal Engineers. These men threw up defences and, when 4,000 of Cetewayo's warriors attacked, poured a hail of bullets into them. They held out for about twelve or thirteen hours until the Zulus retreated at dawn leaving their dead behind. Eleven Victoria Crosses were awarded to the defenders along with a number of other decorations and honours.

The events of Rorke's Drift were superbly recreated in the 1964 Cy Endfield film, *Zulu*, which was followed fifteen years later by a prequel, *Zulu Dawn*, which showed the British command's obstinate and inept handling of the Zulu nation—initially in diplomacy, then in battle at Isandhlwana.

Earlier, both the massacre at Isandhlwana and the subsequent defence at Rorke's Drift were described in a letter written by Derryman, George Babington (dated 3 February 1879), and published in the *Londonderry Sentinel* on Tuesday, 8 April 1879. The following extract details the aftermath of the events at Rorke's Drift:

> …we crossed back into Natal on the morning of January 23rd, at about 7.30 a.m., a smaller and sadder force than left the same place ten days before. When we came to the old mission station, which we had converted into a hospital and commissariat store, where there was a small garrison left to take care of stores and sick, we found they had been attacked the night of the camp affair by a portion of the same force. They had a little time given them to form a kind of rampart, which they did with corn sacks, of which there were plenty, being our horse food, and they made a splendid barricade. These men fought for thirteen hours, with the difference that they lost twelve men and six wounded, and what they killed of blacks they do not know, as they only took the trouble to bury those about the place. Lord Chelmsford went at once to Pietermaritzburg, and has sent for more troops. The other columns have entrenched themselves in Zululand, and can hold out for two or three months, when reinforcements may be expected to arrive, and then I expect and hope there will be an end to the Zulu nation…

On Thursday, 17 January 1946, the *Londonderry Sentinel* reported that Mrs Sybil M. Owens, wife of Captain George Owens, Merchant Navy, 6 Marlborough Avenue, Derry, who had spent over three-and-a-half years in captivity in Hong Kong during the Second World War, was the speaker at a meeting of the Londonderry Soroptimist Club, where she told an interesting story of her experiences in an internment camp.

Mrs Owens was kept in a civilian camp in Stanley, located on the southern end of Hong Kong Island, used by the Japanese imperial forces to hold non-Chinese enemy nationals after their victory in the battle of Hong Kong in the Pacific theatre of war in the east. Almost 3,000 men, women, and children were held at the non-segregated camp for forty-four months, from early January 1942 to August 1945, when Japanese forces finally surrendered. The camp area consisted of St Stephen's College and the grounds of Stanley Prison, excluding the prison itself.

Mrs Owens, who prior to marriage was a nursing sister in the Queen Mary Hospital, Hong Kong, stated that two days after the colony was attacked by the Japanese—on 8 December 1941—and at the request of the local Director of Medical Services, she assumed responsibility for the running of a crèche for children, being assisted by members of the Auxiliary Nursing Staff and the Voluntary Aid Detachment (VAD). The crèche, which was located in the Matilda Hospital, on Mount Kellett, was under the direction of Dr Montgomery, a native of Belfast, and remained in existence until 24 January 1942, when all the children and personnel were removed to the Stanley internment camp.

During the attack on Hong Kong, which surrendered on Christmas Day 1941, the hospital where the crèche was situated and its environs were subjected to severe bombing and experienced many direct hits but, fortunately, there were no fatalities. Talking about life in the camp, Mrs Owens said the internees' greatest hardships were lack of privacy due to the very congested conditions, scarcity of food and monotony of diet, and worst of all, the absence of communication with the outside world.

She paid tribute to the Red Cross, whose supplies only arrived infrequently through no fault of that organisation; however, when they did come they were a marvellous stimulus to the morale of those interned. The administration of the camp changed according to the type of government in power in Japan but conditions were more tolerable under military control than under the civilian or naval regime. Mrs Owens, whose infant son went with her into internment and came safely home again, said the Japanese seemed to be kindly disposed towards children, and they suffered no ill treatment at their hands. Subsequently the speaker answered a number of questions and, after supper, chatted with individual members of the Soroptimist Club to whom she was able, in some instances, to give information about friends who had been interned by the Japanese.

25 JANUARY 1976

Twenty-two-year-old Sergeant Patrick Gerrard Curran died during the Great War from the effects of gas poisoning on 29 April 1916. His remains are interred in Chocques Military Cemetery, Pas de Calais, France, and his name is commemorated on the Diamond War Memorial, Derry. Patrick, who enlisted in Dublin, and two of his brothers, Denis (who rose to become a Company Sergeant Major) and John (who became a Corporal), joined the 8th Battalion Royal Inniskilling Fusiliers, which formed part of the largely Catholic and Nationalist 16th (Irish) Division.

Denis Joseph Curran, who survived the Great War, entered the firm of Hogg and Mitchell Ltd. as an apprentice shirt cutter in 1912, and later went to Bryce and Weston Ltd. on Clarendon Street. He enlisted in July 1915 and was a victim of the first big cloud gas attack at Loos. He was later wounded at the Battle of the Somme, in September 1916, and after having been in hospital in Scotland for a lengthy period he recovered and returned to the Front the following year, this time to the 2nd Inniskillings, which had been merged with the 36th (Ulster) Division. While in this battalion he was shell-gassed on the Belgian coast, and in March 1918, during the last great German advance of the war, he was taken prisoner.

Denis spent the remaining months of the war in a camp near the Danish border. He was repatriated from Denmark and arrived at Leith on Christmas Eve, 1918, being demobbed in Dublin the following year. Back in 'civvy street' he resumed his career in the shirt industry—in Hogg and Mitchell's—and a year later he entered the firm of D.A. Mooney and Co., Foyle Street. He had a very successful career in the firm, and Mooney, who recognised his ability and had the greatest confidence in him, appointed him manager. With Mooney's encouragement and in cooperation with Mooney's son, Arthur, Denis played his part in the expansion of the factory.

It had been Mooney's intention that Denis and Arthur should continue the business after his retirement; unfortunately Arthur died in England, and when Mooney retired, Denis, who had been a partner since 1931, purchased the business. Some years later, Denis bought the shirt factory of S.M. Kennedy and Co. on Magazine Street and made this the centre of the pyjama manufacturing section of his business. He became a Justice of the Peace, and was residing at 'Ash Villa', a distinctive large Swiss-style house on the Duncreggan Road, at the time of his death on Sunday, 25 January 1976.

As well as his participation in the Great War, Denis served as an officer of 21 Platoon, F Company of the 1st Londonderry Battalion, Ulster Home Guard, and second-in-command of the 1st (Cadet) Battalion the Royal Inniskilling Fusiliers during the Second World War.

26 JANUARY 1971

A barricade stretching across the roadway in Aubrey Street, Derry—erected by the residents of the street in protest against the uncompleted demolition of the remains of a factory which was gutted by fire on New Year's Eve, 1970—was still standing on Tuesday, 26 January 1971. A spokesperson for the residents, Nan McFadden, told the *Londonderry Sentinel* on that day that demolition work had stopped over a week previously. Four days earlier workmen arrived to erect an eight-feet-high hoarding on the pavement in front of the factory and they were stopped by the residents. McFadden claimed: 'Once they put up the hoarding it will be the end of the demolition. It'll never be done.'

About fifty jobs were lost in Londonderry following the New Year's Eve fire which destroyed the factory of A. Halliday Ltd.—formerly the box-making factory of George Davin & Sons Ltd. Leather and plastic goods were produced at the factory and, during the previous year, the production of protective clothing such as sou'westers had also commenced. Eight fire appliances—four from Londonderry, two from Strabane, and one each from Limavady and Dungiven—raced to the scene when the alarm was raised at about 6.30 p.m. The fire had started in the stock room in the top floor of the three-storey building which was situated in the cul-de-sac street in the heart of the then thickly populated Fountain area.

Residents of about a dozen houses situated opposite, as well as on the same side of the street, were evacuated by parties of men who assisted about thirty people from their homes. For some of the elderly and invalids who had to be carried to neighbours' houses it was a nerve-wracking experience with the roaring flames from the blazing building only about twenty feet away. The fire was tackled from three sides, including Harding Street, by fifty firemen who got the blaze under control after nearly an hour's strenuous work. The blaze engulfed the whole forty-feet-high, eighty-feet-long building, providing a spectacular sight for hundreds of people as the towering flames roared into the night sky.

A chief concern was the danger of the fire spreading to neighbouring houses and the firemen worked tirelessly, succeeding in preventing this from happening with another laborious struggle. They were hampered by low pressure in the water mains and had to pump additional supplies from Carlisle Square, about 300 yards away. James Harvey, the Divisional Commander, was in charge and directed hoses on the flames from the high turntable ladder and from a ladder against the gable of a house opposite the factory, as well as from street-level jets.

While the firemen were fighting the factory fire, a malicious false call was received and a unit was sent from the Northland Road Station to St Mary's Boys' Club at Creggan Estate. Two genuine fire calls were also received concerning chimney fires in Lawrence Hill, almost across the street from the fire station, and Knockwellan Park in the Waterside.

27 JANUARY 1869

On 27 January 1869 the *Londonderry Journal* carried a report that James F. Warden, the lessee of the Belfast Theatre Royal, had taken the Corporation Hall for 'Eleven first-class Dramatic Performances' including the 'charming Comedietta of *The Lady of Munster; or The Cork Leg*'. Puns like that were common in theatre posters of the time but whatever the quality of the joke, Warden was a showman supreme and the season of plays proved extremely popular with the hitherto rather staid and sober citizens of the Maiden City. He had in Jenny Bellair a delightful and beautiful leading lady, one whom he had the luck and the good sense to marry.

It was a temporary closing of his usual venue for painting that brought Warden to the western city and he was gratified by the reaction to his venture. The *Journal* announcement took up only eight square inches of space but, using 8-point print like most of the rest of the compact paper, he was able to get a fair amount of information in with the words 'ELEVEN' and 'DRAMATIC PERFORMANCES' shrieking in full capitals. The advertisement began with a nod towards the civic authorities whose approbation he needed. Derry had then a strong reputation for public piety and theatres were still regarded by many as the 'Devil's Playhouses'. It was a tribute to Warden's reputation that permission had been given. The Corporation Hall had been hired with the authority of 'the Right Worshipful the Mayor, Thomas H.

Babington MD', and to please other authority, Warden announced that 'on SATURDAY evening the Performance will commence under the distinguished patronage of Major Probart and the officers of the 64th regiment'. The large Ebrington Barracks was home to many military men on circuit and, as Thackeray had found out twenty-seven years previously, their entertainments were considerably less Puritanical than those afforded the townsfolk.

The eleven 'first-class' dramatic performances included several farces including *Hunting the Turtle*, the aforementioned Munster lady, and *Woodcock's Little Game*, but the high points of the week were the several performances of *Richelieu, or The Conspiracy*, written thirty years earlier by Lord Lytton and featuring Warden himself as the clever Machiavellian cardinal. The leading lady's name appeared twice in the advertisement, both times as Mrs J.F. Warden (née Miss Jenny Bellair). He had brought with him specially designed sets by Richard Thorne, the resident scenic artist of the Theatre Royal; these were vital to the popularity of the 'sensation' theatre of the time when there were as many special effects as later graced an episode of *Star Trek*. Warden had also brought the Royal's orchestra to give the provincials a taste of urban sophistication and establish a yearning for a proper local theatre.

He had indicated as much, offering that 'should his exertions to cater for the public be rewarded with liberal patronage, this visit will be but the forerunner to future ones on a more extended scale'. The signals of approval were strong, so he built the Derry Opera House eight years later.

28 JANUARY 1927

A savage gale swept northwest Ulster on Friday, 28 January 1927, causing widespread devastation in Derry, Tyrone and Donegal. Commencing in the early hours of the morning, the storm gradually increased in ferocity until, soon after daylight broke, it had reached hurricane dimensions. Attaining its maximum around noon, it persisted with sporadic short intervals of relative calm until a late hour in the afternoon when it gradually spent its force, although occasionally sudden gusts would sweep along the countryside adding to the harm already wrought in Derry city as well as in many of the towns and villages of Counties Donegal, Tyrone and Londonderry. From all districts came a multitude of similar stories of storm havoc: buildings damaged and in some cases blown down, roofs stripped, chimneys cut in half, windows blown in, trees uprooted, and fences and palings carried away.

Commenting on events three days later the *Derry Standard* reported:

'Occurring in daylight, the effects of the storm were immediately noticeable, and consequently aroused keener anxiety and nervousness than would have been felt had the damage been done during darkness, as was the case on most previous occasions.'

'It was with no inconsiderable risk that citizens ventured forth,' the newspaper continued, 'as slates were falling from the houses in some thoroughfares almost as quickly and regularly as though they were being flung down by workmen engaged in stripping the roofs. Some of these missiles skimmed gracefully through the air before alighting on the streets or footpaths, and not a few ended their flight against the windows or doors on the opposite side. Others descended as though shot from a powerful catapult and buried their sharp edges in the streets or in any woodwork with which they came in contact. A direct hit would have pierced the thickest human skull. In one case a flying slate almost cut off a horse's ear and the poor animal dashed wildly along the street leaving behind a trail of blood. Everyone who could do so wisely took shelter. Falling bricks, chimney-pots, and spoutings, and the crash of glass as window panes were suddenly torn out added to the peril and alarm of those who were outside. Indeed, those fortunate enough to be inside were not without their share of danger, for one never knew the moment the window would be blown in or the chimney-pot come hurtling through the skylights. It was a nerve-wracking experience while it lasted, and there were nearly twelve hours of it.'

Widespread damage was done in Derry city, although happily the storm was not attended by any loss of life. Quite a large number of people, however, were injured and were treated at the City and County Infirmary. Among the buildings damaged was the Opera House in Carlisle Road. The roof covering the stage at the rear was stripped of slates, completely exposing the performance area, with the result that it was utterly impossible for any shows to take place on the Friday and Saturday.

29 JANUARY 1934

The Bishop's Palace, the residence of the Anglican Bishop of Derry and Raphoe, Dr Peacocke, was the scene of an alarming outbreak of fire on the night of 29 January 1934, when one-third of the roof was destroyed by flames. The fire brigade, watched by an enormous crowd, extinguished the fire in a few minutes but had it not been for the vigilance of a police constable on duty at Bishop's Gate and his prompt action the consequences might have been disastrous. The cause of the fire was believed to have been the gradual ignition of a beam in a large chimney and its quick spread to the roof. Following over an hour's work the firemen, having cut away over 120 square feet of the roof, ceased operations but men remained on duty all night.

The outbreak was discovered at exactly ten o'clock when Constable Norman, who was on beat duty, observed a red glow and vapourish smoke on the roof of the wing next to the Gate. He immediately rushed through the stable gate of the palace grounds and over the lawn where his impressions of a fire were confirmed. He went into the palace by the front door and informed the bishop who had just arrived from Belfast by car with his wife. The bishop went out with the constable to the garden and on looking up they saw a slight blaze.

The constable rushed into the palace again and upstairs on to the roof, which he found burning. Seeing that the situation might become very serious, and that single-handed action would be useless, he dashed down again and telephoned the fire brigade a few minutes after ten. Both sections of the brigade were on the scene, under Superintendent Peter Gaylor, in a few moments.

When the brigade arrived the roof was well alight and the firemen ascended to the roof with buckets of water and hand pumps. With the use of the hand hose they got the blaze under control in a comparatively short time. The news of the outbreak spread rapidly over a large area and people, attracted by the dash of the fire engines, came running from all parts; soon a large crowd filled the whole of Bishop Street. A number of police kept the crowd in order while others went to the assistance of the brigade.

Among the early arrivals at the palace were the maids who were off duty at the time and had returned on hearing of the fire. They gave valuable assistance in running with the buckets of water from which the firemen worked their hand hose. After a few minutes' work the blaze was put out and the firemen began cutting away the damaged part of the roof. This was a big task as it was discovered that over one-third of the spacious roof would have to be removed. The slates were stripped from this portion and the rafters sawn off where dangerous.

30 JANUARY 1924

William Buchanan served his business apprenticeship in the pork-curing establishment of W.F. Bigger before helping to found the firm of Buchanan Brothers in Foyle Street, Derry. In a life that spanned sixty-seven years he was also a city magistrate, a member of the Harbour Board, a trustee of the Savings

Bank, a president of the North Ward Unionist Association, and vice-president of the City of Londonderry Unionist Association. In addition, he served as an elder in the First Derry Presbyterian Church and had attended service on the Sunday before his death, on Wednesday, 30 January 1924, after succumbing to an attack of double pneumonia.

In the course of an eloquent tribute to Buchanan in the church a few days later, on Sunday, 3 February, the Reverend Dr McGranahan said:

> Jesus Christ enriches life and enhances death, robbing one of its stain and the other of its sting. This morning, as we recall memories of one who was suddenly called away from the midst of life's activities to learn the great secrets of the Unseen, let us rejoice in the light of revealed love and give thanks to God for a fellowship that makes life fruitful. For many years Mr Buchanan has been associated with the work of this church, and everything that made for its interest met with his hearty support. His cooperation and sympathy and generosity were never wanting in furthering any beneficent schemes that made for the uplifting of men or the relief of distress.
>
> For sixteen years he acted as secretary of the Presbyterian Old Age Fund, and spared no pains to see that First Derry contributed to its support a sum worthy of the church. In nothing, however, did he take a deeper interest than in our praise service. Even when he thought it well that younger people should occupy the choir seats, he was ever ready to render assistance and encourage those who devote their gifts to the ministry of music. Whilst a lover of old tunes and an admirer of venerated ways, yet he was much alive to the necessity of considering modern demands. He was never afraid to declare his views frankly, but he made every allowance for the position of those who had a different outlook.
>
> When this congregation elected him to the eldership he did not accept office without much misgiving and hesitation but once he made the decision he abided by it and proved himself worthy of the trust you committed to him. The House of God was to him a place of renewal. After the worries and cares of a week's business he felt, as he said to me once, that he got something to help him. His seat was never vacant. He had too much consideration for the toil and thought a minister expends in preparation to place himself among those who forget to assemble themselves together.

At the monthly meeting of the Londonderry Port and Harbour Commissioners, held the following Friday, the chairman, Mr A.A. Crockett, also made sympathetic reference to the death of Buchanan.

The objects of the Women's Volunteer Service for Civil Defence (WVS) were explained to a female gathering in Londonderry's Guildhall on Friday, 31 January 1941, where it was made clear that this organisation had achieved remarkable results in the relief work following enemy air activity in Britain. At the conclusion of the meeting all the women present volunteered to enrol for service in whatever duties they might be assigned. Her Grace the Duchess of Abercorn, who became president of the WVS in Northern Ireland, was in attendance. The Minister of Public Security (Major J.C. MacDermott) and Lady Stronge, chairman, were also present, and the chair was taken by Lady Anderson, CBE.

The latter said the value of civil defence could not be over-estimated, and it was worth every minute that one could give to it. Who could say that Derry might not be attacked by the enemy, and so preparations must be made to meet all eventualities; lack of preparation could result in the loss of life being much heavier and the destruction much greater than otherwise. Lady Anderson added: 'I cannot think we are very far down [Hitler's] list for bombing.'

The objects of the WVS were explained by Mrs Huxley, OBE, Chief Regional Administrator, London, who stated that in Great Britain they had started their preparations before the war and members there now numbered 850,000. Their organisation was to the Civil Defence Services what the Auxiliary Territorial Service (ATS) was to the Army and the Women's Royal Naval Service (WRNS) was to the Navy. Volunteers in their services were not paid and they would be required to serve in their own locality. The WVS afforded an opportunity to women, forced to remain at home due to personal ties and unable to enter into national service, which was of vital importance in these dangerous times. Members of the WVS might serve in all branches of the Air Raid Precautions (ARP) services, but in addition they were providing a double function which was absolutely essential. First, they were to set up rest centres for persons made homeless as the result of enemy action; staff would be required at these centres to look after the people brought in. Secondly, they would provide a 'Housewives' Service', organised in all cases under the wardens' service, and built up street by street.

Mrs Huxley, continuing, said the organisation would have to keep a check on the numbers of people in houses and deal with incendiaries. Nothing had contributed more to the general safety of the population than this service. Civil Defence Volunteers would have to be fed while on duty and the WVS would help here with mobile canteens. It would be the women's special contribution to the war effort.

FEBRUARY

1 FEBRUARY 1842

Reverend Professor A. Loughridge of Glenmanus Reformed Presbyterian Church, Portrush, was the special preacher at the centenary services held on Sunday, 13 April 1958, which commemorated the opening of the Reformed Presbyterian Church, Clarendon Street, Londonderry, for public worship on 3 January 1858. Professor Loughridge was welcomed at both morning and evening services by Reverend H. Wright, who had been minister of the congregation for almost twenty years. Speaking before a large gathering in the building, Professor Loughridge said that though at that present day they thought in terms of a century of history, the congregation in Londonderry was considerably older.

From an early date there was a Covenanted witness in this city, said the Professor. Before the Siege, districts surrounding the city were peopled with Presbyterians, many of whom had sworn allegiance to the Scottish Covenants. As had been the case elsewhere in Ulster, the Covenanting Church developed more rapidly in country districts. There were congregations in Bready and at Faughan almost two hundred years before.

The links between Faughan and Londonderry had always been very close, continued the Professor. It was during the ministry of Reverend John Alexander in Faughan (1803–1825) that the congregation was organised in Londonderry. The church was built in 1810 in Fountain Street at a cost of £450. It must have been a rather poor building, he said, for a note in the press on 1 January 1858 stated: 'The Reformed Presbyterian Congregation in this city has hitherto laboured under a great disadvantage in being obliged to meet in a place so uncomfortable and out of the way as they had in Fountain Street.' Reverend Alexander ministered to the joint congregations of Faughan and Londonderry until his death in 1825.

Professor Loughridge said the congregation had no minister until 1831, when Reverend Gordon T. Ewing was appointed stated supply. That appointment, to the 'evident delight' of the Presbytery, was continued on an annual basis for the next nine years. Mr Ewing, a native of Portglenone, was a licentiate of the American Reformed Presbyterian Church. He ministered in Canonsburg Reformed Presbyterian Church for five years before coming to Londonderry. He later served for a year at Grange Reformed Presbyterian Church, near Cookstown. The congregation in 1842 was 'greatly blessed' by the ordination as pastor of Robert Nevin, a licentiate of the Northern Presbytery. He was ordained on 1 February 1842, and ministered with 'great fidelity and power' for fifty-one years until his death in 1893.

During his ministry the congregation decided to provide a more central and accommodating place of worship, and a 'glowing account' of the building of the church and details of the architecture and furnishings appeared in the press of 1 January 1858. The church was opened for public worship two days later. Professor James Dick, of Kellswater, preached at 11 a.m. and Reverend William Toland, from Kilraughts, at 2 p.m. The weather was most inclement and affected the congregation. In the evening, however, the service was held in Great James Street Presbyterian Church.

2 FEBRUARY 1915

Captain Valentine Knox Gilliland, Royal Irish Rifles, was the younger son of George Knox Gilliland, of Brook Hall in Londonderry, and Frances Jane Gilliland. He was killed in action at Ypres on 8 May 1915, aged twenty-five years, and his name is inscribed on St Columb's Cathedral (Church of Ireland) Memorial to the men connected with that cathedral who died during the Great War, and on the famous Menin Gate Memorial in Ypres, Belgium. He is also commemorated on Derry's Diamond War Memorial.

Gilliland, who was educated at Foyle College, was a graduate of Trinity College, Cambridge, where he was a member of the Officers' Training Corps, receiving a commission in the Reserve of Officers on leaving university. In the Ulster Volunteer Force he commanded a company in the 5th Battalion of the Donegal Regiment. At the outbreak of the war he was posted to the 3rd (Reserve)

Battalion Royal Irish Rifles stationed in Dublin, and was one of the first officers to benefit by the War Office order permitting the promotion of second-lieutenants in the Special Reserve to the rank of captain. He proceeded to the Front on 18 January 1915, two days after receiving his captaincy, to join the 1st Battalion of his regiment and was slightly wounded around April of the same year.

A week before Captain Gilliland's death news reached Londonderry of the death of his cousin, Lieutenant W.M.M. Gilliland, 2nd Battalion Royal Inniskilling Fusiliers, who was killed in action at the Dardanelles on 30 April, having been previously wounded at the Battle of Le Cateau in August 1914. On the very day that Val Gilliland's mother received the news of her son's death she also received a letter from him, dated 8 May 1915, in which he mentioned that the battalion was going into action.

A few months prior to his death, Valentine Gilliland had written a couple of letters describing some of his initial experiences at the Front. A letter dated Tuesday, 2 February 1915, read: 'We got back to billets last night about 9.30 p.m. I went up to the trenches on Saturday night. A shell had struck the trench and knocked a good deal of it in, but had done no harm fortunately, so we spent most of the night building it up... They put about eight shells all round us, four of them being those very big shells called Jack Johnstons. One lit behind my dugout and stunned some men.'

Valentine's brother was Captain Frank Gilliland, who later became a President of Londonderry Chamber of Commerce. Around the beginning of November 1916, it was reported in the *Londonderry Sentinel* that Sub-Lieutenant Frank Gilliland, Royal Naval Volunteer Reserve, recently promoted to the rank of lieutenant, had been in command for some time of an armed vessel employed in the auxiliary patrol stationed since the beginning of 1916 in Mediterranean waters. Lieutenant Gilliland had previously held a commission in the 11th Inniskillings.

3 FEBRUARY 1916

On 3 February 1916 the *Londonderry Sentinel* reported that a portrait of David Cairnes, a distinguished citizen of Derry prior and subsequent to the Siege, which had been presented to the Corporation by Henry Cairnes Lawlor of Belfast, had just been received by the Town Clerk. Around the time of the presentation a descendant of Cairnes furnished the *Sentinel* with the following biographical sketch:

David Cairnes, of Knockmaney, county Tyrone, and Londonderry, was the second son of David Cairnes, Lord of the Manors of Killyfaddy and Cecil, near Augher. David Cairnes the younger was born in 1645. He practised in Derry as a barrister, and was elected a burgess in 1680, having a residence and some property in the city. It was not he but his nephew, William Cairnes, who took the leading part in closing the Gates of the city against Lord Antrim's Regiment; but David Cairnes was the first gentleman of position in the surrounding counties to come to the support of the Apprentice Boys in their plucky action. He arrived in the city that afternoon, having hastened there on receipt of a despatch from the Earl of Mount-Alexander, containing a copy of the famous anonymous letter associated with his name. On his arrival he found that the prominent citizens of Derry, under the guidance of the Bishop and the Church clergy, were actually holding a conclave and drawing up a memorial to the Lord Deputy Tyrconnell repudiating the conduct of the Apprentice Boys. He at once called a meeting of the citizens in the Diamond, and explained the seriousness of the situation. His influence had immediate effect, and many notable citizens, who had at first sided with the Bishop, endorsed his views. The meeting was adjourned to the following morning. Meantime Cairnes caused an inventory of the city's arms and ammunition and provisions to be made. These proved to be hopelessly scanty, and at the adjourned meeting next morning, attended by practically all the prominent citizens, who had until the arrival of Cairnes sided with the Bishop, a memorial was drawn up praying for aid from William of Orange and the English Government. The Bishop fled to England. The meeting requested Cairnes to convey their petition in person to King William, and he proceeded that evening in his own ship and at his own expense to convey the message of Derry to the King. It was in response to his representations that the relief ships were sent. It is not known exactly when Cairnes got back to Derry, but there is no doubt that but for his timely arrival in the city after the Shutting of the Gates this brave action of the Apprentice Boys would have been overridden by the Jacobite leaders of affairs in the city.

After the Relief, Cairnes sent a herd of cattle from Knockmaney as a gift to the starving population. He was sent to Parliament as a member for the city, and represented it for several years. In his dual capacity as a member for the city and agent for the Irish Society he was mainly responsible for the financial aid, scanty as it was, granted for the relief of the citizens in their sufferings from the effects of the Siege. On retiring from Parliament he became Recorder of the city, dying in the year 1722.

4 FEBRUARY 1916

Private William Coulson, Royal Inniskilling Fusiliers, died on 4 February 1916 of exhaustion through inability to take nourishment, as the result of swallowing poison while under the influence of deep depression caused by the disappearance of his wife. The tragic circumstances of his death were the subject of a coroner's investigation in the Derry Infirmary on 8 February.

William Miskimmin, Coleraine, stated that Coulson, who was his brother-in-law, enlisted in Coleraine the previous November. His wife had been in delicate health for a considerable time. Coulson was stationed in Derry until 6 December 1915, on which date he returned to Coleraine as a result of a message he received from Miskimmin that his wife had gone missing the previous day. He remained with Miskimmin for two days, and made inquiries into his wife's disappearance but had been unsuccessful when his leave expired. The military authorities refused an extension of leave. Coulson seemed a bit disheartened at that but otherwise he appeared to be all right. That evening Miskimmin heard that Coulson had taken ammonia. He went on to state that Coulson's wife had not turned up yet, and he was in a very depressed state when she disappeared.

Sergeant Henry Holmes, Coleraine, gave evidence of Coulson being charged with attempted suicide and appearing before the Recorder, who directed him to be sent back to the hospital until the doctor could certify that he was fit to travel. Coulson was evidently very sorry that he took the poison because he immediately ran to a woman next door to tell her what he had done. Evidence was given by Lance Corporal Harrison as to the removal of Coulson from the workhouse infirmary in Coleraine to Derry. He was very weak during the journey and had to be assisted into a car.

Dr Cooke, house surgeon in Derry Infirmary, said when Coulson was admitted on 24 January, he was in a very weak condition and badly emaciated. He was at that time unable to swallow more than a few drops of liquid, and after consultation he was considered too weak to undergo an operation. He was then treated by rectal feeding until 29 January, when an operation was performed and an opening made in the stomach, through which food was passed. He improved for a few days, but began to decline on 3 February, and died the following day. The jury returned a verdict of death from exhaustion consequent upon a stricture of the throat which prevented Coulson from taking nourishment.

A juror remarked that it was astonishing the military had moved Coulson when he was in such a weak condition, but the Coroner said the operation had been indispensable and the only question was could Coulson have been brought to the infirmary sooner? Nevertheless he believed that everything possible had been done for the unfortunate man.

Lieutenant James Hamilton Barr, Royal Irish Rifles, was born on 5 February 1897 and died at the Belgian village of Neuve Eglise, situated three miles southwest of Messines, on Sunday, 1 September 1918. He was the son of William and Henrietta (nèe Hamilton) Barr, who resided at 9 Aubrey Street, Londonderry, and his remains are interred in Wulverghem-Lindenhoek Road Military Cemetery, Heuvelland, West Vlaanderen, Belgium.

At the end of August 1916, it was reported in the Londonderry press that Cadet James Hamilton Barr had been given a commission in the Royal Irish Rifles. Less than twelve months before, at an examination held in connection with Queen's University, Belfast, for twelve entrance scholarships, he secured second place. He had a distinguished career at Foyle College, gaining medals in intermediate Latin and Greek in 1913, and exhibitions in junior, middle, and senior grades. On leaving Foyle, he won an Irish Society scholarship of £120. The Governors of Foyle and the Academic Council of Queen's reserved the scholarships until Lieutenant Barr was released from military service.

On joining the colours in October 1915, he was attached to the 18th Royal Irish Rifles as a cadet at Clandeboye, where he was stationed for three months. He then went to the Curragh, where he remained for five months. On receiving his commission he was again transferred to Clandeboye. At the annual distribution of prizes in Foyle College, held on Thursday, 19 December 1918, the headmaster, Mr R.F. Dill paid the following glowing tribute to James:

> Most of those who are here present do not need to be told that James Barr was one of the most brilliant pupils who passed through this school in recent years. It would be impossible to give in detail all his achievements. Suffice it to say that in one memorable year, 1913, he carried off the medal for both Latin and Greek. He became editor of the school magazine in 1914, and brought it up to a high standard of merit. He left us carrying with him the Irish Society's Leaving Scholarship to Belfast University, where he gained a scholarship at entrance. Immediately afterwards he volunteered for the army, and in due course gained his commission in the Royal Irish Rifles. When he entered the army he had only drawn one year of the Irish Society's Scholarship, and it was suggested by his mother, Mrs William Barr, that the Irish Society should be petitioned to allow the amount of the three outstanding instalments, a sum of £90, to be devoted to the founding of a memorial prize in classics. The Irish Society has graciously assented to this proposal. Our gratitude should go out not only to the Irish Society for their great generosity but also to Mrs Barr for making a suggestion which, if I knew James Barr, might have come straight from the true and loyal heart of her son.

Derry's first bridge was a wooden structure begun in 1789 by Lemuel Cox, of Cox and Thompson, Boston; by the following year it was ready for foot passengers. In the spring of 1791 it was opened for the 'vehicles' of those days. Detailing the construction of the bridge an authority later wrote:

> The piles are made of oak, and the head of each pile is tenoned to a cap piece, seventeen inches square, and forty feet long, supported by three sets of girths and braces. The piers, which are sixteen and a half feet asunder, are bound together by thirteen string pieces, equally divided, transversely bolted, and on the string pieces is laid the flooring. On each side of the platform there is a railing four and a half feet high, and a broad footway, provided with gas lamps. At one quarter of the length of the Bridge, measured towards its western extremity, a turning bridge has been constructed in place of the original drawbridge: some contrivance of this kind is necessary, and the inhabitants of Strabane having a right to the free navigation of the Foyle. There is a toll house at the end next to the city.
>
> The city and its reservoir being at opposite sides of the river, the water has to be conveyed across the Bridge. As both the water and gas pipes pass along the Bridge, it is necessary that they should be separated whenever it is opened for the passage of barges. This is effected in the water-pipes by compass joints at the side of the draw opening, round which turn two movable pieces of the pipe, being drawn up by a wheel and pinion, acting on a chain. Stop-cocks, at each side, cut off the communication of the water during the operation, and the pipes, when lowered, meeting with a ball and socket-joint, &c., must form an oblique angle, the vertex being upwards.
>
> In the gas pipes, the separation is effected by a movable piece bent at right angles at each end, and thus capping, as it were, the ends of the stationary pipes, also bent at right angles in an opposite direction, being made airtight by a simple lute.

On 6 February 1814 part of the bridge was torn away by masses of ice.

Before the Corporation disposed of their interest in the bridge they contemplated the creation of a new one. Plans and estimates were obtained, and soundings of the river taken. But years elapsed until real steps were taken to replace the Wooden Bridge. It was not until 1859 that things began moving, but then another problem arose when the railway companies refused to contribute towards the cost, although the structure was to incorporate special facilities for them.

The Bridge Commissioners obtained power to borrow £90,000, of which £60,000 was for the actual bridge and £20,000 for the approaches and abutments. To celebrate the opening of the Bridge on 25 September 1863 by Lord Carlisle, who was then Viceroy of Ireland, the Bridge Commissioners permitted both bridges to be used free of tolls for the remainder of the day.

On 7 February 1936, Paul Robeson, the world-famous black singer, who was to sing in Londonderry the following night, arrived in the city from Belfast, making the City Hotel his headquarters. It was his first time in Derry, and in the course of an interview with the *Londonderry Sentinel*, he displayed an intense interest in the folk songs of the world, which, he said, all seemed to have something in common.

'In fact,' he remarked, 'it has almost appeared at times, so striking is the resemblance, that those of one country have been copied from another country. These are the real folk songs of the people. People of my race in America still retain these songs, which were such a source of comfort to their ancestors in the days of slavery. They have their origin in Africa. The Negroes who live close to nature still sing them.'

The son of an escaped slave who later became a Presbyterian minister, Robeson was a graduate from law school. 'Every Negro has to start at the bottom. There is nothing else for it there,' he said. 'I am trying to impart the dignity of the Negro spiritual which it deserves. I have been criticised for not singing a Brahms or Schubert group... I could do it, but why should I? Thousands of other Negroes could do it but the fellow countrymen of those composers could do it better. We have our own beautiful folk songs. They are fine, and I am proud to sing them as my programme, and not as an apology at the end. If they want to hear me they will have to listen to these.' He explained that Negro spirituals were not essentially sad. Two-thirds of them were humorous.

Robeson sang to the people of Derry on the Saturday evening, 8 February. At least 1,000 people gathered to hear him and they were warm in their applause. Reporting on the event, the *Sentinel* wrote: 'By general agreement it seemed that one of the singer's most appealing numbers was the favourite "Ol' Man River" from *Showboat*. Although it was not a Negro spiritual it revealed to the fullest extent the richness of his voice. In his reading of William Blake's poem, "The Black Boy", he showed that his speaking voice has the same breadth, musical sweetness, and the same simplicity and sincerity that make his singing so attractive. This thought-provoking little poem was beautifully spoken—a delightful interlude. In "Poor Old Joe" and "My Old Kentucky Home" the emotional appeal of his artistry was demonstrated. "Swing Low Sweet Chariot", "Ezekiel Saw de Wheel", and "Water Boy", authentic Negro spirituals, saw the artist at his finest as he sang the songs of his own people.'

Residents of Culmore Road were surprised and delighted on that Saturday morning to see this man of culture, talent and magnificent physique jogging along behind an old Austin Saloon—a normal routine of the singer's before a concert.

The eldest son of a coachbuilder, James McElmunn Wilton was born in Derry in 1870, and after receiving his early education at the Londonderry Academical Institution (amalgamated with Foyle College in 1896), he went to Magee University College in the city and Queen's University, Belfast, before subsequently serving in the legal firm of Patrick Maxwell. During the Third Home Rule crisis in 1912 Wilton became prominently identified with Unionism and was secretary of the Londonderry Ulster Volunteer Force. At the outbreak of the Great War, he organised the Londonderry section of the 10th Royal Inniskilling Fusiliers, 'The Derrys', and served in France under Colonel Ross-Smythe, who recommended him for a commission. He was severely wounded at the Battle of the Somme in July 1916, but was promoted to captain and awarded the Military Cross for conspicuous gallantry on that occasion. On his return to France after convalescence he was again wounded, at Cambrai in November 1917, and mentioned in dispatches.

Returning to civil life, Wilton devoted most of his activities to the welfare of ex-servicemen, serving four years as secretary of the Londonderry War Pensions Committee. Later he was appointed chairman of the Northern Ireland War Pensions Committee, a position he held until his death. For several years he was president of the Londonderry branch of the British Legion and oversaw the civic Armistice Day Commemoration Ceremony. He was also president of the Inniskilling Old Comrades Association.

Throughout his life Wilton was a dedicated Unionist, and in 1923 entered municipal politics as a councillor for the North Ward. Three years later, following a by-election, he succeeded Sir John McFarland as an alderman for the same ward. He was Mayor of Derry between 1935 and '39, and was also an Ulster Unionist Ex-Officio Senator at Stormont at this time. In 1937 he was knighted by King George VI.

Wilton was also Chairman of the Londonderry Education Committee; President of the Council of Education Authorities of Northern Ireland; Chairman of the Finance Committee of Londonderry Corporation; Chairman of the Transport Committee; and one of the Corporation's representatives on the Council of Municipal Authorities of Northern Ireland. In addition, he was Life Governor of the Londonderry City and County Hospital, having formerly been a member of both its Committee of Management and the Committee of Management of the Londonderry Mental Hospital. During the Second World War he was Chairman of the Londonderry City and County War Savings Committee.

Wilton was Lieutenant Governor of the Apprentice Boys of Derry for many years and President of the Apprentice Boys of Derry Club. He also belonged to Foyle Loyal Orange Lodge, 1495, and St John's Masonic Lodge, 196.

He had received nine football caps for Ireland between 1888 and 1893, and was later President of the Irish Football Association. He was also a rugby enthusiast, having captained the City of Derry XV, and was Vice President of the North West Cricket Union.

He died at his home on 8 February 1946.

9 FEBRUARY 1977

On Wednesday, 9 February 1977, the *Londonderry Sentinel* published the memories of Fountain Street resident, George Wray, whose career in the fire service had lasted nearly thirty-two years, beginning in April 1938. George had spent eight years as a butcher before joining the Londonderry Corporation's Fire Brigade, which was then stationed in Hawkin Street. At that time there were very few full-time firemen and they all lived at home. 'We each had bells in our houses,' George explained. 'We operated on a twenty four hour basis.'

The first 'really good' fire in which George was involved was at Lough Eske Castle, a hotel about three miles from Donegal town. Although the fire brigade was expected to cover only the Londonderry area, and a guarantee of payment had to be provided before the men could be called to fires outside the city boundary, George explained that they were frequently expected to travel to County Donegal. 'There was no fire brigade, as such, in Donegal, although they had the odd fire hose. The Corporation was paid a yearly retaining fee to ensure that the firemen could be called immediately if there was a fire anywhere in Donegal. As a result we did a lot of fires over the border,' he recalled. Another blaze in those early years which left an indelible mark on George's memory was the burning of the old Opera House in Carlisle Road which razed the building to the ground.

When the Hawkin Street Fire Station was in operation, there were only fourteen full-timers and eighteen retained men, who also had other jobs, in the whole of the city. The outbreak of the Second World War and the expansion of industry soon meant that a much larger force was needed; in a short time the service was increased to 300 full-time men and 100 women. During the war years George moved to the Waterside and was stationed in a building known as Desmond's Factory on Prehen Road, adjacent to the former County Donegal Railway Station. The National Fire Service was introduced in 1942, and soon afterwards provision was made for the men to sleep at the station.

Further changes followed at the end of the war and the Northern Ireland Fire Authority was created. It divided the province into four areas. The Londonderry Headquarters covered Enniskillen, Dungiven and Limavady and each town in that area had a station with part-time officers. Full-time officers were needed to run the new system and George was appointed Training Officer for Strabane, Castlederg, Limavady and Dungiven, a post he held for ten years. George looked back on his years as a fire-fighter with a great deal of pride and pleasure: 'They were thirty-one years I'd start again tomorrow,' he said. 'I enjoyed every minute.'

10 FEBRUARY 1173

The Annals of the Four Masters record the events of Irish history from the earliest times up to the year 1616. Conscious of the great changes in Irish life that would inevitably follow from the Tudor and Stuart conquests, a Franciscan brother and three lay scholars decided to write down from contemporary sources the story of their country. They were Mícheál Ó Cléirigh, his cousin Cúchoigríche Ó Cléirigh, Fearfeasa Ó Maoilchonaire, and Cúchoigríche Ó Duibhgeannain. They worked at the friary of Bundrowse on the Donegal/Leitrim border under the protection of Fearghal Ó Gadhra of Coolavin, County Sligo. These were the 'four masters' of the popular title but because of the wearisome work of inscribing, extra help was sought from Conaire, Mícheál's brother, and Muiris, the brother of Fearfeasa Ó Maoilchonaire.

Their purpose was to demonstrate that Ireland, far from being the barbarous country portrayed by the English, had a noble and cultured past. The first complete translation into English was by John O'Donovan between 1848 and 1851, but the following account, concerning February 1173, is from a translation by Owen Connellan in 1846:

> Murragh Ó Cobhthadh [Coffey], Bishop of Derry and Raphoe, died. He was a man of pure chastity, a precious stone, a transparent gem, a brilliant star, a treasury of wisdom and chief conservator of the canons of the church, after bestowing food and raiment on the poor and needy, ordaining priests, deacons and clergymen of every degree, repairing and consecrating many ecclesiastical establishments and cemeteries, building many monasteries, performing every clerical duty and gaining the victory of devotion, pilgrimage and penance, his spirit departed to heaven in the Black Church of Columcille at Derry on the 10th day of February.

O'Coffey, a canon regular of the Augustinian Order, was born in Maghera,

County Derry, once the expected episcopal centre for the diocese. His burial was at *Dubhregles*, the 'Black Church of Columcille' mentioned in the passage, and situated just inside the west wall where the present-day St Augustine's Parish Church is built. As befitted such a paragon, who had ordained seventy priests and was held in great regard for his learning, his passing could not take place without a portent as an example to his flock. The *Annals* further record:

> A great miracle was performed on the night of his death... the dark night became bright from dusk till morning and it appeared to the inhabitants that the adjacent parts of the globe were illuminated, a large body of fire moved over the town and remained in the southeast; all the people rose from their beds, for they thought it was day; and it [the light] continued to eastward along the sea.

11 FEBRUARY 1974

The appointment of the Reverend Edward Daly, former curate of St Eugene's Cathedral, to be Catholic Bishop of Derry in succession to Most Reverend Dr Neil Farren, who retired the previous year, was announced in Rome on 11 February 1974. The new bishop, a native of Belleek, County Fermanagh, had become world famous as a consequence of his actions in January 1972 when thirteen young men were shot dead by the army in the Bogside. Daly had been filmed waving a white handkerchief as he, alongside other priests, was helping wounded from the scene. He went to the United States just afterwards on a mission, sponsored by the Irish Government, to explain the situation in Northern Ireland.

Educated at St Columb's College, Derry, he was ordained on 16 March 1957, and served in Castlederg, before going to St Eugene's in 1961. He was diocesan representative on the National Communications Council, and was Chairman of the Irish Delegation to the European Council of Priests. In July 1973, he was appointed Religious Adviser to Radio Telefis Éireann, a post that necessitated his taking up residence in Dublin. In a statement after the announcement from Rome, the new bishop said:

> I am still a little shaken and overawed by the appointment. I am very well aware of the responsibilities of the task that has been entrusted to me. However, I will endeavour to serve the people and priests of the diocese to the best of my ability. I look forward very much to returning to Derry. There is a great body of priests in the diocese and the people have always held a very special place in my affection. It will be a great privilege to serve them as Bishop. I hope and pray that, with

God's help, I can fulfil the trust that has been placed on me by the Holy Father. I look on this appointment, not as a personal honour, but a recognition of the work that has been done by priests in the troubled areas in the North over the last few years. They have shown a great dedication and commitment, and a great love of their people and loyalty to the Christian message. I hope that I can help them and encourage them to continue this work.

In a tribute to Dr Farren, his predecessor, Bishop Daly said:

He has served the Derry diocese as Bishop for almost thirty-five years and has had a most difficult episcopate, starting with the outbreak of war in 1939, and the problems that created, particularly in Derry City. In the 1950s and 1960s— even up until today—he has undertaken a massive programme of school and church building and, at a time when he should have been able to relax, the present troubles broke out five years ago.

At the end of my term of office I hope I can look back with the knowledge that I have served my people and my Church as well as he did.

12 FEBRUARY 1937

At Dungiven Petty Sessions, on Friday, 12 February 1937, before Captain P.S. Bell, RM, George Ferris Beedham from Great James Street, Londonderry, was summoned for driving a motor car without due care and attention. Mr E.G.C. Browne appeared for the defendant and District Inspector Wolsey prosecuted.

Evidence was given by George Stewart that on 2 January about 1 p.m. he was driving along the Maghera–Dungiven Road towards Dungiven on his proper side of the road, when without warning he was struck by another car and knocked into a ditch. The other car passed on and stopped about one hundred yards further on. Four people got out of the car, and one of them told Stewart he should be more careful. The driver of the car told Stewart that he'd turned on his lights to warn him but Stewart did not see them. Another man in the car said a gust of wind must have blown Stewart's car back into the path of Beedham's vehicle. Stewart denied that he had swerved into the left-hand side of the road or that he was swept back to the road by a gust of wind.

Beedham stated that he was driving his father from Magherafelt to Londonderry. The accident occurred on a straight part of the road, and the other car, a Morris Minor, was in front. Before attempting to pass the other car Beedham sounded his horn and when that had no effect he switched on his headlights and saw the reflection clearly in the mirror of the other car, which swerved to the left. A high wind was blowing at the time. Beedham drew out to pass the Morris Minor and, as he came close to it, it car came out again and it was impossible for Beedham to avoid an accident. The front mudguard of Beedham's car struck the rear mudguard of the Morris Minor, and Beedham went in front, stopped, and then came back. The driver of the other car seemed to be excited and asked Beedham what was wrong.

Captain Bell asked Beedham why he had switched on his lights in the daytime, to which Beedham replied, 'It was so stormy that I thought the driver might not hear the horn.' Captain Bell said a map produced by Sergeant Carson, the officer at the scene, seemed to establish that the Morris Minor car was not where it should have been and the case would have to be dismissed.

13 FEBRUARY 1854

When Francis Kelly became Bishop of Derry in 1849 he was faced with many difficulties. The Famine years had brought refugees from Donegal and poverty was widespread. He turned for help to the Irish Christian Brothers, which had been formalised in 1808 by Edmund Ignatius Rice, inviting Brother Francis Larkin to set up a community of brothers in Derry so that they might establish a school 'for the poorest of the poor' for whom the existing 'pay-schools' were unaffordable.

Larkin had been trained in Waterford by Rice himself and was the ideal man for the Derry enterprise. He and a fellow brother arrived in the city after a bitterly cold twenty-four-hour coach journey from Thurles via Dublin on Monday, 13 February 1854. They were greeted by Bishop Kelly who showed them their new home, the diocesan house known as 'The Brow o' the Hill', which had been built by an alderman, Hogg, the owner of the quarry at the south-western end of the 'Bog'; his efforts, at great expense, to reclaim part of the quarry to build his new home on had caused the local wits to name it 'Hogg's Folly'. Hogg responded with equal wit by bestowing the same name on the blocks of terrace houses he built for his workers. The house had been bought by the diocese in 1846 as the bishop's residence and as the site of a long-overdue junior boys' seminary, but the school failed due to the Famine and the death of Kelly's predecessor, Edward Maginn, of typhus.

The Brothers opened their school on 13 March, exactly four weeks after their arrival. They had hoped for a small number of pupils to begin with and to slowly increase their intake but 290 boys presented themselves on that first day. Such eagerness was gratifying but the Brothers were swamped; while Larkin managed the hundred oldest pupils on the second floor, another hundred were shepherded into the ground floor, while the ninety youngest were supervised in the basement by some of the more responsible seniors until a third Brother arrived from Thurles a fortnight later.

In spite of a building not fit for purpose and a teacher–pupil ratio that would alarm today's HM Inspectorate, the school was a success. The Brothers lived lives of monastic asperity, becoming famous around town for their 'green coats', as they could not afford to replace their original garments, but the changes they brought among 'the poorest of the poor' were miraculous.

Larkin moved to Australia in 1860 where he founded two communities and schools, both of which are still flourishing. He died there in 1889.

14 FEBRUARY 1928

On Tuesday, 14 February 1928, the *Londonderry Sentinel* reported that Major-General Sir W.B. Hickie had, on Sunday night, addressed a meeting of men of the 10th, 16th, and 29th Divisions in the Ancient Order of Hibernians Hall, Strand Road, in connection with the newly-formed 16th Irish Division ex-Servicemen's Association. There was a large attendance.

Captain J. McManus, chairman of the Belfast branch, said he was glad to have the pleasure of meeting his old Derry comrades, who formed a not inconsiderable percentage of the 16th Division which had forged such a great reputation for itself under General Hickie's able leadership. Captain McManus went on to state the aims of the association, which, he said, had been started by Lieutenant Burns in Belfast. It was formed for three reasons: to help those comrades who needed assistance in getting work or pensions; to foster and keep alive the companionship formed during the war; and to encourage social intercourse among the men and their families. General Hickie had very willingly agreed to become president.

Lieutenant Burns stated that, in General Hickie, they had, so far as Ireland was concerned, another Earl Haig. This was not a land fit for heroes to live in; but only heroes could live in it. Hickie, at whose request the audience stood for a moment in memory of Earl Haig, said he had been all along the line in France lately, from the Somme to the Seine, and had found the names of all the divisions had been forgotten with the exception of the 16th Irish. Why should this be? Because, he said, the men of that division were gallant, religious, and God-fearing. Conditions in the South of Ireland as regards the ex-servicemen had been very much improved of late, but he was utterly shocked to see in the North cases of men who had served being neglected and forgotten.

Hickie intended to get in touch immediately with London, as he thought the condition of some of the men in Derry and Belfast was a disgrace, and would request that representatives from the British Legion come over to witness the plight of ex-servicemen in the hope that more could be done to help them. In the meantime, it was the duty of everyone to join the Association so that, within a few months, it would have grown in strength. It was quite wrong, he remarked, that the St Vincent de Paul Society should have so many of their men and families to look after.

15 FEBRUARY 1913

The artist, William Scott, was born in Greenock, Scotland, on 15 February 1913, to Scots-Irish parents. The family returned in 1924 to their home town of Enniskillen, where William's father died three years later while trying to save lives in a fire. William was initially attracted to sculpture but soon turned to painting, and received training at the Belfast College of Art and the Royal Academy, London.

In 1941 he began teaching at the Bath Academy of Art and held his first solo show in London the following year. After active war service he returned, in 1946, to Bath, and taught there for the next decade. He joined the London Group and, in 1950, exhibited in the Irish Exhibition of Living Art in Dublin. His almost abstract still-lives of this period were painted from frying pans and saucepans hung on the walls of his studio which were grouped firstly with fish or fruit. Steadily the objects moved half off the canvas or receded into it as Scott became interested in the 'half-said', the inexpressible.

During the 1950s he visited New York, meeting abstract impressionists Pollock, de Kooning, Rothko and Kline, encounters which influenced the enlargement of his own canvasses on his return to London. The primitive paintings in the Lascaux caves in France led him to reduce colour and image again, and with palette knife and brush to lay more stress on textural marks. In 1958 he was rewarded with a retrospective at the Venice Biennale.

That same year he was commissioned to paint an abstract mural for Altnagelvin Hospital in Londonderry. The mural measured 13.7 metres (46 feet) long and 2.7 metres (9 feet) high, and was painted on fifteen plywood panels at Hallatrow, near Bristol, where Scott worked on it for two years in a converted stable. The work was shown for a few weeks at the Tate Gallery, and was installed in 1962, but is now at Belfast City Hospital. A pattern of rectangles and round figures, it arrived in Altnagelvin on Monday, 15 January 1962. At the time the Hospital Secretary, R.F.N. Taylor, said: 'The mural is in crates and it is a specialist job to unpack it. We will await instructions from the Hospital Authority before it is taken out of the crates for erection.'

The wall of the hospital's main hall had been prepared for the mural, which was unveiled on the afternoon of Tuesday, 27 February 1962, by Mrs Scott, wife of the artist. O.A. Davis, representing the architects, engineers and quantity surveyors engaged on the construction of the hospital, presented the mural to the Hospital Authority, whose chairman, William McKinney, formally accepted the gift and asked Dr M.F. Leslie, Chairman of the North-West Management Committee, to accept the custody of it.

16 FEBRUARY 1944

Four Canadian sailors—Richard Kelso, George Hornett, Alfred Walker and Paul Benoit Vigneau—were summoned to Londonderry Petty Sessions on Wednesday, 16 February 1944 as a result of their riotous and disorderly behaviour in the Victoria Bar, Orchard Street.

The barman, James Bradley, said when the defendants came into the premises already under the influence of drink he refused to serve them. Walker pulled him from behind the bar and struck him on the side of the head two or three times, while another of the defendants struck his brother. While the sailors were fighting, three glasses and the glass of the cash register got broken. They also used some expression about 'the dirty Irishmen being no good'. The police were called, but the men resisted arrest.

Sergeant Murdock said Walker tore his revolver holster and overcoat, and tried to push a glass into his face. Another policeman had to strike Walker with his baton. On the way to the barracks the defendants used filthy language towards the police. Resident Magistrate, Captain P.S. Bell, asked, 'They had a very poor opinion of the Irish?' to which the reply was 'They had.'

Constable Boyd said on the way to the barracks the defendants attacked Sergeant Murdock and himself, while Constable Chesney stated that Kelso tore his ammunition pouch. All the defendants declined to give evidence but an officer stated that they had good characters. As a result of this incident their leave and pay had been stopped.

Captain Bell reminded the Canadians that there were large numbers of Irishmen in the Royal Navy and Merchant Navy; there always had been and there always would be, and they were just as good sailors as any Canadians. If an Irishman in Montreal were to talk about 'dirty Canadians', he continued, how long would it be before he would be thrown into the river? The police had their duty to do, and the publican had his living to earn, as he was entitled to do.

Walker was fined 21s for assaulting Bradley, 10s for riotous behaviour, 10s for refusing to leave licensed premises when requested to do so, 1s for malicious damage to Sergeant Murdock's overcoat (with 6s compensation), and 40s for assaulting Sergeant Murdock. Vigneau, Kelso and Hornett also received fines, but the charges of smashing the glasses and cash register were dismissed.

17 FEBRUARY 1911

On Friday, 17 February 1911, the *Derry Journal* and the *Derry Standard* announced that all local railway companies would be making special arrangements in light of the visit to the city of John Philip Sousa, the 'March King'. The Londonderry and Lough Swilly operator assured its passengers that a train for Buncrana would be ready to leave, after the evening concert, from the Strand Road Station at 11 p.m.

Sousa had been born in Washington D.C. on 6 November 1854, the son of a Portuguese father and a German mother. By the age of six he had perfect pitch and an extraordinary capacity for mastering musical instruments. He was a prodigious violinist but was equally adept at brass and woodwind instruments. To prevent his joining the band of a travelling circus at the age of thirteen his father enrolled him as an apprentice in the United States Marine Corps, where he stayed until 1875. It was in tribute to his time with the Corps that Sousa composed the regimental march of the Marines, 'Semper Fidelis', which was second only in popularity to his own favourite, 'The Stars and Stripes Forever'.

After a spell as the conductor of a theatre pit orchestra he returned to the Marines as musical director, before retiring to form his own Sousa Band, which was renowned for its elaborate uniforms, immaculate white gloves, and its members' proficiency in 'triple-tonguing'. The band travelled the world from 1892 until Sousa's death in 1931, garnering universal acclaim for its distinctive brass ensemble playing and its rendition of romantic tunes. Waltzing to the Sousa Band was a recognised treat in those days. To achieve a special musical effect, Sousa designed a greatly enlarged tuba with a much bigger bell, the 'Sousaphone', which was worn like a harness.

The Sousa Band gave two concerts to capacity audiences that Friday afternoon and evening in St Columb's Hall, finishing in time to catch the Laird liner *Rose* to Glasgow.

When America entered the First World War, Sousa was made a Lieutenant-Commander in the Navy, with responsibility for the regimental band. On retiring he donated all his salary, less one dollar, to the Sailors' and Marines' Relief Fund. He continued to wear his naval uniform at concerts for the rest of his life. He died on 6 March 1931 in his home in Reading, Pennsylvania, and is buried in the Congressional Cemetery (reserved for known patriots) in Washington D.C.

18 FEBRUARY 1965

On Wednesday, 17 February 1965, the *Londonderry Sentinel* announced that, in the light of the Northern Ireland Government's decision to grant a university campus to be set up in Coleraine, over 'Londonderry, ancient seat of learning, second city of Ulster', there would be a mass demonstration on the Thursday outside Parliament Buildings at Stormont, involving 'thousands of people from the West'. A 'monster motorcade' would wind its way across the province to Belfast and Mayor A.W. Anderson would deliver a letter of protest at the government's decision. All walks of life from the Maiden City—clergy, business and professional organisations, trade unions, and social organisations of every kind—would be represented in the motorcade.

The Mayor and Corporation had asked for a public holiday in Derry, excepting essential services. Many shops were planning to close for the day, and the industry and business sectors had united in giving the University for Londonderry Action Committee their full support. Public houses would stay closed until 5 p.m.

The *Sentinel* reported a leading citizen saying: 'The city is in revolt. Never in the history of Derry has there been such deep feeling aroused as by the Government's strange decision to site the university in Coleraine…' John Hume, Chairman of the University for Londonderry Action Committee, said: 'It must be dignified.' No flags or emblems would be carried.

Everybody in the city was willing to make the demonstration effective. The managements of BSR, Du Pont, and British Oxygen had pledged their support for the campaign, and one thousand Du Pont workers had volunteered to distribute stickers to cars in the motorcade.

Clive Burcher, manager of Monarch Electric Ltd, said if the university did not come to Londonderry one could only conclude that the North West area was not destined for any future expansion. 'It is time … the formidable power of united public pressure [was] brought to bear on the Government departments concerned,' he commented, adding: 'A university is a prestige symbol to a population centre as large as Londonderry, and its hinterland.'

Members of the St John's Ambulance Brigade and the Order of Malta were to be present and vans from city garages would provide 'mechanical first aid' if required. The Londonderry Shirt Manufacturers' Federation urged support for the protest, as did the Licensed Vintners' Association, and on the previous Thursday night both unionist and nationalist shades of political opinion in Derry had endorsed the campaign to bring the university to the city.

19 FEBRUARY 1906

On Monday, 19 February 1906, the *Derry Standard* newspaper reported that, on the previous Saturday, the wreckage of a vessel, presumed to be the brigantine *Scotsman* of Derry, had washed ashore some little distance north of Maryport in Cumbria. Subsequent information left little doubt that the vessel had perished in the gale of the previous Thursday night with the loss of all hands on board.

The *Scotsman*, which had been laden with coal and was returning to the Maiden City, had left Maryport at tide-time (5 p.m.) on 15 February, and in the ordinary course of events should have reached Derry on the Saturday afternoon. The weather had been fair when she set out on her voyage, but approximately two hours later, a furious gale had sprung up, the wind veering round from south-west to west. The unfortunate vessel was in all probability driven on to the coast before managing to steer clear of it. A message from Captain Kane, master of the SS *Templemore*, arrived in Maryport on Saturday evening, stating definitely: '*Scotsman* gone, with all hands.' This confirmed the worst fears of the vessel's owners, Messrs. George Howatson & Co. of Abercorn Quay.

There had been a crew of six on board. Captain James Rochfort, an elderly navigator, was a particularly well-known figure in Derry shipping circles and had been contemplating early retirement from the sea so as to set himself up in business in the city. The *Scotsman* had been regularly trading as a collier with Londonderry since 1879, and Rochfort had been employed on the boat for the previous twenty-two years. The *Standard* gave the names of the remainder of the crew as Daniel Begley (mate), Edward Smith, John Steel, Hugh Donnelly, and John Ryan. The captain, Begley, and Donnelly had been Greencastle men, while the three others hailed from Derry.

On 21 February, the *Standard* stated that some of the crew's personal effects had been discovered washed ashore. Amongst them were papers which revealed that a man named Patrick McGonigle had shipped in place of Edward Smith. McGonigle, a nephew of the captain, had been making his first voyage on the ill-fated vessel.

20 FEBRUARY 1923

On Tuesday, 20 February 1923, the *Londonderry Sentinel* reported that the news of the tragic death of George Conaghan, principal of St Columba's Boys' National School, Long Tower, Derry, had been 'received in the city and district during the week-end with sincere sorrow by a wide circle of friends'. Conaghan had accidentally fallen from a Great Northern train carriage while returning to Derry from Belfast on the previous Saturday evening. His body was picked up on the railway line on the Sunday morning.

Mr Conaghan, a native of Castlefin in County Donegal, had been in the teaching profession for more than four decades, holding the position of principal at St Columba's since 1913.

An inquest held on 19 February 1923 at Newtownstewart was attended by Mr John Elliott, district coroner, with Mr J.F.A. Simms representing the Great Northern Railway Company and Mr C. McCormack the deceased's next of kin. Thomas E. Conaghan, solicitor and son of the deceased, identified his father's remains.

Conaghan had left Derry on Saturday by the 7.25 a.m. train to attend a teachers' meeting in Belfast. William McClintock, a ticket collector from Omagh, stated that, a little before 8 p.m. that evening, Conaghan and two other men had come up to the Omagh platform barrier and Conaghan had inquired about the train to Derry. McClintock asked him for his ticket, which Conaghan produced. McClintock identified the ticket, which bore the Belfast barrier check, and Conaghan and the two men proceeded to the platform. One of the men explained to McClintock that he had just driven Conaghan from Ballygawley. Conaghan had reached there from Dungannon, where he had been left behind by the train on which he'd been travelling. Millar Hamilton, a farmer from Lisnatunny, deposed that he had found the dead body of a man lying on the right hand side of the line leading to Derry. He was lying on the broad of his back with his feet towards and close to the rails. The jury found that George Conaghan died at Lisnatunny from shock and fracture of the base of the skull caused by falling while the train was in motion.

For many years after this tragic event which claimed their principal's life, St Columba's continued to be known as 'Conaghan's'.

A meeting of the Londonderry City and County Anglers' Association was held on the night of Monday, 21 February 1910, in the Bond's Hill Rooms. Dr Charles A. Stevenson presided. The chairman, addressing the members, said there would soon be a commission sitting to investigate the possibility of extending the season in their district so that it came more into line with the fishing season in the neighbouring County Donegal.

In Donegal the season lasted from 1 February until 1 November, while in the Derry district it did not start until 1 April, lasting only until 10 October, so that it was not really worth a man's while taking out a licence for all the salmon he got. The case was discussed of a man who had recently been angling in Cork, and had come north to Faughanvale for the purpose of taking a house and fishing in the Faughan; as soon as he discovered that the season was so short he abandoned the idea and left the area.

Dr Stevenson stated that the salmon seemed to be running later every year, and were also getting harder to kill; whether that was caused by the outside nets he could not say. He remembered when there was good fishing in the Faughan in the middle of July but now a fish could hardly be got until the end of August.

Another grievance raised by the chairman concerned brown trout fishing, which he considered finer sport than salmon fishing. He remembered when the season for this type of angling had started in the Faughan on 1 March and there was very good fishing then. But now, brown trout was becoming scarcer, and no doubt one of the reasons for the decrease in the number of salmon was the havoc wrought by the trout on the fry.

Mr W.L. Perry, the honorary secretary for the district, read a letter from the department notifying the association of the forthcoming inquiry, and stating that any alteration of the season that might result would not come into force before 1911. Major Boyle from Limavady wrote supporting the proposal to have the season extended, mentioning that he had killed clean fish on the Roe when the season had been extended until 31 October.

The question of taking out licenses for the season was also discussed at some length. Mr E. Gallagher of Strabane proposed that the licenses be taken out from the Letterkenny Board of Conservators. He stated that, at a recent meeting, Strabane anglers had decided that they would not be taking out licenses from the Londonderry Board that season on any account, owing to the way the last election of conservators was carried out. In his opinion, Strabane members had been treated most unfairly, although they contributed £120 revenue during the season to the board. Mr Hill seconded and Mr Starritt supported the motion, which was unanimously passed.

James Gilbert Paton was born in the Free Church Manse, Chapeton, Lanarkshire in Scotland, where his father was minister, and was brought up in connection with the Great James Street Presbyterian congregation in Londonderry, where his grandfather, Aaron Baxter, a former Mayor of Derry, was an elder. He studied at Foyle College, and afterwards in Magee College. Graduating with honours from the Royal University of Ireland in 1903, he obtained his MA in 1904 and secured his BD degree in 1909 from the Presbyterian Theological Faculty. Licensed by the Derry Presbytery in 1906, he was called the following year, unanimously, to Ballykelly congregation, where he remained for four years. Experience gained in congregations in Newry and Coleraine led to his being called to the Malone Presbyterian Church in Belfast in 1920.

Paton played a leading part in the building of the Presbyterian War Memorial Hostel in Howard Street, Belfast, and served as Chairman of the Hostel Committee. His devotion to his Church reaped its rewards in 1931 when he was elected Moderator of the General Assembly. That same year, Queen's University awarded him a Doctor of Divinity degree and he was invited to visit India by the Indian Mission Church. The Moderator's tour of the Indian mission stations was greatly appreciated by the native churches.

During the Great War, Paton was a real soldier's padre. His first contact with troops was during his ministry at Coleraine where, for three months after the outbreak of hostilities, he engaged in YMCA work. His congregation agreed to his request that he might be permitted to offer his services to the army, and he was appointed chaplain to the forces, serving in the 10th Battalion Royal Inniskilling Fusiliers (Derry Volunteers). One of the men wrote of him: 'He is round the firing line every night, especially if the enemy is shelling us. The boys think the world of him as the best man out here.'

Paton was awarded the Military Cross with two bars. He won the Cross in 1917 for great gallantry, and in the summer of the following year was awarded the first bar for what the *London Gazette* regarded, on 16 September 1918, as 'fine disregard for personal safety': 'Under heavy shell and machine gun fire he helped to evacuate wounded, and in one instance assisted to carry a seriously wounded case four miles to an aid station.'

Exactly a month after the publication of the above, and during the attack on Mooseele, Paton's great courage brought him the second bar for his Military Cross. 'He never spared himself,' said the *Gazette*. 'He worked continuously through the operations, carrying in and tending wounded, frequently passing through heavy fire to forward positions to reach the wounded. His gallant conduct and untiring efforts were admirable.'

James Gilbert Paton died on Saturday, 22 February 1936, after an illness of some months.

23 FEBRUARY 1903

At Londonderry Petty Sessions, on Monday, 23 February 1903, before Alderman Bell (presiding), Colonel Tynte, Resident Magistrate, Alderman Breslin, and Bernard Doherty, an adjourned case came before the Court in which Betty Hegarty of Eglinton Row was charged on two summonses with offences against the Licensing Act. In the first she was charged with 'keeping for sale intoxicating liquors, her not being duly licensed to sell the same', and on the second the charge read 'selling or exposing for sale by retail intoxicating liquor without being duly licensed to sell same'. District Inspector McHugh prosecuted, and Patrick Maxwell appeared for the defence.

Sergeant Lappin said he, with Sergeant Boyd and four constables, entered the house of the defendant and asked her if she had any drink in the house, to which she replied she had not. They then proceeded to search the house and seized 168 full bottles of porter, twenty-three empty porter bottles, one pint of whiskey and some tumblers and glasses. Six bottles were found in the kitchen, in a hole cut in the wall with some old clothes on top of them; thirty bottles of porter were found in a kitchen dresser under some oilcloth; six bottles were discovered between two bed-ticks, and another six bottles were spotted under the same bed with a piece of cloth nailed to the wall overhanging the bottles, which stood close to the wall. Lappin also discovered six bottles in the sleeves of a jacket which had been sewn up to contain them; seven bottles under the stairs; six bottles in the back room; and eighteen bottles, all full of porter, under the floor in this room, the boards having been cut into short lengths. He also found a half-pint of whiskey in the pocket of a coat, a half-pint in the clock, and twenty-three full bottles in different places.

Sergeant Boyd said he found half a dozen bottles in a box in the front bedroom. When he lifted the floorboards, which had been cut, he found three dozen bottles, all full. He found a man named Charles Hegan, from Rosemount, in the kitchen, with a bowl full of porter before him, which Hegan drank before he left. There was also a jug and a couple of bowls with fresh porter. Constable Young gave evidence of more finds in the yard. District Inspector McHugh proved a conviction against Hegarty for the same offence on 14 June

1900. Alderman Bell announced that under the summonses brought against the defendant she would be fined a total of £10 or two months. The man Hegan would be fined five shillings and costs.

Mrs Hegarty applied for time to pay the fine. The magistrates refused and she was placed in the dock.

24 FEBRUARY 1904

On Wednesday, 24 February 1904, the annual meeting of the Londonderry Branch of the Society for the Prevention of Cruelty to Animals was held in the Mayor's Parlour, Guildhall. There was a large and representative attendance which included the Mayor, M.A. Ballantine. On the motion of R.S. Smyth, seconded by Dr McCurdy, the Mayor was called upon to preside.

On taking the chair, Mr Ballantine referred to the success of the Society, and added that he knew something of the working of it. As a large employer of labour, and especially in connection with carting, he believed he had been somewhat under the supervision of the Inspector. But he regarded that as rather a benefit since it ensured that men not only keep their harness in order but took better care of the horses of which they were in charge. The Inspector acted with great discretion, and no prosecution was brought unless there was an actual case of cruelty. The Society, the Mayor continued, besides prosecuting when necessary, also wanted to foster the growth of a feeling of kindness for and sympathy with dumb animals, and it was succeeding in doing that.

Mr J.S. McMillen submitted the annual report to those gathered. The number of cases of cruelty to animals reported and investigated during the previous year was 101, showing a decrease over the previous year of twenty-one cases. Four of these cases were prosecuted, convictions being obtained in each one, and fines imposed varying from ten shillings to five shillings.

No cases of cruelty of 'more than ordinary character' came to the attention of the Society during the year but a large number of what would have been cases of cruelty had been prevented by the Inspector, who had been most 'assiduous and energetic' in the discharge of his duties. The Inspector had met with an accident just before Christmas whilst overlooking the shipping of cattle to Glasgow, and this had laid him aside for some time; thankfully, he had almost recovered and hoped soon to undertake his duties in full with his usual energy and ability.

It was reported that, at the riding and driving competitions at the North West Shows, held on 30 June and 1 July, the usual prizes were offered for the best presented and well-kept donkeys belonging to working men within the city boundary. The turnout was above the average of former years. Pupils from the Derry and district schools were again invited to submit essays on 'The Rights of Animals to be Humanely Treated' to the Society, and the committee had much pleasure in stating that this competition was becoming more popular every year.

25 FEBRUARY 1998

On Wednesday, 25 February 1998, the *Londonderry Sentinel* published an appreciation, written by a 'friend and colleague', of Dr Desmond Whyte, who had died on the tenth of the month. 'With his death,' wrote the friend, Northern Ireland had 'lost one of its most respected and talented medical practitioners'. As a consultant radiologist at Altnagelvin Hospital, from the time of its opening, continued the writer, Whyte had a major and continuing influence on the development of the hospital, and was highly regarded by his colleagues for the excellence of his speciality work and his lifelong commitment to a range of medical organisations and charities.

When Altnagelvin Hospital was opened, Whyte realised that it would be the major teaching hospital outside of Belfast. He rapidly set about establishing a Postgraduate Medical Education Centre and Library and the School of Radiography. The latter soon gained a reputation for its high standard of training, and Whyte took great pride in the ongoing success of students and their tutors; he particularly enjoyed tutoring doctors in training for higher diplomas in medicine, surgery, radiology and anaesthetics.

In his work, Whyte set very high personal standards. He pioneered the introduction of open access radiography to general practitioners, ensuring that patients got X-rays quickly, and he was in the forefront of the development of interventional techniques in radiology. He would never leave his department, no matter how late the hour, until all radiographs of the day had been reported on. In retirement, he paid close and admiring attention to the further development of the Department of Radiodiagnosis.

His professional diligence and determination was undoubtedly influenced by his experience in the Royal Army Medical Corps. As a Lieutenant Colonel in a Chindit Long Range Penetration Group, working behind enemy lines in Burma in 1944, he practised under conditions of extreme deprivation and danger. A fellow officer, Richard Rhode James, in his book *Chindit*, wrote of him: 'Doc Whyte worked all through the day and most of the night still whistling to himself "Moonlight Becomes You", and still hopelessly out of tune. He used to go about clad only in the briefest of loincloths and carrying his carbine. I half expected him to take to the trees, until I saw him handle his patients and then realised where he belonged!'

Whyte's commanding officer, Colonel John Masters, considered him as 'the one man above all others who has kept the brigade going, not dashing out to rescue one wounded man under fire but two hundred over a hundred days, calm and efficient and cheerful while shells blast the bodies to pieces under his hands'.

Although being nominated for the Victoria Cross, Whyte was awarded the Distinguished Service Order in respect of his gallantry and service.

26 FEBRUARY 1942

On Thursday, 26 February 1942, the *Londonderry Sentinel* reported that suggestions made at the meeting of Londonderry Corporation two days previously that guns used at the Siege of Derry should be disposed of as scrap for war purposes were received with feelings of incredulity by the citizenry, and the general opinion was that the scrap metal salvage campaign must have been pushed to the utmost extremes in the city (without anyone hearing about it) if use had to be made of these 'priceless relics of the Maiden City's glorious part in the fight for liberty'.

At the meeting of the Corporation, after a reference to a German Great War gun, the only one of three in the city which had not been broken up for scrap, an Alderman Little said: 'Another Association is quite prepared to hand over a few other scrap guns they have, too.' The Mayor, Senator F.J. Simmons, responded: 'You mean "Roaring Meg"?' to which Little said: 'No, sir, but another four or five guns we have there.' Alderman Wilton interjected, 'Where?' to be informed by Alderman Little that he was referring to 'Inside the Bastion.' The Mayor warned Little that he was 'treading on dangerous ground'.

Alderman Little later stated: 'There was no decision taken by the Apprentice Boys to hand over any of the guns in their custody as scrap, but from conversations I had last Saturday I believed they would be willing to part with four old guns which had been collected by the late Mr W. Kyle, Spencer Road, from people who used them as protection at gateways against damage to walls by traffic, and handed over to the Apprentice Boys after Mr Kyle's death. I had no definite authority for saying the Apprentice Boys were prepared to hand over a few guns for scrap, but I was speaking from what I had gathered from the conversations I had. In these it was thought it would give a lead to the rest of the city.'

Matthew Kerr, Governor of the Apprentice Boys, when interviewed later, declared: 'Nobody had any authority for saying the Association was prepared to hand over Siege guns for scrap.' He added: 'If the Government really wanted these guns as scrap we would give them gladly, and we would take the roof off the [Apprentice Boys'] Hall and give all the steel in the building itself if such were necessary. But I hardly think things have gone so far that we would have to give up relics handed down by our forefathers for 252 years. It would be a poor look-out if this was necessary.'

27 FEBRUARY 1807

One of the most popular of all American poets, Henry Wadsworth Longfellow, was born in the seaport and forest frontier of Portland, Maine, on 27 February 1807. In 1836 he became professor of modern languages and literature at Harvard, and retired in 1854. He died at Cambridge, Massachusetts, on 24 March 1882. Longfellow's poetic genius is preserved in such well-known works as 'The Wreck of the Hesperus', 'The Village Blacksmith' and 'The Song of Hiawatha'.

What is less well known is that there resided in Derry, in 1890, an old lady who was for many years in the service of the poet's family as nurse. Mrs Rachel Kernaghan, the lady in question, was then over eighty years old, and lived in Bishop Street with her nephew, Samuel McGuinness. She was born in the neighbourhood of Molenan, a few miles from the city, and reared in William Street, her father being a painter. At an early age she went to America and spent forty years in Boston. She entered the service of the Longfellows at their residence, Craiggy House, Cambridge, shortly after arriving Stateside and remained in the family's service for fourteen years. She nursed the poet's three daughters and two sons, and was in the house when Mrs Longfellow was accidentally burned to death.

The above revelation appeared in the *Londonderry Sentinel* on 9 September 1890. Mrs Kernaghan spoke of the Longfellow family with enthusiasm. She had then been home about two years.

The newspaper also revealed that a James Kent of Derry, on a recent visit to America, called at the famous Longfellow residence at the request of Mrs Kernaghan. The family happened to be away at the time but on communicating with them he subsequently received a very kind and courteous letter from the poet's daughter, Edith—then Mrs Dana—who thanked him for his visit and inquired very sympathetically about 'our old nurse, Rachel Kernaghan'. Mrs Dana said they were all very anxious to hear about her, as they had been very much interested in her return to Ireland. She expressed the hope that her old friend was contented and happy, and begged Mr Kent to satisfy her mind on the subject.

Mr Kent's visit to the Longfellow residence was one of the most interesting of his journey. He was in Longfellow's study, and also in the room known as 'Martha Washington's Room', from its having been occupied by the wife of General Washington. Craiggy House had been Washington's headquarters during the American War of Independence.

Mr Kent also possessed a miniature anvil made from the wood of the spreading chestnut tree which overshadowed the smithy immortalised in Longfellow's poem. He saw a chair, made out of the chestnut tree, which local schoolchildren presented to Longfellow; also an autograph album, presented with the chair from the children, and in front of same a cutting, made out of the wood, representing the smith working at his anvil, with the children looking in when passing.

28 FEBRUARY 1878

Born in Dublin in 1845, Thomas Barnardo, the great Irish philanthropist and founder and director of homes for poor children, had a religious experience in early life which led him to offer his services as a medical missionary in China; for this purpose he enrolled as a medical student at the London Hospital. In the capital, however, he discovered the streets of the East End teeming with children—dirty, ragged, hungry and neglected. Yearning to do something for them he hired a donkey stable and opened a 'ragged school'.

One cold, wintry night a small boy, aged about ten, clad in rags, begged to be allowed to sleep in the stable. His name, he said, was Jim Jarvis. He had no father, no mother, no home, and there were many others like himself in London. Barnardo took the youngster to his own home for supper and at midnight the two of them went out to track down some of these homeless lads. On the roof of the old rag market in Houndsditch, Jim revealed to his astonished companion eleven boys, fast asleep.

Barnardo related the above story in more detail on 28 February 1878, when he gave a lecture in Derry's Corporation Hall, during a two-day visit to the city. The lecture was entitled 'Arab and Gutter Children' and there was a large audience in attendance. The work in which he was engaged, said the speaker, did not apply to the children of humble parents, who were apt to suffer occasionally from depression in trade—it reached a class still lower, a class of destitute boys and girls who were called in common expression 'arab, or gutter children': 'A large number of boys and girls in London live on the streets, by the streets, and for the streets. It may be said that they have no certain dwelling place in the great metropolis which they can call their own; no door to open at their advance. They wander about all day and seek shelter at night in empty boxes in the market place, loiter about wretched courts, and occasionally seek shelter from the blast in the entrance to hall doors. A few of their number find at times their way to lodging houses when they succeed in gathering during the day as much money as pays for their beds, and the moment the morning light shines they prepare to begin again the wretched and objectionable practices upon the success of which depended their previous night's shelter… The lodging house affords them shelter, but it brings them in contact with depraved, immoral men and women, who have spent their lives in vice and crime, and thus they are gradually and instinctively prepared for leading lives of immorality, depravity, and shame.'

It was no wonder that Dr Barnardo (a courtesy title) made it his life's work to help these urban 'arabs'. And more than a hundred years after his death, the work continues.

29 FEBRUARY 1920

Elizabeth McGahey, who resided at Clarence Place, died on 27 February 1920, after meeting with a serious accident. Elizabeth was subject to occasional weak turns, and it appears that she succumbed to just such a turn and fell backwards down the stairs in a neighbour's house—a Mrs Jackson—and fractured the base of her skull. A doctor was in immediate attendance, but the injured woman remained in an unconscious condition for a couple of hours and then passed away. She was interred in the City Cemetery on Sunday, 29 February 1920.

Elizabeth was the mother of six sons who joined up at the outbreak of the Great War, an act acknowledged by Sir Edward Carson in a letter to the sons' mother around December 1914. The letter read:

It gave me great pleasure to learn that your six sons have joined the Army—three of them in the Ulster Division of Lord Kitchener's Army, one in the 6th Battalion Inniskillings, one in the 3rd Battalion, and one at the front with the Canadian contingent. You must be very proud of the record of your family. I am sure that your brave lads will cover themselves with renown, and will fully maintain the great Ulster traditions of devotion to their King and country, undaunted courage in the face of their enemies, and a stubborn endurance of all the trials which await them. Your sons have set a fine example for others to follow, and I hope they will all return to you in safety at the end of the war. I shall be glad if you will tell them that they have my best wishes in the noble task they have undertaken.

One of the sons, Private James (Jamie) McGahey, 10th Battalion Royal Inniskilling Fusiliers, died on 16 July 1916 in Germany from war wounds received in action fifteen days previously. He was a prominent footballer in Derry before the war, and his remains are interred in Niederzwehren Cemetery, Kassel, Hessen, Germany. Ten years after Jamie's death, one of his brothers, Charlie, placed the following tribute to his dead brother and other fallen comrades from the Fountain Street area in a Londonderry newspaper:

> Just a thought in passing for my brother Jamie and my good old pals Billy Ballantine, Jamie Gilliland, Nicky Maxwell, Jamie Glenn, Tommy McElhinney, Lindsay Moore, who died that we might live. After all, patriotism, like love, is self-sacrifice.

Charlie McGahey died after a period of failing health at the Waterside General Hospital on 22 October 1957, aged sixty-eight. He was an ex-councillor, and also ran a furniture business in John Street, from which he had retired some years prior to his death. Keenly interested in sport, particularly football, Charlie had played for the old St Columb's Court, Institute, and Corinthians football clubs. Another of his brothers, William, was also a soccer enthusiast, and was one of the prime movers involved in the formation of Derry City FC.

MARCH

A fire at the Methodist Church, East Wall, in Derry on the evening of Saturday, 1 March 1890, caused great commotion on the city streets. On hearing the fire-bell, people crowded to the scene in significant numbers, totally blocking the thoroughfares in the neighbourhood. Luckily, the flames were soon put out and little damage was done.

The drama began when Reverend John O. Price, who occupied the manse adjoining the church, was in his sitting room at eight in the evening and became aware of the smell of burning wood. He and Mrs Price made a careful search of the room, but finding no cause for the smell, thought there was no danger. Shortly afterwards smoke was spotted oozing through a press in the wall; while Reverend Price went to look for the fire, Mrs Price rushed to the nursery, quickly dressed the children and ushered them to a place of safety.

On entering the yard, Reverend Price saw that the building was on fire. He alerted the sexton, who resided at the back of the premises, as well as the Macrae family next door, and sent for the police and fire brigade. Donald Macrae, Reverend Price and servants from both houses entered the church and ascertained that only one corner of the building was on fire, but not one moment was to be lost if the sacred edifice was to be preserved. Buckets and basins filled with water were passed from hand to hand to quench the flames, and Macrae, at great personal risk, stood as close to the fire as he could to better extinguish it. The flames were soon prevented from spreading.

William Barker soon arrived on the scene armed with two Miller's 'handy' extinguishers, each of which was charged with carbonic acid, and helped to finally extinguish the fire. A hose at St Columb's Temperance Hall was also swiftly put into action, and several people who were in the hall helped to prevent further damage. In fact, by the time the fire service appeared on the scene, they were not needed. Reverend Price asserted that it was chiefly down to Macrae's exertions that the church was saved.

2 MARCH 1811

John Samuel Bewley Monsell, the second son of Thomas Bewley Monsell, the Anglican Archdeacon of Derry, was born on 2 March 1811 at Chatham House (now St Columb's House) in Derry. He entered Trinity College, Dublin, on 2 July 1827 at the age of sixteen, gaining his BA in 1832 and LLD in 1856. Ordained for the Curacy of Templemore (Diocese of Derry) in 1834, he remained there until 1836, when he was nominated Chaplain of Chapel of Ease (St Augustine's), where he stayed until 1838. He was Rector of Ramoan (Diocese of Connor) until 1839; Chaplain of Magdalene College, Belfast from 1843 to '46; Rector of Dunaghy from 1846 to '47; and Chancellor of Connor from 1847 to '53. In 1853, he began the first of twenty years as Vicar of Egham in Surrey, before finally moving to St Nicholas's in Guildford. He married Anne, daughter of Bolton Waller, of Shannon Grove and Castletown, on 15 January 1835. Their eldest son Thomas, aged eighteen, died in a shipwreck off the coast of Italy in 1855 while on the way to the Crimean War.

Monsell was a prolific writer of hymns, including 'Worship the Lord in the Beauty of Holiness' and 'Fight the Good Fight', the title of which is derived from 1 Timothy 6:12: 'Fight the good fight of faith, lay hold on eternal life, whereunto thou art also called, and hast professed a good profession before many witnesses.' Monsell's lyrics were to be set to the music of William Boyd, who later recollected: 'One day, as I was walking along Regent Street I felt a slap on my back, and turning around saw my dear old friend Arthur Sullivan [the musical half of the famous Gilbert and Sullivan partnership, who was then editing the book, *Church Hymns*]. "My dear Billy," he said, "I've seen a tune of yours which I must have." "All right," I said, "Send me a cheque and I agree." No copy of the book, much less a proof was sent to me, and when I saw the tune I was horrified to find that Sullivan had assigned it to "Fight the Good Fight"! We had a regular fisticuffs about it, but judging from the favour with which the tune has been received, I feel that Sullivan was right in so mating words and music.' The hymn became a favourite of Winston Churchill and was sung at his funeral on 30 January 1965. It also featured in the Academy Award-winning film *Chariots of Fire*. It was believed that Monsell was inspired to write the hymn, a rousing battle cry of faith, by the spirit of those who had defended Derry during the Siege of 1689.

Monsell died on 9 April 1875 from an infected wound received after a fall from scaffolding while repairs at St Nicholas's in Guildford were being carried out.

3 MARCH 1747

On 3 March 1747 William Barnard succeeded George Stone as Anglican Bishop of Derry when the latter moved to Armagh. Born circa 1697, William Barnard was the son of John Barnard from Clapham in Surrey. Educated at Westminster School and Trinity College, Cambridge, he became chaplain to the Duke of Newcastle in 1726, and chaplain to George II two years later. He was also Prebendary of Westminster and Dean of Rochester, and was appointed to the See of Raphoe in May 1744, with George Stone assisting as Bishop of Kildare at his consecration. William even married Anne, Stone's sister.

Barnard spent less than three years in Raphoe, but more than twenty in Derry. He erected the Chapel of Ease (later St Augustine's Church of Ireland) and the Bishop's Palace (later the Londonderry Masonic Temple). He was eulogised in his epitaph for his benevolence towards the poor, and for his munificence in restoring and adorning the churches of his dioceses. John Wesley mentions him with enormous respect as the 'good old Bishop of Londonderry' and states that 'he waited on the Bishop at Bristol in 1766, and spent two or three hours in useful conversation'. He died in London on 10 January 1768, and was buried in Islip Chapel, Westminster Abbey, where a monument was erected to his memory. He bequeathed £1,000 to provide from the interest thereof a salary for the chaplain in charge of the Chapel of Ease. By a deed of charge Barnard's son, Sir Andrew Francis Barnard, granted the Reverend John Hume, Dean of Derry and his successors a yearly rent of £50 on the lands of Templemoyle, reserving to himself, his heirs and assigns, the right of *advowson* to the church.

Another son of William's, Thomas, was successively Archdeacon and Dean of Derry, and afterwards, in 1781, Bishop of Killaloe, from which he was translated to Limerick in 1794. He was frequently mentioned in Boswell's *Life of Johnson*, being intimately acquainted with the biographer and lexicographer. In fact, the following charade, composed by Dr Johnson, contains a play on the Barnard family name:

My first shuts out thieves from your house or your room;
My second expresses a Syrian perfume;
My whole is a man in whose converse is shared
The strength of a Bar, and the sweetness of Nard.

4 MARCH 1971

On 4 March 1971, after two years of searching, the City of Derry Sub-Aqua Club claimed to have finally found (in Glenagivney Bay, County Donegal) wreckage of the Spanish Armada armed merchantman which sank on 16 September 1588 in the bay where it had sought shelter from a gale. 'Time and tide had taken their toll of the ship since 1588,' remarked the *Londonderry Sentinel* on 10 March, and all that remained was scattered debris in less than seventy feet of water.

The club planned to maintain their search for a further two years. The members had found and recovered part of an iron swivel gun, a copper kettle, a vase, and a piece of broken pottery. Dr Keith Lindley, of Magee University College in Derry, said the ship, the *Trinidad Valencera*, was the second largest of the Armada ships to come around the Irish coast, and one of the largest of the Armada as a whole.

The *Trinidad Valencera* was one of five Venetian traders requisitioned by Spanish authorities in Sicily for use as an armed transport with the Armada. When the fleet sailed, she was the most heavily armed ship in Martin de Bertendona's Levant Squadron. In addition to her own armament, she carried four of the King's guns and a complement of seventy-nine seaman, 281 Neapolitan soldiers, and a cadre of officers.

The *Trinidad Valencera* saw action off Portland Bill, the Isle of Wight, and in the rear-guard action fought at the Battle of Gravelines, just before the Armada sailed into the North Sea for the return to Spain. On 20 August, the *Trinidad Valencera*, the *Gran Grifón* and two other hulks parted from the main fleet off the northern Scottish coast. On 12 September, the *Trinidad Valencera* was caught in a storm off the northern coast of Ireland and, leaking badly, came to anchor on 14 September. Two days later, she split in two and sank.

Most of the ship's company appears to have made it safely to shore, but were tricked into laying down their weapons. Stripped of their clothes and other possessions, three hundred of the soldiers and sailors were killed by an Anglo-Irish force. Thirty-two of the surviving crew eventually made it to Scotland and, with safe passage granted by James VI, moved on to France. The officers were marched to Dublin, where all but two were executed on orders from the Lord Deputy, Sir William Fitzwilliam.

Parts of the Armada wreckage found were to be handed over to the Irish National Museum in Dublin, but it was hoped that a museum would be set up locally to display the objects. Dr James Whelan, chairman of the Sub-Aqua Club, said: 'We would like to stress that this historical wreck was found by an Irish sub-aqua club in Irish territorial waters. The benefit will go to the Irish people in that a period of our history is vividly brought to life.'

5 MARCH 1891

The great Harry Houdini was undoubtedly the most influential illusionist of the twentieth century. His speciality was escapology: slipping out of ropes, chains and handcuffs while locked in trunks and milk cans or underwater. In an age before television, he became world famous travelling across America and around the globe to demonstrate his skills. Less well-known is the man who apparently inspired the young Houdini, a certain Dr Lynn, a performance by whom Harry (then just plain Erich Weiss) witnessed as a young boy.

Dr Lynn was a successful nineteenth-century magician who, for a time, was a chief rival to John Nevil Maskelyne, magician and inventor of the pay-toilet and other Victorian devices. Lynn's featured illusion, Palengenesia (invented by the gifted mechanical engineer Thomas William Tobin), involved taking a human body apart, limb by limb, and then putting it back together again. He toured the world between 1862 and 1895, performing under the names of Washington Blythe, Washington Simmons and finally Dr H.S. Lynn. Early in his career, he devised an illusion he called 'The Indian Box Trick' and sold the secret to P.T. Barnum, the great American showman, in 1873 for a reported $25,000. Barnum then exhibited the trick in his museum, billing it as the '$25,000 Box Trick'.

Dr Lynn gave the first of three nightly performances before a crowded house in the City Hall on Thursday, 5 March 1891. Commenting on this performance the following day, the *Derry Standard* wrote:

> The entertainment was certainly one of the most humorous and mystifying ever submitted to a Derry audience. We have had Dobler and Hartz and other conjurors performing from time to time, but Dr Lynn eclipses them all both in the skilful manner in which his tricks are done, and in the amusing explanation of 'how it's

done' with which he accompanies them. County Inspector Hayes and another gentleman took their seats on the platform to watch the doctor, and good humouredly contributed largely to the enjoyment of the audience, whose merriment at some of the incidents found vent in roars of laughter. Tricks were done with hats, handkerchiefs, watches, coins, cards, and other articles, each being more mystifying than its predecessor, the 'bouquet extraordinaire' feat being past comprehension.

The newspaper continued by remarking on the versatility of the show:

To give variety to the performance, a number of well-known gentlemen took seats around the table on the platform, when an exhibition of 'spiritualism' took place. Each person placed his hands on the table, making a connection with each other by means of their little fingers. After the requisite lapse of time the table began to move, and the 'mediums' rising to their feet were dragged by the table round and round the platform, to the great amusement of the audience.

Finishing off their review the *Standard* wrote that 'no better performance of its kind was ever given in the city'.

6 MARCH 1930

Three privates belonging to the 1st Battalion York and Lancaster Regiment, Joseph Johnston, Rodger B. Weston and Frank Wigglesworth, appeared in the dock at Derry on Thursday, 6 March 1930, charged with breaking and entering the Hipps Ltd. shop and stealing two suits of clothes, four overcoats, one vest, two pairs of trousers and other articles. They were also charged with breaking a glass door.

John Armstrong, manager of the firm, stated that the premises were properly locked up on the afternoon of Thursday, 27 February, the half-holiday. At nine o'clock the following morning, when opening the shop, he found that one of the locks of the wicker gate had been tampered with and the glass of the vestibule door was considerably damaged, the hole being large enough to admit a man. On examining the shop, in company with Constable McGowan, he found it in a state of great disorder, with garments strewn over the floor. On the shop table lay a military cap while a military great coat was found in a corner. In one fitting room Armstrong discovered a belt, a cane and a tunic, and in another a second military cap, a tunic, belt, cane, and overcoat were revealed. Hanging on a hall stand was a civilian coat which did not belong to the shop. A cash drawer had been forced open and the contents scattered about. No cash had been taken but insurance and postage stamps had disappeared from a small tin box.

Edward Rodgers, of Ferguson Street, stated that, on 28 February, at 11 o'clock, he met the three defendants on the Derry side of the Kildrum Post Office. They asked if he wanted to buy a blue suit and a blue coat and vest, but he replied that he could not and suggested that they could either sell them or pawn them in the city. They gave Rodgers the clothes and told him he could have the coat and vest if he could get them money for the suit. Rodgers took the clothes to Barr's pawn shop in Rossville Street, giving his name as Wilson. Asked why he gave that name, Rodgers replied to prevent getting into trouble.

Detective Inspector Dykes gave evidence of arresting the defendants at 12.30 p.m. on 28 February at Termonbacca. When charged and cautioned they made no reply. Johnston was wearing a brown suit and a red cloth overcoat; Weston had on a pair of grey flannel trousers, a blue serge coat, and a blue grey overcoat, and had in his possession one insurance stamp and some postage stamps; and Wigglesworth was wearing a black Melton overcoat, with a white raincoat on top. On the application of District Inspector Ferris, the prisoners were returned for trial to the Assizes in Derry.

7 MARCH 1950

On 7 March 1950, the *Londonderry Sentinel* reported that a thirty-year-old Derry pilot, Flying Officer Instructor Sidney T. Bryans, of the Northland Road, and two other students of Queen's University, Belfast, had lost their lives two days previously at Sydenham airport when the training machine in which they were flying crashed on the aerodrome and burst into flames. Both Flying Officer Bryans and Cadet Pilot W.A.L. Morrison, aged twenty-one, were killed instantly. The third occupant, Cadet Pilot E.H.G. Porter, was pulled from the aircraft by a fireman but never recovered consciousness.

The machine, a Proctor, crashed to the ground just after it had taken off at 1.25 p.m. It had reached a height of about fifty feet when it suddenly nose-dived on to the runway, only a few yards from the fire brigade station. Thomas Stephens, a fireman who was employed by the Admiralty, witnessed the accident as he strolled outside his headquarters in the warm sunshine. He saw flames shooting from the machine as it turned over and then spiralled slowly to earth a short distance from him. As he ran to the aeroplane he shouted 'Crash, crash' to his comrades, and they turned out immediately. In less than half a minute he was at the side of the Proctor. Courageously opening the door as flames shot all over it, he seized Cadet Porter by the legs and began dragging him away. The petrol tank burst and there was a tremendous flash of flame. For a moment Stephens was blinded, and though he was burned about the face and head, he kept hold of the cadet and pulled him from the machine which, by this time, was burning furiously.

The airport fire engine arrived on the scene in a few seconds and smothered the flames by foam extinguisher. The two other bodies, unrecognisable but for the name tabs on their shirts, were then recovered. The Proctor itself had practically disappeared with only ashes remaining. Cadet Porter was rushed to the Royal Victoria Hospital but died within five minutes of reaching the ward. Stephens was also taken to hospital to have blisters on his head and face dressed. As soon as he received attention he insisted on returning to his duties at the airport.

Flying Officer Bryans had been educated at Foyle College and had entered the Belfast Bank before signing on as a Cadet Pilot at the outbreak of the Second World War, rising eventually to the rank of Flight Lieutenant. He returned to bank duties after the war, but re-joined the RAF almost a year before his death, and was commissioned as a Flying Officer stationed at Sydenham Aerodrome.

8 MARCH 1884

The photographer Alexander Ayton was born in Denny, Stirlingshire, around 1829. He established a photographic studio in Londonderry circa 1859, and died in the city in 1901. Ayton took many photographs in Donegal and one of these, 'Open Air Mass', has been reproduced on numerous occasions. On Saturday, 8 March 1884, the *Londonderry Standard* reported on the internal construction of Ayton's newly-erected photographic studio in Shipquay Place, having previously published a piece on the external design by architect, John Guy Ferguson.

At the entrance was a recessed vestibule with show windows filled with plate-glass and enclosed on sides and back with richly-embossed glass. The entrance hall and stairway had the floors inlaid with the richest and most expensive description of Minton's tiles. In the hall stood the hot-water register, the improved system of Keith of Edinburgh, by which the whole house was heated. The fittings were of highly polished teak, pitch pine, and ebony; the ceilings had enriched cornices, and there was a handsome archway opening on the stairway filled on either side with the monogram of the proprietor.

This apartment on the ground floor formed an admirable showroom, containing specimens of photographic art or portraits, landscapes, and views of buildings and places of interest, mostly in the north of Ireland. The portraits were mainly of gentlemen and ladies of the city and neighbourhood who had since passed away.

Passing by a staircase with massive walnut newels and handrails and beautifully polished pitch pine balusters and steps, the visitor was conducted to the portrait gallery on the first floor. This was a very handsomely proportioned apartment, forty-eight by twenty-three feet, and fifteen feet high, with a panelled ceiling enriched by very elaborate cornices and centre flowers. The cornices and plaster ornamentation of the apartment was brought out with great skill in colours and richly etched with gold. The walls were hung with a rich design of paper specially manufactured in Paris which toned with the carpet (itself enclosed in a border of oak paiquetry) and the furniture.

This department was devoted chiefly to the exhibition of oil paintings copied from photographs, which were richly framed and hung around the walls. Here too were displayed different styles and sizes of photographic pictures, from the small *carte-de-visite* and miniature vignette to the large cabinet portrait, and still larger development of pictures in oil. A portion of this apartment was reserved for dressing rooms, which were enclosed with a screen formed of pitch pine panelling and moulded teak framing. On the upper floor, reached by a richly carpeted flight of stairs, was the photographic gallery.

9 MARCH 1895

Dame Isobel Baillie, the renowned soprano, was born in Hawick in Roxburghshire, Scotland, near the English border on 9 March 1895, the youngest child of a master baker and his wife. Originally called Isabella, she used the name 'Bella Baillie' early in her career but changed it to Isobel at the suggestion of conductor Hamilton Harty, who felt that Bella Baillie sounded too much like a music hall performer.

She was a characteristic 'Scottish lass' with reddish hair and a fair complexion. Displaying early musical talent, she had singing lessons from the age of nine and won a scholarship to the High School in Manchester, where her family had settled. In 1918 she wed entertainer Henry Leonard Wrigley, who was severely wounded in the Great War, and in 1921 made her debut with the Hallé Orchestra. She won instant success in her opening season in London in 1923, and during 1925–26 studied with Guiglielmo Somma in Milan.

Her favourite work was Handel's *Messiah*, which she performed first at the age of fifteen, and subsequently over 1,000 times during her career. She was frequently sought after for choral works. Apart from *Messiah*, she was celebrated for performances of Haydn's *The Creation*, Felix Mendelssohn's *Elijah*, and Johannes Brahms' *A German Requiem*. In 1933 she became the first British performer to sing in the Hollywood Bowl in California. Four years later Arturo Toscanini chose her to sing Brahms' *Requiem*.

Her performances in Gluck's *Orpheus* (always in English) and Charles Gounod's *Faust* were extremely popular. However, her forte was in British music, including Ralph Vaughan Williams' *Serenade to Music* (of which she was one of the original singers) and Edward Elgar's *The Kingdom*. On 6 February 1947 the famous lady performed a carefully chosen group of songs —which ranged from works by Bach and Handel to Scottish ballads—in the Guildhall in Derry.

She taught at the Royal College of Music (1955–57, 1961–64), Cornell University in Ithaca, New York (1960–61) and the Manchester School of Music (from 1970). She was appointed a Commander of the Order of the British Empire (CBE) in 1951, and promoted in 1978 to Dame Commander (DBE). She passed away in Manchester on 24 September 1983, the year after the publication of her autobiography, *Never Sing Louder Than Lovely*.

10 MARCH 1940

On 10 March 1940 the midnight sky over the Maiden City was lit up by a fearful conflagration as Derry's Opera House was consumed by flames.

Derry's custom-built theatre had for seventy-three years been the venue for the likes of the Carl Rosa Opera Company, the D'Oyle Carte Company, and the Charles Doran and Frank Benson companies who specialised in Shakespearean productions. It also attracted many and various travelling variety shows from across the water who performed for a week and, during the second house on a Saturday night, had many of their props taken out the scene-dock door by Wordies, the local carriers, and loaded on to the *Lairds Loch* steamer for transportation back to Glasgow later that night.

In 1938 it had been fitted out as 'the most modern, luxurious, well appointed cinema in the city capable of seating 1,500', becoming Derry's seventh 'picture house', as they were called in that golden age of 'going to the flicks'. Ironically, it was this refurbishment that contributed to the Opera House's demise. The original ornamented interior walls of the theatre had been sheeted over and when a wiring fault caused a fire, the spaces between these and the screen battens acted like flues; in less than two hours there was nothing left of the dream palace but the standing walls and the girders that supported the balcony.

In the previous weeks the management had been warned by the IRA not to show what they termed British propaganda films (including newsreels), and members of the RUC were on duty at front of house. In fact, that same night an incendiary device had been thrown on to the roof of the Midland cinema in Bond's Hill but it caused no damage. IRA threats notwithstanding, the Opera House's fiery end was entirely accidental.

The fire brigade were assisted in their attempts to contain the blaze by the special volunteer wartime Auxiliary Fire Service. Police were supplemented by members of the B-Specials who forced the large crowd that had gathered away from the scene. Inevitably they were greeted with less than enthusiasm by some youths 'who had been shouting remarks at the firemen as they were engaged on their task'.

Though this was the only fire in the Opera House's long history, it was also the last. The costly renovation had left it vulnerable to the kind of freak accident that had destroyed it so rapidly. Eventually the gaping hole left in Carlisle Road, where so many players had strutted and fretted their hour upon the stage, was converted to a car park.

11 MARCH 1924

On Thursday, 13 March 1924, the fervently Protestant and Unionist *Londonderry Sentinel* paid glowing tribute to the impartiality of Hugh C. O'Doherty, a former Nationalist Mayor of Derry from 1920–23, who had passed away two days earlier in Buncrana, County Donegal.

The newspaper said that 'a highly-strung man of strong feelings, he took his official work very seriously, and he remarked more than once that he felt the effect on his nervous system of the constant, conscientious attention which he gave to the affairs of the city.'

The paper continued:

> It cannot be said that his difficulties were increased by those members of the Corporation to whom he was politically opposed. His trouble was with the extremists of his own household politically, who resented the strictness with which he kept them to the rules of debate, and his refusal, in the interest of the city's welfare, to adopt a Republican policy. In the Council Chamber, but more notably at the private meetings of the Sinn Féin–Nationalist members, Mr

O'Doherty was girded at in a most unpleasant way by some of those who placed him in the Mayoral chair, and he frequently expressed in private his gratitude to the Loyalist members for the sympathetic consideration they invariably extended to him... His three years' period of office gave him the opportunity to show his exceptional ability, his courage, and his fairness. If he found it expedient at times to deliver political speeches from the Mayoral chair, it was sometimes suggested that his main object was to consolidate his party by emphasising the points on which they were agreed. Mr O'Doherty's eloquence was little short of remarkable. Many of his most effective speeches were made on the spur of the moment, and obviously without preparation. With his widow and family there is profound sympathy in their loss, which is also a loss to Derry.

At the meeting of the Londonderry Corporation Committee on Tuesday, 11 March, the Unionist Labour Association councillor, Mr Greenaway, said he would like to express sympathy with the deceased's widow and family in their sudden bereavement. He had sat under the late mayor for three years and observed that he was very impartial in the discharge of his duties; Greenaway further commented on the fact that, with regard to the working people of the city, Mayor O'Doherty was more or less always in their favour. Another Unionist, Councillor Magee, said he was shocked to hear of the sad and sudden end of Mr O'Doherty, who had filled the chair of the Chief Magistrate with distinction for three trying years. In that time he had the misfortune to be deprived of the services of the Town Clerk for some months, and though a very busy man, Mr O'Doherty had nevertheless found time to spend hours daily in the Guildhall carrying on the civic affairs.

12 MARCH 1765

William Scott, the man credited with founding Derry's once proud shirt industry, was born on 12 March 1765 at Ballougry, the son of Presbyterians. He was trained in the art of linen, cotton and woollen weaving as an apprentice in Gilmour's linen establishment in Artillery Street. He subsequently became a master weaver and from his premises in Weaver's Row he produced linen cloth on a hand-loom. With the creation of a regular steamboat service between Derry and Glasgow in 1829, Scott began to journey to Glasgow to sell his webs of linen cloth to the firm of William Gourlie & Son. Whilst there, Scott noticed that there was a demand for linen-breasted shirts and so in 1831 began the shirt industry in Londonderry, recruiting his wife and daughters to make some garments which he brought with him on his next trip to Scotland. The shirts were snapped up by his Scottish clients and he returned home with more orders.

To deal with the increase in business, and to provide work for those skilled in sprigging, an outworker system was created. Stations were established in the countryside, where girls skilled in shirt-making were based. These station girls supplied local girls with the means to make shirts in their own homes. On completion, the station girls collected and examined the shirts and paid the workers. The ready-cut materials were delivered to the stations and the finished shirts collected from them were carried by horse and cart from Scott's factory in Bennett's Lane. This factory, set up in 1840, had room for weavers, cutters, sewers, examiners and packers, as well as stables for the fleet of horse and carts.

By that year Scott had stations scattered all over the country: in County Derry, in the Inishowen peninsula, in the towns of St Johnston, Milford, Ramelton, Raphoe and Castlefinn (all in County Donegal), and in Strabane, County Tyrone. As this outworker system was established prior to the advent of the railway to Derry, it was dependant on the road network to and from the city.

Scott retired in 1850 at the age of eighty-five, handing the business over to his sons. In spite of the introduction of the sewing machine, the sons persisted in using Bennett's Lane as a delivery centre. The Scott method of hand-stitching shirts in the homes of outworkers became antiquated and in 1859, the year following his death, the Bennett's Lane premises ceased trading. It was Scott's success nevertheless that attracted Scottish entrepreneurs to Derry, who with their modern ideas and methods of production allowed the city's shirt industry to continue expanding.

13 MARCH 1890

Marie Roze, the French operatic soprano, was born Maria Hippolyte Ponsin, in Paris, on 2 March 1846. At the age of twelve, she was sent to England to be educated, staying two years. She then studied with Mocker and the French composer, Daniel Auber, at the Paris Conservatoire, where she gained her first prize in singing in 1865. That same year, she made her debut at the Opera-Comique in the French capital. Her achievements there led to positions with the Paris Opera and subsequently in London. In 1877, she was engaged by the Max Strakosch Opera Company and made her US debut on 8 January 1878 in Philadelphia as Leonara in Donizetti's *La Favorita*.

She toured North America with the Carl Rosa Opera Company from 1883 to 1889. On Thursday, 13 March 1890, as part of an Irish tour, she performed in Derry's Opera House. The *Derry Standard* had announced her coming to the city a month previously by declaring that 'the people of Derry will… have an opportunity of hearing the world-renowned prima donna, Madame Marie Roze…'

On 7 March, the newspaper informed the public that the booking of seats for the concert had been 'unprecedented, nearly every seat reserved having been secured'. Special late trains would run from Buncrana and other places to 'enable the people in the neighbourhood to attend the concert, which, as a musical treat, is expected to be superior to any which the people of Derry have ever been invited. The programme bears out this statement. Marie Roze will make her first appearance in the scene from *Oberon* singing "Ocean, thou mighty monster". The prima donna will also sing Lady Dufferin's song, "Terence's Farewell", and Michael Watson's new song, "Babylon", besides taking part in Caldicott's well-known prize glee, "Humpty Dumpty"… We advise lovers of good music not to miss this concert, that is, if seats can be secured…'

On 14 March, the *Standard* gave a lengthy and positive review of the previous evening's concert: 'Every available space was occupied in the Opera House last night on the occasion of a concert given by the Marie Roze Opera Company. It was a suitable acknowledgement of the abilities of the famous cantatrice, who made her first appearance before a Derry audience. Seldom, indeed, has this city been favoured with a performance by a concert party in which such merit exists as in that which bears the name of its principal artiste, and the people are under a debt of gratitude to Mr R. Motherell, who engaged the party and made so complete and satisfactory arrangements. Of Madame Roze herself little need be said, as her accomplishments are familiar to all musical people. As a vocalist and actress she is well known here by repute, and her contributions to the programme last night amply confirmed the most favourable opinion…'

14 MARCH 1890

Baron Richard Dowse died at Tralee on Friday, 14 March 1890. He was born in more humble circumstances in 1824, the son of Mr W. H. Dowse from Dungannon, and received his early education at the Royal School in the town. He later entered Trinity College, Dublin. In 1852 he was called the Irish Bar, and in the same year married the daughter of Mr George Moore. He went to the North West Circuit, and rapidly won a common law practice. In 1863 he was called to the Inner Bar.

Five years later he entered Parliament as the Liberal representative of Londonderry. The election had been a heated one. His opponent was the Tory, Lord Claud Hamilton, and as a matter of tactics Nationalists supported the Liberals. The *Londonderry Standard* of 22 July reported that twenty Protestants had marched from their hall in London Street to the Diamond and attempted to gain entrance to the Corporation Hall, where Dowse was to speak. The Liberals, sensing trouble, had brought fifty working class men and placed them inside the hall. They were unarmed but when the opposing group tried to gain entrance, they tore down the banisters of the hall staircase, used these as weapons and repelled the onslaught.

Bricks and stones were thrown through the windows of both the Corporation Hall and First Derry Presbyterian Church, as a large number of active supporters of Dowse belonged to First Derry. The Reverend Robert Ross of Carlisle Road Presbyterian Church supported Dowse; when Dowse won the election the church was deserted by half its congregation, causing a severe financial loss for Ross. Dowse was accused of bribery and undue influence during the election and there was a twelve-day hearing early in 1869. On his election, however, a procession thronged the streets outside the walls to celebrate the victory.

Dowse's debating prowess attracted the attention of Liberal leader, William Gladstone, and he was appointed Sergeant-at-Law, and soon after Solicitor-General. In 1871 he conducted the prosecution of Robert Kelly for the murder of Head Constable Talbot, an informer against the Fenians, on the streets of Dublin. The latter lingered for some hours with a bullet in his spine while doctors pondered whether to remove it or not; they did, and the patient died. Isaac Butt, who defended Kelly, cleverly placed the blame on the doctors, and spared the life of the prisoner.

In 1872 Dowse became Attorney General and was raised to the Bench as Third Baron to the Exchequer. He was considered one of the finest and wittiest Parliamentary speakers of his age, and his obituary notice in *The Times* of 15 March 1890, read:

> Mr Baron Dowse was a self-made man, who, without social advantages, forced his way by his own merit to the eminent position which he occupied... He gave at all times free and vivid utterance to his thoughts, without waiting to examine critically the terms in which he should mould them...

One day in February 1768, so the story goes, a number of Church of Ireland clerics could have been observed playing leapfrog in the gardens of the palace of the Bishop of Cloyne in north County Cork. One of the most boisterous of the divines, the bishop himself, having reappeared from his house, announced his retirement from the game, which he had initiated and in which he insisted his clergy take part: 'I have surpassed you all! I have jumped from Cloyne to Derry.' The story was typical of many legends that attached themselves to him like burrs.

Frederick Augustus Hervey was born in the family home of Ickworth, Surrey, on 1 August 1730, the son of the 2nd Earl of Bristol. He was rich; apart from income from family land his stipend from the richest parish in Ireland was considerable. It allowed him to indulge his taste for designing and building mansions and filling them with priceless works of art acquired from mainland Europe.

Ordained in 1754 he was appointed chaplain to George III (1763) and when his brother George Hervey, 3rd Earl of Bristol, was appointed Lord Lieutenant of Ireland, he became Bishop of Cloyne in 1767 and eased from the deep south to Derry. He was enthroned there on 15 March 1768 and became exceedingly popular with all denominations in the city and throughout the diocese. He made a large contribution towards the building of the Long Tower Catholic church, the first post-penal-days church in the city, and was one of the main sponsors of the first bridge across the Foyle. As part of his estate that held his mansion at Downhill he built a cliff-top temple to one of his many mistresses, and allowed the despised Papists to use its basement as a place of worship.

He became the 4th Earl of Bristol on the death of his brother in 1779 and, having designed and built two more mansions, at Ballyscullion, near Bellaghy, County Derry, and Ickworth, where he rebuilt the ancestral home, became known as the 'Edifying Bishop' (a pun on the word 'edifice') and after 1779 the 'Earl Bishop'. He was a strong advocate of Catholic Emancipation and a leading light in the Irish Volunteers, wearing a startlingly gorgeous self-designed uniform. He was notorious for his resource to prostitutes both at home and on his frequent continental tours, and his public relationships with such notorious women as Lady Hamilton, later the mistress of Lord Nelson, and the Countess Lichtenau. He gave his name to many 'Hotel Bristols' in the cities to which he came looking for the artistic booty that made the great mansions seem more like art galleries than habitations.

He made his last trip to Italy in the summer of 1803 and, succumbing to a sudden attack of gout at Albano near Rome, took shelter in a barn because none of the Catholics would allow the notorious 'heretic' to enter their houses. He died there on 3 July and his body was shipped home to Ickworth, disguised as one of the pieces of sculpture he used to import so often. He was buried the following April in the family vault at Ickworth. He is commemorated there by an obelisk subscribed by Derry friends, including the Catholic bishop and the chief Presbyterian minister of the city.

16 MARCH 1913

On Sunday evening, 16 March 1913, William Pearson, the temperance orator, whose stirring addresses had been listened to by large audiences in various parts of the city during the previous week, concluded a successful campaign in the Guildhall, his subject being 'The Church and the Liquor Traffic.'

Pearson said the question of temperance reform was essentially one for the churches. The progress of good movement was hindered not so much by the wickedness of the bad as by the indifference of the good. As soon as ever the good people of the country did as well as they ought to do in this matter the days of intemperance would be numbered and ended. In order to save people from this curse the Church must teach the whole truth on the subject, for people were destroyed for lack of knowledge. The pulpit should speak with no uncertain voice, and that much more frequently than the institution of what was known as Temperance Sunday allowed; but the most powerful teaching of the Church was through the lives of its members.

Everything which it was proper for the pulpit to preach was right for the people to practise. There were no two standards of conduct—one for the pulpit and one for the pew. Christian people should be abstainers for the sake of the example they could thereby set to the young. It was not the example of the drunkards which enticed young people to begin taking drink. It was the influence of the little drop-drinking of otherwise respectable Christian people. The drink evil was certainly of sufficient magnitude to call forth the energies of the Christian Church in seeking its destruction. Mr Pearson went on to point out that £163,000,000 was spent in one year on alcoholic liquors, a sum nearly double the house-rent of the nation, and more than double the entire cost of the upkeep of the British army and navy. The eight great naval powers of the world combined spent £16,000,000 a year less than the United Kingdom spent in intoxicants.

Over 300,000 cases of drunkenness came before the magistrates in the course of twelve months. At least ninety per cent of the crimes of violence in the nation were occasioned by drinking, while the Right Hon. John Burns (then President of the Local Government Board) had stated recently that of 100,000 paupers passing through the poor law union of the parish in which he resided the medical officer said that not twenty-five persons were teetotallers. To put an end to the cause of an evil of this character, said Mr Pearson, was a crusade in which all sections of the Church, Protestant and Roman Catholic, might fitly unite.

The Chairman, Alderman R.N. Anderson, in conveying the vote of thanks, said the work which Mr Pearson had been carrying on in their midst for the past week could not be overestimated.

17 MARCH 1951

Until the beginnings of the Northern Ireland 'Troubles' Derry was a remarkably peaceful place but occasionally the nationalist people grew frustrated at what they saw as an unreasonable refusal to express their politics 'on the street'. On one noted occasion a number of them risked violence by insisting on their right to march within the walls of the city and display the flag to which they professed their allegiance. The small party included Edward McAteer, the Nationalist MP for Foyle (known to friend and adversary alike as 'Big Eddie'); Alderman Frank McCarroll, whose father J.J. McCarroll had been an MP and proprietor of the *Derry Journal,* the leading nationalist voice west of the Bann; and James Doherty and James Hegarty, both elected councillors to the Corporation of the city. These men attempted to lead a small crowd from the Diamond down Shipquay Street carrying the Irish tricolour on St Patrick's Day in 1951.

All attempts at obtaining permission from the police to hold a march in non-nationalist parts of the city in the past had been vain; it seemed that for a majority of the population certain parts of Derry were out of bounds for any peaceful march that could be deemed 'likely to give rise to violence'. Indeed on that day a few people not connected with the small colour party smashed the window of a parked police car and the driver was cut by flying glass. As the tiny procession moved down Shipquay Street a detective in plain clothes ran into the group and tried to wrest the tricolour from James Lynch, and he was joined by several uniformed colleagues wielding batons. In the struggle Hegarty managed to get hold of the flag and ran the rest of the way down the steep street. When it slipped from his hands a scrum ensued and the detective who secured it was surrounded by members of the gathering crowd.

A solid phalanx of RUC officers tried to prevent the scrum from pushing its way through Shipquay Gate and into the hallowed precinct of Guildhall Square. Among those arrested were Doherty and Hegarty, who were questioned in the main RUC station, Victoria Barracks. Doherty told a *Journal* reporter that he had been struck three times across the face during interrogation in an interview room in the building as well as being assaulted when he refused to get into the police van at the corner of Customs House Street. He told the reporter that he would be laying formal charges against the RUC. He and Hegarty were released after an hour to be greeted by a huge jubilant crowd. When the cases came to be heard on 7 November 1951 the police had dropped all charges, so depriving the frustrated men of their day in court which they had hoped would help reveal to the world the true nature of local politics in the city.

18 MARCH 1944

On Saturday, 18 March 1944, the *Londonderry Sentinel* announced that the Londonderry Methodist City Mission, Clooney Hall, was to celebrate its fiftieth birthday that weekend, and a special jubilee anniversary programme had been arranged. The preacher that Sunday was to be Reverend Hugh M. Watson from Bangor, and on Monday night there would be an anniversary tea and social hour, followed by a public meeting, at which Reverend Watson would be the speaker and Charles W. Gordon would preside.

At the morning service on Sunday, the Mayor of Derry, Senator F.J. Simmons, and members and officials of the Corporation would attend, and there would also be a parade of RAF personnel. At the evening service, there would be a parade of the Girls' Life Brigade, the Boys' Brigade, and members of the Ulster Home Guard. The offerings over the weekend were to be devoted to a Special Jubilee Fund, and it was hoped to raise £2,000 to be used in renovating and modernising Clooney Hall. The booklet containing the annual report was larger than normal that year and included among other retrospective items a short history of the mission by a well-known Londonderry Methodist, C.W. Gordon, alongside a list of ministers who had graced the Clooney Hall pulpit.

The mission was the outcome of the 1859 Evangelical Revival when the only Methodist church in Derry was situated on East Wall, and the first record of any membership from the Waterside area was in 1860. A year later a meeting of interested Methodists was held in Duke Street to consider erecting a building on that side of the river. It was announced that Sir William McArthur (later

Lord Mayor of London and a former Derry man) had written promising £400. This generous offer so inspired those gathered that another £400 was promptly donated. A site was secured shortly after and a neat building, seating 160 people, was erected. It was opened on Friday, 11 May 1862.

The coming in 1893 of Reverend Patrick Ernest Donovan, a converted Catholic, established the church as an active mission centre and eventually it was felt a bigger building was needed. The premises were enlarged slightly, adding another hundred seats. These were fully taken advantage of. Donovan's successor was Reverend E.B. Cullen, who did solid work with increasing success; and during his time Clooney Hall was erected. The foundation stone was laid on Tuesday, 5 May 1896, and the building was opened for public worship on Friday, 25 September, that same year. There was seating for over six hundred people, but a few years later an annexe was added, providing two hundred additional seats.

19 MARCH 1980

On Wednesday, 19 March 1980, the *Londonderry Sentinel* reported that there had been little worth seeing in the boxing ring that dominated Glasgow's Kelvin Hall on the previous Friday night after Derry man Charlie Nash's bid for the World Lightweight crown was thwarted by referee Sid Nathan. The 6,000-plus crowd clambered atop their seats for a better view, and what looked like *Z Cars* policemen, complete with gingham bands on their hats, formed a uniformed cordon around the ringside, preventing anybody who wasn't meant to be there from entering the ring.

In the opening round a right hand by Nash had opponent Jim Watt's backside on the canvas, dumfounding the Glaswegian's supporters and delighting Nash's followers in equal measure. That first round belonged fairly and squarely to Nash but by the second it was clear that things had changed. Nash was no longer employing his trademark neat footwork and flashing right hand, and Watt was keeping his hands much higher and seemed more composed than at the bout's beginning. The fighters clashed repeatedly, exchanging blows in the centre of the ring and, despite it being a difficult call, it seemed that Watt just had the upper hand.

In the third, Charlie was fighting to go forward but was being forced on to his back foot all the time. It was another round for Watt. The fourth was a disaster for Nash; he was backed on to the ropes and as Watt followed up both fighters went down heavily. Charlie was winded and received a standing count.

Watt went on the offensive and had Charlie in trouble immediately. He went down again and the crowd rose, almost taking the roof with them. They had no sooner settled into their seats again when it was all over. After taking two rights to the head which had pushed him to the canvas again, Charlie was examined by the referee, who called a halt to proceedings. The ring was suddenly full of people and the Irish contingent, stunned by disbelief at seeing their boy beaten, was making more noise than ever. As Charlie Nash left the ring draped in his emerald green robe the master of ceremonies was announcing the next fight. The small party made their way through the crowd to the vast empty space behind the seats where the 'doubles only' bar was doing a brisk trade.

Two more fighters made their way to the ring, but hundreds of seats had by this time been left vacant by departed fans. Charlie Nash accepted his defeat with no complaint other than the referee had stopped things too soon.

20 MARCH 1879

'It must, indeed, be a source of gratification to the eloquent and zealous pastor of Fourth Presbyterian Church to find that, after the labours of upwards of a quarter-of-a-century, both in season and out of season, among the flock that values his ministerial devotion, he can cast his eyes around the handsome temple which has just been completed for further extending his usefulness, and to meet the wants of an increasing congregation...'

With these words the *Londonderry Sentinel* of Thursday, 20 March 1879, referred to the planned opening on the following Sunday of the new Carlisle Road Presbyterian Church, which was described as 'one of the most substantial, commodious and elegant Presbyterian Churches in the North of Ireland... The cost of the building will fully reach £6,000, a sum considerably above the original contract. To defray this large outlay the congregation have liberally subscribed and contributions have not been confined to the members...'

The minister to whom the report referred was the Reverend Robert Ross who had been installed in March 1850 and remained in charge of the congregation until July 1894. Dr Ross was, in fact, the third minister of the congregation which had been established in June 1838; nine years later, when Robert Simpson published his *Annals of Derry*, the church was 'situated in the lane hitherto known as The Widows' Row, and is constructed out of a portion of that which was once the Derry Theatre'.

The first minister, Reverend John McFarland, remained for four years and was succeeded by Reverend Marcus Dill Reid, Licentiate of Limavady Presbytery, who was installed in May 1843, and remained until his death on 2 August 1849. Under the ministry of his successor, Mr Ross, the congregation increased to such an extent that the new Carlisle Road Presbyterian Church was built.

Commenting on the move from the former theatre to the new church, the *Sentinel* reported on 4 February 1879 that the previous Sunday had seen farewell services conducted in the old church building on Artillery Lane. The new church would not be opened until the following month, the *Sentinel* related, but in the meantime the congregation would meet for worship in the hall of the Young Men's Christian Association, the use of which had been kindly granted by the committee. There was a large attendance at the farewell services, including representatives of other Presbyterian congregations in the city.

21 MARCH 1943

Twenty-one young Irish Republican internees in Londonderry Jail made one of the biggest prison breaks then on record on Saturday morning, 20 March 1943, in daylight, after making a sixty-foot tunnel direct from a cell to the backyard of a house in Harding Street, completing the getaway in a Belfast furniture van. Twelve of them and one of the escorts on the van had been recaptured by Tuesday, 23 March, twelve in Éire and one in Northern Ireland, and the question of destination of the former had raised a problem for legal experts in Dublin and Belfast. Éire captives were detained in Rockhill Military Barracks, whilst the Ulster prisoners had been returned to the jail.

It was believed that sixty others were due to follow the twenty-one whose escape took place after breakfast when the cells had been unlocked for the day but there was such an air of tension in the prison grounds that a warder became suspicious and on following other internees discovered where they were going. He found some in the act of letting themselves down the tunnel by means of sheets. At the time over 250 internees, all in civilian clothes and under none of the ordinary prison discipline, were strolling about and the departure of the first batch was unnoticed. The alarm outside was given by a passer-by, who ran to the prison front in Bishop Street and warned the police guard.

How the tunnel was constructed had excited the interest of the whole British Isles, stated the *Londonderry Sentinel*: first the prisoners bored a shaft to a depth of about fourteen feet and then tunnelled horizontally for about forty feet or more until outside the forty-foot high prison wall, rising again at a slant to emerge into a coal shed. It was surmised that the noise of the hammering and scraping each night was drowned by the playing of bagpipes and other musical instruments over a period of many weeks. The clay must have been disposed of by scattering it over the prison grounds, down lavatories, etc. The final signal to outside men that the escape was under way was said to have been a series of catcalls.

The furniture van was brought from Belfast on a bogus order, and once in Londonderry the driver was seized, trussed up, thrown under sheets in the back of the van, and not released until the vehicle was abandoned between Strabane and Newtownstewart, where he reported to police. Eleven of the men were rounded up on Saturday evening on Kinnacally hill-top, near St Johnston, by over a hundred Civic Guards from all over East Donegal and military from Letterkenny, after five hours' careful approach work. No resistance was offered but shots were fired at two men seen escaping over a neighbouring hill. A twelfth man, alleged to have been one of the escorts, was also captured, and on Sunday night, 21 March, another internee was caught by a police patrol while trying to get back into the city on the Letterkenny Road.

22 MARCH 1850

The Friday evening edition of the *Londonderry Sentinel*, 22 March 1850, stated that reports had just arrived at 2 p.m. concerning an inquest held near Culmore which had excited some interest. The inquest was held on the body of Eliza Ann Reid, who appeared to have died on 9 March, and rumours circulated that she came by her death from undue means. The Coroner, Mr M. Lloyd, repaired to the spot, and having made a careful inquiry he was satisfied that an inquest on the body was unnecessary.

The constabulary in charge of the station at Muff, Donegal, however, reported the matter to Sub-Inspector Smith of Buncrana whose duty it was to direct the attention of the County Inspector to the circumstance, and the result was that the case was brought under the consideration of the local authorities who directed that an inquest should be held. Accordingly, at eleven o'clock on 22 March, a jury was sworn. Reports were to the effect that Miss Reid was pregnant, and on this coming to the knowledge of her parents, they not only ill-used but administered poison to her.

Elizabeth McIlwain, one of several people examined, said that she knew Miss Reid and saw her last alive on Friday, 8 March. She had known her since she was a child; Miss Reid was of delicate constitution and was in poor health since the previous May. From August on she had complained more than formerly, but did not state what was making her ill. McIlwain was of the opinion that Miss Reid died naturally and didn't believe the rumours going through the country about her death.

A Dr Forsyth said he viewed the body before interment, examined it carefully, and found no marks of violence. Death resulted from the gradual decline of nature, and he had no reason to believe that medicine was administered. Mr Lloyd, the Coroner, then briefly addressed the jury, remarking that he was satisfied from the first inquiry he had made that it was unnecessary to hold an inquest; but, as reports had gone abroad that the deceased came by her death from undue means the authorities had ordered an investigation and he was there, in his official capacity, to make the most searching inquiry. On his first examination he was perfectly satisfied that death arose from natural causes, and therefore, he was unwilling to put the county to the expense of holding an inquest owing to the groundless and perhaps malicious reports of certain parties. It was for the jury to return a verdict in accordance with the evidence tendered and he left the matter in their hands.

The jury at once returned a verdict: 'Died by the visitation of God.'

23 MARCH 1970

On Saturday, 21 March 1970, in Amsterdam the last entrant in the fifteenth Eurovision Song Contest was an eighteen-year-old Derry schoolgirl, Rosemary Brown, performing under the Celtic name 'Dana'. She sat perched on a cylindrical stool in an embroidered white mini-dress, and many in the audience thought her position a little bit unsteady. However, 'All Kinds of Everything' written by Derry Lindsay and Jackie Smith became the first of several Irish entries to win first prize in the contest.

The whole of Derry seemed to be celebrating the victory but what amazed and almost terrified the youngster as her plane landed at Dublin Airport on Monday, 23 March was the sight of the thousands of well-wishers waving flags and carrying banners. 'Operation Dana' was in full flow and though the object of all this adulation wanted to 'lock myself in the loo' she pulled herself together and entered the crowded Arrivals area. As she put it in her autobiography: 'The cheers broke like the roar of the sea over my ears and I found bouquets of glorious flowers thrust into my hands as I acknowledged the wonderful welcome.' After a hectic press call she was aloft again for RAF Ballykelly (Derry's airport had not been built) where another crowd waited on the tarmac to greet their new hero, insisting she sing the victorious song again on the steps of the plane. The fifteen miles of road into the city were lined with more well-wishers, crying: 'Dana, Dana, we love Dana!' When she reached Guildhall Square, there were so many cheering fans that not a square foot of ground was to be seen. Her limousine could not move through the throng and was stalled about twenty feet from the front steps of the Guildhall. The headline: 'Eurovision Star Crushed to Death in Welcome Home' flashed into Dana's head and she was relieved when an army officer persuaded her to climb on to the roof of the car from where she would be carried into the hall. She was passed bodily from shoulder to muscular shoulder, along with her father, safely to her destination. Then the celebrating really began; two hours later, speech slurred from exhaustion rather than champagne, and with her jaw aching from too much smiling at gathered press and dignitaries, she and her parents were shouldered 'like carcases of meat' back to the car and securely deposited at her home in the Bogside. Dana sang a few more verses of her song from the balcony of her parents' flat before finally catching up on some well-earned sleep.

24 MARCH 1917

The Diamond War Memorial in the centre of Derry contains on its four bronze plaques the names of 756 ill-fated individuals who died as a consequence of the bloody and brutal conflict posterity has labelled the Great War. All but one of those names are male, the only female being Nurse Laura Marion Gailey, a member of the Voluntary Aid Detachment (VAD), who died of pneumonia on 24 March 1917 at the City Hospital in Fazakerley, Liverpool.

In 1910 the VAD, officially approved by the War Office, was organised by the Territorial Army and managed by the British Red Cross and St John's Ambulance. Like the territorial force it was thought the VADs would only be called out if Britain was invaded but in 1914 they were asked if, in the event of an emergency, they would consent to serve overseas; the majority agreed to do so. Theoretically, VADs could be either men or women, but as their most suitable employment seemed to be as nurses, a VAD soon became a term for a woman nurse. They were, needless to say, voluntary and unpaid.

Laura was the youngest daughter of William Gailey, a stationer, and Margaret Elizabeth Gailey of Bayview Terrace in Londonderry. Miss Gailey had been engaged in military hospital duties, and some four weeks before her death had an attack of measles which developed into pneumonia; this proved fatal.

On Thursday, 29 March 1917 the *Londonderry Sentinel* announced that the remains of Miss Gailey had been interred the previous day with full military honours. The coffin was borne to the cemetery on a gun carriage covered with the Union Flag and after the interment the 'Last Post' was sounded by buglers. The chief mourners were the deceased's sorrowing mother and sister, and representatives were present from Fazakerley Hospital in which the deceased had nursed for eight months before taking ill.

More details of Miss Gailey's funeral were given in a letter from an English gentleman to a friend in Londonderry: 'I have just come from attending the funeral of Nurse Gailey, a most impressive and solemn spectacle. Ranking as an officer, the deceased lady was entitled by King's Regulations to a funeral with full military honours. The firing party and band numbered about eighty, and there were about 200 nurses present to pay the last tribute to a dead sister, whom everybody in Fazakerley Hospital liked for her gentle disposition and ready sympathy. The band and buglers belonged to the Welsh Fusiliers. Many of the officers were present, and RAMC non-commissioned officers acted as bearers. On the Union Jack covering the coffin were many wreaths. I shall not soon forget the inspiring effect of the moving procession, the measured tramp, tramp, tramp of the soldiers, or the sad yet lofty music of the "Dead March" with muffled drums.'

25 MARCH 1937

On Thursday, 25 March 1937, the *Londonderry Sentinel* reported that a young woman named Jeannie Waugh, who resided in a caravan in Duke Street, had appeared before Mr Justice Brown at the City Assizes the previous day charged with having attempted to commit suicide by drowning in the River Foyle the January before. When arraigned the accused, who was not professionally represented, said: 'I plead guilty under the influence of drink. I did not know exactly what I was doing.' Mr Justice Brown returned: 'If you say that you did not know what you were doing that is a plea of not guilty' to which Waugh responded: 'I plead not guilty. I was drunk when it happened.' His Lordship directed that a plea of not guilty be entered.

Harbour-Constable McKinlay gave evidence that on the evening of 23 January previously, when he was returning off duty along the subway of Craigavon Bridge, he heard a woman shouting that she was going to drown herself. He saw the woman crossing the wooden gate at the railway line and running along the track. He then heard a splash and procured a life-saving pole. Two men came to his assistance, securing a boat and succeeding in reaching the woman. She was about fifteen yards from the bank and was unconscious when taken from the water. When she was brought ashore first aid was applied before she was taken to be detained at the City and County Infirmary. McKinlay confirmed that the water at the place was about twelve to fourteen feet deep and that the accused was swimming against the tide in the direction of the fishery station. Asked if she had any questions to put to the witness, Waugh replied she had none; she did not remember seeing him at all.

Samuel McDermott said he was standing at the end of Craigavon Bridge when he saw the accused. She seemed to be in a hurry and practically ran down the brae. He heard the splash and assisted the harbour-constable in taking the woman from the water. She had been in the water for about twenty minutes and was fully dressed. In reply to the accused, McDermott stated he did not hear her shouting nor did he see her stagger. 'You were running,' he added.

Waugh told the jury that, on the day in question, she'd had a very bad cold and thought she was taking the flu. She had a considerable quantity of drink taken and did not know what she was doing. She was a stranger to the city, and instead of going down Duke Street she must have taken the wrong turning. When she found herself in the water she did her best to keep afloat. She remembered putting her arm around one of her rescuers but the rest of her memory was a blank.

After a brief absence the jury found the prisoner not guilty, and she was discharged.

26 MARCH 1953

On Thursday, 26 March 1953, two days after reporting Queen Mary's death, the *Londonderry Sentinel* recollected the only visit of Her Late Majesty to the city, in 1897, the year of Queen Victoria's Diamond Jubilee. As Princess Mary, she had accompanied her husband, then the Duke of York (later King George V), and following a short stay at Baronscourt as guests of the Duke and Duchess of Abercorn, their Royal Highnesses travelled by train to Londonderry on Saturday morning, 4 September. The tremendous scenes of enthusiasm as they departed from Newtownstewart were repeated all along the route, and big crowds turned out at Sion Mills, Strabane, and St Johnston.

There was unparalleled delight and enthusiasm when the royal visitors arrived at the GNR Station in Derry. Reports of the occasion say that a 'seething mass of humanity' thronged John Street, Carlisle Road, Ferryquay Street, the Diamond and Bishop Street, as the royal couple made their way to the Cathedral accompanied by the Abercorns and by Mayor J.B. Johnston and his wife. There was a procession of fourteen carriages, the last of which was that occupied by their Royal Highnesses. The Nationalist members of the Corporation took their places in the procession.

When 'the beauteous Princess May' walked up the churchyard, children strewed flowers in her path, and she and her husband were presented with an address from a deputation representing the Diocesan Council of Derry and Raphoe. While the Cathedral joy-bells rang out in appropriate melody, the royal couple inspected Siege relics and other objects of interest. Dr Jones, the organist, played the National Anthem. Before leaving by the private exit leading to the city wall, the Duke and Duchess signed the visitors' book.

Under the guidance of John Guy Ferguson, Lieutenant-Governor of the Apprentice Boys of Derry, the distinguished visitors inspected the Walker Pillar. Later, while still on the walls, opposite First Derry Presbyterian Church, they were presented with an address from the Derry presbytery. The royal party then drove through the streets, lined by cheering thousands, to the Guildhall where in the presence of a large assembly they were greeted by the mayor. The town clerk, Sir Newman Chambers, read an address of welcome from the Corporation stating that the people of Londonderry had 'longed to see His Royal Highness, and the fair and gracious Princess, His Royal consort, so well known and loved throughout the realm as Princess May'. His Royal Highness replied and afterwards received addresses from the Harbour Board, the Chamber of Commerce and the Apprentice Boys.

At a subsequent luncheon, the Duke of York mentioned that several times previously he had been on Lough Swilly and once on Lough Foyle when he had been in command of a torpedo boat. The Duke and Duchess left, again amidst great enthusiasm, on the Northern Counties Railway in the Waterside.

27 MARCH 1951

On Tuesday, 27 March 1951, an irate *Londonderry Sentinel* informed its readership that 'Londonderry Republicans did their utmost to provoke the Loyalist community over the weekend when they forced an entrance to the Walker Memorial Pillar on Mall Wall and hoisted the Éire tricolour on the flagpole at the top of the monument, and then tipped tins of white and yellow paint over the parapet of the ancient City Walls at Shipquay Place opposite the Guildhall.'

'Despite these unprecedented outrages,' the newspaper continued, 'the Loyalists of the city behaved with the greatest restraint and decorum for which they have been praised in the past. That the Walker pillar outrage was deliberately perpetrated to stir up trouble is beyond doubt, and is proved by the fact that its timing coincided with the conclusion of the Saturday evening dance in the Apprentice Boys of Derry Memorial Hall, scarcely a hundred yards away, where several hundred young Loyalists were gathered.'

The *Sentinel* went on to speculate that 'the hoisting of the flag was an open secret in Nationalist quarters because a crowd was on the scene to witness the flying—and the quick removal—of the flag. From the report in yesterday's issue, it is obvious that even the *Derry Journal* had a reporter assigned to covering the insult.'

None of the dancers leaving the Memorial Hall on the Saturday night noticed the flag, but it was spotted soon after eleven o'clock by the police who, when they procured the keys to the pillar, found that the original lock on the door leading to the internal staircase had disappeared, removed by the person who hoisted the flag, and a new one put in its place. This substitute lock had to be cut away before entrance could be gained but it delayed the police only a short time. The tricolour, when hauled down from the flagpole which was mounted at the back of the nine feet high statue of Reverend George Walker, was retained by the police. The crowd of Republicans gathered in the vicinity of the pillar and Mall Wall was 'moved on' by the police.

In Shipquay Place, where the 'despoilers were interrupted in their vandalistic work', two tins of paint—one yellow and one white—were tipped over the parapet of a part of the walls which, throughout the previous week, Corporation workmen had been engaged in cleaning. This cleaning was being carried out on behalf of the Irish Society as part of their contribution to the city's celebration of the Festival of Britain.

28 MARCH 1896

According to an issue of the *Londonderry Sentinel* in May 1956, Eglinton-born, seventeen-year-old Thomas Gallaher 'spun his first Irish Twist' in a small room in 7 Sackville Street in the city in 1857 and thus started the 'one-man' business that was to become the genesis of the company, Gallaher Limited, whose products went on to enjoy worldwide popularity.

In a piece marking the imminent centenary of the firm, the *Sentinel* went on to state that 'Londonderry folk... cannot resist the thought of how much it would have been to the benefit of their city had Thomas Gallaher been encouraged to remain in Londonderry and develop his industry [there].' It was Derry's great loss when, in 1863, Gallaher decided to move his business to

Belfast, though the full extent of that loss—and the corresponding gain for the eastern city—was not grasped at the time or, indeed, for a number of years after. Under his direction and drive the industry progressed and flourished, and in 1896 he formed his business into a private company, incorporated on 28 March that year to 'carry on in all their branches the businesses of tobacco, cigar, cigarettes and snuff manufacture'. The firm had by that time established a solid reputation for its internationally recognised Irish Roll tobacco. By the time of his death in 1927, Thomas Gallaher's 'one-man' concern had grown into a vast business employing some two thousand people, 'a business which in many ways, apart even from the direct employment it gave, proved a great asset to Belfast'.

'The people of Londonderry have reason to be proud of Thomas Gallaher,' concluded the *Sentinel*, 'though it is a matter of great regret to them that he early moved his business to Belfast and did not continue it in Londonderry. But the Gallaher family maintained their close links with the city and district. Mrs Michaels, a sister of Thomas Gallaher, resided at Eglinton for many years, and her son, John, became the first managing director of the new public Company.'

29 MARCH 1957

One of the finest English novelists of the first half of the twentieth century, Arthur Joyce Lunel Cary, was born in the house of his maternal grandfather, who was the manager of the Belfast Bank in Derry, on 7 December 1888. An Ulster History Circle blue plaque commemorating the birth is now located on the spot. At the age of sixteen, he began to study painting in Edinburgh and then in Paris. From 1909 to 1912 he was at Trinity College, Oxford, where he read law.

After Oxford, Cary set off in 1912 for Montenegro, serving as a Red Cross orderly in two Balkan wars. He had by then met his future wife and, when work for Horace Plunkett's co-operative movement in Ireland did not lead to a permanent post, he joined the Nigerian political service in 1913. He served in the Nigeria Regiment during the Great War, was injured while fighting in the Cameroons, and returned to civil duty in Nigeria in 1917 as a district officer.

Determined to become a writer, Cary settled in Oxford in 1920. Although that year he published ten short stories in the *Saturday Evening Post*, an American magazine, he decided he was not knowledgeable enough about philosophy, ethics, and history to pursue writing in good conscience. Learning occupied the next few years, and it was only in 1932 that his first novel, *Aissa Saved*, appeared. The tale of an African girl converted to Christianity but still preserving pagan elements in her faith, it was followed by three more African novels—*An American Visitor*, *The African Witch*, and *Mister Johnson*—and *Castle Corner*, a novel about the twilight of Anglo-Irish ascendancy and other aspects of the erosion of the British Empire. Childhood was the subject of two subsequent novels: his own, spent near Moville, in *A House of Children*, and that of a Cockney wartime evacuee in the country in *Charley is My Darling*.

Cary's trilogy of novels on art commences with the first-person narration of a woman, Sara Monday, in *Herself Surprised* and follows with that of two men in her life, the lawyer Tom Wilcher in *To Be a Pilgrim* and the artist Gulley Jimson in *The Horse's Mouth*, his most famous book. Monday is portrayed as an affectionate, munificent woman who is poorly treated both by the conservative upper-class Wilcher and by the talented but dishonorable artist Jimson. The latter is a social rebel and visionary painter whose philosophy and picaresque adventures in *The Horse's Mouth* established him as one of the most memorable characters in modern fiction.

Similarly, Cary's political trilogy is related from the vantage point of a politician's wife in *A Prisoner of Grace*, the politician himself in *Except the Lord*, and the wife's second husband in *Not Honour More*. He planned a third trilogy on religion but became plagued with muscular atrophy and knew he could not live to finish it. Thus he treated the topic in a single novel, *The Captive and the Free*.

His short stories were collected in *Spring Song*, three years after his death, which was on 29 March 1957.

30 MARCH 1900

By midnight on 30 March 1900 fire had gained a hold on the Foyle Chandlery Works on Strand Road, Derry. The now archaic word 'chandlery' originally meant a place where candles, oils and paints were manufactured and sold. Derry, with its strong maritime connections, had several ship-chandlers that specialised in heavy rope and cable, other nautical equipment, and strong preservative paint for use on board. All of these materials were highly flammable and soon the fire, according to the *Derry Journal*, 'assumed enormous proportions, tongues of flame leaping high in the air, and sparks falling on all sides in a flood of lurid radiance'.

Two members of the independent Harbour Police Service, Constables Graham and Scott, who were on patrol on the quays and noticed flames coming out of the chandlery, rushed to the area to warn the people who lived in the adjoining premises. They stopped two young men who were cycling past and told them to inform the police in the RIC station at Victoria Barracks in Waterloo Place. There was a fire alarm at the gate of the asylum and Constable Greenan, who had arrived on the scene with his partner Constable Hayes, used it to summon the fire brigade from their headquarters in Hawkin Street.

The premises of Philip McLaughlin, cabinet maker, next door was soon in danger of catching fire and volunteers worked throughout the night and early morning to rescue what furniture they could from the store. Though the night was dark the inferno in the chandlery provided all the light that was needed. Firemen first hosed down a number of storage casks of paraffin at the rear of the chandlery. Horses stabled on the other side of the building were rescued, though they were greatly agitated. Two cows belonging to a William Armstrong were also led to safety out of a nearby byre.

The *Journal* listed the stuffs stored in the burning building as including paraffin oil, casks of resin, vitriol, cocoa-nut oil, tallow and soap, all of which were used in the manufacture of the Foyle Chandlery's products. With such volatile material inside, there was no hope for the building's survival. Twenty barrels of resin burned themselves out in a matter of seconds. The remarkable nature of the fire, with regular crescendos of sparks, seemed to the reporter to resemble a 'sort of placid pyrotechnics'.

Not long after midnight the fire abated, having completely destroyed the business that, according to the *Journal*, was 'only in its infancy... not, it is understood, covered by insurance'. Collateral water and smoke damage was sustained by the McLaughlin furniture factory and 'a network of sheds containing great quantities of timber, mostly the property of Mr Joseph Ballintine, were saved only by the energy of the brigade'.

31 MARCH 1930

The crew of the coaster *Wheatplain* which, having been shipwrecked in dense fog off the Donegal coast, was marooned on Tory Island, had both pleasant and unpleasant memories of their life amongst the islanders. Arriving at the Sailors' Rest, Derry, on the night of Monday, 31 March 1930, they told of their adventures.

They had left Birkenhead, Merseyside, on the previous Wednesday for

Westport and Kilrush on the west coast of Ireland with a cargo of flour. As they approached the Irish coast on Thursday morning they encountered the dense fog. The skipper Captain W.P. Glendinning, the mate Mr Lamb, and Able Seaman Gibbons were on the bridge when, suddenly at about 2 a.m., the vessel ran on the rocks on the eastern side of Tory Island. The fog was so thick that it was impossible to see anything, but with high seas raging it soon became evident that there was no hope for the ship.

Captain Glendinning ordered one of the lifeboats to be launched, and it pulled away from the vessel but stood by. It was then quite close to the land which was not visible owing to the fog. The crew remained in the lifeboat until dawn approached to see if it would be safe to go aboard the *Wheatplain* to discover precisely how she lay. As day was breaking a boat put out from the island, about a hundred of the inhabitants, learning of the wreck, having flocked to the shore. This contained fourteen or fifteen of the islanders who made for the *Wheatplain*'s lifeboat from which the crew threw them a rope; the islanders towed them ashore.

Captain Glendinning, a Derry man, asked the islanders to put him on board the vessel again as soon as possible so that he might get some clothes and other necessaries for his crew, some of whom were scantily clad. The islanders suggested that it would be advisable to wait for low water at ten o'clock, and he considered this a reasonable enough suggestion and agreed to it. However, the crew had not been long on the island when two boats pushed off in the direction of the *Wheatplain*; soon afterwards Glendinning saw a light in his chart-room. He enquired angrily why anyone had gone aboard without his permission and succeeded, after some difficulty and in the face of threats, in getting a boat and reaching the stricken ship again. On boarding her he found to his dismay that many of his and the crew's belongings had disappeared.

If there were black sheep on the island, however, these were more than outnumbered by those who were some of the finest people in the world, according to the Captain. This included the Reverend B. Gallagher, whose influence on his parishioners resulted in many of the missing articles being eventually restored to their owners.

APRIL

Public passenger transport in Derry city, which celebrated its Diamond Jubilee on 1 April 1957, was the subject of a talk by the Ulster Transport Authority's Commercial Officer, R. Carlisle, to Londonderry Rotary Club on Monday, 18 March. Referring to the opening of the City of Derry Tramways one hundred years previously, Carlisle pointed out that the line had been constructed by Messrs. McCrea and McFarland, who were paid for their work in shares and so became the proprietors of the tramway, which ran from the Lough Swilly Station to the west end of the then Carlisle Bridge. The single track with intermediate passing loops provided a service which ran mostly on the half-hour. The tramway never knew any form of motive power other than the horse.

'The tramway was closed in 1916 and there then seems to have been something of a hiatus, so that the Diamond Jubilee history of your passenger transport system is not, I am afraid, one of progress which was entirely uninterrupted,' added Carlisle. 'However, in 1918, your Corporation obtained powers by a private Act of Parliament to provide, maintain and run omnibuses within the city and, accordingly, on 1 March 1920, a municipal motor bus service was introduced. This service was confined to that part of the city lying to the west of the river, and, I believe, did not earn any very handsome profit for the ratepayers.

'An agreement was reached with Catherwood Ltd., then one of the principal omnibus operators in the Province, whereby for a period of twenty years from 1 April 1929, Catherwood's should lease from the Corporation the exclusive right to run omnibuses within the city, subject to their having the right to surrender the lease if they so wished at the expiration of ten years. As one of the omnibus operators in Northern Ireland, Catherwood's were acquired by the Northern Ireland Road Transport Board in 1935 and the service previously provided by them in the city was continued by the Northern Ireland Road Transport Board. In 1948 the Board was vested in the Ulster Transport Authority, and that is how we now come to operate the city service in Londonderry.'

Carlisle said that from the establishment of the Northern Ireland Road Transport Board in 1935 until the year ended 30 September 1951, there were surpluses in each year, giving a benefit to the ratepayers for the city amounting at its lowest to £593 in 1936, and at its highest to almost £10,000 in 1944; in the years since 1951, however, there had only been two surpluses. In all, the Corporation had benefited since 1935 by £81,000, which represented about five and a half percent of the gross receipts during the period. In recent years the Lone Moor and Creggan services had started, and there had been the extension to Altnagelvin. 'I think it is quite fair to say that the city bus service plays the ever-increasing part in the life of Londonderry,' he added.

2 APRIL 1934

On Monday, 2 April 1934, the Associated Clubs of Apprentice Boys of Derry from the Maiden City, Belfast and district visited Enniskillen at the invitation of the local Browning Branch Club and a large demonstration was held. A sizeable part of Fermanagh, including several Orange lodges from the surrounding district, turned out to welcome the visitors from all parts of the Six Counties and many from the Free State.

The demonstration was organised by the Amalgamated Committees of Belfast and Portadown and the General Committee, Londonderry. The arrangements at Londonderry in connection with the demonstration were carried out by Mr A. White and a sub-committee. From the Maiden City alone upwards of a thousand people made the journey by special train to Enniskillen. The Londonderry contingent consisted of the seven parent clubs: the Apprentice Boys of Derry Club, the Walker Club, the Mitchelburne Club, the No Surrender Club, the Browning Club, the Baker Club and the Murray Club; in addition there were four bands: the Britannia Brass and Reed Band, the No Surrender Fife and Drum Band, the Molenan Pipe Band and the Churchhill Fife and Drum Band.

Friends and members of other loyal organisations took advantage of the Easter holiday to make the journey. The *Londonderry Sentinel* the following day remarked that seldom indeed was it that the parent clubs left the city: it was generally the case that the branch clubs visited the Maiden City, the home of the Apprentice Boys. 'No other place,' the newspaper stated, 'apart from Londonderry, has such loyal traditions associated with it as Enniskillen, famous also for its defence and brave men who preferred to die rather than sacrifice their principles. It was fitting, therefore, when arrangements were being made for the demonstration that Enniskillen should have been chosen as the venue.'

The Derry contingent had assembled on the Mall Wall in the morning and the procession was marshalled by Brother A. White, who headed it along with the Lieutenant-Governor, Brother A. Birney. Included in the procession was the drum beaten by the Prince of Wales when he opened the Northern Parliament Buildings at Stormont. It marched via Bishop Street, Ferryquay Street, Carlisle Road, and John Street to the Great Northern Railway Station, from which the Apprentice Boys made the journey by special train. Contingents from other places joined the train at various points along the line. As the procession, which was headed by the Britannia Band, passed the City War Memorial all colours were dipped in salute to the fallen.

On arrival at Enniskillen the various contingents were marshalled on the Fair Green and then proceeded on through the main thoroughfare to a field in the vicinity of Brook Street, where a short meeting was held. Brother C.L. Corry presided and among other speakers was the Minister of Agriculture, Brother Sir Basil Brooke. On the march to the field a wreath was laid on the War Memorial in tribute to the Apprentice Boys of Enniskillen who fell in the Great War.

3 APRIL 1925

On Friday, 3 April 1925, the *Derry Standard* reported that at the Derry Recorder's Court the previous day, before his Honour Judge Osborne, KC, John Breslin, a tailor from Capel Street, appealed against the decision of the magistrates which sentenced him to a month's imprisonment as a result of making a false declaration to claim unemployment insurance. Mr J. Young appeared for the Ministry of Labour and Mr A. Robb represented Breslin.

Mr Young pointed out that the chairman of the magistrates stated that he had been present when the appellant was convicted on a former occasion, at which time a warning had been given that he would be sent to prison if convicted again. The appeal was with respect to a conviction that was recorded on 26 February. Young submitted that this was a particularly bad case, but Mr Robb did not dispute the facts: Breslin was a very old man, suffering from bronchitis or asthma which was aggravated by his trade; he had represented that he had been out of work, but the fact was he was suffering from a sort of stupor as a result of taking drink. He asked his Honour to impose a fine, as Breslin had a wife and family.

Mr Young asked: 'Aren't they all working? Mr Robb said that they were not all working. This man had been out of work for a considerable length of time.' Breslin stated that he was sixty-five and had two sons who were not working. Mr Young countered: 'Drawing the dole, I suppose?' to which the witness replied that he had been employed at Mulholland's but had been put out of work. At the time he had been troubled owing to the death of a relative, and was making the funeral arrangements. He took 'a drop too much'. Judge Osborne asked: 'And when you take a drop too much you go and draw the unemployment benefit?'

His Honour said that this Unemployment Insurance Act offered a great temptation to get the dole rather than work, or for people to represent that they were out of work to draw the dole in addition to their wages. That could not be tolerated. Had this been Breslin's first offence, the court would have acceded to the request of Mr Robb, especially as this was an old man; but Breslin had already been warned of the consequences at the time of his previous conviction, and so the original decision of the magistrates to impose a month in prison stood.

4 APRIL 1933

An inquest into the death of a cyclist was resumed at the Coroner's Court on 4 April 1933. The deceased was Michael Farren of Ballybrack near Moville, who had been cycling home from Lifford hospital after visiting his daughter who was a patient there. The journey of seventy-four miles in total was not regarded as being anything out of the ordinary in those years when the bicycle ruled. Farren had been cycling down Strand Road and had come level with the site of the Lough Swilly railway station. Meanwhile a bus being driven in the opposite direction swerved right to avoid ploughing into 'three or four' dogs in a huddle in the driver's path. Farren suddenly realised that the bus had swung in front of him and he quickly swerved to his right, assuming that the vehicle intended to pull into the premises of H.A. Catherwood, who then held the franchise for the city's public bus service. What happened next was never made quite clear: the bus certainly hit the cyclist and he was heard to scream just before impact. He was dragged the length of the bus and when it stopped, his leg was trapped under the front wheel. At this stage he seemed immune to the massive shock and haemorrhage that soon caused his death. He asked for a glass of water, which was given to him.

At the inquest before Coroner John Tracy, Jean McAleese of Shantallow said that she was walking towards Pennyburn on the left pavement of the Strand Road and noticed Farren in front of her, well in on his own correct side. She also observed the two dogs that indirectly caused the accident. She reported that, when Farren saw the bus swerve to his side of the road, he instinctively swung out to the right towards the crown of the road: 'Then he seemed to lose his head and turned to come back. The driver of the bus swung further to the right but struck Farren with his left front wheel.'

The coroner said that in his opinion there could be no responsibility attached to the driver but laid the blame squarely at the door of the dogs' owners: 'My strong opinion is that the owners of these dogs have a great deal to answer for.' The jury found that Farren met his death through shock and haemorrhage received through coming in contact with a bus. Asked if they had anything to add, the foreman George Copeland answered: 'No.'

5 APRIL 1907

On Friday, 5 April 1907, the *Derry Standard* reported that two days previously in the Recorder's Court, Ezekiel Bredin of Drumcorn and Daniel McDaid from Glebe, had been seeking damages against William J. Curry from Melrose Terrace in the Waterside as the consequence of an incident that had occurred on Christmas Eve in 1906.

Dr Alexander, presenting the plaintiffs' case, stated that on the evening of 24 December, Mr Bredin, a farmer, was driving into Londonderry, accompanied by Mr McDaid, who was sitting on the front of the trap with him and two boys who were sitting behind. Coming down Chapel Brae a little after six o'clock, a horse belonging to Mr Curry ran into the trap knocking down Mr Bredin's horse and vehicle. Mr Bredin was thrown off, receiving very severe injuries, and Mr McDaid broke his collar bone; the trap was smashed. The plaintiffs held that the accident occurred through the negligence of the defendant's man, who had been delivering coal but went into a public house and left his horse and cart outside with nobody in charge.

Bredin said he saw the runaway coming behind him and had not time to get out of the way. The animal collided with them, throwing him over his own horse's head. His horse was thrown down, and the shafts of his trap broken, enabling the horse to break free and gallop over its owner, injuring him on the leg and body. As a result, Bredin was laid up for six weeks.

Mr Smiley said the case for the defence was that while John Begley, coal-driver for the defendant, was leading the horse along the Strabane Old Road some boys were playing football in Ashgrove Place and their ball struck the horse on the head, causing it to bolt. Begley held on until the horse came to the corner, where there was an electric lamp, and in order to save himself from being crushed against the pole he had to let the horse go. It then charged down Chapel Road, causing the unfortunate accident.

William Curry remarked that he had bought the horse in June and it had been a quiet animal. Further, he said, Begley was a sober man, or he would not be in Curry's employment. While sympathising with Curry, His Honour ruled that the plaintiffs were entitled to damages. He duly awarded £15 15s in damages to Bredin and £5 5s to McDaid, with 30s expenses and costs.

6 APRIL 1956

In the years after the Second World War, tennis ace Jaroslav Drobny was a force to be reckoned with. As well as winning the Wimbledon crown, he won the French Open twice and the Italian championship three times. Renowned for one of the fastest serves in the game, the left-hander actually competed at Wimbledon for three different countries: in 1938, aged sixteen, 'Drob', who hailed from Prague, made his Wimbledon debut as a Czechoslovakian; the following year, he represented Bohemia Moravia; after the war, Drobny competed on the world-famous court once more as a Czechoslovakian. However, following his defection to the West in 1950, he secured an Egyptian passport and represented that country at the Wimbledon tournament in 1952. He was still an Egyptian subject two years later when he emerged from the London court as men's champion. By the time of his final Wimbledon appearance in 1960 he was a naturalised British subject.

On 6 April 1956, Drobny was officially received at the Guildhall by the mayor, Senator S.S. Dowds, before taking part in a lawn tennis exhibition at Londonderry High School along with three promising British Davis Cup Players: Michael Davies, Billy Knight and Bobby Wilson (all of whom were twenty years of age). A crowd of six hundred attended. The *Londonderry Sentinel* remarked that the court surface did not seem altogether to suit the players and they did not appear to be going 'all out'. Nevertheless, play was of a high standard.

Drobny beat Davies 6-3 in the first set of a singles match, but Davies came back with 6-4 in the second set. Drobny's variety of strokes and shots, noted the newspaper, and his ability accurately to switch play to every part of the court was all too evident. Davies had plenty of speed in getting to the ball and a strong sweeping forehand volley was his most dangerous weapon, but the maestro dictated play all through.

In the other singles match Knight, a powerful hitter and a left-hander like Drobny, beat Wilson 6-3 and 6-1. In the doubles, Drobny and Davies beat Knight and Wilson, 3-6, 3-6, 6-4, 7-5.

7 APRIL 1943

On Wednesday, 7 April 1943, at Londonderry Petty Sessions, thirteen defendants were charged with unlawfully participating in a strike involving journeymen butchers from the city abattoir. The defendants were William Doherty, James Boyle, Arthur Fitzsimmons, Thomas McCourt, Leo McDaid, Edward McDaid, Daniel Boyle, William Boyle, William McDaid, James Cassidy, William Hegarty, Charles Doherty and Patrick Boyle.

Mr P. Maxwell MP, who appeared for all thirteen men, argued that sixteen-year-old Patrick Boyle was only an apprentice who had been left with nothing to do when the dispute began. In Belfast prosecutions against apprentices arising out of the butchers' strike had been withdrawn and he understood the District Inspector was willing to adopt the same course here. District Inspector Dobbin agreed and the case against Patrick Boyle was dismissed.

The Belfast strike, Mr Maxwell explained, had arisen because the butchers held that the tying of sheep for slaughter was not part of their work, and if the practice was to continue they either wanted more money, or other men employed, to do it. Since the Belfast men had not notified the Ministry of Labour of the dispute, it was deemed illegal, thus making the actions of the Derry butchers, who came out in sympathy with their Belfast comrades, illegal also. Mr Maxwell, in a plea for leniency, mentioned that the Belfast strikers were each fined £1. However, District Inspector Dobbin countered that the Derry strikers had had no grouse whatever, and he asked for a heavy penalty.

The Resident Magistrate, Captain P.S. Bell, noted that Mr Maxwell, in his plea for leniency for the defendants, had not indicated any sympathy for the ordinary people of Derry who had been deprived of their food because of the butchers' action. 'I saw an advertisement in the Press,' he continued, 'inviting applications from the veterinary profession for positions under the Ministry of Agriculture. It would cost a man about a thousand pounds to become a veterinary surgeon as well as constant burning of midnight oil, yet the remuneration offered the veterinary surgeons was only a shilling or two above that earned by the men who went on strike... I don't know what sort of world we are coming to. I am told the Court in Belfast imposed a fine of £1 on each of the defendants there. The Court in Londonderry is in no way bound by the decisions of the Court in Belfast, and the Resident Magistrate in Londonderry is a good many years senior to the Resident Magistrates in Belfast. This conduct is anti-social, revolutionary and disgraceful, but in the administration of justice it is desirable that there should be some sort of uniformity; therefore in following the fine of twenty shillings in Belfast, as Resident Magistrate for Derry, I do so with great reluctance.'

8 APRIL 1912

On Tuesday, 16 June 1987, the *Londonderry Sentinel* announced the imminent closure of the Palace Cinema on that coming Saturday. Giving its readers a short history of the Palace, it highlighted the effects of the coming of sound and the introduction of Cinemascope, among other touchstones in the cinema's past. In April 1954, the *Sentinel* noted, an extra wide screen and thirty loudspeakers were put in place to do full justice to Richard Burton's conversion to Christianity in the Roman epic, *The Robe.* That film ran for eight weeks and was seen by 192,000 movie fans.

It had been somewhat different when the 'Picture Palace', as it came to be known, first opened its doors on Shipquay Street on Monday, 8 April 1912. The opening had been anticipated in the local press for weeks and on the afternoon of Saturday, 6 April, a special preview was arranged for Mayor John M'Farland and other city dignitaries (including William Colhoun, the City Sheriff, D.G. Hogg, His Majesty's Lieutenant and their wives), though the *Derry Journal* reported a full house with many children in the audience. The programme included a film of the late king, Edward VII, which was 'not wanting in pathetic interest' showing him in 'quite lifelike manner mounting his horse and starting for sport'; a visit to Antwerp Zoo and a trip down the Zambesi River; and three cine-plays (though the term wasn't used then), *A Signalman's Bride, The Innocent Burglar* and *A Cure for Jealousy,* proved considerably more popular than *Wild Birds at Home*. In the strangely formal parlance of the time the individual items were referred to as 'exhibitions' and there was much praise for the 'Kinematograph'. Speaking after the private showing, Mayor M'Farland congratulated 'the Irish Living Picture Company on the splendid display of pictures to which they had treated the audience'.

There was no mention then of such a thing as a 'film star', yet by the time the Picture Palace had opened Mack Sennett, Mabel Normand, Mary Pickford, Tom Mix and the Gish sisters, Lillian and Dorothy, all had fan clubs and Pearl White was revving up to make the first of the popular serials *The Perils of Pauline*. Within a few decades Derry would have seven cinemas, still called 'picture houses' by the locals: the Strand, the City, the Rialto, St Columb's Hall (its flat floor making sightlines difficult), the Midland, the Opera House, hastily converted, as well as the Palace. Children were catered for with Saturday matinees in the City, Hall and Midland, and film became part of the city's life, even if not always approved of by the Church. When differential certificates U, A and H (for horrific) were introduced for parental guidance they tended to be ignored by cinema staff who argued that if children understood the adult allusions in the fairly staid films of the early decades of the twentieth century they were old enough to see them.

9 APRIL 1953

Joseph Hubbard Welch's association with the Derry shirt and collar industry, which extended over a period of more than six decades, began in 1892 when he first came to the city as a young man of eighteen to visit the Welch, Margetson and Company factory which his grandfather Joseph James Welch had founded, and which his father Joseph had carried on. In 1894, J.H. Welch came to live permanently in Derry as a resident partner in the firm.

The firm of Welch, Margetson and Company was established in the Maiden City in 1846–7 when a depot was opened in two houses in Clooney Terrace. The firm later transferred to more commodious premises in Foyle Street. With the introduction of the sewing machine, business steadily expanded until in 1876 a factory in Carlisle Road was opened to deal with the growing worldwide demand for its products. The firm was the first Derry manufacturer to install electric light and power, around 1886.

By 1900 several major extensions to the Carlisle Road premises had taken place. Under J.H. Welch's guiding hand the firm introduced the conveyor belt system, another first in Derry, which revolutionised the method of production in the industry. About seven years before his death on Thursday, 9 April 1953, Welch retired as an active director of the firm, but he maintained an interest in it to the last. He was also interested in the city's public affairs, entering the Corporation in 1926 as a councillor for the East Ward; later, in 1936, when it merged with the North Ward, he was returned as a councillor for it, remaining a member of the City Council until 1946. He was, for a number of years, chairman of the Electric Lighting Committee.

J.H. Welch was elected as a member of the Londonderry Harbour Board in 1929, becoming a chairman in both 1947 and '48. He took on the office of City High Sheriff in 1928, the same year he was awarded the MBE, and was appointed His Majesty's Vice-Lieutenant during the Second World War, having already been appointed Deputy Lieutenant a short time previously. As a fervent Unionist, Welch had been Honorary Treasurer of the City of Londonderry Unionist Association. He was also involved in the Derry Chamber of Commerce and, as a member of the Church of Ireland, represented Muff parish at the Synod of Derry and Raphoe, becoming a member of the Diocesan Council in 1944.

10 APRIL 1929

On the morning of Wednesday, 10 April 1929, Derry police found the remains of a female infant child in a suitcase in a bedroom at an address on the Waterside. At the subsequent inquest held in the Police Court by Captain O'Donnell, deputy coroner, Head Constable Neely stated that on information received on Monday, 8 April he went to the house of Annie Robinson on Glendermott Road. He told her that the police had been informed that she had given birth to a child, that he was inquiring into the matter, and that any statement she might make to him would be taken down in writing and used in evidence. After she was cautioned, she made a long statement denying the birth had taken place.

On Tuesday evening Annie called at the Waterside Police Barracks, and in a statement to Neely said that, on the Saturday night before Easter, she took ill around midnight. She was alone. The baby was born at 12.30 on Easter Sunday morning. Annie claimed she didn't know there was going to be a birth until she heard the child cry. After it was born, she had it in bed with her, and it died about an hour later. Annie went to work as usual on the Wednesday, leaving the child's remains in the house. Neely discovered the dead child at Glendermott Road when Annie Robinson pointed out a suitcase to him in an upstairs room;

she opened it, revealing a rolled-up cloth like a nightdress. When the cloth was unrolled, the body of the infant was apparent; Neely had it removed to the morgue.

Dr Crosbie said that, in conjunction with Dr J.A.L. Johnston, he carried out a post mortem examination of the body. In his opinion the child had been dead a week, and had not breathed for any length of time. In the absence of any evidence of violence or disease, death in his opinion was due to natural causes. He was asked by District Inspector Dobbin if the woman had received proper attention at the time of the birth, would the child, in his opinion, have lived. Crosbie replied, 'Probably, yes'; he also confirmed that the child was fully developed, but small. As a consequence of the evidence, the jury returned a verdict of death from natural causes.

At a special court afterwards, before Mr Denis Boyle, Annie Robinson was charged with concealment of birth. Dr Crosbie said in his opinion death was not caused by any wilful act or omission on the part of the mother. Dr Johnston corroborated. After the evidence of Head Constable Neely, Robinson was returned for trial at the next assizes.

11 APRIL 1944

On Tuesday, 11 April 1944, the *Londonderry Sentinel* reported that Patrick Thornton, a fifty-one-year-old railway goods checker who was seriously injured as a result of an accident on the previous Thursday evening, had died in the City and County Hospital on Sunday. An inquest was convened on Monday by Captain J.T.E. Miller, City Coroner, with C. McCormick representing Thornton's next of kin and P. Maxwell MP appearing for Michael Doherty, a taxi driver also involved in the accident.

James Thornton, son of the deceased, gave evidence of identification, and said his father was a keen cyclist. Dr H.M. Gault from City and County Hospital reported that Thornton had been conscious on admission to the emergency ward but did not know what had happened to him. He had an extensive lacerated wound on the forehead and a fracture of the skull, and death had been due to shock and haemorrhage following the aforementioned head injury which could have been caused by being knocked down by a motor vehicle.

In reply to District Inspector W. Lynn, Dr Gault revealed the dead man's injuries would indicate that he must have come up against something 'with great force'. Sergeant W.S. Magee, Inspector of Vehicles, described the damage to the taxi, driven by Doherty and owned by Denis Bradley of St Columb's

Street, and to Thornton's bicycle, saying that the damage caused indicated that the force of the impact must have been very severe. Sergeant Lee, answering Mr Maxwell, said the accident occurred on the deceased's wrong side of the road.

Thomas Curran, a lorry driver from Killea, gave evidence that he'd been walking on the road at Foster's Glen when a taxi passed on its own side, and a pony and trap and two cyclists came in the opposite direction. One of the cyclists, the one farthest from the footpath, looked behind as if to speak to the driver of the pony and trap, and swerved across the road in front of the taxi, which struck him. The cyclist, in Curran's opinion, seemed to be at fault. John Doherty, the driver of the pony and trap, said he was driving from Carrigans to Londonderry when a cyclist shouted 'Hello' to him; the cyclist then seemed to go across the road, was unable to get back to his own side, and struck the car.

The Coroner called it 'a very sad accident', expressed his sympathy for Thornton's relatives, but added that he could place no blame on the taxi driver. District Inspector Lynn, who had been at the scene of the accident, commented that it was very sad to see the life of such a loving father of a large family as Mr Thornton removed so.

12 APRIL 1719

Two distinguished officers, Lieutenant Colonel James MacGregor and Brigadier General Matthew Clark, who served during the 1689 Siege of Derry, were both later to enter the gospel ministry. After the Siege, many Ulster Presbyterians sought new lives in America, including Reverend MacGregor who accompanied a number of his flock to the New World in 1718. After many hardships they came to New Hampshire where a tract of land comprising twelve square miles had been assigned to the colonists; they named it 'Londonderry'. On the Sabbath of 12 April 1719, they gathered under a large oak on the west side of Beaver Lake, where MacGregor preached to them from Isaiah 32:2: 'And a man shall be as a hiding place from the wind, and a covert from the tempest; as rivers of water in a dry place; as the shadow of a great rock in a weary land.' The wilderness echoed with the sound of prayer, and what would become the oldest Presbyterian church in New England (and one of the oldest in America) was born, with James MacGregor as its pastor; he would be the spiritual guide and father of the church for ten years, and died on 5 March 1729. The Session, in noting his demise on its records, speaks of 'his merciful and triumphant death, and his victorious entering into the joy of his Lord'.

Anecdotes abound concerning this remarkable man. During the Siege, he was the officer who discharged the large gun from the Cathedral which announced the approach of the vessels under General Kirke which should have brought relief, but did not.

MacGregor's friendship with the French Governor of Canada, the Marquis de Vaudreuil (they had been classmates at Oxford), meant that the Londonderry colonists were never bothered by the Native Americans. During the French–Indian War, the Marquis instructed the French Catholic priests to frighten the redskins and forbid them to attack the Londonderry colony, 'as these people were different from the English'. They were further advised that if they did attack them there would be serious consequences.

After MacGregor's death, Londonderry Church enticed Reverend Matthew Clark from Ireland to be its pastor. General Clark was past sixty when he received ordination, 'laying down the sword of a hallowed defence for the purer service of the sons of Aaron'. He was nearly seventy when he answered the call from New Hampshire. He died on 25 January 1735, and his remains, in compliance with his wishes, were borne to the grave by old soldiers who had served under him in the Siege of Derry.

13 APRIL 1824

William Alexander, husband of the renowned hymn-writer Cecil Frances Alexander, was born in Derry on 13 April 1824, the third child of Reverend Robert Alexander. He was a delicate child with a hip disease that required him to lie for a year on a wooden stretcher, as recommended by the noted novelist Charles Lever, who was the dispensary doctor in Portstewart. The boy spent his ninth year immobilised but reading voraciously and afterwards recovered sufficiently to pile up debts as an undergraduate in Oxford and come down with a poor Fourth in Classics. His first appointment was as a curate in St Columb's Cathedral in Derry and while there was introduced to Fanny Humphreys of Strabane, the daughter of the Marquis of Abercorn's land steward in 1849. She was thirty-one to his twenty-five and already famous as the author of *Hymns for Little Children* (1848). Though there were accusations among the Alexanders of 'cradle-snatching' the two were happily married on 15 October 1850.

He served as curate in Killeter, County Tyrone, for the next five years up to his appointment as rector at Fahan in Inishowen (1855–60), and in Strabane (1860–7) until his prestigious appointment as Bishop of Derry and Raphoe on

20 July 1867. There they lived with their family of two boys and two girls until his wife's death on 12 October 1895. More than a year previously, on Tuesday, 6 February 1894, the *Londonderry Sentinel* reprinted a character sketch of the bishop taken from the *Leeds Weekly Mercury*:

> Dr Alexander is without controversy the greatest orator in his own Church, and since the death of the late Dr Magee, Archbishop of York, but much better known as the Bishop of Peterborough, it is open to question whether even on this side of St George's Channel the Anglican Church can point to his equal in eloquence... In the Bishop of Derry the imagination is so conspicuous, and is allowed so much play on its own account, not in defiance of logic, it is true, but still independently of that the hearer is often reminded of his descent from one of the most poetical and eloquent of races... Dr Alexander is no longer young, for he was born sixty-nine years ago; but in these days, when so much of the world's best work is done by octogenarians, he is still, even reckoned by years, not an old man... and listening to the tones of his splendid voice, it is easy to see that the Bishop is still remote from the time when the years that have been lived are felt as a burden...

Alexander was seventy-one when his wife died. She had been his pillar of strength and continuing inspiration but he still had the comfort of his daughter Nell, who acted as his housekeeper. In March 1896 he was enthroned as Archbishop of Armagh and Primate of All Ireland. He edited Cecil Frances's poems with a moving biographical introduction in 1897 and retired from the primatial see in 1911 to live in Torquay. He died later that year, having been presented by George V with the Grand Cross of the Victorian Order.

14 APRIL 1947

Charles Lynch, a forty-two-year-old labourer, William Duffy, a forty-six-year-old lorry driver, and thirty-one-year-old Thomas Moore, all from Mabuoy, Campsie were at Londonderry Petty Sessions on Monday, 14 April 1947, returned for trial on bail to the Quarter Sessions on alleged charges of breaking and entering a lock-up store at Maydown Aerodrome and stealing various goods, the property of the Air Ministry, and receiving the goods knowing them to have been stolen. Mr P. Maxwell MP appeared for Moore.

Detective Constable McComish gave evidence of examining the store, stating that a window had been broken at the catch. A few yards from the store a bag of nails were lying on the ground and a stove was found on a gun site; another stove was uncovered among some bushes. McComish proceeded to Mabuoy Camp, which was occupied by 'squatters', and entered a hut occupied by Lynch. Under a bed he found two meal bags which contained two pairs of hedge clippers, a Stilson wrench, a stock and die, a breast drill, two waterproof coats, four waterproof caps and two pairs of rubber boots. Comish continued that when he went to Duffy's hut he discovered a pair of rubber boots inside of which was an Air Ministry stamp. In Moore's hut he retrieved a waterproof coat. Returning to Londonderry, the detective met Duffy and Moore; when asked about the boots, Duffy said, 'I have no rubber boots', and 'hung his head and said nothing' when shown those that had been found in his hut. When shown the waterproof coats, Moore simply commented, 'That's all right.'

In statements to the police Duffy said: 'I can't say anything about it: I brought the boots home from the Army.' Moore claimed he 'bought one coat for 12s 6d and the other belongs to Samuel Wiley of Bond's Street, who gave me the use of it'. Lynch said he had nothing to do with stealing the goods from the aerodrome, but had found a bag containing some of the stolen items. Taking the bag home and putting it under a bed, his intention was to report the find to the police; he claimed to have been going for the bus to the barracks when he met the police on the road. When charged, the three defendants denied having anything to do with the theft.

A fifteen-year-old boy working with his father on a farm beside Maydown stated that at approximately 3.30 p.m. on Easter Monday, after crossing the aerodrome with a horse and cart, he met Lynch and two other men. Lynch asked the boy if there were any police on patrol to which the boy replied that there had been none since the navy left. The boy's testimony added to an already air-tight case against the three accused.

15 APRIL 1953

At 11.40 on the night of Tuesday, 15 April 1953 Mrs Johnston of Fountain Villa, Chapel Road, was startled to hear the sound of a snore behind the settee in her living-room where she had gone to close the curtains. When she saw a man sleeping there she screamed and Samuel Johnston, her husband, who had been folding up a card table, came running out, still with the table in his hand. He saw a man in the hall and threw the table at him, at the same time telling his wife to dial 999. They struggled for a while, the man with his hands round Johnston's throat, cutting off his air supply and wounding him above the left eye with his fist. He then ran to the porch door, kicked out the stained-glass window and escaped through the hole. It was later discovered that the door was unlocked and that it was through this that the man had gained entry.

The details of this episode and similar others were revealed when the twenty-eight-year-old Gerard Gallagher, a Derry man 'of no fixed abode', as the homeless were then described, was charged at a special court on Wednesday, 29 April with three counts of breaking and entering. On 24 October 1952, as alleged, he entered the licensed premises of Michael Gallagher on Butcher Street, taking £200 in cash and a pen belonging to the owner valued at £1. He was also accused of breaking and entering at the lock-up shop at 1 Victoria Road, Waterside, the property of William H. Crawford, four days earlier, from where he absconded with a quantity of razors, blades and cosmetics and in excess of £2 in cash.

For the burglary of the pub in Butcher Street he had hidden in the yard until after closing time. He made his way upstairs to the main bedroom in the private part of the house and found Gallagher's bunch of keys in a jacket pocket. Using them to open the safe, he found cash boxes inside and pocketed the contents. Asked in the police station by Head-Constable Carson to make a statement about the most recent incident, Gallagher claimed that he walked into the house when the door was open: 'I went into the sitting-room and was lying down behind a settee. I was dozing over when a woman came into the room and started to squeal. It must have been her husband, I don't know, who came along and fired a big pot at me and lifted a stick. I put up a defence and put my foot through a window and went out.' Gallagher was returned for trial at the next Quarter Sessions on bail of £200 and two £100 sureties.

16 APRIL 1941

By Easter 1941, although the Second World War had been raging for nearly two years, people in Derry still seemed unconscious of the risk of living in a town that was an important naval base with its own graving dock for the refurbishment of damaged destroyers and corvettes used to protect the vital Atlantic convoys. Even when Belfast was bombed by the Luftwaffe on the Tuesday of Holy Week, Derry people showed no alarm. That Easter Tuesday the focus of their attention was the Guildhall where the second day of the intensely popular Féis Doire Colmcille was in progress. So when at 22.40 hours the air-raid sirens sounded they were not unduly alarmed.

Everything was quiet for an hour; the Féis audience had largely gone home and only the people involved in Air Raid Precautions (ARP) remained on watch.

Then two deafening explosions rocked the city and the local anti-aircraft batteries started firing their shells, adding to the noise. Charles Gallagher, the driver of one of the ARP ambulances, drove to the Buncrana Road, then the city boundary. He found himself in a kind of fog and though he was still on a main highway his tyres felt as if they were being driven over a field. Suddenly an ARP warden loomed up out of the artificial haar: 'Corner of Messines Park. Direct hit on two houses... Stand by for instructions.'

It became clear that two landmines had been dropped, perhaps intended for the narrow opening of Ross's Bay where the River Foyle reaches the lough. They could have effectively blocked the exit for the many warships at anchor in the Derry docks. Landmines float down on parachutes and are not susceptible to precise targeting. One landed innocuously in a sandpit, causing the artificial fog. Later a pious parishioner of St Patrick's, Pennyburn, claimed he saw the statue of the patron direct the mine manually away from the church to land in the quarry. Messines Park was not so lucky: the street had been named after a WWI battle near Ypres in 1917 and most of the householders were veterans of the older conflict. The mine had blown a huge crater in the road, which was filling with water from mains and sewers. At least thirteen people were killed, the inhabitants of numbers 55, 57, 59 and 61, and as many seriously injured. One woman's body was found under rubble, still in bed, apparently without a scratch, dead of shock or blast. A crying baby was dug out from between two dead parents and a whole family was saved when the father, a naval veteran, seeing the flares and hearing the Ack-Ack, bundled his wife and six children into one large bed and pushed it between the two bedroom windows. The whole tenor of life in the city changed after that terrible night and though the Luftwaffe never returned, for many weeks there was an evening exodus of Derry people across the border into the nearby safety of Donegal.

17 APRIL 1895

Descended from a long line of distinguished seafarers, William Coppin was born at Kinsale, County Cork, in 1805. While still a young man, Coppin assisted in the rescue of six customs men from the Shannon after their boat had capsized. On leaving school, an invitation to spend the summer with relatives at St John's, New Brunswick, became a prolonged stay when William decided to enter the shipyard there.

After acquainting himself with the techniques of shipbuilding, Coppin boarded a vessel engaged in trade with the West Indies to study navigation.

Derry also traded extensively with the West Indies at this time and Coppin got wind of the fact that a timber merchant in the city had ordered the construction of a new ship; he applied for and attained the post of captain of this vessel and duly arrived on the Foyle in it with a consignment of timber for the merchant. The *Londonderry Sentinel* on 3 September 1831 contained the following paragraph: 'The ship *Edward Reid*, William Coppin, master, from St John's, New Brunswick, arrived in our river on Wednesday last, having made the passage in nineteen days.' The Derry merchant, pleased with the new vessel and her youthful captain, asked Coppin to supervise the building of a new passenger ship.

In 1832, the year after the Derry and Liverpool steamboat service was established, Coppin was appointed master of the *Queen Adelaide*, the first steamer on this route. Some months later he was put in charge of a newer vessel, the *Robert Napier*, and in 1839 he launched his first ship, the *City of Derry*. Two years later Coppin's *Great Northern* was constructed, driven by an Archimedean screw propeller, a technical feat which earned it a feature in the *Illustrated London News* in 1843. Having already turned his interest to salvage work, by the 1880s he was designing and building the triple-hulled iron ship, the *Tripod Express*, for the Atlantic run, and inventing the artificial light fish-catching apparatus which was revealed to the world in 1886. He somehow found the time to take on the responsibilities of a councillor in his adopted city amid all of this activity.

'Captain Coppin', as he was invariably addressed, was married to Dorothea Smith, the great granddaughter of Mary de Courcy (the daughter of Lord Kinsale). He had two sons and four daughters. Retiring from active work many years prior to his death, he passed away on 17 April 1895.

18 APRIL 1689

On 8 April 1689 King James left Dublin and marched with his army towards Ulster. He arrived at Omagh on 14 April. On the night of 16 April, while at Charlemont, James received a dispatch from his army's officers informing him that they had resolved to advance to the gates of Londonderry in expectation of being admitted. On the morning of 17 April another express arrived stating that the Jacobite commanders believed that if the king showed himself before the city, the gates would be opened. James determined at once to follow this advice, and rode to Newtownstewart, then Strabane, where he crossed the river on horseback and overtook his troops advancing from St Johnston about two miles from the city. On 18 April the Jacobite army reached the Upper Strand near Bishop's Gate.

Derry was surrounded, except on the river side, and there was considerable talk within the walls of the council wanting to surrender. It was, however, stipulated that the besieging army should not in the meantime advance to within four miles of the city. General Rosen was positioning the Jacobite forces around the city, and while the king's troops were being deployed into position, the Williamite Colonel Adam Murray advanced with a party of horsemen to a field below Pennyburn Mill. He received a message from Governor Lundy and the council, asking him to withdraw his men, and that preparations were being made to surrender. Murray marched to the city, and arrived at Shipquay Gate. The council sent him a message that he might be taken up alone upon the walls by rope, but the proposal was dismissed, and the gate was opened to him and his troops. The council, however, proceeded in their attempt to surrender. Murray was favourably received by the populace, who implored his assistance. He told them he would stand by them in defence of the Protestant interest, and that his first act should be the prevention of surrender and his next the suppression of Lundy and his council.

While Murray was addressing the crowd about the treachery of their governor, Rosen ordered the troops to advance towards the city. A trumpeter was sent out by the besieged to the king, requiring an hour's time to consider his summons to surrender, and requesting that the troops should advance no farther. Rosen took no notice of this. As the Jacobite army continued to advance with James at their head, a terrific fire belched forth from the walls of the city. This salute was so unexpected that the Jacobite troops were alarmed. The council of the city tried in vain to allay this alarm by laying the blame on a body of men whom they were unable to restrain. James, however, who had spent the whole day without food and on horseback in the pouring rain, decided there was nothing for it but to withdraw his troops.

19 APRIL 1908

On 19 April 1908, Easter Sunday, Derry's eighteen-year-old Guildhall went on fire. The first appearance of smoke was noted around 1.20 p.m. and the alarm was raised. The news was communicated to worshippers at church, and soon all Shipquay Place and the walls commanding it were packed with people. It was in the valley between the rear section of the building and the great roof covering the Assembly Room and corridors that the flames initially became evident through a ventilator on the Ulster Hotel side; a young man named Reynolds was the first to report the outbreak.

There was at the time a high north-north-easterly wind that carried the fire across the hall, and so rapid was its progress that flames were observed bursting through the gallery windows at the front of the building within ten minutes. It was 1.40 before the Fire Brigade arrived and about twenty minutes elapsed before their new motor engine got into working order. Alderman P. Campbell, chairman of the Water and Fire Brigade Committee, hastened to the scene to give valuable assistance. He phoned for the military, and in a short time some four hundred men of the 1st Hampshires had arrived with the regimental fire-extinguishing apparatus. Some were detailed for work in the inner circle, while others performed the duty of keeping the crowds outside the area of activity.

Carried by the high wind, burning sparks also fell in showers upon the roof of Mr McCool's licensed premises at the corner of Shipquay Place and Foyle Street, and it caught fire. There was danger of an extension of the fire, and Alderman Campbell got one of the Brigade men to climb to the roof and cut away the woodwork of the parapet, which was all that had been affected. It was soon reported that Mr Watson's place, which immediately adjoined Shipquay Gate, had also caught fire. This turned out to be untrue, but in checking this out it was discovered that a portion of the roof of Mitchell's premises in Foyle Street had ignited. A small body of soldiers and civilians was detached for service here and the premises were soon made safe.

There was no further extension of the fire, and for the remainder of the evening all the efforts of the military and civilian firemen were concentrated on the Guildhall itself. Afterwards there was much criticism of the Corporation for its inadequate fire provisions. The Guildhall had to be totally reconstructed, not opening again until 1912, but decked out in the same red sandstone with more elaborate ornamental tracery.

20 APRIL 1608

If Sir Henry Docwra had continued as Governor of Derry it is almost certain that Sir Cahir O'Dogherty (to use the contemporary English spelling) would not have gone into rebellion. Docwra's successor, Sir George Paulet, was despised by even his own men, not because he was a martinet, but because he was ill-tempered and cruel. Cahir was deeply indebted to Docwra. On the death of his father, Sir John O'Dogherty, in 1600, when he himself was a teenager, Hugh Roe O'Donnell had appointed Sir John's younger brother to be Lord of

Inishowen. But the boy Cahir had two potent allies—the brothers Hugh Boy and Phelim Reagh MacDavitt, who were bound to him by fosterage. The brothers persuaded Docwra to back Cahir against his uncle and he was pleased to do so. Apart from the policy of divide and rule, it also gave him the opportunity to mould the youngster. Additionally it fitted in with the English law of inheritance, as James I had restored to Cahir his father's lands.

Cahir's relations with Paulet were bad from the start. It was said that the governor had struck him with a riding-whip during an altercation. He also had a material grievance. Just before the settlement of 1603, Inch Island in Lough Swilly, which contained the best lands in Inishowen, was leased to Sir Ralph Bingley. Docwra had protested vigorously that the rights of O'Dogherty had been infringed, but without effect. James I also intervened and ordered that the lands should be returned, but his directive was received after Cahir had gone into rebellion. The truth was that he was as impulsive and quick-tempered as Paulet and, being no politician, he decided on an armed rising.

To capture Derry he needed weapons and a ruse. He was on friendly terms with the Governor of Culmore Fort, Henry Hart. On 19 April 1608, he invited Hart and his wife to dinner at Buncrana. The Harts were hospitably entertained. Just before it was time to go, O'Dogherty took Hart upstairs and complained to him about Paulet's treatment and told Hart that he was his prisoner, vowing that he would put him to death if he did not surrender Culmore Fort. This Henry refused to do, but his wife gave way and she was marched to Culmore where she called out that her husband was lying in a ditch with a broken leg. The gate was opened and Cahir's men entered the fort and gained possession of arms, several guns, and two sailing boats.

Being a humane man, he killed none of the prisoners but marched at the head of 100 men through the night to Derry, only six miles away, arriving at 2 a.m. on 20 April. The whole town was asleep, and the settlement was defended only by a ditch and bank. The defences consisted of a fort at each end. O'Dogherty divided his force in two in order to attack each fort simultaneously. Despite the common surprise, there was some resistance. Paulet died during the struggle, and the houses were burned. When a relief force reached Derry on 20 May, they found the place a complete ruin, except the little cathedral church. Cahir himself was killed in a skirmish near Kilmacrenan in Donegal on 5 July 1608.

Reporting on the opening of only the second photographic studio of its kind in the world—George F. Crook's at Waterloo Place in Derry—the *Londonderry Sentinel* described the premises, which opened their doors on 21 April 1950, as a place where 'the self-conscious, the fastidious, the nervous, can have their photographs taken in the best and most satisfactory possible way by the people who know better than any others just how they want to look—namely, by themselves'. This was made possible due to an invention by Newtownards man Charles Powis, whose revolutionary type of camera dispensed with 'bright lights, stiff poses, and everything which makes the photographer's studio such an ordeal'. A *Sentinel* reporter had the opportunity of seeing the *Fotomatic* studio, and certainly it was a 'departure from the conventional in many ways'. Small and curtained-off, as it was, the sitter was given complete privacy in a three-mirrored room which was comfortable, 'homely to the eye', with no intimidating strong lights. When the sitters were comfortable they pressed a button 'and the photograph is taken, not according to the dictates of a studio photographer, but, precisely as the customers wanted it. The camera itself is fool-proof and no matter how foolishly the subject may take up his instructions, nothing can go wrong. Once he presses the switch his photograph is taken.' In addition, the sitter was spared the strain of sitting under a battery of bright lights because of an instantaneous flash system which didn't aggravate the eye, making the process particularly suitable for children. So fast was the exposure that, if the sitter moved, it made no difference to the perfection of the photograph and the 'most natural results may be obtained'. The first camera of this type was installed for use in a Belfast store, where hundreds of people took advantage of it every month.

Charles Powis, who was accompanied in Derry by his works manager, E.G. Athey, told a *Sentinel* reporter that the first of these cameras to go outside Ulster would be installed in London in the summer. They would also be despatched soon to New Zealand and America, and enquiries had been received from many other interested sources abroad. Powis, a lifetime keen amateur photographer, stressed that the success of his invention meant that he was now concentrating on producing units at his Newtownards factory for distribution over the world.

Monday, 22 April 1935 was a day of sporting triumph for Derry: Derry City Football Club won the Belfast City Cup; City of Derry Rugby Football Club captured the Ulster Provincial Towns' Cup, defeating Ballymena in the final by nine points to six at Ravenhill; and City of Derry Harriers won the Whitehead Cup for the Northern Road Race Championship.

Derry's soccer aces were, commented the *Londonderry Sentinel* the following day, 'winding up the season in a blaze of glory'. At Brandywell they defeated Portadown before a big holiday crowd by three goals to one, and as Linfield and Celtic only drew, this gave the Maiden City lads the Belfast City Cup. They had been 'struggling gallantly', continued the newspaper, for one of the big trophies since the formation of the club six seasons previously, but all eluded them until now.

They had been Irish League runners-up in 1931–32, and again in the present season when they fielded what was perhaps their best team; this had helped them to secure the North West Senior Challenge Cup for the fourth successive year. Three years before they had been strongly tipped for City Cup glory but were beaten in all of their last three games. Showing more consistent form of late they had been undefeated in the eleven matches they'd played so far in the City Cup, having won ten and drawing one (against Glenavon at Brandywell). Derry now had a five-point lead and could not beaten for the title no matter how the remaining games turned out, but the *Sentinel* reported that the team were hoping to emerge undefeated in their games against Newry and Linfield. Arrangements were afoot for IFA and Irish League officials to be at the Linfield match the following Saturday to present the cup to the Derry team.

The City of Derry rugby team's triumph was no less a cause for rejoicing, remarked the *Sentinel*: it had been a quarter of a century since they had figured in the final, and the last time they'd won the Towns' Cup was in 1908 when they had beaten Bangor at Dungannon by eight points to five. Meanwhile, the City of Derry Harriers, in winning the Whitehead Cup for the Northern Road Race Championship, had finished first out of fifteen teams, leading East Antrim, the favourites, by two points.

The heartiest congratulations of the citizens, the *Sentinel* concluded, would be extended to the two football teams and to the Harriers on the honours they had brought to the Maiden City.

General Tom Thumb was the stage name of Charles Sherwood Stratton (born 4 January 1838), a dwarf who gained considerable renown under the famous American showman, P.T. Barnum. Stratton had been a fairly large baby, weighing 9lbs 8oz at birth. He developed and grew naturally for the first six months of his life, at which point he was twenty-five inches tall and fifteen pounds in weight; then he stopped developing. His parents became anxious and took him to their doctor who said there was a possibility Charles would never grow to natural height. By late 1842, Stratton had not grown an inch in height or added a pound in weight from when he was six months old. Aside from this, he was a completely normal, fit child, with a number of siblings who were of standard size.

Barnum, a distant relative, heard about Stratton and, after getting in touch with his parents, went into business with the boy's father. Stratton made his first tour of America at the age of five with an enormously successful act that included impersonating the likes of Napoleon Bonaparte, singing, dancing and engaging in comical banter with a straight man. One year later, Barnum took young Stratton on a European tour, making him a global celebrity with crowds thronging to see him wherever he performed. He appeared before Queen Victoria, and met the three-year-old Prince of Wales, the future King Edward VII.

In 1847 Charles began to grow for the first time since the first few months of his life, but with tremendous slowness. On his eighteenth birthday he was measured at 2ft 8.5in. Two years later, he performed in Derry, gaining the following approbation from the *Londonderry Sentinel* on Friday, 23 April 1858: 'The levees of the little General, whose fame is worldwide, have been attended during the week by multitudes of all ranks and classes. His personal appearance even surpasses the anticipations we had formed. He is remarkably well-made, and peculiarly lively in all his movements; and seems to enjoy an excellent and lively temperament. He sings in character with considerable humour, his voice being shrill and piercing, but not at all disagreeable; while his impersonation of several celebrities drew forth repeated plaudits from the audiences. The entertainment is certainly of a most novel and interesting character, and the General loses no opportunity of affording his visitors a hearty laugh. It will be seen that this (Friday) is positively his last day of appearing in Derry: and we therefore recommend all who have not already visited this renowned General to attend some of his farewell levees.'

The deaths of James McGowan, a thirty-four-year-old storeman, and Laurence, his six-year-old son, on Wednesday, 24 April 1946, brought the total deaths caused by a fire at 11 Eden Place, off Rossville Street, the previous morning, to four. The other two fatalities were Mrs Jane Bradley, an eighty-three-year-old widow, and little Peter McGowan, aged two.

Mrs Bradley occupied the back upstairs bedroom and kitchen, and Mr and Mrs McGowan and their four children had the use of the upstairs front room; the downstairs front room, meanwhile, was let to Mr and Mrs Robert Cooke and their four children, whose ages ranged from fourteen months to eight years. Cooke had moved his family safely to the street when the fire broke out, but his attempts to rescue Mrs Bradley were in vain.

McGowan succeeded in lowering his wife and two of his children from the burning building but was overcome by smoke while carrying his sons in his arms; Peter fell back into the smoke-filled room while his father and brother, Laurence, clung to the window ledge. A neighbour freed Laurence from McGowan's arms and brought him to the ground just before McGowan himself fell to the street.

Giving evidence at the inquest, Dr L. Ganz, a house surgeon at the City and County Hospital, stated that both Mrs Bradley and Peter McGowan's bodies were severely burned; Mrs Bradley had succumbed to shock resulting from her injuries, while Peter had superficial burns on his face and trunk and had perished due to shock and suffocation. Dr Ganz further testified that James and Laurence McGowan had been admitted to hospital at 5.15 a.m. but both died at approximately nine o'clock that morning.

Elizabeth McGowan became the fifth unfortunate casualty of the fire when she passed away on Saturday, 4 May. According to Captain J.T.E. Miller, the City Coroner, death was caused by pneumonia following shock and burns affecting the face, arms and knees.

25 APRIL 1925

On Saturday, 25 April 1925, the *Londonderry Sentinel* reported that the Londonderry City War Memorial Committee had approved the design of the city's memorial to the fallen of the Great War at a meeting held the previous day. A scale model had also been put on show in the Guildhall's council chamber.

The *Sentinel* commented on the very striking design, by Messrs. Sidney &

Vincent March, of Bromley South, London, and said it should be one of the finest memorials in the United Kingdom. It was to be erected in the centre of the Diamond, and would be a worthy reminder of the gallantry and sacrifice of the sons of Derry who had answered the call to arms when war broke out in 1914.

The bronze and Portland stone edifice would be nearly forty feet in height and twenty-seven feet wide at the base. At its summit would stand a figure emblematic of Victory in War, typified by the laurel wreath extended over the four panels which would list the names—engraved in raised letters—of all those hailing from the Maiden City who had died in the conflict. The monument would be additionally embellished with two bronze figures, one of a soldier in the act of taking a trench and the other of a sailor coming hurriedly on deck and pulling on his oilskin. The design was to be submitted to the Corporation for their formal approval; on securing this, the foundations would be laid and work would be completed within twelve months.

That same day, the *Sentinel* also remarked upon the installation of the Londonderry City Voluntary Women War Workers' Memorial Windows in the Guildhall. This 'very fitting' tribute to the city's First World War heroes would mark the completion of the Assembly Hall stained-glass window scheme.

26 APRIL 1947

On Saturday, 26 April 1947, the *Londonderry Sentinel* reported that the law committee of the Corporation were proposing to lease a portion of the vacant ground opposite the Apprentice Boys' Memorial Hall to the Bayview Factory for building purposes. This decision was arrived at by the committee the previous Wednesday, disclosed in the minutes published on the Friday, and due to be passed at the following Tuesday's meeting of the council. The *Sentinel* presented this news with astonishment as many of those who fell in defence of the city in 1689 were buried in this patch of land.

When it had been proposed on an earlier occasion to use this land for building, many human bones (enough to fill two coffins, later interred in St Columb's Cathedral churchyard) and a number of weapons were unearthed. This really was sacred ground to those citizens determined to honour the legacy of Derry's past defenders and the ideals they stood for.

Past opposition by the likes of the Apprentice Boys and Orangemen to building on the site had ensured that the land had remained vacant. Given that there had been so much recent talk of providing much-needed open spaces in the city, the *Sentinel* implored the Corporation to do what it should have done a long time ago and make this sacred plot just such a space. The newspaper reminded its readers that for many years previously this had been the assembly point for the Apprentice Boys and Orangemen for their annual celebrations, and any proposal that could affect this tradition should be resisted.

The *Sentinel* could only assume that Unionists on the law committee had helped to pass this controversial resolution without fully taking into account all of the implications, and after further consideration they would resist its passing when the matter came before the council on Tuesday. Otherwise, the Bayview scheme would, like the construction of the electricity sub-station which currently occupied part of the site, represent yet another encroachment on what was an important physical part of Derry's historical landscape.

27 APRIL 1891

The brothers George and Weedon Grossmith were co-authors of *The Diary of a Nobody* (1892), a comic novel of late Victorian lower middle-class manners which Weedon also illustrated. The humour stems from the narrator, the socially and physically accident-prone city clerk, Charles Pooter, who is oblivious of how ludicrous he makes himself look by his petty snobberies. The *Diary*, which first appeared in the magazine *Punch* in 1888–89, met with immediate success, and has never been out of print; it also spawned the word 'Pooterish' to describe the tendency to take oneself excessively seriously and to worry about trifles.

George (1847–1912) began his career as a police court reporter for *The Times*, Weedon (1857–1919) as an artist. Both later became actors, George creating many of the most famous baritone *buffo* roles in Gilbert and Sullivan's Savoy Operas. In 1891, the year prior to the publication in book form of the *Diary*, George appeared in Londonderry's Opera House on 28 April. The day before the appearance of the then world-famous entertainer, the *Derry Standard* revealed that 'already many of the best seats in the house have been booked, and it is evident that our distinguished visitor will address a crowded audience'. The newspaper continued: 'Last week in Dublin the hall in which he appeared was unable to contain the crowds which sought admittance, and his entertainment was voted to be the best of the kind ever witnessed in the metropolis...'

Two days later, on 29 April, the *Standard* gave a short review of the performance, apologising that 'want of space forbids us giving a longer notice of what was undoubtedly the best evening performance which has been given in Derry for a considerable time'. Grossmith began, related the newspaper, 'with some reminiscences of his Savoy life, interspersed with snatches of his most popular Gilbert and Sullivan songs'. He went on to 'amuse his hearers with ludicrous incidents in connection with his tour'; his impersonation of a lady shopping 'created roars of laughter, as did also his imitation of a melancholy glee party'.

In the second part of his performance Grossmith gave 'a humorous foretaste of the way in which women will propose when their sex assume the upper hand' and 'concluded the imitation with a love song of the future entitled *Oh, take me away* ... The officers' burlesque was another of his funniest caricatures, and his banjo melody was clever in the extreme.'

In the concluding part of the evening 'the audience was fairly convulsed with laughter at his description of how a waltz is composed ... while "Henry Irving and his leetle dog" was keenly enjoyed by those who have heard the great actor'. The idiosyncratic style of Irving's acting was also mildly satirised in *Diary of a Nobody* when Pooter's son brings Mr Burwin-Fosselton to supper, 'who not only looked rather like Mr Irving but seemed to imagine he *was* the celebrated actor ... he began doing the Irving business all through supper'.

28 APRIL 1789

On 28 April 1789, a famous mutiny broke out on HMS *Bounty*, a British armed transport ship in the South Seas. The captain of the vessel, William Bligh, and eighteen loyal crew members were set adrift in a long boat. The mutineers, led by master's mate Fletcher Christian, sailed eastwards to settle eventually on Pitcairn Island.

One of the mutineers, Eglinton-born John Adams, was the subject of an interesting address given by a Mr Sam Henry at a meeting of the Derry Rotary Club held on Tuesday, 4 April 1939. Mr Henry said his interest in Adams—who had sailed on the *Bounty* under the name of Alexander Smith from London—had been aroused by a chance remark of a colleague of his, Mr James Adams, a Customs and Excise official in Derry, that he was a descendant of the same family. After years of research, said Mr Henry, he could prove beyond doubt that Alexander Smith of London was none other than the boy Adams, who spent the early days of his life in Eglinton. The present members of the Adams family, hailing originally from the townland of Tully, about six miles from Derry, were all perfectly cognisant of the story of John Adams, mutineer of the *Bounty*. Mr Henry had obtained his information from the great-great-great-niece of the mutineer.

On joining the *Bounty* on 7 September 1787, Adams had stated his assumed name and gave his age as twenty. It was believed that he took the name of Smith because he was the son of James Adams and Nannie Smith. His heart yearned for his mother, and, indeed, he called his eldest child Hannah (the full name for Nannie). The Adams clan were famous for sandy hair and light blue eyes and, as in Ulster, Alexander is shortened to Sandy: his assumed name may have had a veiled reference to his peculiarity. One of his descendants in Norfolk Island was even called Absalom Caleb Tully Adams, the name incorporating the name of the old home of the Adams family. Although blue eyes were recessive in transmitted eye-colour, it was found, in spite of the universal brown eyes of the Tahiti natives, almost seven per cent of blue eyes among the Adams descendants in the island of Pitcairn and Norfolk. Comparison of John Adams' portrait with family albums showed a marked similarity in the shape of the head, and the strange blue of the eyes was still a peculiarity of the clan.

The story of the Eden set up on Pitcairn, a colony pruned by massacre and trained by circumstance to grow round Adams, was well-known; the roots of that simple oligarchy, ruled in love and wisdom for thirty years, were lesser known. Adams's folk were Ulster Covenanters of the strictest type who worshipped in the little Covenanting Church in Waterside, Londonderry.

29 APRIL 1916

One of the 450 individuals who lost their lives during the 1916 Easter Rising was 2nd Lieutenant Charles Love Crockett, a member of the Royal Inniskilling Fusiliers, who died at King George V Hospital in Dublin. Educated at Foyle College and a member of Strand Road Presbyterian Church, he was the eldest son of Andrew Alexander and Rebecca Love Crockett of 'Mountfield', 7 Templemore Park, Londonderry. Crockett's remains are interred in the family plot in Derry City Cemetery and his name can be found on the Diamond War Memorial.

A member of the Young Men's Christian Association, Crockett was one of many who enlisted during the Great War. He was formerly in the Queen's University Officer Training Corps, and on receipt of his commission was attached to the 12th Battalion Inniskillings. He accompanied a detachment from his battalion at the Enniskillen depot to Dublin during the Rising, where he met his death.

Confusion surrounded Crockett's death. The *Derry Journal* said he had been shot by inadvertence by 'one of the military sentries'—what would now be called 'blue on blue' or 'friendly fire'. The *Derry Standard*, however, contradicted this statement, saying that a medical examination of the wound revealed that it was caused either by an expanding bullet or by a piece of metal fired from a shotgun. The newspaper went on to say that it was known that the rebels employed dum-dum bullets and cartridges filled with small pieces of iron.

The following letter, uncovered in the Public Record Office in London, and written by Crockett's commanding officer at the beginning of May 1916, appears to clear up the mystery as to how Crockett met his end. However, it muddies the water somewhat with regard to the date of death and as to whether Crockett died instantaneously on 27 April, as the letter claims, or from gunshot wounds in hospital on 29 April, as was reported in the Derry press:

> Sir, I beg to report that 2/Lieut C.L. Crockett, of the Battalion under my command, was killed at Dublin under the following circumstances—On Thursday 27th ult. He went out at 10.15 p.m., and was posted at Aldborough House, near Fitzwilliam Street, with the Lewis Gun Section. He was instructed to get in touch with the Officers of the Dublin Fusiliers, whose headquarters were about 100 yards up the Street, and about 10.15 p.m. he left his post to do so. On running across the Street he was fired at and hit by a Sentry, death being instantaneous.

Crockett's funeral took place on Wednesday, 3 May 1916. Full military honours were abandoned at the request of his parents, and no military trappings were in evidence except for four of his fellow officers walking abreast behind the hearse. It being impossible to get a coffin in Dublin, one was conveyed by motor from Derry, and the remains of 2nd Lieutenant Crockett were brought back from the Irish capital to the Maiden City.

30 APRIL 1881

On the evening of Friday, 29 April 1881, Fountain Street resident and army pensioner David Buchanan was found dead. His face was terribly mutilated, the under jaw being completely gone. Far down on his breast, partly covered by a tuft of grey hair which had formerly been a beard, lay the lower portion of his mouth without the teeth. The under portion of the face was a cavity of bloody debris; the nose was gone, but the flesh hung in lappets, torn in every direction. There was, however, what appeared to be a clean cut extending from the outer side of the cheek to the eye.

His wife Elizabeth insisted that he had shot himself with a pistol but this was not supported by the results of the post-mortem examination. Elizabeth was arrested, brought up on 30 April, charged with the murder of her husband, and then remanded. At the subsequent trial the jury concluded that Mrs Buchanan was guilty of murder, but they strongly recommended her to mercy. The judge said that this recommendation would be sent 'forward to the Executive Government for its consideration; but I cannot hold out any hope that mercy will be extended to you …' Putting on the black cap, he went on: 'In this case I have no discretion but to pass upon you the sentence of the law … I do adjudge and order that you, Elizabeth Buchanan, be taken from the bar of the Court at which you now stand, to the place from whence you came, the common gaol of this county of Londonderry, and that you be taken thence on the 23rd day of August next, to the common place of execution within the walls of the prison, and then and there be hanged by the neck until you be dead, your body to be buried within the precincts of the prison; and may the Lord have mercy on your soul.' The prisoner was observed to change in colour several times and repeated the words 'I am not guilty; no, I am not guilty'; she was then removed.

The sentence of death, however, was never carried out. On 30 July 1881, the *Sentinel* reported that the jury's recommendation had been forwarded to the Lord Lieutenant. An affirmation made by some gentlemen in the neighbourhood of Moville, where Elizabeth had resided in her early years, to the effect that she was much below the average in intellectual capacity, was also passed on. Then, on 9 August, the newspaper related that the sentence of death had been commuted to penal servitude for life, and that the prisoner had been removed by train from Londonderry to Mountjoy Prison in Dublin on the previous morning.

MAY

Derry's first female penitentiary was established on 1 May 1829 by the Hon. Mrs William Knox at Hawkin Street—then Cunningham's (later Hawkin's) Lane—which ran from New Gate towards the River Foyle, between Bridge Street and Wapping Lane. The purpose of the penitentiary was 'the reform of unfortunate females' who were there 'employed on plain work' and their earnings were deposited in the savings bank for general purposes.

According to the rules of the Londonderry Penitentiary, which initially housed ten inmates, the women were 'reminded of their voluntary seclusion and enjoined, under certain penalties, to conduct themselves discreetly and, in particular, to avoid any allusion to the past irregularities of each other'. After the inmates retired for the night no talk was allowed, and the rigid discipline stipulated that 'no message can be at any time conveyed but through the matron'.

What was described as 'the period of residence' was limited to three years, 'at the expiration of which, or sometimes, of two years, those who had been well behaved are sent to Scotland, America, or elsewhere, according to their wish, receiving a free passage, with some portion of clothing and sea stores'.

The Anglican Bishop of Derry was the president of the penitentiary board. It was controlled by two secretaries and a committee, all of whom were ladies, but it was also stated that the committee was 'assisted by a body of gentlemen'. Funds for the organisation were collected by a lady and a gentleman in each of the wards of the city. Besides the subscriptions and donations, the institution was also 'supported by the produce of labour'.

The penitentiary seems to have continued to function until about the end of the nineteenth century and, afterwards, it was a working men's club until the Great War when it was used by army units as accommodation. On the formation of the Ulster B-Special Constabulary the building became known as Whitehall and was used as the headquarters of the City and District. The accommodation included the open-air parade ground that was also used as a miniature range for rifle shooting. Indoors there was another miniature range, offices, an armoury, stores and recreation rooms.

During the Second World War, the building became the headquarters of the Londonderry Battalion of the Ulster Home Guard and after the war it was returned to the Special Constabulary, which continued to use the premises until its disbandment in 1970. The premises were also used as a headquarters of the Traffic Wardens service until it was transferred to Waterside RUC Station.

During an IRA bombing campaign shortly after the outbreak of the Second World War, Whitehall was one of two targets in Hawkin Street that was bombed. A bomb was left at the top of the steps leading to the front door but the damage was not extensive. About the same time a similar bomb was left on the windowsill at the former fire station at the corner of Hawkin Street and Lower Fountain Street but only slight damage was caused.

2 MAY 1952

The *Derry Journal* carried a story on 2 May 1952 about a 'domestic' case at Newtowncunningham Court heard the previous day. Jim Harkin from 10 Joseph Street, now disappeared, was charged with 'unlawfully entering a dwelling-house, the property of his sister-in-law, Bridget Harkin, Carrigans, in a violent manner with intent to enter and take possession'. The prosecution case was handled by Superintendent T. Kelly of the Garda Síochána and C.J. Furlong defended.

Mrs Harkin stated that she married John L. Harkin, the defendant's brother-in-law, in 1920. They cohabited for a few months in Derry before each returned to their mother's house. By now she had a son and when her husband migrated to America in 1921 she received no support from him for herself or her child. She had to work to maintain him. When Harkin came back from the States seventeen years later he asked for a restoration of his marital rights and they lived as a family in Pilot's Row, off Rossville Street, in Derry. He stayed for about a year and then, in 1949, returned to America. He was there for about a year, during which time he sent her money totalling £500, which she used to buy the house in Carrigans, the deeds registered in her name.

The husband returned in 1950 but began to ill-treat her, finally evicting her after three months, so that she had to seek shelter with her son. She had not had time to bring the deeds with her when she was 'put out'. Her husband went back to America in February 1951 and when Bridget was able to enter the house again she found that the deeds were missing with other important papers. Also gone were items of clothing and curtain material valued at a total of £40. On 8 April Jim Harkin, her brother-in-law, tried to force his way into the house, struck Bridget on the shoulder, used filthy language and threatened to kill her if she did not leave. He told her that she had no right to be in possession, as the house was his.

When Furlong cross-examined Bridget she denied that she had tried to strike Harkin with a smoothing-iron. The accused had previously admitted to the local Garda sergeant that Mrs Harkin's was the name on the deeds. Mr Justice Ó hUadaigh fined the defendant one shilling for the assault and bound him to keep the peace for a year on a personal bail of £10.

3 MAY 1909

Eighteen-year-old wireless operator Louis Allen Cattley, Mercantile Marine, SS *Geo* (London), was lost at sea after a torpedo attack by a U-Boat near Cape Pelero. On the evening of 29 January 1918, Cattley's transport vessel left Messina and had been at sea for an hour when a periscope was sighted. The transport gunner fired but the *Geo* was torpedoed. Cattley was at his post, sending out an SOS, and remained there until the transport went down. The signals sent out by Cattley attracted another vessel to the scene an hour later where it rescued fifteen of his crew colleagues from the water; the young seaman's staying at his post had saved these men from a watery grave. His name is recorded on the Tower Hill Memorial in London and commemorated on Derry's Diamond War Memorial.

Cattley's death was the second tragic loss for his parents, whose eldest son, Irvine, had died after a few weeks' illness on 3 May 1909 at the age of fifteen. Irvine had been a chorister at St Columb's Cathedral, where his funeral took place two days later. Awaiting the arrival of the remains in the cathedral churchyard were his brother choristers, all wearing their surplices. The oak coffin, topped with a cross of beautiful flowers, was borne by four senior choristers from the hearse in St Columb's Court up the steps into the churchyard; a solemn procession then proceeded into the cathedral.

Behind the choir, and preceding the hearse, were the officiating clergymen, Reverend Canon Hayes, the rector, and Reverend W.G. Murphy, who repeated the opening sentences of the burial service as they entered the church. The chief mourners followed the coffin, and while the choir and clergy walked up the nave, the organist Dr Jones played 'O rest in the Lord'. The coffin was then placed upon draped trestles at the church steps. Very slowly, to a minor chant, the 39th Psalm was sung by the choir; then the rector read the lesson taken from the 15th chapter and 13th verse of 1st Corinthians.

In Reverend Hayes' address he remarked that it seemed almost an impertinence to add anything to the beautiful words of the burial service, but he wished to emphasise the words of the lesson just read: 'We sorrow not as others which have no hope.' He referred to an inscription he had seen on a broken pillar in a graveyard in Syria—the place where the demoniac of Gadara had his dwelling 'among the tombs'. Etched over a boy's grave were the words: 'Titus, son of Malchus, farewell. Thou didst die before thy time being only twelve years of age. Farewell.'

4 MAY 1942

At a special court in Londonderry on Monday, 4 May 1942, the Resident Magistrate Captain P.S. Bell returned Annie Robinson, a native of Drumahoe and inmate for nine years of the Londonderry Union, for trial on the charge of concealment of the birth of her stillborn female child. Robinson had given birth to the child in a women's dormitory, put it in an attaché case, and kept it from 1 December until 1 May, when the matron (Miss Annie Ritchie) noticed a smell and made the grisly discovery.

Sergeant Hunter gave evidence that, on the previous Friday evening, he had gone to the Union on Glendermott Road, cautioned the accused, and took her statement in which she said: 'On 1 December I gave birth to a female infant at seven o'clock in the evening. It was dead-born. If it had been alive I would not have interfered with it. There was no person near the bed and none of the other inmates knew about the birth. I occupied the women's dormitory. I don't know how many women were in the place at the time. I kept the infant in bed with me and got up at eight o'clock on the following morning and put the body in a suitcase and kept it there from that until this.' The sergeant also said that Robinson told him she did not know the identity of the child's father.

Annie Ritchie testified that, on 1 May at 10 a.m., she was making the usual daily inspection of the dormitories in the body of the house when, in one dormitory occupied by a number of female inmates, she noticed an unusually heavy smell in consequence of which she examined a small attaché case concealed behind a partition. It was here that she discovered the unfortunate child's corpse. Noticing Annie Robinson, who was sweeping at the time, Ritchie asked if she knew anything about the case, to which Robinson replied: 'It was me who put it there, as I did not want anybody to know about it.'

Dr B. Deeny, the medical officer at the Union, confirmed that it was a full-term infant and stillborn, and that there were no marks on the body, which was considerably mummified with recent evidence of decomposition. It appeared to have been born at least two months previously, but the birth could have been at any time in the cold weather, which would have preserved it.

5 MAY 1945

Councillor James Hamilton of Edenmore, Northland Road in Derry, died on the evening of Saturday, 5 May 1945. He had been in indifferent health for some time and passed away in a Belfast nursing home where he had undergone an operation. A native of County Donegal, Hamilton had come to Londonderry as a boy from the Killea district and began his career with a business firm in the city. His industry and energy were irrepressible and he soon prospered. At his death he was senior partner in the then flourishing shirt manufacturing firm of Messrs. Hamilton & Sons on John Street.

Hamilton had been a member of the Corporation from 1918, and had held the office of Mayor from 1926–28. He had also been chairman of the Public Health Committee; was appointed a Justice of the Peace in 1920 and often adjudicated at the local Petty Sessions; was President of the Londonderry Unionist Association for many years; and had been a Children's Guardian, a member of the board of management of the City and County Hospital, of which he was also a Life Governor, a Past Master of Harmony Masonic Lodge No. 63, and an EK of the Royal Arch Chapter.

Hamilton was a lifelong temperance advocate, and his name was strongly associated with the Independent Order of Good Templars. He held the office of Grand Chief Templar of Ireland, and was a valued member of the Londonderry Temperance Council. He was also deeply interested in the activities of the Presbyterian Working Men's Institute, of which he was President in 1928. Outside business and public affairs, Hamilton's chief interest centred around Carlisle Road Presbyterian Church, of which he was a member of the church committee and for a time its secretary. He was also a senior elder of the church, and for many years the Clerk of Session. He worked particularly hard for the well-being of the Sabbath School, and for a long time was superintendent of the Morning School.

Paying tribute to James Hamilton at a memorial service in Carlisle Road Presbyterian Church on Sunday, 6 May 1945, the Reverend S. McVicker said: 'No one could have taken a greater interest in its welfare and in the welfare of its members than he did, and many have reason to thank him today for the positions and work he helped them to get. He was a generous supporter of our church funds and of every good cause. He had strong convictions on many subjects, and was not afraid to let them be known and to stand up for them … It will be hard to fill his place but may his passing be a challenge to others to come forward to carry on the work of Christ and His Church. We will miss him, but how much more will he be missed by loved ones…'

6 MAY 1926

The 1926 General Strike was a national stoppage of work by members of Britain's major industries, lasting from 3 to 12 May. The strike began when the Trades Union Council (TUC) called out its members in support of the miners, who had refused to accept a reduction in wages. It extended to all forms of transport, the iron and steel industries, the building and printing trades, and gas and electricity workers. Over two million men were out.

On Thursday, 6 May, the *Londonderry Sentinel* reported that a definite assurance was given that the supplies of commodities were ample and that Londonderry householders need have no anxiety of a shortage of any description. In the majority of cases merchants had taken the precaution of laying in exceptionally large stocks and these were considered sufficient to tide over the strike period. The only trouble likely to arise, the newspaper commented, was from people who, in a state of panic, were placing orders in excess of their normal requirements. With the object of dealing with these people, the organisation established by the Northern Government for the controlling of supplies of coal and essential commodities had issued directions regarding the sale of coal, flour, and sugar in the Londonderry area.

In respect of coal, a permit system had been established. No coal was to be supplied or acquired for domestic consumption where the stock already on hand exceeded five hundredweight. If the quantity the householder already possessed fell short of five *cwt*, a further supply could be obtained under permit up to a maximum of one *cwt* per week. In the case of factories and business premises, permits could be obtained for a supply not exceeding fifty per cent of normal requirements. In regard to the sale of flour and sugar, restrictions, it was understood, would be enforced, and wholesale merchants would be unable to sell their customers more than fifty per cent of the quantities normally supplied.

The Harbour Commissioners placed the Committee room of the Harbour Office at the disposal of the organisation, and on 5 May, over 300 permits for coal were issued. At times during the day a queue of applicants was in waiting. The following day the issue of coal permits was to be from the Custom House, while the office of the Food Committee would remain at the Harbour Office. Wholesale merchants would be prohibited from selling flour and sugar, except under permit from the Food Committee.

Derry, in almost every branch of its industrial activity, was gradually feeling the effects of the trade paralysis across the water. The quays were deserted of shipping, with only one vessel arriving from Mulroy on 5 May. Hundreds of dockers had been rendered idle, and, of course, with no shipping there was less work for carters. Cattle coming from Donegal and Tyrone for shipment had to be turned back. Londonderry pork curers had also stopped buying until shipping was resumed.

7 MAY 1980

Most Reverend Dr Neil Farren, Catholic Bishop of Derry from 1939 to 1974, died on Wednesday, 7 May 1980, at Nazareth House in the city. His remains were removed to St Eugene's Cathedral on Friday, 9 May, where he lay in state on Saturday and Sunday. The funeral took place after Solemn Requiem Concelebrated Mass in the Cathedral on Monday, 12 May.

A native of Buncrana, Dr Farren was born on 25 March 1893 and received his early education in St Mary's National School, Cockhill. His long association with St Columb's College, Derry, began in 1906. He completed his studies there in 1911, when he won a Donegal County Council scholarship, but was not allowed to go to Maynooth College, a constituent university, having to carry on his education at University College, Dublin instead. Specialising in moral philosophy, Farren secured a BA degree with first class honours and took first place in ethics. He entered Maynooth College in 1914 to study theology, and as at UCD, he was the head of his class. After two years he was awarded his BCL degree and, in 1918, he took the BD degree. Ordained in 1918, he was chosen for a place in the Dunboyne post-graduate establishment where, in 1919, he secured the Licentiate after a special study course of the new Code of Canon Law which had just been promulgated.

Shortly afterwards he was appointed lecturer in Dogmatic Theology in Maynooth. In 1920, he made ecclesiastical history by having the Doctorate in Canon Law conferred on him. He and a Dublin priest were the first students to be thus honoured in Maynooth. His thesis on Domicile and Quasi-Domicile became an essential reference for students of Canon Law. In 1920, he returned to St Columb's College as professor, taking time in 1921 to go to Rome for a special course in theology; the following year he became a Doctor of Theology. He returned to St Columb's College as a teacher of mathematics and science.

Dr Farren became President of St Columb's in July 1927, the youngest man to attain that post in any Irish college; later he became the youngest Irish bishop. He was appointed Bishop of Derry in 1939 in succession to the Most Reverend Dr Bernard O'Kane, and was consecrated on 1 October 1939 in St Eugene's Cathedral. In 1942 he was appointed the Northern Ireland representative of Cardinal Spellman of New York, and Ordinary of the United States Forces; he was awarded the US Medal of Freedom after the Second World War.

Dr Farren retired as Bishop of Derry early in 1974 after almost thirty-five years. On 31 March 1974, he was assistant consecrating prelate at the installation of his successor, the Most Reverend Dr Edward Daly. On his retirement Dr Farren returned to his native Buncrana, and there, in St Mary's Oratory, the diamond jubilee of his ordination to the priesthood was celebrated in May 1978.

8 MAY 1724

George Berkeley, the Irish philosopher and Church of Ireland clergyman recently appointed to the valuable deanery of Derry arrived there in May 1724 to pay a visit. In the ecclesiastical and political culture of the period a visit was not strictly necessary but he decided to see for himself the source of his valuable sinecure. His diary entries reveal his impressions:

8 May 1724

My house is a fashionable thing, not five years old, and cost eleven hundred pounds. The Corporation are all good churchmen, a civil people, and thoroughly English, being a colony from London. I have hardly seen a more agreeable situation, the town standing on a peninsula in the midst of a fine spreading lake, environed with green hills, and at a distance the noble ridge of Ennishawen mountains and the mighty rocks of Magilligan form a most august scene.

Later he noted on 5 June 1724:

The city of Londonderry is the most compact, regular and well-built town, that I have seen in the King's Dominion; the town house (no mean structure) stands in the middle of a square piazza from which there are four principal streets leading to as many gates. It is a walled town, and has walks all round on the walls planted with trees, as in Padua.

Unlike many of his contemporaries he had an interest in Ireland and Irish affairs. In his publication, *The Querist* (1735), he asked many sharp questions:

Whether there be upon earth any Christian or civilised people so beggarly wretched and destitute as the common Irish?
Whether there be not every year more cash circulated at the card-tables of Dublin than at all the fairs of Ireland?
Whether if there was a wall of brass a thousand cubits high round their kingdom, our natives might not nevertheless live cleanly and comfortably, till land and reap the fruits of it?

He was born in Dysart Castle, County Kilkenny, on 12 March 1685 and educated at Trinity College, Dublin, where he remained as fellow until 1713. In 1709 he published an *Essay towards a New Theory of Vision* as a prelude to his masterwork *A Treatise Concerning the Principle of Human Knowledge* the following year. It was a typical production of the age of enlightenment, offering an overarching view of reality: 'we live, move and have our being' in a divine mind that perceives everything in the universe. This Supreme Reason is theologically known as God. Our own ideas and perceptions of experience are merely imperfect apprehensions of a fuller reality. It was a view that greatly influenced later philosophers like David Hume and Emmanuel Kant who did not fully comprehend it. It is usually totally incomprehensible to the layman and rejected by the realist. The impatient Dr Johnson kicked his foot vigorously against a large stone, shouting, 'I refute it thus!'

Berkeley spent the last years of his life as Bishop of Cloyne (now part of the diocese of Cork) still deeply concerned with philosophy and ways of the improving the lives of his flock. He died on 14 January 1753.

From 1913 until 1928 Derry had no first division football team. An earlier club known as Derry Celtic had been voted out of senior football eleven years after its foundation in 1902. The years between had seen the horrors of the Great War abroad and the Easter Rising and the Tan War at home, followed by the creation of the Northern Ireland state. These cataclysmic events tended to put professional football far down the citizens' list of priorities but early in 1928 a group of fans, from all classes and creeds, met to try to establish a team of which the city could be proud. The first hurdle was the name; the 'Celtic' element was regarded as divisive so the intended new team should now be known as the neutral Derry City.

On 9 May the club affiliated to the Northwest Football Association, with Norman McClure, the son of one of Derry Celtic's directors, as Club Secretary; but it still had to be confirmed in status. The Derry delegates, led by William Arthur, made the attempt on 25 May but along with Crusaders and Brantwood their application was unsuccessful, perhaps because the forms did not arrive until two days after the deadline. It was a disappointment but it had the effect of making the committee more determined than ever to succeed. They *were* ultimately successful, as the crowd attending a match at the Brandywell between Derry Celtic and Richmond on Friday, 29 May 1929, learned at half-time.

Joe McCleery, a Derryman, then managing Dundalk FC, became the first manager of the new senior team. Negotiations for the purchase of a suitable venue began but nothing could be found in time for the start of the new season. The stadium at Brandywell had been used for football and other events for many years but it was strictly the property of the Honourable the Irish Society, the company of London guilds who had been assigned the county of Coleraine and the city called Londonderry in the society's honour at the time of the Ulster Plantation.

A working arrangement that still exists was agreed and, on 22 August 1929, the players of Derry City FC ran on to the turf wearing shirts of claret with blue sleeves and white not-very-short shorts. (The traditional red candy stripes were not worn until 1934.) Their opponents were Glentoran and the first score was a goal against the Belfast team by Peter Burke, who had served in the Free State army. Glentoran rallied in the second half and won the match 2–1. It was not until the evening of 7 September that Derry City had their first win, defeating the premier team Linfield 3–1. Derry were at last regarded as a side to follow and it is reckoned that in their first four home fixtures there was a total gate of 36,000.

1st Earl, Viscount St Pierre, also called (from 1892) Baron Roberts Of Kandahar, was born on 30 September 1832 in Cawnpore, India, the son of Abraham Roberts and great-grandson of John Roberts. After a military education, he served as an officer in the Indian army for a quarter of a century. He commanded the British forces in Afghanistan in 1881–82, and was later the Commander-in-Chief, India (1885–93), in the South African War (1899–1902) and finally Commander-in-Chief of the British army (1901–1904). Among the most respected officers of the British army, Roberts was awarded the Victoria Cross, Britain's highest award for gallantry, while serving as a lieutenant in the Bengal Horse Artillery during the Indian Mutiny.

The citation reads: 'Lieutenant Roberts' gallantry has on every occasion been most marked. On following the retreating enemy on the 2nd January, 1858, at Khodagunge, he saw in the distance two Sepoys going away with a standard. Lieutenant Roberts put spurs to his horse, and overtook them just as they were about to enter a village. They immediately turned round, presented their muskets at him, and one of the men pulled the trigger. Fortunately the caps snapped and the standard-bearer was cut down by this gallant young officer, and the standard taken possession of by him. He also, on the same day, cut down another Sepoy who was standing at bay, with musket and bayonet, keeping off a Sowar. Lieutenant Roberts rode to the assistance of the horseman, and, rushing at the Sepoy, with one blow of his sword cut him across the face, killing him on the spot.'

In 1899, his son, Fred Roberts, was also awarded the VC for his actions at the Battle of Colenso during the South African War. In the same year, on Wednesday afternoon, 10 May, Lord Roberts arrived in Londonderry for the purpose of inspecting troops in the garrison and the forts of Lough Swilly. He travelled by the 11.20 train from Belfast, and on arrival shortly before three o'clock at the Great Northern Railway terminus, was received by the Mayor (Alderman McLearn), Sir Newman Chambers, Town Clerk, and Colonel Wace DSO, commanding the troops in the North West district. The Commander of the Forces, who was accompanied by Colonel W.F. Kelly and Major H. Streathfield, assistant military secretary, drove at once to Ebrington Barracks, where the troops of the garrison were drawn up in line for inspection.

Four companies of the Royal Inniskilling Fusiliers, under the command of Major Sandes, and some fifty men of the Royal Artillery, commanded by Major Wright and Captain Hamilton Moore, were under arms, and the Field Marshal, having passed through the lines, the artillerymen were dismissed and the infantry marched past in companies. Afterwards the Inniskillings were put through manual and firing drill and bayonet exercise. Lord Roberts subsequently made an inspection of the barracks. Later he had afternoon tea with the Mayor and Mayoress in the Guildhall, and left by the 6.35 train for Buncrana to inspect the fortifications on Lough Swilly.

11 MAY 1899

Clara Butt was born in Sussex in 1872, and trained with the bass Daniel Rootham in Bristol. She won a competition organized by the Royal College of London in 1889, and in 1892 appeared in the title role of Gluck's *Orfeo ed Euridice*, performing the same role at the Lyceum Theatre in London. She went to Paris and made further studies with the Belgian baritone, Jacques Bouhy, and later with the celebrated soprano Etelka Gerster in Berlin. Saint-Saëns wanted her to study Dalila, but owing to laws then existing prohibiting the portrayal of biblical characters on the British stage, nothing came of it.

From 1895 she began a celebrated career, appearing almost exclusively on the concert platform. Her repertory was comprised of Bach, Handel, a little Lieder, but above all, of the popular ballads of the day. Clara 'created' Elgar's *Sea Pictures*, a piece especially written for her. She appeared in a few opera performances in one single role, as Orfeo, but triumphed in all the famous concert halls, making tours to Australia, Japan, Canada, the USA and many European cities.

Married to baritone Kennerley Rumford (called 'Bertie'), who accompanied her on most of her tours, she was one of the most distinguished singers of the time. In 1920 she was created 'Dame of the British Empire' for her charitable services during the Great War. Clara's three sisters were singers as well. One of them, Ethel Hook, became a famous contralto in her own right and made some solo recordings.

In later life Clara Butt was plagued by tragedies. Her elder son died of meningitis whilst still at school, and the younger committed suicide. During the 1920s she developed cancer of the spine, but her faith gave her the strength to continue working. She made many of her later records seated in a wheelchair, and died in 1936.

Clara performed in Londonderry's Guildhall on the night of Thursday, 11 May 1899, as part of a short Irish tour, which also included Cork, Dublin and Belfast. The building was packed to capacity. Several pieces preceded the first appearance of Butt, who sang Schubert's *Der Wanderer* in German with the finest effect. When about to leave the platform Butt was presented by the manager, Mr Henry B. Phillips, with a beautiful bouquet in the name of the audience amid the warmest applause. Having bowed to the audience, she retired, but was recalled again and again until she consented to the encore, and sang Alicia Adelaide Needham's beautiful Irish melody 'Husheen'.

Her next performance was in a duet with her husband singing Goring Thomas's 'Night Hymn at Sea'. After this the cry for 'more' was so persistent that both returned to the platform and gave the duet 'O, That We, Too, Were Maying' to the great delight of the audience. She then sang Henry Francis Lyte's well-known hymn 'Abide with Me'. Finally, after singing Frederick Crouch's 'Kathleen Mavourneen', the lady retired amidst immense applause.

12 MAY 1911

On Friday, 12 May 1911, thirty-eight young Derry women bound for Australia had an enthusiastic send-off from the Midland Railway Station, Waterside. They left by the 4 p.m. Larne express, but before the hour of departure the station and its precincts were crowded with people. The emigrants were the nucleus of the staff of a new shirt factory established at Melbourne by Welch, Margetson and Company. Each girl as a condition of her emigrating was advanced £4 or £5 with which to purchase an outfit, and received a guarantee of twenty-five shillings a week for three years. Passages were secured for them and suitable lodgings at the journey's end recommended. When the factory was in full working order the wages obtaining in Melbourne were to be paid.

As the time of leaving approached the throng increased. The ticket checkers were brushed aside in the rush of people at the platform gates and soon the departure platform was packed to capacity. Even the emigrants had enormous trouble in reaching the carriages, but the overcrowding became less severe when many of those present passed on to the outer end of the platform and up the embankment that skirted the river in order to get a better view of their friends' leaving. This vantage point also became also packed with people as far as the first signal box. Many had to content themselves with viewing the departure from the opposite platform. Mr Candy, the stationmaster, and his staff had an onerous task on their hands, and it was to their credit that the train left in good time and without any serious incident.

As the *Queen Alexandra* moved out of the station, detonators which had been positioned on the line gave the signal to vessels at the harbour and every available siren filled the air with prolonged shrieks, cheer upon cheer went up from the mass of people, and many a tear-stained handkerchief was waved in farewell from the carriage windows and platforms. The size of the crowd was partly accounted for by the fact that the firm the girls worked for had allowed as many of their fellow-workers who wished to join in the send-off to leave the factory at half-past three.

The emigrants left Tilbury, on the River Thames in Essex, on the morning of Saturday, 13 May aboard the Aberdeen liner *Moravian*, which was due at Melbourne on 18 June. On 28 June, the *Melbourne Age* newspaper covered the luncheon held in honour of the Derry girls in the Federal Coffee Palace, which had occurred the previous day. The Minister of Lands, Mr McKenzie, who gave the girls a hearty welcome to Victoria, expressed the hope that the most sanguine anticipations which the girls had of their adopted country would be realised.

13 MAY 1915

Commanded by Captain Thomas Lawrie Shelford, *Goliath* had been part of the Allied fleet's naval operations in the Dardanelles during the landing at Cape Helles on 25 April 1915. On the night of 12–13 May that year, she was stationed in Morto Bay off Cape Helles, along with HMS *Cornwallis* and a screen of five destroyers. Around 1 a.m., the Turkish torpedo boat *Muavenet*, which was manned by a combined German and Turkish crew, eluded the destroyers HMS *Beagle* and HMS *Bulldog* and closed on the battleships. *Muavenet* fired three torpedoes which struck *Goliath* causing a massive explosion and the ship capsized almost immediately taking 570 of the 700-strong crew to the bottom.

Among those who died on board the *Goliath* were three Derry men: Leading Seaman John Doherty, Private Robert Hutchinson and Seaman-Gunner John Joseph (Jack) Dennis. Their names are commemorated on the Plymouth Naval War Memorial in Devon and on Derry's Diamond War Memorial.

Thirty-four-year-old Doherty was the son of John and Bridget Doherty from Daisy Hill Cottages, Boom Hall, on the Culmore Road. Thirty-two-year-old Hutchinson, a member of Great James Street Presbyterian Church, was the son of shopkeeper Fanny and carpenter Robert Hutchinson, 125 Creggan Road, Rosemount. Private Hutchinson had been in a previous engagement off the German South West African coast on board the *Goliath*. His name was read out during a memorial service held in St Columb's Cathedral in his native city on Sunday, 1 August 1915, to commemorate the officers and men of the city of Derry who had died during the first year of the Great War.

It was also read aloud in First Derry Presbyterian Church on Friday, 4 August 1916 in a service paying tribute to Londonderry's Presbyterian soldiers who had made the supreme sacrifice thus far in the war. Seaman-Gunner Dennis, whose exact age was unknown but who was born around 1894–95, was the son of James, who worked as a railway engine driver for the Midland Railway, and his wife Mary, who resided at 43 Clooney Terrace, Waterside. Dennis had been engaged for over four years with the Cunard line, and his last position, before being transferred to the *Goliath*, had been as wireless operator on the *Asquitania*.

14 MAY 1977

Derry's Guildhall, which was badly damaged by two bombs within five days in June 1972, was officially re-opened in a simple ceremony on Saturday afternoon, 14 May 1977, when Mayor James Hegarty unveiled a commemorative plaque on the main staircase. Alderman Hegarty, who said that the Guildhall had always had 'a very special place in the hearts of the people of this city', commented that when he looked back on his term of office as Mayor, the unveiling ceremony was one which would rank very highly amongst those which had given him greatest pleasure.

'It is most gratifying to see it restored to its original state,' said the Mayor. 'It is a great credit to the consultants, the contractors and the craftsmen who have done such a marvellous job in carrying out this work.' Alderman Hegarty said he felt very honoured to be Mayor on that particular occasion and described the opening ceremony as 'a fine way to round off my year of office': 'I am sure I speak for all who will shortly be facing the electorate when I say that the work of the council will have a new dimension for those of us who may be returned for another term. I sincerely hope and pray that the Guildhall will be fully operational in the not too distant future, and enjoyed by all the community. It is also my hope that the re-opening of the Guildhall will see the beginning of the restoration of our city centre.'

Welcoming the guests, who included many members of the City Council, Mr Patrick Devine, Chairman of the Technical Services Committee, said it was a pity that the general public could not be involved in the re-opening of the Guildhall at that stage. He congratulated the contractors on the magnificent job they had done, particularly in relation to the stained-glass windows, and said the resurrection of the Guildhall was something that would be appreciated by everyone. Mr Devine went on to congratulate those who had striven to complete work on the famous landmark on time: 'It seemed remote that we could open on schedule a year ago but with the complete co-operation of everyone concerned the schedule has been kept.' Referring to the original clearing-up operations and the recovery of all usable materials, in which the Development Commission had also been involved, Mr Devine described the saving of a section of the stained-glass windows as 'one of the crowning achievements' of the restoration work.

The cost of restoring the Guildhall had been approximately £1,250,000, and had taken four years.

15 MAY 1920

Derry in the late spring of 1920 was a city of unbearable tension. The War of Independence, that outside of Ulster was a straightforward clash between the IRA and the security forces, inevitably, in the northern province, became a sectarian struggle between Catholic and Protestant with a one-sided reaction from the government forces. Tension in the city was further increased by a strike by bakery workers and threatened industrial action by railwaymen.

On 15 May Detective Sergeant Denis Moroney was RIC Chief of Detectives in Derry and, with other plainclothes detectives, led a charge of uniformed police officers carrying bayonets to scatter rioters. The trouble had begun around 10.30 a.m. at a well-known flashpoint at the top of Carlisle Road where the other end of the Protestant Fountain Street opposed the Catholic Bridge Street. It was early on in the mini civil war that heralded the setting-up of the Northern Ireland state. As was the standard tactical move in those days the police attacked the nationalist crowd, who scattered at the bottom of the hill where it reached Foyle Road, opposite the Great Northern Railway Station. A group of people were chased down the now-vanished Fish Lane on to the quay. Some were armed and, after firing a few shots as they ran, hid behind barrels and goods wagons à la the OK Corral and continued to shoot at the police. Suddenly Moroney gasped to his aide, Detective Constable Patrick Kelly, 'My God, Kelly, I'm shot.' Kelly and Detective Constable Darragh caught Moroney as he fell and helped him to the nearby Metropole Hotel on Foyle Street, where he died of his wounds.

He had lived at 16 Grove Place, off the foot of Carlisle Road, the other end of the shop-filled street where the trouble had begun, and three days later, at 11.20, his remains were carried by his former comrades down John Street to the station followed by as many policemen that could be spared from duty in those troubled times. The coffin was then taken by train to Ballinrobe in County Mayo for later interment at Roundford, Hollymount. Members of Moroney's family later had the body exhumed for re-interment at his native Tulla, ten miles east of Ennis in County Clare. Moroney had been a farmer there before serving nineteen years in the force. He was the first member of the RIC in Ulster to be killed in the Tan War, though two constables, Peter Henley and Richard McLaughlin, had been shot on 1 May but escaped serious injury.

16 MAY 1769

John Wesley, the religious reformer and founder of Methodism, was born in Epworth, Lincolnshire, in 1703, the fifteenth of the nineteen children of Samuel Wesley, the local rector, and Susanna Annesley. He studied at Oxford, was ordained deacon in 1725, a Fellow of Lincoln College and lecturer in Greek in 1726, and a priest in 1728. In 1729 he joined with his brother Charles, who became one of the finest and most voluminous (more than 5,500 pieces) of English hymnists, to form with others the movement known mockingly as the 'Holy Club of Oxford Methodists'. The nickname arose from their claim to be methodical in observing the proper devotional requirements of the Church of England, which they claimed had fallen into abeyance.

The result was a separate, virtually independent Protestant church, characterised by open-air meetings to which Wesley's genius as a preacher drew huge crowds. By 1767, after many tours throughout these islands, he could count on at least 75,000 members, poorer people, on the whole, who found greater empathy with the humble mien of the Methodist clergy than with the condescending Anglicans. The reformed creed did well in western counties, Cornwall and in Wales, where people's adherence to 'chapel' or 'WC'—the shorthand for their more rigorous and egalitarian faith—was widespread. Wesley ordained his first Methodist clergy in 1750, one hundred men who would follow a highly structured ministry that involved much travel and adult education.

Wesley made several visits to Derry, notes of which he kept in his *Journal.* The first mention on 20 May 1769 refers to the previous Saturday when, he had 'as usual a full house… in the evening and again at eight on Sunday morning [16 May]. In the afternoon we had a brilliant congregation. But such a sight gives me no great pleasure, as I have very little hope of doing them good: only "with God all things are possible".' Realist that he was, he well understood that his preaching had become an event—almost a form of entertainment. That evening he found 'the audience in general dead as stones. However, we are to deliver our message; and let the Lord do as seemeth him good.'

Another visit was on 28 June 1773 and this time his interest was horticultural rather than spiritual. He was being shown round the garden of the Earl Bishop's palace and had an argument with the gardener about the name of one of the plants:

> Here I innocently gave some offence to the gardener, by mentioning the English name of a Greek word. But he set us right, warmly assuring us that the English name of the flower is not Crane's bill but Geranium!

Wesley, of course, was correct but so was the gardener: 'geranos' is the Greek word for 'crane' and the Latin word for the flower clearly comes from it.

17 MAY 1937

How a young Derry man met his death in the River Foyle on the afternoon of Saturday, 15 May 1937, was described at the inquest at Newbuildings two days later. Richard Henry, aged twenty-five and married, who resided at Bond's Place, had been employed in a Londonderry garage, and had gone to Newbuildings to visit his mother when he met his death. His body was recovered on Sunday morning by the Waterside police and civilians who had assisted in dragging operations. The inquest was conducted by Dr W.P. Colhoun, the deputy coroner for the Liberties.

Dr W.G. O'Doherty testified that he had examined the body of the deceased on Sunday afternoon, and there were no marks of violence on it, though there were post-mortem marks on the right elbow; the body was that of a well-developed young man. Robert Henry, brother of the deceased, gave evidence of identification and said he'd met Richard on Craigavon Bridge on Saturday afternoon. As far as he knew his brother could swim a little and had bathed at this place since he was a boy.

John Miller, a blacksmith from Newbuildings, stated that he saw two people bathing, and one of them was on a sand-bed which was covered by about two feet of water and was about 150 yards from the shore. There were some holes beside the sand-bed. Miller heard a shout, and when he looked round one person had disappeared. Miller asked a friend who was with him where the man had gone and the friend replied that perhaps he had dived. There were two other men who had been bathing, and they were still undressed; they got a boat and looked for the missing man, but could not find any trace of him. On Sunday morning Miller went out in a boat with a grapple, and about thirty yards from the place where the bather had disappeared a body was found in six or seven feet of water.

John McGlinchey, a motor mechanic who worked with Richard Henry, said that he'd accompanied Richard, along with Stephen Brown and Samuel Mitchell, to Newbuildings. They went to the river, where Richard, Stephen and John went in for a bathe. The deceased went to the sand-bed and John tried to follow him, but was unable to do so. John went out about twenty yards and Stephen about forty, but Richard remained in the water after they had come ashore. John McGlinchey was dressing when he heard Richard shout for help, and when he looked towards the sand-bed he could see no sign of his friend. John was unable to swim, and he could not say with certainty if Richard could. After hearing some more eyewitness evidence, the jury returned a verdict that death was due to accidental drowning.

18 MAY 1931

In spite of being the hilliest town in Ireland, Derry always prided itself on its bus service. At first the city service was run by private operators, usually with Corporation subvention. On 12 May 1931, when Catherwood's were the main operators, a letter sent by them was being considered by the members of the Corporation's Bus Committee, comprising Aldermen Moore, Wilton and Bradley, and Councillors Caldwell, McMenamin, Duncan and Kerr. The letter concerned Catherwood's request to the Ministry of Home Affairs to curtail, as from 1 June 1931, the service on the Rosemount–Glendermott Road. The committee imposed the following conditions: a month's trial, at the end of which Catherwood's would furnish a return showing total passenger usage; and the guarantee that the full service was restored on 1 October for the winter months.

A second item before the committee that day concerned a letter from the ministry regarding the operation of double-decker vehicles on the following routes: Lough Swilly Railway Station (Buncrana Road) to the west end of Carlisle Bridge, the forerunner of Craigavon Bridge, via Strand Road and Foyle Street; Glendermott Road (or the city boundary on the Limavady Road) to the east end of Carlisle Bridge; and Beechwood Avenue to the west end of Carlisle Bridge, via Foyle Street, but not via the Diamond. The ministry did not consider the bridge suitable for 'double-deck omnibuses'.

The Bus Committee's report was then considered by the Corporation at its full session on 18 May. They accepted the sub-committee's recommendations but began to enquire about a balance sheet. Councillor Cochrane wanted to know what profit, if any, the Catherwood's operation had made. Phillips, the assistant Town Clerk, reported that the returns had arrived the day before and they were being examined. Councillor Healy persisted: the returns had been promised three months previously; thirteen unfortunate tenants of subsidy homes had been prosecuted because they would not pay three months' rent; yet here was a man running the city's bus service who owed them two years' money, probably £2,000. He suggested that they prosecute Catherwood but the Unionist members all claimed that such an action was unthinkable.

It was turning into a good old-fashioned Corporation slanging match with an accusation that Phillips had asked that the Rosemount bus terminus be changed from Glendermott Road to May Street for his convenience. This was greeted with laughter and a heated denial from the assistant Town Clerk. More serious was the news that the fares paid by factory girls had been raised with the result that there had been a falling-off in bus usage. In conclusion, when Councillor McFarland asked the Corporation members gathered if Catherwood's provided a reasonable service, most agreed, including (with certain reluctance) Councillor Healy. In 1935 the semi-state body, the Northern Ireland Road Transport Board, assumed general responsibility for the province-wide (but not cross-border) transit network and it did not dominate council debate as before.

19 MAY 1966

The act of personation, by which someone votes in the name of another person, usually dead, has never really been regarded as a crime in Ulster. As one neutral humorist once put it, almost quoting Shakespeare: 'The graves stood tenantless and the sheeted dead did vote right often in the Derry booths.' In one Belfast election for Westminster the Unionist candidate for North Belfast got in by a margin of twenty-five votes. In the senior common room in Queen's on election night there was great excitement, the non-Irish members of the faculty being particularly impressed. 'Think of the excitement,' said one politically naïve English lecturer, 'of being one of those twenty-five!' 'Think of the excitement,' said a cynical Irish colleague, 'of being all twenty-five of them!'

Ulster today has the most rigorous system of identity establishment at polling stations in the United Kingdom, requiring photographs in many cases. The attitude of both sides towards personation as a kind of local harmless sport died hard but as the Troubles intensified the matter became more serious and the draconian legislation with serious fines was introduced. Back in 1966, during the period of political stasis, a personator when challenged and caught got off with a £25 fine, which even at today's buying value of £346, is considerably less that the current fine of up to £5,000.

Dermot Samuel Morrow, a nineteen-year-old man from Derryowen, Coshquin, thought it worth the risk to personate on 19 May 1966, but in a very unusual way. The person he claimed to be was not dead but the polling agent, Thomas Drought, of Belmont, who had been assigned to the station at the annexe of the city technical school in Strand Road. Morrow's deception had nothing to do with the actual voting, but was, in fact, a minor case of identity fraud. What gave the case an extra flavour was that the Independent Unionist candidate for a seat on the Londonderry Corporation was Ruth Morrow, the defendant's mother. When the mother realised that Drought had not appeared on Election Day, nor did it seem likely he would appear to help at the polling station, she sent for her son and asked him to do the work. It was a venial offence because the remuneration would have been small, if there was any payable.

Dermot Morrow later admitted to making a false statement that he was Thomas Drought, contrary to the Perjury Act of 1946, and a further charge of completing and signing a form in the name of Drought. He committed the second misdemeanour when he took his impersonated role too seriously and challenged a voter for personating; when asked by the presiding officer to sign the necessary form, Morrow signed it in the name of Drought. As his solicitor Herbert Montgomery judiciously phrased it: 'It was a very technical case. The fact that the defendant was the son of the candidate made him more enthusiastic than would normally have been the case.'

20 MAY 1939

On Saturday, 20 May 1939, the *Londonderry Sentinel* reported that at Coleraine Petty Sessions the previous day, before Major McLean, RM, the case was heard against defendants Linton Selfridge, Hugh Glass and Herbert Johnston, all of whom hailed from Coleraine, and who were summoned on charges of disorderly conduct at the close of the drawn semi-final of the North West Senior Cup between Coleraine FC and Derry City Reserves on 18 April.

Head Constable Fulton said the referee on the occasion was John Finlay, a harbour constable from Londonderry, whose decisions throughout the match were met with apparent dissatisfaction by the spectators. Finlay was attacked on leaving the pitch at the end of the match, despite having police protection. Hugh Glass was seen to hit the referee with his fist on the back of the head and Selfridge was just prevented from attacking him; Johnston had been found outside the ground after the match with a stone in his pocket. Some stones had been thrown at the conclusion of the game and a Sergeant Elliott was severely cut on the hand by a missile. Fulton stated there could not be a recurrence of such scenes at football games in Coleraine, otherwise decent people would not attend. Sergeant Elliott described the spectators involved in the 'demonstration' as a 'howling mob'.

The referee testified that he awarded a penalty kick to Derry Reserves near the end of the game, which caused numbers of disgruntled Coleraine supporters to congregate round the touchlines; although extra time should have been played, Finlay decided that it would not be advisable to continue the match in light of the attitude of the crowd. While he was leaving the field, he continued, stones were thrown and he was struck by someone. When he got to his dressing room stones were flung on top of it.

Johnston denied in evidence that he had any wrongful intent at the football match. He claimed to have heard two boys saying they were going to throw a stone and he took it from them. It was this stone which had been found in his possession by the police. Glass denied striking the referee, claiming he had been pushed against the official by the pressure of the crowd behind him. He had merely raised his arm when a Derry player assumed a confrontational attitude towards him. Selfridge accepted the charges against him as had been detailed by the Head Constable.

Major McLean said there was no justification for the attack on the referee by the three defendants, or by any other members of the crowd. He did not think it acceptable that football teams visiting Coleraine should be subjected to such treatment as that displayed in this case, and for that reason imposed the maximum penalty of £2 on each defendant.

21 MAY 1932

On Saturday, 21 May 1932 a little red monoplane, a Lockheed Vega, flew very low over Derry and eventually landed in a field on the northeast outskirts of the city. The plane was piloted by Amelia Earhart, and its arrival on the city's edge caused a tremendous stir.

Amelia Mary Earhart Putnam, to give her married title, was an aviatrix, to use the title used for women fliers in those sexist days, and it was her ambition to emulate 'Lindy's' transatlantic flight to Paris. Charles Augustus Lindbergh had been the first person to fly solo and non-stop from New York in his specially modified plane *The Spirit of St Louis* five years earlier in May 1927.

On 20 May Amelia took off in her plane *Friendship* from Harbour Grace in Newfoundland and in spite of icy conditions and contrary winds reached the Irish coast in safety. Heading for Paris she changed her mind when she felt petrol dripping down the back of her neck and realised that the fuel gauge was broken. She opted instead for an emergency landing, having followed the Great Northern railway tracks to choose a fairly flat green field at Springfield, Ballyarnett. The landing at 1.30 p.m. was a bit bouncy but brilliant in the circumstances. She had flown 2,026 miles in a little over thirteen hours, and was greeted by Dan McCallion, the resident of the first house at which she knocked. Robert Gallagher, the owner of the field, soon came on the scene and asked where she had come from; he was suitably impressed when she answered that she had flown from America and could she wash her hair. She is also reported as having said, as she climbed from the cockpit, 'Surely this must be the prettiest spot in Ireland.' Souvenir hunters appeared like locusts at the landing field. One contemporary photograph shows a group of smiling men holding the detached red tail-plane of the *Friendship*. Another has no less than three RUC constables guarding the plane.

In Derry her first action was to cable her husband G.P. Putnam, the US publisher, about her safe arrival, and she was able to book a transatlantic call to speak to him. (The many clamouring newsmen had the tact to leave the room in the Northern Counties Hotel while they talked.) Next afternoon, after an exhausting on-going press-and photo-call, she returned to Springfield and in the presence of a mob of well-wishers took off exactly twenty-four hours after touchdown. Her meteoric visit to Derry was soon over but she left behind her a reputation for imperturbable charm and the information that she did not 'use' tea, coffee and cigarettes. Michael C. Friel, the local representative of Pratt's oil company that had supplied the fuel for the flight, brought a tanker out to Springfield to fill up the tanks. She landed in Blackpool a few hours later.

Amelia Earhart set off on a round-the-world flight with navigator Ted Noonan on 2 July 1937. They left New Guinea on 2 September, flying east across the Pacific, and were not heard of again in spite of many searches and great speculation about their fates.

On Thursday, 22 May 1952, the *Londonderry Sentinel* reported on the inquest held the previous night concerning William Robinson, a forty-two-year-old clerk in the Rates Department of the Corporation, of 75 Chapel Road in the Waterside, who died in Londonderry's Eye, Ear and Throat Hospital on the Tuesday shortly after a routine operation.

Dr S. Ernest Bolton, consultant surgeon, said when he first saw Robinson in December 1947, he found his tonsils were very large and subject to a high degree of chronic sepsis. Bolton explained to him that this highly poisonous material would affect his general condition and recommended that he should have his tonsils removed. Dr Bolton did not examine Robinson again until 9 May 1952, when he found that he was still suffering from quinsy and tonsillitis. He once more urged his patient to have the tonsils extracted.

Bolton told him he had been carrying out tonsil operations for twenty-five years without fatality, and he had removed tonsils in a worse condition, and from older people, without ill effects. He did add, however, that there was some risk involved in dealing with tonsils with a long history of sepsis. Robinson had been anxious to have them removed and Bolton dissected his tonsils. The operation duly went ahead, with no glitches, and Robinson had been returned to his ward in a good condition.

Bolton left the hospital at 1.14 p.m., but at 2.05 p.m. received an urgent message stating that the patient had collapsed. Bolton went to the hospital immediately, where he found that Robinson's pulse was weak and that he was showing signs of heart failure. Bolton did everything possible to revive Robinson, giving him artificial respiration and administering oxygen. Dr J.C. Clark arrived five minutes later and joined in attempts to save the patient but he passed away at 2.30 p.m. Bolton persisted with the treatment until about 2.40 p.m. when it was apparent that nothing could be done. In his opinion, death was caused by cardiac failure due to toxic myocarditis.

Dr Clark confirmed that he had given Robinson an anaesthetic before the operation, and at no time did his condition cause the slightest concern. The total amount of the ether used was between three and four ounces, which the doctor considered was small for the physical size of the patient and the duration of the operation. He corroborated Dr Bolton's evidence of their efforts to revive Robinson.

On Wednesday, 23 May 1888, the Presbyterian and liberal *Londonderry Standard* newspaper became the *Derry Standard*. Not only did the newspaper relinquish the reference to the English and United Kingdom capital city on its front page, it also simultaneously erased Siege-related images of Walker's Pillar, the 'Roaring Meg' cannon, a flag bearing the year '1688', and the homely proclamation 'Our Faith and our Firesides'. Although the pillar and proclamation were later re-introduced, why the *Standard* did this remains a mystery. It provided no explanation for the name change at the time, not even after the following criticism of it appeared in the *Londonderry Sentinel* on Thursday, 24 May:

> What is this that has happened to our excellent contemporary and neighbour, the *Derry Standard*? Is it to the heat wave or to the loss of that North-West Show contract that we are to attribute the greatest change—and there have been many of them especially lately—that has taken place in our contemporary these forty years? What is it that has caused the *Standard* to abandon 'Our Faith and our Firesides', pull down Walker's Pillar, 'strike' the flag of 1688, and abolish Roaring Meg? They have all disappeared in one cataleptic shock, and not a trace of them remains; there is not a wrack behind. We refer, of course, to the pictorial representation of these interesting relics that has been the only distinctive feature about the *Standard*—except its protean changeability—for the last half century. Without the slightest warning they have all been annihilated at one fell swoop. What will become of 'our faith and firesides' now? The *Standard* has protected them long, but now they have been bereft of its guardianship and left to take care of themselves. Why our contemporary should choose this particular moment for so relentlessly and recklessly throwing up the sponge as the champion of 'our faith and firesides' we are at a loss to understand. We thought this was a time when our faith and firesides particularly wanted looking after, but the *Standard* has abandoned them to their fate. If it is heartless and cruel to abandon our faith and firesides it is shabby to lower the flag of 1688, which has been kept flying on the front page of the *Standard* for forty years or more. Perhaps it was considered too much a sign of 'ascendancy', and, therefore, had to be lowered in deference to the feelings of the Nationalists, upon whom our contemporary was recently bestowing its favour and approval, and to whom it may be meditating an early return. Roaring Meg was about as harmless in the columns of the *Standard* as she is on the Wall, and that she should be so unceremoniously 'discharged', after doing duty so long, is a signal instance of human ingratitude. It is true that Walker's Pillar was beginning to have a battered and dilapidated appearance, and wanted renovation like the original, but a little patching up would have improved it wonderfully. But this is an age of Philistinism and Vandalism, and our contemporary has been seized with the spirit of demolition ...

In the year 1860, St Columb's Cathedral was closed for renovation and the congregation held their services in the old Corporation Hall in the Diamond. As a result of the renovations, the old box pews, the Corporation seats, the Bishop's, the Dean's, and the Mayor's thrones were removed, the windows taken out and the flooring torn up in preparation for the installation of a new heating apparatus. The earth was excavated to a depth of some feet, and during its removal a large quantity of human bones was discovered. These were carefully collected, placed in six large coffins, and re-interred in a special grave under the third window of the north aisle on Friday, 24 May 1861.

The grave took the form of a mound (measuring 44 feet in circumference and 14 high) which was surmounted by a stone pillar ten and a half feet from its base, stood at the east corner of the Cathedral churchyard. Panels of stone were placed in the monument at the four cardinal points. The inscription on the south panel stated that the monument was erected by the Apprentice Boys of Derry, assisted by Harvey Nicholson, Esq., and other friends, in memory of the gallant men who fought in the defence of Derry in 1688–89. The north bore an appropriate scriptural quotation, the east the Nicholson Arms, and the west the Derry Arms. John Hempton greatly assisted this undertaking:

Here rest to be disturb'd no more,
Till come the resurrection day,
The bones of men who fought or yore,
And perill'd life in deadly fray,
The rights of conscience to secure,
And laws place on a basis sure.

No common conflict here they wag'd,
War, pestilence, and famine dire,
Around them in a fierce fury rag'd,
Their faith and fortitude to tire;
But, trusting in the Lord Most High,
Still 'No Surrender' was their cry.

Contending valiantly they fell,
And weeping friends interr'd them here;
How doleful rang the funeral knell
Of each when stretched upon his bier,
And when the grave had on them clos'd,
'Twas thought in safety they repos'd.

Yet strange and dismal sight to view,
Their bones, which moulder'd in the clay
For more than eight score years and two,
Were rudely raised from where they lay,
And thrown in heaps the churchyard o'er,
Like common earth, and nothing more.

But soon the brave Apprentice Boys
Restor'd them to their former place,
Honour'd by cannon's booming noise,
Their second burial rights to grace:
Whilst citizens of every grade,
Deserv'd respect have to them paid.

In 1861 the population of Derry was 20,153 and there were only six Apprentice Boys' clubs: the Walker Club, the Murray Club, the Mitchelburne Club, the Williamite Club, and the Apprentice Boys of Derry Club, comprising an active membership of three hundred. The mound is of great interest to tourists visiting the city walls and the graveyard of St Columb's Cathedral.

25 MAY 1943

John Miller Andrews was the second Prime Minister of Northern Ireland. He was born in Comber, County Down in 1871, the eldest child of Thomas Andrews, flax spinner, and Eliza née Pirrie, a sister of Lord Pirrie, chairman of Harland and Wolff. He was educated at the Royal Belfast Academical Institution. In business, he was a landowner, a director of his family linen-bleaching company, and of the Belfast Ropeworks. His brother, Thomas Andrews, who died in the 1912 sinking of the *Titanic*, was managing director of the Harland and Wolff shipyard in Belfast; another brother, Sir James Andrews, 1st Baronet, was Lord Chief Justice of Northern Ireland. In 1902 John married Jessie, eldest daughter of Bolton stockbroker Joseph Ormrod, at Rivington Unitarian Chapel, near Chorley in Lancashire. They had one son and two daughters. His younger brother, Sir James, married Jessie's sister.

Andrews served as an MP in the Parliament of Northern Ireland from 1921 until 1953 (for County Down constituency from 1921–29 and for Mid-Down from 1929–1953). He was a founder member of the Ulster Unionist Labour Association, which he chaired, was Minister of Labour from 1921 to 1937, and Minister of Finance from 1937 to 1940. On the death of Lord Craigavon in 1940 he became leader of the Unionist Party and the second Prime Minister of Northern Ireland.

In 1943 backbench dissent forced him from office. In the same year, on Monday, 24 May, he was made a Freeman of the city of Londonderry. Commenting on the ceremony the following day, the *Londonderry Sentinel* wrote: 'With dignified ceremonial appropriate to the occasion, Londonderry Corporation, as representatives of the citizens, yesterday bestowed on one of Ulster's most distinguished sons, Right Hon. John Miller Andrews, CH, DL, MP, the highest honour which it is in their power to give, namely the freedom of this ancient and historic city, "in recognition of his outstanding and successful statesmanship in guiding the destinies and protecting the interests of the Imperial province of Northern Ireland." The ceremony took place in the Council Chamber of the Guildhall, scene of so many other memorable episodes in the life of the city, and present were not only representatives of the business and professional life of the city but representatives of the British and American armed forces and of the public life of the Province as a whole.'

Mr Andrews, having taken the oath admitting him an Honorary Freeman of the City, signed the 250-year-old Freemen's Roll, adding his name after that of Sir Charles Batho, who when Governor of the Honourable the Irish Society, was admitted to the Freedom of the City in July 1937. The Mayor (F.J. Simmons), who presided over the ceremony, at the commencement of the proceedings, said this was, perhaps, the proudest day of his public life, when as mayor of this most ancient and truly historic city, he was permitted to be the medium of adding the name to their list of one beloved by all who had the great privilege of his friendship.

26 MAY 1938

On Thursday, 26 May 1938, the *Londonderry Sentinel* reported on J.J.S. Barnhill's arbitration inquiry, held the previous day, on the proposed acquisition by the Corporation of Riverview, Abercorn Road, in the old East Ward, and Watt's Field, in the old West Ward, and the property at the corner of Spencer Road and Simpson's Brae. The Corporation wanted Riverview to develop as recreation grounds and to establish offices for the Medical Officer of Health to carry out clinics; Watt's Field to provide playing fields and an open space; and the Spencer Road and Simpson's Brae sites for road widening.

During the inquiry, and in response to the claim by W. Lowry that the townland in which Watt's Field was located would be Templemore, Barnhill stated that Templemore was the name of the parish on which the city was mainly situated, but that there was no such townland of that name in Northern Ireland. Lowry said the townland would be Londonderry, but Barnhill responded by saying that if they went far enough back they would find Derry was built between the Foyle and the watercourse which formerly ran from Sackville Street to the Great Northern Railway workshops, and it was, therefore, built on an island. It was once known as the Termon-of-Derry, and later it became 'the Island-of-Derry'; Barnhill recalled how old documents referred to property as being situated on 'the island of Derry'. When the townland became the unit of taxation it became the townland of Londonderry, and this still extended only as far as the western watercourse, which was known later as Mary Blue's Burn and ran through Watt's ground. It was wrong to say that Watt's Field was in Templemore, Londonderry, as part of it was in Templemore, or the townland of Londonderry, and the remainder across the stream was in Edenballymore. To the amusement of those gathered, Barnhill reiterated that it was wrong, of course, to call Templemore a townland, as the nearest townland of that name was in Tipperary.

W. Finlay Bigger, the owner of Riverview, had claimed £4,698 compensation, and arising out of this there were several subsidiary claims, which included those by William J. Burns for £4,615, and Samuel Stewart for £1,613 and loss of prospective building profits; these latter claims arose out of agreements to take part of Riverview for building purposes, although Burns and Stewart had been previously notified that the Corporation intended to acquire the property. The trustees of the Watt property claimed £3,700, and there were additional claims from property tenants. Captain W.A. Lane, who appeared for the Honourable the Irish Society, said that body was seeking only nominal compensation in respect of the head rents. F.L.A. Harrison said it was agreed that £35 should be paid to the representatives of Captain F.J. Montgomery for these.

27 MAY 1936

On Wednesday, 27 May 1936, the trial began in Dorset Assizes, Dorchester, of thirty-three-year-old Charlotte Bryant, a native of Derry, who was accused of murdering her husband, thirty-nine-year-old cowman Frederick John Bryant. The couple had been married in 1922, and their five children were unaware that their mother, who pleaded not guilty, was at the centre of a sensational trial.

Presenting the case for the Crown, the Solicitor General, Sir Terence

O'Connor, began: 'Administration of poison by a person who wishes to kill another is usually the concomitant of cruelty and of character and mind that do not usually go with a high degree of cunning, and it may well be that in a case of this kind you will have to delve a good deal beneath the surface in order to find where the truth lies. This is not the kind of case where I am in a position, on behalf of the Crown, to say this: On a certain day at a certain place this woman went and bought some arsenic; she took the arsenic home; she put it in her husband's tea, milk, or whatever it might be, and he consumed it, and of that consumption he died. If you accept the evidence on behalf of the Crown you will have no doubt that on at least four occasions during 1935 this unfortunate man was the victim of the administration of very large quantities of arsenic.'

Sir Terence went on to point out that Charlotte had become acquainted with a man named Leonard Edward Parsons, who was also known as 'Bill Moss'. He had lodged with the Bryants, and if the jury accepted Parsons' evidence (as corroborated by several other witnesses) they would conclude that Mrs Bryant had been his lover for a considerable time.

'I am afraid,' said Sir Terence, 'that what dramatic writers call the eternal triangle is not absent from this case. If you accept the evidence which I put before you, there is a woman here with the strongest of human motives for destroying her husband in order that the marriage might take place.'

'You are not a Court of morals,' observed the Solicitor-General. 'Mrs Bryant had said to more than one person that the youngest child of the family was a child of Parsons. In November 1935, Parsons took himself off, and so far as was known, Mrs Bryant never saw him again. Whether that accelerated Parsons' departure or not I do not know, but some time before he went the prisoner told him that before long she would be a widow.'

Charlotte Bryant was found guilty of her husband's murder, and was subsequently hanged on 15 July 1936.

28 MAY 1931

On Thursday, 28 May 1931, the *Londonderry Sentinel* reported on an inquest held two days previously concerning a thirty-eight-year-old seaman, Michael Brady, believed to have hailed from Mayo but who had been living at 45 Wamsley Street, Fleetwood. Brady had received injuries while on the Fleetwood steam trawler *Somersby* in the vicinity of St Kilda. The trawler made for Inistrahull and Brady was landed at Moville on 15 May before being conveyed to Derry Infirmary, where he died on Monday, 25 May. Mr John Tracy, City Coroner, presided over the inquest and District Inspector Lynn represented the police.

George Steen, a fisherman from Moville, who was also a steam trawler agent for the Boston Deep Sea Fishing Company in Fleetwood, said he believed Brady was a single man and had been in the Australian army. The *Somersby* had been fishing recently off St Kilda, and on 15 May had come to Moville, where Brady and another injured man had been put ashore. A Dr McKenzie rendered medical assistance to the men, and Brady told Steen that he'd been pulling up ashes when the captain called, 'There's a sea coming.' With the noise of the bucket, Brady did not hear until it was too late. He was half roads forward when the sea came on him, and he was washed through the boat, which had shipped water, and swept across the deck. The other man was washed overboard but was picked up again. Brady was taken to Derry Infirmary.

A juror remarked that Steen was only telling what he had heard, and not what he had seen for himself, to which the Coroner replied, 'If the jury consider an eye-witness necessary we shall adjourn the inquest.'

District Inspector Lynn responded, 'I suppose this will be the subject of a Board of Trade inquiry elsewhere. I think we should simply find the cause of death. There is no suspicion of foul play. I don't think there is any necessity for an adjournment.'

Dr D.J.C. Dawson, house surgeon, said Brady had been admitted to the infirmary at 1 p.m. on 15 May. There was an incised wound on the right side of his scalp, a deep wound on the outer side of his left thigh, and one behind his right shoulder. He had rib fractures on the right side, and one rib had perforated the lung, which collapsed. The cause of death was cardiac failure, stated the doctor, and the wounds were absolutely consistent with Mr Steen's story.

The Coroner, Mr Tracy, believed there was sufficient evidence to form a verdict. The police had been active in procuring Mr Steen as a witness, and no others were available as the *Somersby* had gone. The jury found in accordance with the medical evidence that the accident arose when the deceased was in the discharge of his duty.

The foreman of the jury, Mr O'Hare, then expressed sympathy with the relatives.

'Unfortunately,' replied George Steen, 'we cannot trace the relatives.'

'Who is to bury this man?' asked the Coroner.

'I am supposed to bury him,' said Steen.

'Where?'

'In the Derry Cemetery.'

On Friday, 29 May 1925, the *Derry Standard* reported on the Derry Petty Sessions from the previous day, presided over by Mr H.W. Porter. John McClay of 1 East Avenue and his sister, Mrs Caroline Johnston, had summoned Robert Simpson of 4 East Avenue to answer charges of assault; Simpson, in reply, had issued cross-summonses. Mr McDermott appeared for the complainants and Mr Conaghan for the defendant.

McClay stated that when he went to attend to one of his goats which was grazing at the head of the street, Mrs Simpson came along and ordered him to take his 'f———g goat' away; she threatened if he didn't do so she would put a knife in it. Robert Simpson then appeared and began to kick a tin at the goat and when the animal reared up at him he kicked the goat itself. He also struck McClay on the mouth and blackened his eye. When Mrs Johnston came out Simpson struck her also and kicked her on the shin. He threatened to turn both of them into mincemeat. Mrs Johnston said she witnessed the assault on her brother, and was attacked herself when she called Simpson a coward for striking a boy like him. Constable Magill's testimony confirmed that, after the incident, he saw McClay whose mouth was bleeding and who appeared to have been hit on the eye, and that Mrs Johnston's face was bruised and ruffled.

Mrs Simpson's version was that McClay's goat was grazing on the playground and had reared up at her children when she sent them out to play, frightening them in the process. She asked McClay to secure his goat in the garden but he refused and told her children to leave the street. His attitude to the children became threatening and Mrs Simpson called out her husband. McClay caught him by the vest, and her husband hit him with his hand. Mrs Johnston ran up with a knife in her hand and threatened to stick it in Mr Simpson, who gave her a push, causing her to fall on the street. Robert Simpson corroborated his wife's evidence. He added that the McClays wanted to get his house for Mrs Johnston, and made his life a regular hell. Mr Conaghan said it was a regrettable thing—and he hoped the Corporation would note it—that there were no open spaces where children could play. The owners of goats, he continued, apparently thought that the children should get no fresh air but that they were entitled to put their goats on the ground where the children played.

Robert Simpson was fined twenty-five shillings in total for assaulting John McClay and Mrs Johnston. His cross-cases were dismissed.

A member of a family of Scottish origin, Dudley Evelyn Bruce McCorkell, was born on 22 February 1883, and died on 30 May 1960. His father was David Browne McCorkell, a barrister-at-law from Ballyarnett, and his mother was the daughter of T.S. Pakenham of Crumlin in County Antrim. Dudley was educated at Shrewsbury College, Pembroke College and Cambridge University, where he graduated with a BA. He played hockey for Cambridge and had the distinction of representing Wales in internationals on a residential qualification basis. In 1909 he married Helen Elizabeth Usher from Terenure in Dublin.

Dudley was Chairman of William McCorkell and Co. Ltd., the Derry firm of grain importers and millers founded by his great grandfather in 1778, and which had formerly imported supplies in its own sailing ships. The company's ships also developed the passenger traffic, particularly towards America.

In 1918 Dudley received the MBE for his work during the Great War; he had applied for active service but was declined on medical grounds. He then devoted his time to the British Red Cross Society and the Order of St John. He was knighted in 1933, during one of his terms as Mayor of Derry. While holding that office the previous year, Amelia Earhart had completed her first solo transatlantic flight when she landed at Ballyarnett in Culmore. As Mayor, and owner of the Ballyarnett lands, which he'd inherited in 1897, Dudley welcomed Amelia after her successful flight.

Dudley's association with local government had begun with membership of Londonderry County Council. In 1925 he served as County High Sheriff, and he was a member of Londonderry Corporation until 1946.

In 1933 Dudley was nominated as a member of the Pigs Marketing Board, subsequently the Bacon Marketing Board. He was the first chairman of the Pig Industry Council, which superseded these bodies, and functioned until 1954. The Pigs Marketing Board was then reconstituted and he became its chairman, resigning the post in 1958. He was a practical farmer and retained his acreage at Ballyarnett.

Personal tragedy struck when his only son, Lieutenant F. Dudley Pakenham McCorkell, was killed in action on 6 August 1944 while serving with the Irish Guards in France.

During his life, Dudley was also an Ulster Unionist Ex-Officio Senator at Stormont; a Justice of the Peace and Deputy Lieutenant for County Londonderry; a Commander of the Order of St John of Jerusalem; a director of the Bank of Ireland; a member of the Ulster Transport Authority; a director of Londonderry Gaslight Company; a chairman of the Belfast Board of the London and Lancashire Insurance Co. (Northern Ireland); a director of

Industrial Finance, Northern Ireland; a president of both City of Derry and Culmore Horticultural Societies; a senior member of the Londonderry Harbour Board; a member of Derry and Raphoe Diocesan Council; a president of Londonderry YMCA; a director of Derry City FC; and a member of the NCC of LMS Railway.

31 MAY 1916

Lance-Corporal Francis Ledwidge of the Royal Inniskilling Fusiliers, which he had joined on 24 October 1914, was ordered to report to Ebrington Barracks in Derry on 18 May 1916. Though a committed nationalist he'd volunteered for service, answering John Redmond's call for enlistment of Irishmen, 'neither for a principle nor a people nor a law, but for the fields along the Boyne, for the birds and the blue skies over them'. He also commented: 'I joined the British Army because she stood between Ireland and an enemy common to our civilisation and I would not have her say that she defended us while we did nothing at home but pass resolutions.'

He was already known as the composer of poems about his native County Meath and had become a friend of Lord Dunsany, the local landlord, who did what he could as an officer to get him out of scrapes that caused him several times to lose promotion, reduced again to the ranks once for drunkenness, but usually for 'insubordination' in the eyes of English officers, who regarded him as a truculent, uppity 'Paddy'. He had survived the hell of Gallipoli but was severely depressed at the British reaction to the Easter Rising and the general harrying of Irish enlisted men after the executions.

One of his finest poems was written about Thomas MacDonagh, who was shot on 3 May 1916 during the first round of executions:

> He shall not hear the bittern cry
> In the wild sky, where he is lain,
> Nor voices of the sweeter birds
> Above the wailing of the rain.

He was in Dublin when the orders to report to Derry came through, his mind troubled by the different pulls of instinctive nationalism and his duty as a soldier. This showed itself in what would later be called 'bolshiness' and an undesirable independence of mind in one from the 'other ranks'. He had lost two days' leave while waiting for a passage in the boat from Manchester and said so to the C.O. in Richmond Barracks in Dublin, who refused to grant an extension. This man made some slighting remark about the Rising and Ledwidge responded by saying he had fought in France and the Dardanelles. It was an acrimonious encounter and the brass hat sent a damning report to Derry where he would be dealt with on arrival. It was typical that he took the train from Amiens Street Station for Belfast instead of Derry. He stayed for several days with friends called Christie and did not arrive at Ebrington until 31 May, where he was immediately court-martialled for overstaying his leave, 'for insubordinate talk and behaviour in the presence of the commanding officer in Dublin'.

His single lance-corporal stripe was removed and it was as Private Francis Ledwidge, Fifth Company Inniskillings, that he was sent to the front in Belgium for the third battle of Ypres. He was blown to pieces by a shell in the Boesinghe sector near the Ypres canal on 31 July 1917, just nineteen days before his thirtieth birthday.

JUNE

With the headline 'The Missing of a Tailor in Derry' in reticent 12-point, the *Derry Journal* of 1 June 1900 told the sad story of the inquest on Neal Boyle, a tailor, aged fifty-two, of Foster's Terrace, Lecky Road, whose body was found floating in the river at the quay 'in proximity to the large grain steamer at present lying there'. Boyle had been missing for nearly a week, having been last seen on Saturday, 28 May. When the body was discovered the state of decomposition necessitated a speedy interment, and an inquest was ordered immediately.

It was held, in those informal days, in the public house of Matthew McCloskey, of Kildara Terrace, not far from the deceased's own home. The coroner Thomas Lindsay swore in the jury of twelve, with the owner McCloskey as foreman. They all had the dubious pleasure of having already had to view the corpse. Sergeant Morrow of the Bishop Street police barracks 'represented the Crown'.

The first witness was Edward Owens, who had formally identified the body as being that of his friend, a widower whose wife had died six months earlier. He had seen him between five and six on the Saturday afternoon. Boyle had taken the death of his wife very badly but though he 'fretted a great deal he was not in the habit of drinking'. When Owens and he parted he went off alone and was perfectly sober. John Glenn of Bluebell Hill, on the opposite side of Lecky Road, was with Boyle from about 9.30 p.m. until 10.40 p.m., during which interval they had walked down to the Rock at the edge of town at the end of the Strand Road, where a Mrs Lally kept a boot store. He testified that Boyle had been in jovial mood, making a joke about a German band that was playing in Shipquay Street. (These travelling brass and woodwind bands were a popular public diversion at the time.)

Matthew Lally, a further witness, said that he and Glenn had left Boyle at his wife's shop, but he later learned that Boyle had not spoken to his wife but had headed with his dog towards the quay. Sergeant Morrow said that Boyle had made a practice of hunting rats with his dog in the quay sheds. Another witness, Edward Owens, offered his theory that, since Boyle was short-sighted, 'the deceased stumbled over some articles near the berth of the Donegal steamer and fell into the water'. The dog that had accompanied Glenn and Boyle on their evening walk returned home at two o'clock on the Sunday morning. Glenn observed that though there had been recent rain his coat was perfectly dry.

The last witness was Edward Hassan of St Columb's Wells, who described how he had found the body that morning about 6.10 at a point opposite McCorkell's huge grain store on the Derry side. The jury returned promptly with a verdict of 'found drowned'.

2 JUNE 1912

Sir Edward Reid, a former Mayor of Derry, died at his residence in Hampshire, England, on Sunday, 2 June 1912. He was the son of the Reverend Edward Reid, a minister of First Ramelton Presbyterian Church, County Donegal, and the nephew of James Seaton Reid, the renowned Presbyterian historian. Both the Reverend Edward and James Seaton were the sons of Forrest Reid, master of a grammar school in Lurgan, County Armagh. After their father's death, James Seaton Reid, at the age of eight, was sent in 1806 to Ramelton to be under his brother's care.

Following in his father's footsteps, the Reverend Edward Reid opened a grammar school in Ramelton, and it was here James Seaton Reid received his early education. The building in which lessons were held later became part of cottage tenements. Others who attended the school were the future Sir Edward Reid and his brother, Forrest, who became Crown Solicitor for County Londonderry.

Sir Edward came to Derry, and with his partner, Mr Joseph Orr, he extended the firm of Messrs. Reid, Orr and Co., one of the business establishments which rose out of Derry's rapid advancement, particularly in shipping, in the middle of the nineteenth century. The characteristics which made him a good businessman also commended him to the citizens of Londonderry, and for a long series of years he was a member of the Corporation; he received the honour of knighthood in 1868. It was during one of his five years' Mayoralty that the market which bore his name was opened by the Duke of Abercorn, the occasion being that of a ball, carried out on a scale of much splendour.

He once stated that one of the highest compliments which he had ever received came to him from Bishop Higgins, a former Anglican Bishop of Derry, who had said of him, 'Here is a man whose word is as good as his bond.' As secretary of the Gwyn Trust, when the beneficiaries of the Trust were housed in a building which stood in what is now Brooke Park, he showed a kindly concern in the welfare of the boys. When Brooke Park was formally handed over to the Mayor and Corporation of Londonderry in trust for the citizens in August 1901, he addressed the gathering as the only survivor of the original trustees of the Park.

In politics a Liberal, he was the last of the group of merchants who supported Baron Richard Dowse as the city parliamentary candidate in 1868 when he defeated the Tory, Lord Claud Hamilton; but like the majority of the group, he became a Unionist when William Gladstone turned Home Ruler. He retired from the Corporation in 1889, and upon his decision being notified, the secretary of the Irish Society wrote a letter expressing the Society's high appreciation of his character. His removal from Londonderry, in 1894, to live in London was celebrated by a public dinner.

3 JUNE 1960

In 1948, as part of a general reorganisation of transport in the north, the Ulster Transport Authority (UTA) was generated out of the Northern Ireland Road Transport Board (NIRTB) and the Belfast and County Down Railway (BCDR) by the Transport Act passed under instruction by the Labour government at Westminster. In 1949 the Northern Counties Committee (NCC), once part of the old London, Midland and Scottish Railway (LMS) that had been nationalised the previous year, was added. The effect was to bring all these transit systems under the one bureaucratic umbrella. New fleets of buses were purchased and, in time, diesel trains were introduced to run on the same routes as the coal-burners. All of this expense inevitably meant an increase in fares and a decrease in services.

The decades-old problem of the border—Derry only three miles away at its nearest point—complicated the issue. The Great Northern Railway (GNR) was still the main line connecting Belfast to Dublin—and Derry to Dublin (with a change at Portadown). Many Derry workers who lived in Donegal relied heavily on the Lough Swilly service and the County Donegal rail and bus services for such destinations as Buncrana, Moville, Letterkenny, Ballybofey, Donegal and Sligo. The only UTA railroad serving the northwest was the LMS, as people persisted in calling it. It took rather more than two hours to travel to Belfast via Coleraine, Ballymena and Antrim. By the 1960s the car, once the privilege of the rich, was virtually within every adult's grasp, and the UTA found it was catering more and more for the very young and the very old.

The edition of the *Derry Journal* published on Friday, 3 June 1960, had a headline that fifty-three years later would have shocked people into laughter: 'Transport Authority Announcement: Derry Bus Fares To Go Up A Halfpenny.' A halfpenny (pronounced 'haypnee') was a coin to be reckoned with then. It was, as the name implies, half of a penny, and two and a half of these made up one new penny when decimalisation arrived in February 1971; so a halfpenny was one-fifth of 1p—not shattering by today's inflationary standards.

The announcement was made by James Houston, the Derry Traffic Manager, who said that all city fares would rise by the halfpenny. He reminded the public that the last increase had been on 31 December 1956. In those days one could travel from the Rosemount factory to Glendermott Road or from Pennyburn to Ebrington on a single ticket. And the UTA would soon extend the bus service to the newly-opened Altnagelvin Hospital. Houston went on to say that the cost of fuel and maintenance had risen sharply and these increases had been met so far by internal economies: 'The search for economies is a continuous one but unfortunately the latest rise in expenditure is of such magnitude that it cannot be met within the resources of the undertaking.'

4 JUNE 1939

The business of the summer Crown Court, as reported in the *Derry Journal* of 4 June 1939, was the usual mixture of the funny, the sad and the bizarre. James Moore of Cliftonville Avenue, Waterside, had been found guilty of assaulting Annie McShane at Foxe's Corner, at the foot of Fahan Street on 6 February that year, and was sentenced to fourteen days' imprisonment.

Mary Ann Moore, the wife of the appellant, had engaged in a squabble with

McShane, who lived nearby in St Columb's Wells. J. Lynn, acting for Moore, managed to persuade the judge that he was not a chief participant and His Honour, while confirming the validity of the conviction, did at least rescind the imprisonment. He had, of course, to make his judicial mark and his bench comment: 'I cannot have these squabbles going on and disturbing the peace of the district.' He ordered the Moores and McShane to enter into bail each of £5, and to be of good behaviour for six months.

Michael McDevitt of Boomhall appealed against a ten-shilling fine for driving, as alleged, without due care and attention. McDevitt had hit the front of a lorry that, having momentarily stopped on the right-hand side of the road prior to turning left, was preparing to reverse through a gateway. The lorry driver had given a 'slow-down' signal but, it was claimed, he had not given any indication that he was turning briefly to the left. McDevitt then tried to pass on the left but struck the lorry as he moved forward. The judge upheld the conviction because the appellant had taken a risk in trying to pass between the front of the lorry and the pavement.

The next case heard involved a collision with a cyclist in Waterloo Place, just at the foot of Magazine Street, on 22 March. Thomas Hamill from the Culmore Road appealed against a conviction and a ten shilling fine for striking Walter Jeffers, who while cycling towards the Guildhall, had put out his hand to indicate that he intended turning right into Magazine Street. He was struck by Hamill's car and fell against it. Hamill's counsel, C.A. Nicholson, suggested that as the car passed Jeffers the rear wheel of his bicycle wobbled. Hamill claimed to have stopped the car, and the bicycle then skidded, and that was why Jeffers fell against the vehicle. His Honour was not convinced and he affirmed both the conviction and the fine.

5 JUNE 1886

On 5 June 1886 the *Londonderry Sentinel* reported the death of James Allender, 'the Derry Giant' or 'Irish Giant', who had just passed away in South Shields Workhouse.

Allender, who was only thirty-eight, had lived for a considerable part of his life in Derry and was remembered for his inoffensive manner. As a boy he was admitted to Gwyn's Charitable Institution for orphans, where he grew with remarkable speed to an abnormal height. Believing that outdoor employment might benefit him, he was apprenticed to the gardener of the institution. This occupation was not entirely successful in one respect: Allender found it necessary to go on his knees to perform work for which ordinary men could stoop. He eventually reached the height of seven feet and nine inches.

Allender was consistently harassed and taunted by crowds of boys who followed him when he went through the streets, and in order to minimise bringing attention to himself and his height he regularly assumed a stooping manner of walking. Soon, however, he came up with the idea of using his height to its best advantage, and sought a career as a public entertainer. Unfortunately, by this stage, Allender had been so used to adopting a cramped position, his chest had become dwarfed, and his lungs refused to expand when he straightened himself.

When he was twenty-one years of age he took ship, it was believed, with Captain Cassidy in one of the ocean-going vessels belonging to Messrs. McCorkell, and was engaged as an 'Irish giant' barman in a large New York drinking saloon. The famous American showman Phineas Taylor Barnum discovered him here, and Allender was secured by the novelty-monger and exhibited as an 'Abyssinian chief' at the Philadelphia Centennial Exhibition. He was also put on display at the Paris Exhibition in 1878.

Subsequently he went on tour throughout the main towns of the United Kingdom with a 'fat woman', whom he was said to have met in Derry. On returning to the city he resumed residence in William Street, his birthplace, and obtained employment as a 'ham-hanger' in Henry Lecky's curing company in Foyle Street. The hooking of hams to the ceiling normally needed a stepladder, but Allender was able to dispense with this aid.

Allender's mother, who kept a dairy in William Street, died in the early 1880s and left him some money. He was soon married, by the Reverend F.L. Riggs, to a domestic servant named Mary Elkin. The marriage was celebrated in Christ Church, and was the occasion of extensive rejoicings in the Lower Road and William Street. Six months later he again went on exhibition in England and Scotland. He was subsequently employed to stand in front of the Crompton House, Liverpool, to attract the attention of passers-by, and at the door of Messrs. Hyam Brothers, also in Liverpool.

6 JUNE 1957

A verdict of accidental death was returned at an inquest in Derry on Thursday, 6 June 1957, concerning a forty-one-year-old window cleaner, William McCloskey, of 3 East Wall, who had fallen twelve feet from the window of an Academy Terrace house two days earlier. At the close of the inquest, Mr P.

Maxwell, who appeared for the next of kin, said he had been asked by the relatives to make a complaint in this matter in order to ensure that the same thing did not happen again.

'I am told,' said Maxwell, 'that this man was found to be dead at the hospital at 5.15 p.m. on Tuesday. The remains were not removed from the hospital by his relatives until today (Thursday) at 2.30 p.m. A certain procedure, as we now know, had to be gone through but the complaint of the relatives is that in answer to all inquiries at the hospital no information had come out... as to what was happening, arrangements and times fixed, so that the relatives could make the necessary arrangements for the funeral. Not until they approached the District-Inspector had they been able to get the information they wanted from the hospital offices.

'It is to be regretted that the complaint had to be made on an occasion like this, but they wanted the coroner to convey their complaint. They think a considerable amount of anxiety, which was unnecessary, was caused to the widow. Had the information been given, that anxiety could have been allayed.

'They ask the coroner to see that anxious relatives be kept in touch with [at] the various times that things were done.'

The City Coroner, Mr C.A. Milligan, admitted that the blame lay with him, but the case was rather different from the usual. What was regarded as a straightforward fall was followed by evidence that the man had had an illness beforehand. In order to make sure that McCloskey's fall had not been occasioned by this or some other illness, a post-mortem was carried out. Steps were taken to get in touch with the pathologist, Captain Hopkins, but there were delays. Milligan was not trying to excuse himself for this; he just believed the matter could have been speeded up somewhat.

'Certainly the relatives had every right to the fullest information,' Milligan said, 'and it is the duty of everyone concerned to give them the fullest information as to what is happening. I explained to the relatives that a post-mortem might be necessary. I am deeply sorry for any anxiety that might have been caused to the relatives, especially to the widow on this occasion. I will certainly make sure the relatives, as I have always tried to do, will be kept fully informed as to what exactly is happening.' Milligan confirmed that McCloskey had appeared to be in good health and that his fall had been purely accidental and not caused by any pre-existing illness.

A special sitting of Derry Recorder's Court held, unusually, on a Saturday was reported on in the newspapers on Monday, 7 June 1937. One subhead read 'Woman Tries on Coat in Court', making up in mystery what it lacked in drama. The case was brought by John Kelly and Francis Guckian, two partners in Kelly & Son, a tailor's firm in Foyle Street. They were suing Constable Michael Brennan to recover £5 10s for goods 'sold and delivered'. The plaintiffs' solicitor, C.A. Nicholson, produced a lady's coat that was at the heart of the case. He advised the court that there had been a similar case a few days previously in London but involving a coat valued at over £800.

Kelly described how Mr and Mrs Brennan came into his shop to buy a coat, and how the wife chose the pattern and material for it. The necessary measurements were made and work on the coat was started. Mrs Brennan returned on several occasions for fittings and necessary alterations, and eventually the coat was ready and was delivered to her home in Mount Street. It arrived on a Friday but Mrs Brennan returned it the following Monday with a note saying it was too tight about the shoulders and sleeves. In light of this, she wished to cancel the order. Kelly wrote back to say that the order could not then be cancelled but, receiving no answer, wrote to Mr Brennan only to get a letter from Brennan's solicitor in reply.

At this point the Recorder suggested that Mrs Brennan retire to the solicitors' room to put on the coat. She complied and the court waited, as if in a theatre, for her entrance, though they withheld any applause. After some scrutiny, Judge Osborne said that it seemed to be a good fit. The defendant disagreed, insisting that it was too tight: 'It is not a good fit!' At this point Nicholson remarked: 'Do you know it gives you a very nice figure.' Mrs Brennan replied sweetly: 'Thanks for the compliment, but the coat doesn't fit me no matter what compliment you pay me.'

Osborne was silent for a moment and then stated that the lady's real objection to the coat was that she had made a mistake in the material she had chosen. He gave a decree for the full amount.

Dr James McKnight, a name strongly associated with nineteenth-century Ulster tenant-right agitation, died in Derry on 8 June 1876. The agitation was a potent means of producing crucial Acts of Parliament to safeguard the rights of

Irish tenant farmers, which, unique to Ulster, were jealously guarded by northern farmers.

The son of an Ulster Presbyterian who could speak Irish, McKnight was born at Rathfriland in County Down on 27 February 1800. His preparatory education was received at the school of a Mr Henderson in Newry. His later studies were conducted at the Belfast Academical Institution. He entered the Collegiate Department of that seminary in November 1825.

He began, around 1828, during his leisurely student life, to send some contributions to the *Belfast News Letter*, which led to an acquaintance with Mr Macky, its proprietor, and in the end to an appointment on its staff; in time, he became its editor. The *News Letter* was then published only twice weekly, the duties of the editor were not heavy, and time was left at his disposal for private study. His connection with the newspaper ceased around 1845, and some time later he moved to Derry to edit the *Londonderry Standard*. He returned to Belfast where, for five years, he was in charge of the *Banner of Ulster*. On the *Banner* becoming a tri-weekly journal, he was afraid that more time would be required for its editorial work than he was willing to spare from his books, the study of which was his great enjoyment, and he gladly accepted a re-appointment to the *Standard* in 1853. From that time until his death he resided in Derry and conducted the literary department of that paper.

It was soon after McKnight first became editor of the *Standard* that he commenced the great tenant-right agitation which made him famous. At that time Tory landlords held the parliamentary representation of Ulster. Not a single representative of the farming population could hope to secure a seat, and the farmer's rent was fixed by the landlord. The Presbyterian farmers of the North feared eviction without compensation so much that they dreaded facing the landlords. James McKnight determined to do battle and, in the summer of 1846, with the assistance of a few tenant farmers and Presbyterian clergymen, he founded a Tenant-Right Association.

The agrarian movement in Ulster placed Presbyterians again in the ranks of agitators. Some of the Southern leaders, such as Charles Gavan Duffy, hoped, through McKnight, to win over the North to their own political principles, but McKnight, while he agreed to act with the Southern leaders on a tenant-right platform, rigidly insisted that the idea of Repeal of the Union be excluded. The Southern desire for Repeal and the Northern wish to remain part of the Union eventually tore apart the tenant-right movement, and hindered the progress of reform.

A lengthy explanation was given by the *Derry Journal* on Friday, 11 June 1897, of the outbreak of religious fervour that had gripped the Catholic community in Derry in the run-up to, and actual celebration of, the Columban feast on 9 June:

> The thirteenth centenary of Derry's patron saint has come and gone, and the important event has been celebrated in a manner and in a spirit worthy of the city of St Columbkille. Fame, we are told, is but an empty breath afforded a mortal, or his deeds, and can give him no solace in eternity, but the fame of a soldier of Christianity is not a perpetuation of his name, but a perpetuation of the Faith and principles that animated him in his lifework for God. Man's work dies with himself—the work of God's chosen minister never dies. Time has forged thirteen hundred links since the noble youth Columba resigned all that this world could give to plant the standard of Apostleship amid the green oak groves of Derry. Since then great conquerors and greater tyrants have arisen and passed away... Yet the faith that Columba preached is still practised in the same purity, with the same devotion, and with intense magnificence on the hill of Derry, and for nights past around the Stone where St Columba knelt, Catholics of Derry recited the prayers of the Catholic Church in the very tongue in which Columba prayed. Of all the thousands now living in Derry... not one shall see the next centenary—yet St Columba's work will not die, and Catholics more numerous and as faithful will celebrate St Columba's memory with equal fervour and in greater magnificence.
>
> > For on the Faith must go
> > Amidst joy or weal or woe.
>
> That is the heritage of the Irish people; it is the one thing of which they could not and cannot be bereft. It is only in the light of these considerations that the extraordinary outburst of religious enthusiasm on the occasion of St Columba's centenary can be properly appreciated. Unbelievers may not approve, but they must admire—Catholics alone can understand. In what other light can it be viewed when it is known that although it was not a church holiday, not a Catholic man, woman or child in Derry failed to go to Mass, or to pay a visit to the Blessed Sacrament which was exposed for adoration in all our churches. Five thousand persons received the Holy Communion in the Long Tower, twelve hundred at the Cathedral, and a like number at the Waterside... Within the last few days there have been many evidences of the vitality of Catholicity and unaffected piety in Derry.

There were, indeed, 'many evidences of the vitality of Catholicity and unaffected piety' to be found in June 1897. Besides the aforementioned religious services, which attracted vast audiences, it could also be evidenced in the scores of decorations that adorned Catholic areas of the city.

10 JUNE 1940

An inquest in the Londonderry City and County Hospital, held on Monday, 10 June 1940, attempted to make sense of the deaths of Head Constable Thomas Dempsey and Constable Edward Corr at the Liverpool Shed on Queen's Quay on the previous Saturday night. The coroner presiding was Captain J.T.E. Miller.

Constable Corr had been on harbour duty from two o'clock and was due to be relieved at ten o'clock. At a quarter to ten Head Constable Dempsey attended to his rounds and accompanied Corr towards a yacht which he wished to inspect. Dempsey and Corr went through the Liverpool Shed, engaged in normal conversation on the wharf. When Dempsey turned to walk away Corr drew his revolver and fired at him. Dempsey, who was unarmed, attempted to escape, but Corr fired two more shots into him as he lay on the wharf. Constable Corr then turned the revolver on himself, missing with the first shot, but shooting himself through the head with the second. When a doctor arrived both men were found to be dead.

Head Constable Dempsey, who was forty-seven, was a native of Ballinasloe, County Galway, and had joined the RIC in 1913. After transferring to the RUC he was promoted to sergeant in 1922 and became head constable six years later. One week before his death he had succeeded an Officer Hueston as senior head constable in Londonderry, and had already successfully completed the examination for promotion to the rank of District Inspector. He had been stationed in Kilkenny, Cork, and Antrim before coming to Derry in 1934. He left a widow and two daughters.

Constable Corr, who was forty-nine, came from Ballinaugh, County Cavan, and had been in Donegal before moving to Derry in 1922. He left a widow and six children.

Constable T.J. Moran testified that on Saturday night at 9.55 p.m., after being paraded for night duty, he was told to go to the Liverpool Shed, as something was wrong. On his arrival, he saw the bodies of the two policemen, Dempsey lying on his right side with his head in a pool of blood nine feet from the edge of the wharf; and Corr, who was lying on his left side with his feet towards the edge of the wharf.

Given the circumstances of the double tragedy, and with no real evidence to

186

account for Corr's state of mind, a doctor said that he had probably had a 'brainstorm' and did not know what he was doing. Captain Miller added that the 'brainstorm' may have been caused by the heat.

11 JUNE 1959

On 17 April 1959 Margaret McLaughlin of 183 Foster's Terrace, Lecky Road (one of many 'disappeared' Derry streets) stepped unheeding into the road in William Street and was knocked down by a motorcycle. Her leg was broken and she was rushed to the City and County Hospital. She died there on 3 June of sepsis and toxaemia after nearly seven weeks of confinement in bed during which period, as the medical report presented at the inquest put it, she resembled 'an elderly, debilitated person showing changes of senility'. The inquest was held on 11 June, C.A. Milligan, the City Coroner presiding, and the jury returned a verdict that accorded with the medical evidence. They exonerated Hugh Kelly, the rider of the motorcycle, from any blame for her death.

The autopsy was performed by Dr R.J.W. Ryder who said that cause of death was not directly related to the fractured leg, but it did accelerate the effects of certain aspects of congenital debility. The body was identified by Mary Gallagher, Margaret's niece, whose house in William Street she had been visiting just before the accident occurred. Two eyewitnesses corroborated existing evidence. Elizabeth McBride of Dawros Gardens saw Margaret step off the footpath into the road without looking. In her opinion the motorcyclist had very little chance of stopping; he braked hard and had almost stopped when the old woman 'just walked into him'. Catherine Coyle of Bolies, Prehen agreed that Miss McLaughlin had stepped into the path of the motorcycle, not giving Kelly any chance of avoiding her.

Kelly stated that the deceased was about three feet from him when he saw her heading across the road. He was travelling at about 15mph and braked, swerving sharply to the right. In spite of this she kept moving forward and 'walked into his machine'. Milligan summed the situation up 'as a simple accident which in other circumstances would not have had a fatal ending', and used the opportunity to extend sympathy to the relatives of the deceased and also to the driver.

The fact that the patient was 'elderly, debilitated and showing changes of senility' was then taken as a sufficient cause of death. Both the medical and legal establishments accepted that toxaemia and sepsis would be the inevitable result of 'a prolonged confinement in bed'.

On Monday, 10 June 1929, at Derry Crown Court, Mrs Margaret Rabbit from the Collon area of the city was charged with the mild-sounding offence of 'receiving'. However mild it sounds the offence was regarded with the utmost seriousness, since the 'fence' was an essential part of the criminal structure in the city. From the report of the proceedings in the *Derry Journal* of 12 June it seems clear that from the start Mrs Rabbit had been guilty of nothing more than carelessness and mild greed, having made no real attempt to discover the provenance of the 'received' goods when they were offered to her.

The thief who needed to dispose of his unlawful goods was John McDermott; he had already been sentenced at the Petty Sessions Court on 6 June to six months' imprisonment for the theft of two pairs of ladies' shoes from Andrew D. Kennedy, who kept a shop in Duke Street. Kennedy in his evidence stated that on Saturday, 25 May he had sent a message boy with the shoes, each worth £1 5s, to Mrs Brown of Linenhall Street. He had not seen either pair since, except the pair he had identified at the police station that had been obtained from Mrs Rabbit. It became clear that McDermott had somehow obtained the shoes from Kennedy's message boy, assuring him that he would deliver them to Mrs Brown, whom he claimed to know.

McDermott, who had already pleaded guilty to the theft, stated that he sold one pair to 'a country man' for two shillings and had taken the parcel to the Collon where Mrs Rabbit kept a little shop. McDermott noticed her chatting to another woman on her doorstep and when he offered the shoes for sale cheaply, she expressed an interest. There was little haggling; McDermott was too anxious to get his price and disappear. She agreed to pay the two shillings for the shoes and had given McDermott two packets of Woodbine cigarettes 'as a present'.

Detective Constable Murphy stated that as a result of information received he had visited Rabbit's house after midnight on 26 May. He asked her if she had bought shoes the previous day but she denied it. She did, however, say that there was a parcel in the shop that she thought might contain shoes. These she handed freely to the constable who was able to have them identified at the police station as belonging to Kennedy.

Mrs Rabbit's defence counsel was allowed to reveal something of McDermott's criminal past. He had been convicted ten times in Northern Ireland for larceny, and once in the Free State. In the seven years since 1922 he had served forty-three months in prison. It was the contrast between the convicted thief and the shopkeeper who had merely taken the opportunity at a time of deep recession to buy cheaply that swayed the jury, and they returned a verdict of 'not guilty'.

13 JUNE 1949

One of the purposes of the local press is to celebrate the achievements of local people. It was perfectly appropriate for the *Derry Journal* of 13 June 1949 to use fifty square inches in 9-point font in a story of a Derry man who was playing an important part in running the mighty and complicated Greater London transport system.

Patrick McElwee had been born in Derry and educated at St Columb's Boys School, Long Tower, and like so many before and since, he had found it necessary to emigrate to Britain to find work. In 1925 he began a career in transport management as controller of London's 5,000 buses. He himself lived in Lewisham and his office was at the tube station at Kennington Oval, the nerve centre of the services that carried 6,640,000 passengers in the metropolis each day. With such an area to be covered and so many vehicles involved he had to be prepared each day for road repairs, punctures, minor mishaps, breakdowns, diversions and accidents. Though having nothing of the volume or complexity of today's metropolitan transport, even then there was a string of telephone calls waiting to be answered. On his capacious desk was a plan of the city's bus routes but he rarely had to consult it. The location of every bridge, junction, roundabout, fire station, police station and shopping precinct was already mapped in his brain; he could actually visualise the scene from the co-ordinates given by his drivers or conductors.

A bus had a puncture, for example, on Cambridge New Road. Within minutes McElwee sent a recovery truck from the nearest transport garage. Before the breakdown had been attended to he had rearranged the schedule. Each incident was dealt with appropriately. When a conductor was assaulted by a passenger and word got back to the controller, he had the police on the job within minutes.

As McElwee described his life to the *Journal* reporter he recalled the kind of incident that presented him with most trouble—the cat that held up a No. 37 bus by refusing to move out from under the wheel, Oswald Mosley's Fascist marches in the East End, the dreaded frost and snow—though he admitted that London rarely suffered from too much disruption.

He had begun to work with the old London General Omnibus Company when some of the 'generals' still had open tops. His first work had been as an Inspector-Interpreter at the 1924 Wembley Exhibition (he was fluent in French, German and Dutch and had run the system all through the terrors of the Blitz). His tensest time was when a V2 rocket landed at a bottleneck at New Cross Gate, wrecking buses and trams, and killing more than a hundred people. Teased about 'the knowledge', the intimate 'savvy' of the capital's topography that all London cabbies must acquire, he said he had had it for years but that the only thing that prevented him from putting it to best use was the fact that he could not drive.

14 JUNE 1951

A rally of Pioneers (those who have made a promise to abstain from alcoholic liquor for life) was held in St Columba's Church, Long Tower, on 14 June 1951. Temperance movements in Ireland were nothing new, beginning with the effective crusade of Fr Theobold Mathew in Cork from 1836. Derry had its own teetotal movement, the St Columb's Total Abstinence Society, founded by Fr Walter Elliott. By the 1950s the many different societies were brought under the general umbrella of the Pioneer Total Abstinence Association of the Sacred Heart. The members wore lapel pins to indicate membership.

The rally was addressed by the guest speaker, Reverend Daniel Dargan, SJ, Assistant Director of the Pioneer Association, and he pulled no punches:

> There was a time Ireland was regarded in the eyes of the nations of the world as a nation of drunkards. Now intemperance is not merely an Irish problem, it is a world-wide problem, and today we see those nations turning to Ireland to give a lead, an inspiration, in the virtue of temperance. These countries saw what the Pioneer movement has done here.

He gave a brief historical survey of the dire effects of drunkenness half a century before, when the number of prosecutions for over-imbibing averaged about 100,000 a year. Now he could claim with some satisfaction that the figure had fallen to 4,000 and he insisted that the Pioneer movement had been one of the main agencies of this improvement.

The membership of the movement was then half a million, probably the peak figure. Growing affluence and a more sophisticated lifestyle may not actually have increased the abuse of alcohol but it served to decrease the number of people prepared to make the heroic personal sacrifice of abstinence. The

Golden Jubilee of the Pioneers had been celebrated in Dublin in 1950 but even ten years later the numbers had fallen. This possibility clearly had not occurred to the members in the church or to those who had marched down Fifth Avenue in New York on the previous Sunday week, carrying the Pioneer banner. Dargan did not hesitate to present another side to the picture. He adverted to the disturbing fact that while Ireland had an exemplary record for teetotalism, drinking to excess was becoming characteristic of young people of both genders. He produced the interesting statistic that Ireland ranked seventh in the world for its people's consumption of port wine. His strongest fulminations were directed at young women:

> Are these stupid girls to be the future mothers of Ireland? Are we to depend on girls like that to raise up future priests and nuns and Catholic laymen and women. The whole future of our country is affected.

He finished by emphasising the importance of members repeating the Heroic Offering prayer each day, of wearing the pin, and taking time to explain its significance.

15 JUNE 2010

On 15 June 2010 the square in front of Derry's Guildhall was crowded with people, largely silent, but with a sense of expectation of imminent revelation. Inside the ninety-eight-year-old civic building, a much smaller group of people waited with an agonising intensity for the news that, they hoped, would vindicate and reward them for thirty-eight years of grief, frustration and agitation. Lord Saville of Newdigate was about to reveal the findings of the enquiry into the events of 30 January 1972 in the Bogside area of the city—the 'Bloody Sunday' that saw the deaths of thirteen unarmed civilians, in the wake of a civil rights march, at the hands of soldiers of the British Parachute and the Royal Anglican Regiments. A fourteenth victim died later. A tribunal chaired by Lord Widgery had largely exonerated the army in its report published on 18 April 1972, but this was immediately and correctly dismissed as a whitewash.

Successive British governments had refused to overturn Widgery or revisit the event that had benefited the Provisional IRA greatly in terms of prestige and recruitment to its ranks. The relatives of the fourteen victims continued their campaign for justice until, in 1992, as one of the early acts of his newly-elected majority Labour government, Tony Blair asked Saville to inquire into the matter. Saville's deliberations lasted twelve years, and now the findings were to be made public, simultaneously to the House of Commons and in the Guildhall, where the relatives had gathered. To a packed house in London, Prime Minister David Cameron apologised on behalf of the United Kingdom to all concerned; Saville had found that all of those shot were unarmed and that the killings were 'unjustified and unjustifiable'.

A large screen had been set up beside the Guildhall and people gathered there were able to see images of Cameron addressing MPs in London, but after the initial important sentences, his words were lost as a mighty roar came from the throats of the Derry crowd. The government were at last prepared to listen to the words of Lord Saville as he concluded: 'What happened on Bloody Sunday strengthened the Provisional IRA, increased nationalist resentment and hostility towards the Army, and exacerbated the violent conflict of the years that followed. Bloody Sunday was a tragedy for the bereaved and the wounded, and a catastrophe for the people of Northern Ireland.' Among those who were inside the Guildhall and aware of the embargoed findings, before Cameron made the formal announcement, was Bishop Edward Daly, pictures of whom, carrying a bloodstained handkerchief as he ministered to the dying on that fateful day, had been broadcast round the world. His joy was palpable as he welcomed the findings.

A last act, as if of exorcism, took place on 30 January 2011, also a Sunday. A large crowd, including many of the relatives of the dead, retraced the route of the original civil rights march on its thirty-ninth anniversary. There was not the same surge of joy as on the sunny June day of the publication of the report, but there was a kind of peace.

16 JUNE 1915

Captain Edward George Harvey, Duke of Edinburgh's Wiltshire Regiment and Royal Flying Corps, was killed in action near the Belgian village of Hooge on 16 June 1915, aged thirty-two. His name is inscribed on St Columb's Cathedral (Church of Ireland) Memorial and on the famous Ypres Menin Gate Memorial in Belgium. He is also remembered on Derry's Diamond War Memorial.

Educated at Foyle College, Harvey was only eighteen when he enlisted in the Argyll and Sutherland Highlanders. He served with them in South Africa, and subsequently as a sergeant in India, where he obtained his commission in the Wiltshire Regiment in 1905. In 1913 he was seconded for service with the

Royal Flying Corps in which he was promoted to flight commander in 1914, and subsequently to captain in his regiment to which he returned at the end of that year, joining its 1st Battalion at the Front in February 1915. Captain Harvey was at the head of his company leading an attack on the third line of German trenches when he was mortally wounded.

A brother, William Francis Harvey, served in the Great War with the Canadian forces but died afterwards at Victoria, British Columbia, on 25 March 1922, aged twenty-eight. Harvey's cousin, Major F.H. Harvey of the East Yorkshire Regiment, and younger son of Colonel Edward Harvey, Royal Engineers, featured on a list of honours included in Field Marshal Sir Douglas Haig's despatch in January 1917; he had already been awarded the DSO. At that time Major Harvey was serving on the Headquarters Staff of the Fifth Army, commanded by General Sir Hubert Gough.

At the sitting of Lifford Quarter Sessions Court, held on Tuesday, 22 June 1915, Judge Cooke said it was only fitting that he should express deep sympathy with Mr J.G.M. Harvey on the death in Flanders of his son, Captain Edward George Harvey, which had been announced in the papers that morning. The captain's father was constantly represented in that court and, although resident in Derry, was intimately connected with the county of Donegal as a grand juror. J.G.M. Harvey, the youngest son of Commander Edward Harvey, RN, belonged to an old and highly esteemed Donegal family, who had been granted estates and settled in the Malin district about the year 1618. J.G.M. Harvey was directly descended from John Harvey, who had been Chamberlain of Derry and had commanded a company of volunteers during the Siege of 1689.

17 JUNE 1952

St Patrick's Day 1952 was a time of rioting in Derry, just as it had been the year before. Three months later to the day, at the Recorder's Court in the city, a large number of claims for personal injury and damage to property were placed before Judge Copeland. Two claims were made by RUC constables for injuries received. The first, by Alexander Newell, who claimed £5,000, was adjourned until the next session. A similar postponement greeted a claim for £500 by Special Constable John Ross. The hearing was even delayed for an hour to accommodate negotiations which were taking place between interested parties, and before the court convened settlements had already been made in practically every case, amounting to £600. Daniel James Craig of Strand Road claimed £100 for the smashing of a plate-glass window and accepted £30 16s

10d, while Alexander Canning of Butcher Street received £18 15s 7d for a window he'd valued at £20. Butcher Street had taken quite a battering and six residents lodged claims that were nearly fully compensated. Margaret McMonagle and William Gallagher, who claimed £42 13s 3d for six shop windows, three dwelling-house windows, a fanlight, three window screens, a curtain and a barometer, were awarded the full amount, as was S.S. Thompson of Sackville Street, who got £16 10s 6d for a broken window. Twenty-three such cases were dealt with to the claimants' reasonable satisfaction.

Two Maghera farmers, John Molloy and James McCusker, had gone with their wives to Derry for the day when they got caught up in a crowd of people. Molloy had been 'knocked on the head' and was required to spend a night in hospital. He was still being treated for the effects of the blow. He asserted that he had been hit by a policeman's baton, but the case was dismissed. The judiciary tended in those years to be strongly on the side of the police 'acting in the execution of their duties'. McCusker had a similar story to tell and had his case similarly dismissed.

Special Constable Kennedy of the RUC in Claudy claimed £100 for personal injuries. He had been mobilised for service to Derry for the day and had been called out from Victoria Barracks to 'quell some riots'. There were several baton charges and during the disturbances he had been struck on the mouth 'with a bottle or stone or some missile'. It cut both his lips and 'a tooth came out subsequently'. The injury had been sustained during a mêlée at Littlewood's corner when rival crowds struggled with a tricolour. R. Lowry, who appeared for Derry Corporation, agreed that Kennedy was entitled to compensation, and Judge Copeland issued a decree for a quarter of the amount claimed.

18 JUNE 1949

During World War II, Derry played an important part in the Battle of the Atlantic. Ships from the Royal Navy, the Royal Canadian Navy and other Allied navies were stationed in the city where the United States military had established a base. The reason for such a high degree of military and naval activity was that Derry was the United Kingdom's westernmost port. Indeed, the city was the westernmost Allied port in Europe. Thus, Derry was a crucial jumping-off point for the shipping convoys that ran between Europe and North America.

On 18 June 1949, the *Londonderry Sentinel* announced that the last remnants of a once proud and deadly fleet, that for years had sailed from the

Londonderry naval base to guard the convoy routes from practically mid-Atlantic to the shores of Britain, had just departed down the Foyle to begin life anew as whaling ships.

The previous day, the first of the last four corvettes which had been berthed at Abercorn Quay since they were 'taken off the mud' at Ross's Bay, made her final trip down the river, shorn of all her glory and livery, a deserted hulk. The ship, formerly the Flower Class corvette, HMS *Sweet Briar*, didn't even make the trip under her own steam. She was made fast alongside the Norwegian *Jason* of Bergen which was an ex-Dancing Class minesweeper-trawler, and had also been in the service of the Royal Navy before her conversion to a tug. At Moville the *Sweet Briar* was taken in tow for the remainder of her voyage to Sandefjord, where she would be fitted out for her new purpose.

'Ships,' noted the *Sentinel*, 'always regarded as having a close connection with the sentimentality of the humans, can present just as pathetic a sight as the humble trap or the down-at-heel beggar. It was such a sight that several hundred people along the Foyle saw the previous day as the *Jason* and the *Sweet Briar* slipped their moorings and slowly made the voyage down the Foyle, past the glistening destroyers and subs, still in commission. It was in sharp contrast that the *Sweet Briar*, rusty, with twisted deck rails, slack rigging, and flapping canvas bridge screens, limped to sea without the glamour or excitement that were a vital part of her a few years before when she was bristling with armaments.'

A fortnight later another of the Flower corvettes, the former HMS *Primrose*, was also to be taken by the *Jason* to Larvik for her Norwegian buyers. The London firm, Faulkland Shipowners, would remove the last of the vessels, the *Columbine* and the *Wallflower*, to re-join their sister ships in the hunting of whales in due course. A number of obsolete submarines which had been lying at the naval base, and at Lisahally, had also been towed to cross-channel breaking-up yards at this time.

19 JUNE 1920

It was during sectarian trouble in the Diamond area of Derry on the night of 19 June 1920 that forty-five-year-old Unionist, Edwin Andrew Price, was fatally shot. He had come to the door of the Diamond Hotel, where he resided, when a bullet struck him in the abdomen. After penetrating his body, the shot pierced a two-inch door and became embedded in the woodwork inside. With no ambulance available at that time, a number of people carried the injured man to the fire station, where he lingered for about an hour, dying shortly before midnight. Mr Price had come from America at the outbreak of the First World War and served with the Ambulance Corps of the 36th (Ulster) Division. He was about to return to the States when he was shot.

At the inquest into Mr Price's death, on 28 June 1920, Dr J.E. Miller said he was called to the fire station on the night of 19 June and found Price lying on the floor bleeding from two wounds on the lower part of the stomach. He was beyond medical aid, and death, which took place a few minutes after the doctor's arrival, was due to internal haemorrhage.

John Buchanan, proprietor of the Diamond Hotel, said that he'd seen Price about 10.20 on the night in question when he walked from the hotel door towards the middle of Shipquay Street. He went out of Buchanan's sight for a moment, and then returned to the door. On arriving back, he said, 'Mr Buchanan, I'm shot', having been hit by a bullet as he was entering the hotel. The Coroner asked Buchanan if he had heard the shot. Buchanan replied that he had; Mr Price had indicated where the bullet had lodged in the door after passing through him. Buchanan held out his hand to him to support Price as he was falling and brought him into the hotel before he was subsequently removed to the fire station.

Hugh McElgunn testified that he'd been standing with Price at the head of Shipquay Street. They walked back together to the hotel, where McElgunn entered, leaving Price at the door. The next thing McElgunn heard was that Price was lying shot in the hall. McElgunn afterwards helped to remove him to the fire station.

The jury returned a verdict that Edwin Price met his death from wounds from a bullet fired by some person or persons unknown, and that person or persons unknown were guilty of murder.

20 JUNE 1915

A Derry lieutenant named on the Diamond War Memorial and killed at Gallipoli in 1915 was the grandson of a chief pioneer in the field of photography. Richard Brendan Buchanan, of Chiswick Lodge, Templemore Park, in the city, died on 20 June 1915. The son of Robert Eccles and Ethel Maud Buchanan (nee Williams), he had reached the age of twenty-one just a month before his death. Richard received his early education at Foyle College and subsequently at Bedford School, where he was a member of the Officers' Training Corps. He entered Edinburgh University Medical School in October 1911. On the day after war was declared he applied for a commission and was made a lieutenant in the Royal Army Medical Corps on 16 August 1914. He applied for transfer to the Royal Scots Fusiliers, and was in due course made second-lieutenant. About mid-May 1915, he proceeded with his battalion to the Dardanelles and, landing on 30 May, went almost at once into the trenches. Buchanan's remains are interred in Lancashire Landing Cemetery in Turkey.

Richard's mother was the daughter of Thomas Richard 'T.R.' Williams, who was among the first people to be designated as an official press photographer, and had been appointed as royal photographer to Queen Victoria. Ethel Maud Williams arrived in Derry with her brother Herbert in the 1880s. On 1 April 1891, at St Mary's, West Kensington, London, she was married to Robert Eccles Buchanan, a civil engineer from Fintona in County Tyrone. Richard Buchanan was born on 6 May 1894 when his parents lived at 12 Harding Street, Londonderry.

Richard's grandfather T.R. Williams was born in England in 1825. In 1854, while working for Phillip Henry Delamotte, he made his celebrated stereograph daguerreotypes of the Crystal Palace, some three years after its opening at the 1851 Great Exhibition. Some commentators consider him to be one of the first photographers to record events as they happened, making him the original press photographer. By the mid-1850s he had turned his attention to portrait photography and later to still-lives, in which field he enjoyed great artistic success. Much of his personal history, however, remains elusive.

Brian May, renowned guitarist with the rock group Queen, has an almost obsessive interest in Williams, of whom he has written: 'Williams succeeded on his reputation by word of mouth. His portraits of Royalty, including Queen Victoria and her daughter Princess "Vicky" were evidently highly prized by the Queen herself, who ordered duplicate copies in case they should fade.'

Yet, such was the quality of Williams's work that the prints have never faded and are in existence to this day. He is now widely recognized as a pivotal figure in the history of stereoscopic photography since his stereo cards were the first examples of photographic art for its own sake ever to achieve wide commercial success.

21 JUNE 1891

On Sunday, 21 June 1891, John McNair and James Wray, the driver and fireman of the engine *Donegal*, had taken the regular 10.15 train to Buncrana and were given orders that on their return, with three empty carriages and a tender, they should await one of two special troop trains at the junction at Tooban where the Londonderry and Lough Swilly Railway headed west to Letterkenny. They were intended to hook on to the troop train and so shorten the time for the journey to Letterkenny. The extra trains had been commissioned to return the militia, known as the Letterkenny Artillery, to their headquarters after annual training at Harwich. Their transport, the *Hirondelle*, had arrived twelve hours earlier than expected, and both the local police and military authorities thought it wisest to send them home as quickly as possible, nobody relishing the prospect of turning 600 militiamen loose on the Sabbath city. Two special night trains had been scheduled to take them from the station by the graving dock on Strand Road and it was just there in the marshalling yard that two emergency specials were being coupled.

The railroad was single track as far as Tooban, about eight miles to the northwest where the Letterkenny line and the one to Buncrana separated. It was vital to keep that eight-mile section clear of oncoming traffic. For some reason, due to his misunderstanding his orders or an error on the part of the guard, or even forgetfulness, the thirty-five-year-old McNair, with his nineteen-year-old fireman, continued along the track towards Derry. Less than a mile from the terminus, where the Springtown industrial estate is located today, the *Donegal* met the second troop train carrying more than 250 soldiers in a head-on collision. It happened just past a road bridge where the Buncrana Road passed over the rail track. James Deeney, the driver of the special, had seen the smoke of McNair's train and immediately jammed on the steam brakes. He succeeded in bringing the train almost to a dead stop, enabling himself and his fireman, John Murdoch, to jump to safety.

McNair and Wray were not so lucky. From the position of McNair's body it was clear that, while trying to jump clear, his leg had been caught between the two engines and completely severed at the thigh. His death was almost instantaneous. James Wray was impaled by the broken metal at the front of the engine and was scalded by the escaping steam from the tubes that had burst when set on fire by the blazing coals from the firebox. He died in hospital at 4 p.m. In the special, the impact was lessened by the fact that the first two wagons behind the tender were full of luggage. The third wagon back held the horse belonging to Major Hicks of the Donegal Artillery and its groom, but neither party was other than grazed.

On 22 June 1985, the Londonderry Young Men's Christian Association (YMCA) opened its new building at Drumahoe in the Waterside. The association had been established on the other side of the River Foyle on 9 December 1856, on the site of an old theatre situated just off the city wall. It used a room in the theatre, which stood on the corner of London Street and Artillery Lane (now Artillery Street). It is believed that it was established by twelve young men who were members of Third Presbyterian (Great James Street) Church.

Just over a decade earlier, in 1844, the YMCA had been founded in London by Sir George Williams from among apprentices and other young men in the drapery trade. The restriction as to trade was soon removed, and the association expanded to include any young men of Protestant denomination.

In the 1860s, after some time using meeting rooms in Linenhall Street, and later in Sackville Street, the Londonderry YMCA acquired a site on East Wall, near the house where they had conducted their first meetings, and began building the hall that was opened on 14 November 1867.

Its architect John Guy Ferguson was a local man of some renown, responsible for the re-building of St Augustine's Chapel of Ease inside the city walls; the original Guildhall that was burned down in 1908; the Apprentice Boys' Memorial Hall; and Welch Margetson's factory. The YMCA building on East Wall had the distinction of being the first purpose-built premises for the organisation in Europe. It missed by a mere two months the distinction of being the first in the world; that had opened in America in September 1867.

Describing the new edifice on East Wall, the *Londonderry Sentinel* wrote: 'The building occupies the site of the old Linen Hall, with a principal elevation to the East Wall. The various requirements of the Association have been carefully studied in design. The rooms are lofty, spacious, and well heated and ventilated. And while no extraneous ornament is lavished externally, the finish is of a neat and most substantial character. The edifice has a frontage to the wall of 37 feet, by a depth of 65 feet, and the internal arrangements comprise a spacious corridor, a lofty and well lighted reading room, committee room, and classroom on the ground floor; with a large and handsome lecture room in the second story and the libraries in the mezzanine. While studying economy in the erection of the new hall, the architect has managed to give a handsome character to the details of the principal front, which presents a very pleasing and effective elevation, and style. The frieze of the main cornice is enriched with medallions containing the heads of the most celebrated reformers—Luther, Calvin, Knox and Cranmer...'

The Diamond War Memorial, erected by the people of Derry to 756 citizens killed in the Great War and 4,000 men and women who volunteered for service, was unveiled on Thursday, 23 June 1927, by Major-General F.F. Ready, General Officer commanding the Northern Ireland district.

Long before the unveiling ceremony every part of the Diamond and adjacent streets was crowded, and all points of vantage above ground, such as shop windows and even rooftops were occupied. The bereaved relatives, representatives of disbanded regiments, ex-servicemen's associations, public bodies, and clergy occupied places of honour near the memorial. Major-General Ready, accompanied by Mayor James Hamilton, the Town Clerk, Sir Henry Miller, and members of the Corporation, marched at 12.15 from the Guildhall to the Diamond where Major-General Ready inspected the guard of honour.

Lady Anderson, who occupied the chair in the unavoidable absence, through illness, of her husband Sir Robert Anderson, chairman of the War Memorial Committee, said:

> During the long and strenuous years of the war the men and women of Londonderry, as in her historic past, played their part nobly and heroically, and when the call came for service they rushed to the ranks of the fighters and workers on sea and land, with glowing enthusiasm and with hands and hearts ready for work and sacrifice. They lived, they served, they died gloriously. The record for the city of over 4,000 volunteers is something of which we, and posterity, may ever be justly proud, and the 756 names of our honoured dead inscribed on this our memorial will show that these brave and noble ones came from all creeds and classes, so that every citizen can join today when we proudly commemorate their glorious deeds.

Lady Anderson then asked Major-General Ready to unveil and dedicate the memorial.

Major-General Ready referred to the honour conferred on him in being asked to unveil the memorial and said he should be proud to do so in any city, but much more so in Derry, 'whose history is an example to the whole Empire for its loyalty and devotion to the Crown'. He continued:

> On an occasion such as this we are stirred by two great emotions. We are moved to a great feeling of pride in that these sons of Londonderry have shown how they were prepared to sacrifice all in order to carry on this glorious heritage of devotion to the Crown handed down to them by their fathers, and we are moved to a great feeling of sorrow, knowing full well the grief and suffering which the loss of these brave lives has caused and indeed still causes to their sorrowing friends and

relations. But besides recording these feelings of pride and sorrow, this memorial so skilfully designed and executed, and so beautifully sited, fulfils still another role. It stands for all time to remind those that come hereafter that, should ever the just cause again arise, the men of this city will come forward as fearlessly as they have done in the past.

24 JUNE 1920

Augustus Austin, a convert to Catholicism residing at Cross Street, Waterside, was shot and fatally wounded on 24 June 1920. Hailing from Newcastle-on-Tyne, and formerly in the ranks of the Royal Scots Fusiliers, Austin was employed, after his discharge from the army, by McKeown's boot manufacturers in William Street. He had resided in Bond Street in a house belonging to a Protestant family but was forced to flee when the owner of the property received a letter warning him to clear out the 'turncoat', and the house was attacked by an angry crowd. He and his wife and their three children then took refuge in a house belonging to a John Muldern.

On the evening of 24 June, the supply of household coal ran out and there was no fuel available for cooking. After seven o'clock Austin and his brother-in-law ventured out to secure some supplies. When Austin turned the corner of Union Street he was shot by a sniper. Friends secured the body and he was conveyed to a house, but died within half an hour.

Mrs Austin declared that: 'They may have wounded his body but his soul is safe and he died a martyr for his religion… He is one of the men they started the war over and now that they have murdered him they should be satisfied. He was confirmed at the last Confirmation, and was a frequent communicant. When attending the Retreat in St Columb's Church he was jeered at by gangs of Unionists…'

On 6 July, in the Police Court, Mr J.P. Thompson, deputy coroner, presided over the inquest into Augustus Austin's death. Austin's widow gave evidence that, at 7 p.m. on the evening of 24 June, she heard a shot and ran to the door, saying, 'That is a deadly shot; someone belonging to me has been killed.' She saw her husband's body being pulled into the house of Mrs Murphy on Union Street and ran to find him lying on the floor. She said, 'Speak to me; are you dying?' but got no reply. When Head Constable O'Donohue asked Mrs Austin where the shot came from, she replied it had been fired from the foot of Bond Street. The Coroner asked how she knew where the shot had come from if she was in the house; Mrs Austin stated she was judging by the sound of the shot where it had originated from. She added that there had been gunshots earlier in the day, between two and four in the afternoon, but no other shots had been fired after that time until the one that claimed her husband's life.

A doctor revealed that Austin had received a gunshot to the chest which had penetrated the heart, thus leading to his death. The jury returned a verdict of murder, and expressed their sympathy with Mrs Austin.

25 JUNE 1920

On the morning of Wednesday, 23 June 1920, an elderly Catholic labourer, John (Jack) McKinney of Cross Street in the Waterside was shot in the throat and conveyed to the military hospital, and later the Infirmary, where he died the following morning. On Friday, 25 June, an inquest was opened at the County Infirmary concerning the cause of his death, with Sergeant Dillon representing the constabulary, and James McDaid of Long Tower Street having identified McKinney's body. Dr A.J. Morrison said McKinney came there from the military hospital on 23 June suffering from a bullet wound on the right side of the neck, and died about nine o'clock on 24 June from shock and haemorrhage due to the wound.

On Thursday, 8 July, Mr John P. Thompson, Deputy Coroner, resumed the inquest into McKinney's death. Head Constable O'Donohue represented the Crown. The first witness was a servant girl named Maggie Murphy of 6 Clooney Terrace, who stated that on the morning of 23 June, at 7.30, while standing at the door, she saw a man walking on the far side of the street towards the military barracks. Three shots were fired and the man fell. He called to her 'for God's sake to come over' but she was too frightened.

Mr Florence O'Sullivan from 16 Clooney Terrace stated that on the morning of 23 June he heard shots across the terrace, where shooting had been a regular thing for a few mornings. As O'Sullivan was getting out of bed his mother came to the room and told him that a poor man had been shot in the street and that he was lying there. O'Sullivan pulled on his trousers and coat and ran out to where the man was lying. He asked the man his name, and he replied he was Jack McKinney, adding that he wanted a drink. Two girls went for Dr Malseed, who came and attended to the man who was afterwards taken to the military hospital.

The coroner said O'Sullivan certainly did a great deal in trying to aid this poor man. He showed great pluck and deserved great credit. Staff Sergeant Cooper, Royal Army Medical Corps, said after medical treatment at the military hospital the man was conveyed to the City Infirmary, where he later died. Expressing sympathy with McKinney's family, the coroner mentioned that the deceased's wife had died only five months before. The jury returned a verdict of murder committed by some person or persons unknown.

26 JUNE 1877

On Wednesday, 27 June 1877, the *Londonderry Sentinel* related that on the previous Sunday evening a fire had broken out in the extensive range of stores in Foyle Street and Sugarhouse Lane belonging to Mr W.F. Bigger, which in a few hours reduced the buildings to a pile of ruins and caused damage to the extent of £60,000. From the time the fire was discovered it was impossible to contain it, and the flames were allowed to burn themselves out.

At about ten o'clock in the evening flames were first observed coming from the second flat of what was known as the smoking department, in Sugarhouse Lane, a few yards off Foyle Street. No time was lost in raising the alarm and, in a short time, all the obtainable hoses in the city were brought to bear on the flames which had spread with much speed. They soon enveloped the greater part of the buildings on Sugarhouse Lane which were also used as a drying loft and packing loft.

It became apparent that nothing could save the stores; the flames had spread beyond control and the water supply was faulty rendering the hoses next to useless. Leaping from flat to flat, and from room to room, the fire consumed the entire block in the lane, and thence to the inner range which contained as much flammable stock and materials as the first block.

The bacon and other produce contained within fed the fire, and the efforts of the fire-fighters shifted towards saving those portions of the building so far untouched. Men belonging to the 23rd Fusiliers, who were early on the ground, worked with commendable courage and doggedness. Eager volunteers, including most of Mr Bigger's employees, lent their assistance, but their cause was doomed.

The fire continued to burn throughout the night with unabated fury, but exhausted itself by early morning, leaving the greater part of the stores nothing more than a mass of smoking ruins. During Monday and Tuesday the hose was kept on the heated stones in case of a fresh outbreak, and by 26 June workmen were engaged in pulling down walls deemed unsafe.

St Eugene's Cathedral, the foundation stone of which was laid on Saturday, 26 July 1851, had been opened in 1873 but lacked a spire. Its odd truncated appearance was regularly commented upon, especially by the caretaker of its Protestant opposite number, in Bishop Street within the walls. As he led parties of sightseers round his own building he added a visit to the little church of ease of St Augustine, built in 1750, and sited on the western wall. From there the tourists would have a clear view of the incomplete building and their guide, in a mixture of pity and derision, would shake his head and say: 'There will never be a spire on thon papish building.'

He did not live to see his statement disproved on 27 June 1903 when the spire, designed by George C. Ashlin of Dublin and E.J. Toye of Derry, and begun in 1900, was finally complete. It was 256 feet high, at least sixty-five feet higher than that of St Columb's. A granite cross, some eight feet high, was placed on top that summer's afternoon; it weighed fifteen hundredweight (764 kg) and was supported by a gunmetal rod sunk thirty feet into the spire, secured by a cradle of the same material. It was decided that two curates from the cathedral should make their way up the ladders by different levels of scaffolding to the very top to install and bless the cross that would be the cathedral's crowning glory. John Keys O'Doherty, the Bishop of Derry, was three months short of his seventieth birthday and there was no possibility of his making the ascent. By today's health and safety standards it might not have been permitted at all. Then, however, it seemed paramount that the cross should be blessed *in situ*.

The two priests chosen were Laurence Hegarty, who was then thirty-seven, and John O'Doherty, already at age twenty-nine showing signs of the muscular dysfunction that would afflict him for the rest of his life. The task completed without any apparent vertigo the priests returned to the ground and the bells that had been installed rang out for the first time; as a local writer put it: for almost three decades the cathedral 'had demanded its bells'. Now they were 'ringing out their peals of joy over the hill of Calgach and the city of Columbkille'. The great bell still rings; it is inscribed: '*Ad gloriam Dei et in honorem Sancti Eugenii me fieri fecit, Rvdmus Joannes K. O'Doherty. Eps Derrensis anno rep sal 1902, Leone XIII, feliciter regnante.*' This may be translated as: 'The Most Reverend John K. O'Doherty, Bishop of Derry, in this year of 1902, in the benevolent papacy of Leo XIII, caused by me to be made to the glory of God and in honour of St Eugene.'

Lieutenant Chester Hamilton Irvine, 31st Battalion Canadian Infantry, was born on 29 September 1893, and killed in action on 25–26 June 1918. He had been previously wounded by shrapnel circa June 1916. His remains lie interred in Wailly Orchard Cemetery, Pas de Calais, France. His name is inscribed on the St Columb's memorial to the men connected with the cathedral who died during the 1914–18 conflict, and is also commemorated on Derry's Diamond War Memorial.

Chester Irvine was killed alongside Lieutenant Norman Mee, also of the 31st Canadians, and at a special meeting of the Council of Londonderry Chamber of Commerce held on Tuesday, 23 July 1918, the Mayor, R.N. Anderson, referred in emotional terms to the death of Lieutenant Mee, son of W.H. Mee, secretary of the chamber, and to the death of Lieutenant Irvine, brother of David S. Irvine, also a member of the chamber. His Worship said Lieutenant Mee, with his brother Lieutenant E.C. Mee, who had also been killed, played a fine part in connection with the struggle, had upheld the honour and maintained the fine traditions of the city of Londonderry. Lieutenant Irvine was another fine Derry lad who had given his life in the cause of freedom, and Mayor Anderson was sure the council desired to express their deepest sympathy with the relatives of these gallant young men. The motion was passed in silence, the members standing. Mr Irvine, in thanking the members for their sympathy, said he had a letter from the chaplain stating that these two Derry boys had fallen together, and lay side by side in the same cemetery.

Tribute was also paid to Chester Irvine when his name was read out during a memorial service held in St Columb's Church of Ireland Cathedral on Sunday, 28 June 1918 in remembrance of those Derry soldiers who had been killed over the previous twelve months.

Chester's father, David Irvine, a Freeman of the city of Londonderry, had died on Sunday, 17 March 1912, at the age of eighty-one. Apprenticed to the printing business, David Irvine had spent his early business years in the *Derry Standard*'s office, and subsequently with the *Journal*. He dabbled in newspaper publishing for a while when he helped purchase the *Derry Guardian*, changing its name to the *Derry Chronicle*, but gave this up to concentrate on his printing business which he rapidly developed with the assistance of his son, David S. Irvine, who succeeded him and moved the firm from its original address in Castle Street to Waterloo Street.

Private Thomas Alexander Mills, Royal Marine Light Infantry, was killed in action on 3 May 1915 while serving in the Dardanelles. He was a member of Ebrington Presbyterian Church and the Murray Parent Club of the Apprentice Boys of Derry. His parents Alexander and Margaret resided at 6 Orchard Row. Mills' name is recorded on the Helles Memorial in Turkey and commemorated on Derry's Diamond War Memorial.

Private Mills joined the colours a few weeks before the declaration of war in 1914, being then engaged as an apprentice cutter in the factory of Messrs. Lowry & Porter in Bishop Street. He was part of the 29th Division engaged in the landing operations at the Dardanelles. His father had served with the 1st Inniskillings through the South African War and held the King's Medal with two clasps, the Queen's Medal with five clasps, and the Distinguished Service Medal.

Mills' mother was fatally shot on Wednesday, 23 June 1920, during sectarian unrest in Derry. At the opening of the inquest into her death, on Friday, 25 June, evidence of identification was given by her husband. The coroner, Mr John P. Thompson, expressed sympathy on behalf of himself and the jurors with Mr Mills and the relatives of the deceased. It seemed to him from the investigations he had made that it was the innocent, to a great extent, who were suffering during these troubled times.

In addition to her son, Margaret Mills had also lost two brothers in the Great War. Private Joseph Mowbray, 10th Battalion Cameronians (Scottish Rifles), was killed in action in Flanders on 29 June 1917, aged thirty-six. His remains lie interred in Ypres Town Cemetery Extension, Ieper, West Vlaanderen, Belgium, and his name is commemorated on the Diamond War Memorial. Sergeant Thomas Mowbray, Royal Inniskilling Fusiliers, had been earlier killed in France, on 16 May 1915. His name is recorded on the Le Touret Memorial in Pas de Calais. Sergeant Mowbray was almost certainly killed at Festubert, a village situated three miles west of La Bassee, and which figured prominently in the conflict. He had been a well-known and popular figure in football and athletic circles in the North West, being a member of the old North End team, and was the battalion gymnasium instructor. He had over twenty-one years' service, spending fifteen years in India as well as some time in Egypt. He was in India at the time of the South African War, and accompanied one of the later drafts to the Transvaal. He had been awarded the South African Queen's Medal with two clasps, the Northwest Indian Frontier Medal with two clasps, and the Meritorious Service Medal. He had been in France only a month when he was killed.

On 30 June 1921 two memorial windows and a tablet in St Columb's Cathedral were unveiled and dedicated in the presence of bereaved fathers, mothers, brothers and sisters of eighty-three members of the congregation who had made the supreme sacrifice in the Great War. It was an impressive ceremony. Tickets had been issued to the relatives of the fallen and subscribers to the memorial, and these were provided with seats in the nave, the public being admitted to the other parts of the church.

The two windows taken together, one being the complement of the other, formed a conception in harmony with the spirit of the memorial, for while one window typified burial, the central idea being the entombment of Jesus Christ, the suggestion symbolised by the second window was victory. The first window was a memorial of the dead. The grave was hallowed by the fact of Christ's burial. The inscription across the lights was: 'In that He died, He died unto sin once.' The second window, Victory, had as its main feature the angel at the empty tomb: 'He is not dead. He is risen.'

The side lights in both windows illustrated the women with St Peter and St John looking on. The inscription on this window read: 'In that He liveth, He liveth unto God.' The base of each window followed an idea very common in Italian art through the introduction of a predella, the object of which was to supply, as it were, a commentary upon the subject treated in the main lights. Thus the predella in the Entombment window represents the first fall, by which sin was introduced into the world. An angel, with the scourge, represents suffering, and the portrayal of the scene in Gethsemane, with the angel comforting, suggests the mothers and relatives praying that this cup may pass.

In the predella of the Victory window could be seen the angel with the sword and olive wreath of victory. Another light showed the angel with the palm branch and crown, while in the centre light was the white horse described in *Revelation*, with him that sat upon it going out conquering and to conquer, having the heavenly armies behind him.

The tablet, containing the names of members of the congregation who fell in the Great War, was of bronze, and occupied a position between the memorial windows. The intention was to complete the memorial by encircling the windows and tablet with a suitable surrounding. The inscription on the tablet was: 'To the glory of God, and in thankful remembrance of all the loyal men connected with Derry Cathedral who, not counting their lives dear unto them, went out to fight for us in the great war, 1914–1918. Remember especially the loved ones whose names are recorded here who were themselves called into the larger life.'

JULY

1 JULY 1916

Among the units that advanced at the Somme on 1 July 1916 was the largely Protestant and Unionist 36th (Ulster) Division, who held a section of the line from the north-east of Thiepval Wood. Initially the Ulster Division achieved its aims, but elsewhere the British were repelled by the unrelenting fire of German machine guns, and suffered the heaviest losses it had known in a single day—20,000 men dead and an additional 40,000 wounded. Among the dead on the opening day of the battle were approximately 115 men associated with the city of Londonderry and its immediate environs. The overwhelming majority of those men belonged to the Protestant Unionist tradition.

The sheer scale of loss and suffering experienced by the Unionist community on 1 July 1916 has virtually eclipsed reference to—and rendered almost forgotten—the death and suffering of Irish Catholics on that same day. At least eleven of the 115 men referred to above were Derry Catholics, and ten of those were members of the 1st Inniskilling Fusiliers.

The 1st Inniskillings were in the first wave of the July attack, north of the 36th Division. The small number of men who made it to the German lines found the wire there almost uncut; nevertheless they made a courageous but ineffective attempt to push on without support. Crowded together at the only gaps cut in the wire, the men made easy targets for the machine guns, and the casualties swiftly escalated.

Among the ten Derry Catholics, and members of the 1st Inniskillings, who died, was Private Bernard (Barney) Donaghey. Barney was born on 23 December

1882. His name is recorded on the Thiepval Memorial to the Missing at the Somme in France, and commemorated on the Diamond War Memorial in Derry. Barney was a well-known and popular footballer, having played for Derry Celtic, Belfast Celtic, Glentoran, Hibernian, Manchester United, Burnley, and other teams. Records indicate that his appearance against Scotland on 9 August 1902 at the Balmoral Showgrounds was the only time he played for Ireland. This game has only recently been declared an official international game by FIFA; at the time no caps were awarded for it. Barney, around this time, was a member of the Belfast Celtic squad. He also made two appearances for the Irish League representative side while registered with Derry Celtic, playing against the Scottish League in a 3-0 defeat on 15 February 1902 in Dundee, and against the English League in a 4-0 defeat on 14 October 1905 in Manchester.

On the battlefield, Barney had previously been wounded in the head by shrapnel and spent time recovering in a hospital at Tanta, Egypt. On that occasion he wrote a letter home saying that he was on his way to recovery, and added: 'The other four soldiers that were beside me were killed. It was an awful sight. I am sure it was the prayers that saved me.'

2 JULY 1933

The great transatlantic flight from Orbetello in Italy to Chicago, USA, by the Italian air armada of twenty-five seaplanes, under the leadership of General Count Italo Balbo, began on Saturday, 1 July 1933. The Italian airmen had waited at Orbetello for three weeks, initially detained by the difficulty which their supply ship *Alice* had in getting through ice, followed by a spell of unfavourable weather. At 4 o'clock on the Saturday morning General Balbo was informed that favourable weather reports had been received. Within twenty minutes all the men had reported and the ceremony of hoisting the flag was performed. After this the crews boarded their machines and at 5.34 a.m. the flight began. In order to cross the Alps they had to rise to a height of 13,000 feet. Afterwards the route was down the Rhine, and they flew in groups of three at a height of between 4,500 and 4,600 feet. Over French territory they were accompanied by an escort of twenty French chaser planes.

General Balbo and his aviators were welcomed in Amsterdam. First in the brilliant sunshine, there appeared six black machines flying in formation of three; these were followed successively by six red, six white, and six green machines, making up the colours of the Italian flag. Turning towards the water, the planes began to land. The first machine to glide down on to the water was that of General Balbo. A motorboat went to the spot carrying Dutch officials and the Italian Minister. All the other machines, except *I-Dini*, which was commanded by Flight Lieutenant Baldini, alighted safely. *I-Dini* came down at too great a speed. It nosedived into the water and capsized. A Dutch naval motorboat dashed to the spot and gave prompt assistance. The cockpit of the seaplane was completely wrenched away, and the two engines were wedged in the petrol tanks. Flight Lieutenant Baldini was found to be suffering from concussion, the second officer had an arm and leg fractured, and a third member of the crew had his jaw and shoulder broken; a fourth man was rescued uninjured. It was thought that all the crew had been saved, but later the body of Corporal Quintavalle was found in the wrecked machine.

At 7.14 a.m. on Sunday, 2 July, General Balbo gave the signal, and the machines began the second stage of their flight. Later that day, the armada alighted on Lough Foyle in brilliant sunshine and within sight of thousands of spectators gathered from all over the northwest of Ireland. In an interview with the press, General Balbo said that when the planes ran into the fog bank near the Irish coast, it was decided to alight on Lough Neagh if conditions were no better over Lough Foyle. A little later, however, a report was received from the Italian base at Londonderry intimating that Lough Foyle was clear, and the airmen then decided to come straight ahead.

3 JULY 1953

George VI died on 6 February 1952 while Elizabeth, his beloved daughter and heir, was on a Kenyan tour with her husband Prince Philip Mountbatten. She was crowned queen on 2 June 1953 and spent the summer touring her realm. Her visit to Northern Ireland included a visit to Derry, where she spent two hours on the afternoon of Friday, 3 July 1953. She and her husband had spent the previous night in Government House in Hillsborough and boarded a special train at Lisburn that was to take her on a whistle-stop journey through Ballymena, Ballymoney and Coleraine. Philip wore the uniform of an Admiral of the Fleet and, as the *Irish Times* reporter took pains to advise, the queen 'wore a coat of steel grey taffeta with a full skirt and a small hat covered with emerald green feathers. Her dress was pale green and her accessories were black.'

The royal couple left the train at Lisahally to travel the remainder of the journey by ship, boarding the destroyer HMS *Rocket* after a reception by Admiral Sir Maurice Mansergh, Commander-in-Chief of the Plymouth station and Captain D.H. Connell-Fuller, Senior Naval Officer in Northern Ireland. The *Rocket* was flanked by two naval launches as it entered Rosses Bay and berthed at the quay just behind the Guildhall. As the couple were piped ashore they were greeted by Alderman Sir Samuel Orr, Mayor of Derry, and other civic dignatories. The Guildhall Square was packed with cheering people and the parts of the city's walls overlooking the square were also dangerously crowded. Also present were the Governor of Northern Ireland, Lord Wakehurst and his wife, the Prime Minister Lord Brookeborough and Lady Brookeborough. Queen Elizabeth and the Duke inspected a guard of honour of local servicemen from HMS *Sea Eagle* and the RAF station at Ballykelly under the command of Lieutenant-Commander C.R. Simms.

After the inspection the royal motorcade headed for a garden party in Brooke Park via Great James Street, moving quite slowly because the estimated 1,300 police officers on duty in the city that day could not prevent the crowds on the pavements from drifting on to the roadway. At the party Pearlie Wilson, an industrial nurse from nearby Marlborough Street, presented a bouquet to the queen and then as the cameras clicked and flashed the royal couple planted two commemorative trees. On her return to the Guildhall the queen formally conferred a knighthood on Samuel Orr, even though he had already grown used to the title.

It was now nearing five o'clock in the afternoon and after the presentation of souvenir gifts by the Mayoress, the royal party set off by car on the eight-mile journey to the Royal Naval Air Service base at Eglinton, where they boarded the plane back to London. The queen sent a signal from the plane to Lord Wakehurst expressing her gratitude to the many people in Northern Ireland who had gathered to meet her and her husband.

4 JULY 1899

Moville is a pretty seaside village on Lough Foyle, 25.5 kilometres northeast of Derry. It is famous for its views of the wide sea lough and the north Derry hills of Benevenagh and Benone. It was known in slightly uncomplimentary language in Irish as *Bun an Phobail* ('the bottom of the parish') that was anglicised in the eighteenth century as 'Bonifoble'. Before the Second World War it was the port of call for transatlantic liners, fed by paddle steamers from Derry Quay. Like Buncrana on Lough Swilly it became a popular resort for Derry citizens, and not just for day-trippers. One of its enthusiastic visitors, an amateur poet called Mat McNeary, entranced by the beauty of the surroundings and the perfect summer weather, was driven to celebrate it in verse with a poem called simply 'Moville'. It was published in the *Derry Journal* on 14 July 1899, ten days after its composition:

The golden sun, with radiant beam, was rising far away
To bless the world with gladness in a glorious summer day;
And I saw him kiss the hilltops and I saw him higher soar
Till he burst in laughing splendour on the village by the shore.
As I gazed in admiration at this tranquil happy scene
The wild flowers nodded greetings from the beauteous bed of green;
And high in heaven's ethereal dome, far over vale and hill,
The lark's mellifluous song proclaimed a sunrise at Moville.

Oh! The pleasure when the hedgerows tell of One who is Divine
And the woodbines' scented tendrils with the wild rose intertwine.
When the gorse with floral rockets decorates its hillside home
And the lilies by the swirling pool hold revel in its foam;
When the buttercups and daisies smile through pearly tears of dew
And nature's myriad leaves unfold to paint the world anew;
When the merry humming bee begins his storehouse to fill;
'Tis then I wish the sun could shine forever on Moville.

On yon verdant hillside nestling by the lake's sequestered nook,
Where curling wavelets ripple when joined by the chattering brook;
'Mid heathery hills and sylvan dells where sightless zephyrs croon,
And perfume-laden fan the cheek with their cooling breath at noon.
Such is the scene where the town I love in modesty still shines,
A rival for the Orient lands or South'rn home of vines.
Far away from the city's throbbings, where peace is with me still,
In the bow'ry glens amid the ferns adorning sweet Moville.

When eventide comes on apace from each fragrant flow'ry spray,
God's harmonised 'Farewell' is sung to the ruddy king of day
And the clustering, blushing blossoms, the dainty warblers know
Will their little fledglings shelter and provide for winter's snow.
There the balm of quiet gladness lulls the weary soul to rest,
Where the slanting sunbeams sparkle from the glowing ruby west;
When the singers tuned in heaven all their joyous anthems trill.
Oh! 'tis rapture, sweetest rapture then to linger near Moville.

On Saturday, 29 June 1912, there occurred what the Unionist *Belfast News Letter* described in its strap as 'Disgraceful Affair at Castledawson', and deplored the 'Hibernians Cowardly Conduct'. An Ancient Order of Hibernians procession complete with bands was on its way back from a Home Rule rally in Maghera when it meshed with a Sunday school outing from Belfast. There were a few scuffles, no injuries, and an apology from 'Wee Joe' Devlin, the president of the AOH, who banned all AOH events for the summer. Word travelled swiftly back to Belfast that a Sunday School party had been attacked by a drunken party of the dreaded Hibernians, armed for battle, and though the minister pleaded for calm and no action against Catholic neighbours, the plea was ignored by the Protestant shipyard workers in Workman Clark, 'the wee yard'.

By the morning break on Tuesday, 2 July, Catholic workers were surrounded by knots of grim-faced, foul-mouthed Protestants who ordered them to leave the yard. As they did so they were beaten and kicked and forced to run away from the lethal metal discs, the detritus from the riveters' punches, and the rivets themselves. There were twenty-five assaults inside the yards and fifty-five about the city, and the Catholics dared not return.

Of the 2,300 Catholics attacked and expelled during that week, twenty-five were from Derry and they, too, were forced out on the Friday, 5 July. It was the febrile summer when there seemed real danger that Ireland would at last achieve Home Rule, and Carson and Craig had shouted themselves hoarse at a huge meeting when Ulster showed itself ready to fight because Ulster was right. September would see the signing of the Ulster Covenant, and the Derry tradesmen realised how lucky they were to have escaped the dreaded 'Belfast confetti'.

They told their stories to a *Derry Journal* reporter whose shaken prose in the edition of the following Monday showed how unaware Derry people were of the deep-rooted fear, hatred and suspicion of the opposing tribes in the other city. One man reported: 'A friendly Protestant gave me the tip to clear out and I had barely time to jump from the boat I was working on, a distance of twelve feet, pursued by the "black squad", who are mostly ironworkers. I managed to escape by rushing into a crowd and they lost sight of me.' The discovery of Catholics was implemented by 'spies' who named certain workers as 'suspected'. In one incident two detectives sent on observation were surrounded by a crowd of Shipyard Unionist Club members who threatened them until they cursed the pope. Socialists, trade unionists and so-called 'rotten Protestants' also ran the same danger as their nationalist brothers. Another member of the Derry 'Twenty-five' told the *Journal* reporter that as he left the troubled city, he saw a notice chalked on a wall: 'Protestant Home Rulers, your turn comes next.'

6 JULY 1809

William McArthur, the fifth child of the Reverend John McArthur, Methodist minister, was born in Malin, County Donegal, on 6 July 1809. While an infant of a few weeks he moved with his parents to Newtownstewart, where his father had been appointed by the preceding Methodist Conference. Some years later, the family again moved, to Stranorlar, where William was sent to a school run by a Mr McGranahan. At that time another pupil of the school was the future prominent Protestant Home-Ruler, Isaac Butt, with whom McArthur formed a friendship that continued throughout Mr Butt's career.

In 1818 William's father, through failing health, retired from the active duties of the ministry, and with his family went to reside at Miltown Cottage, Ardstraw. At twelve years of age William McArthur's school education ended, and he was apprenticed to Mr Hugh Copeland, a woollen draper in Enniskillen. His business abilities became so evident that he was offered a partnership in a new establishment in the town, but declined, not wanting to damage Copeland's trade. On 25 November 1827, he set out for Lurgan to keep the books of a Mr Johnston. This Mr Johnston seems to have been a manufacturing tobacconist and spirit merchant, and sent his new chief clerk out as a traveller. In 1830, William moved to Dublin to re-engage in the business for which he had been trained. His employer, Mr Samuel Steele, kept a woollen drapery shop and warehouse in Wellington Quay. McArthur spent only a year in the capital, his employer having closed his business in 1831. That same year William McArthur and Joseph Cather entered into a partnership and opened a woollen drapery shop in the Diamond in Derry. The qualities that McArthur displayed led to prosperity and a natural desire to enlarge the business, contrary to his partner's ambitions, so an amicable dissolution of the partnership occurred on 15 November 1835.

McArthur was a man of religious zeal, and his exertions, along with Alex Lindsay, later Mayor of Derry, led to the creation of the Methodist church on East Wall. On the day of the opening McArthur marched through the streets, at the head of a procession of Sunday school children, from the old chapel in Linenhall Street to the new building.

In 1857 McArthur moved his business to London, where he became involved in politics, and at the 1868 general election was elected Member of Parliament for Lambeth. Twelve years later, on 20 September 1880, he became Lord Mayor of London. He returned to Derry in August of the following year as part of a deputation of the Honourable the Irish Society, and again in 1887, when he was present at the laying of the foundation stone of the new town hall in the centre of the Diamond where he had once had his store. Later that same year, on 16 November, he passed away in a carriage on London's Metropolitan Railway, at or near Praed Street Station, Paddington.

7 JULY 1933

For six days Derry had gone Italian. Twenty-four Savoia-Marchetti twin-hulled flying-boats, the pride of Mussolini's Italian Air Force, lay at anchor in the Foyle at Lisahally, en route to the Centennial Exhibition in Chicago. The planes had only a limited flying range and refuelling stops were set up at Amsterdam, Rejykavik, St John's, Newfoundland, as well as Derry, so that they could land safely on Lake Superior. The commander, General Count Italo Balbo, dressed in a sky-blue uniform, dripping with gold braid, was a strong supporter of *Il Duce*, though he disapproved of his meetings with Hitler. He had become Secretary of State for Air in 1926 and the Chicago exhibition gave an ideal opportunity to demonstrate the power and elegance of Fascist Italy.

Balbo was straight from Central Casting: handsome, bearded, and the lead pilot with the letters I-BALBO painted on the side of the vanguard aircraft. The Italian community in Derry were feted as well as the fliers with many photocalls at dinners and on the steps of the Guildhall, formally welcomed by Sir Dudley McCorkell, the mayor, and Sir Henry Millar, the town clerk. Some local members wearing the black shirts of the *Fascisti* movement paraded with young girls in Italian national costume. The whole affair was a deliberate and effective piece of propaganda and the displays of precision drilling with gleaming boots, shining white belts and perfectly angled rifles by the British army, and music by their regimental band, showed that the old sweats could put on just as good a show as the 'Eyeties'. Derry's Italians, in the person of Vittorio Fiorentini, presented gifts to the visitors.

Autograph hunters had several field days as riggers, fitters and air-crew members signed books, slips of paper, and even cigarette papers, thrust towards them by children of all ages. In those years the paddle steamer *Seamore* plied between Derry and Moville, partly as a pleasure boat but more soberly to take Irish emigrants to the transatlantic liners that lay at the head of Lough. The wash of the *Seamore* paddles caused the twenty-four planes to dance elegantly as it passed, and the rush of passengers from port to starboard as it circled the anchorage caused the ship to cant to that side, lifting the opposite paddle clear of the water.

On Friday, 7 July the weather had improved sufficiently for the air armada to take flight for Iceland. The sight of those giant birds taking off was as impressive as that of their landing. They turned into the wind and, flying over Inishowen Head, set out west by north for Reykjavik to refuel. The last drone of their engines disappeared and Derry settled back into its characteristic 1930s torpor. In 1934 Balbo was made governor of the then Italian colony of Libya but was killed in an plane brought down by 'friendly' anti-aircraft fire from Italian shore batteries.

8 JULY 1912

The adventure of a man named Edward Duffy, from the St Columb's Wells area of Derry, unfolded before the magistrates at Londonderry Petty Sessions on Monday, 8 July 1912, when the defendant was charged with breaking and entering the public house of Richard McDaid, Holywell Street, near his home.

Head Constable Gillis, who prosecuted, said the shop was a lock-up, and early on Sunday morning, the previous day, a passer-by heard screams in the house. He alerted the proprietor and brought the police. They found the defendant so tightly stuck in the chimney of the public house that he had to be dug out. He asked the magistrates to deal with the defendant under the Vagrancy Act or on the charge of breaking and entering the public house. The evidence pointed to the defendant having climbed to the roof of the public house, and then attempting to get inside through the chimney. The clerk jokingly said perhaps the charge should be trying to break out of the public house, which was greeted with laughter.

Richard McDaid, of Bishop Street, stated he was awoken by John Glenn about 3.30 on Sunday morning, and told there was someone in his public house in Holywell Street. He went down with the keys, opened the shop, and Glenn, who went up to the loft above the kitchen, returned and told him someone had got stuck in the chimney. The police were sent for, and the defendant was released from the chimney. There were no marks of the house having been broken into and the defendant must have got into the chimney from the roof.

John Glenn stated he was passing the public house and heard screaming.

He roused McDaid, and subsequently when he entered the public house he heard screaming in the chimney. He was there when the police got crowbars, and they dug the defendant out of the chimney. Constable Canning said he saw the man's feet dangling at the fireplace. They got crowbars, and succeeded in getting the defendant out. He was all black, with the exception of the white of his eyes, a remark that caused laughter in the court. He asked the defendant what he had been doing there, and the defendant replied that the police had chased him and he must have accidentally fallen through the chimney. The defendant was not wearing boots, and a search located them about thirty or forty yards away from the public house.

Mr Butler, the RM, asked the defendant could he give any explanation of how he got into the chimney. The defendant repeated he had been chased by the police; he had some drink taken, and as he was climbing over this house he must have fallen into the chimney. Duffy's explanation was, not surprisingly, rejected by the magistrate who, finding the defendant guilty of breaking and entering, sentenced him to one month in prison.

9 JULY 1948

Back in the days when Latin and Greek led the curriculum in secondary school, the St Columb's College student who obtained the highest mark in Ancient Greek in Senior Certificate exams won the Semple Prize. In 1949 it was two guineas, a handy amount of cash in those Spartan days. The donor was Patrick Semple, DLitt, an old boy of St Columb's who, after holding the chair of Classics at the Royal University, had become Professor of Latin at University College, Dublin (UCD) in 1909.

On 9 July 1948 his retirement was celebrated at an event presided over by Michael Tierney, president of the university, who presented to Semple the portrait painted by Sean O'Sullivan, for whom Maud Gonne, Yeats, Joyce, Larkin, Hyde and de Valera had also sat. In his encomium Tierney observed that Semple was the first Catholic Irishman of modern times to win international recognition as a classical scholar. He also made it clear that Semple had been one of the strong foundations upon which UCD in its early years had flourished; he had devoted his life to the manifold activities of the university while distinguishing himself for the lucidity of his lectures.

Semple was born in Derry and went to St Columb's after primary education at the Christian Brothers' school at the 'Brow of the Hill'. He seems to have been an exceptionally gifted student, winning the Gold Medal for attaining first place in Latin in the whole of Ireland in the Intermediate Examination, and an additional Gold Medal for coming first in each of the examinations as a whole. In 1894 he began his third-level studies at the Royal University, from which he graduated with first-class honours, joining the staff immediately upon graduation. With the setting up of the Oireachtas in 1923 he was elected to the upper house and continued actively to serve after the constitutional changes in 1936.

His retirement dinner was covered by the *Derry Journal* which, with admirable economy, reported that after Tierney's speech, 'Dr Semple suitably replied.' The doctorate was an honorary DLitt conferred in recognition of the prominent place he held in the classical world. As he might have observed one of the measures of worth that such an academic might claim was the number of students who 'passed through his class-hall' and 'occupy high places today in Church and State, in the professions and diplomacy'. As the *Journal* reporter put it: 'All of them had for him not only the greatest admiration but an abiding affection and they will join with his other friends—and none more so than his old schoolfellows in Derry—in wishing him many years to enjoy the rest earned by a long and fruitful career in the great work of higher education.'

10 JULY 1902

On Thursday afternoon, 10 July 1902, Mr William Mitchell, a Londonderry merchant, came by his death in Carlingford Lough under tragic circumstances. About a week earlier, accompanied by his wife and some of his children, he had gone to Warrenpoint, then a popular resort, on his annual holiday. Also accompanying him was his brother-in-law, Dr Charles Hurford, and on Thursday morning the two men had visited Rostrevor. They decided to return by steamer, and took passages on the *Pilot*, the vessel which plied between Rostrevor and Warrenpoint during the summer season.

The day was rough, with a fresh northerly wind, and the fatality occurred when the *Pilot* was about a mile out, standing towards the Greenore shore. It was rolling heavily, and Mr Mitchell, who was standing on the bridge, was pitched into the sea. He was thrown off his balance by an exceptionally heavy lurch of the vessel and fell against part of the passenger drop rail, which became free. As he was falling over the side, Dr Hurford managed to catch his waterproof, but the coat was not able to stand the strain, and the gentleman fell into the sea. He almost immediately rose to the surface, and Dr Hurford saw him swimming after the steamer, which was stopped by the captain. He then cut a lifebuoy off its lashings and gave it to a sailor to throw to Mitchell but when he looked again Mitchell had disappeared.

William Mitchell's body came ashore six weeks and two days later at Barrow-in-Furness, Cumbria, on Saturday night, 23 August. The Barrow police were able, by papers found in Mitchell's pocket book, to identify him, and Mrs Mitchell received confirmation in the form of a letter from Barrow giving a description of the crest on Mr Mitchell's watch.

Mitchell occupied a prominent position in Londonderry's commercial life. Born in Hull, he came to Derry with his father, who was for many years commodore of the fleet of ships owned by Daniel Baird, an extensive merchant engaged in trade with the West Indies and the United States. He commenced his business career in John Christy's, Foyle Street, and after serving his apprenticeship there he was for some years in William McCorkell & Co.'s shipping offices when that firm had a large fleet of ships in the American passenger and goods trade.

It was in these two businesses that he gained the knowledge and experience which proved of such value to him subsequently. Afterwards he entered into partnership with Mr John Cunningham, but when the latter retired on being appointed a Land Commissioner, Mitchell carried on the business of importer and general merchant on his own account. About this time he erected the fine premises in Foyle Street known as Commercial Buildings. A strong desire to maintain the trade of the port influenced him to establish a line of Londonderry-owned sailing ships, and several vessels were built in the shipyard when it was run by Charles J. Bigger.

11 JULY 1911

On 11 July 1911, an anonymous American visited Derry and made some slightly amusing and sardonic criticisms of the city which were published in the *New York Evening Post* and later replicated in the *Londonderry Sentinel* on 6 February 1912.

'On the afternoon of 11th of July,' he wrote, 'after ten days sailing, we came within sight of Tory Island and the wild headlands of Donegal. We passed Malin Head, and were soon turning southward into Lough Foyle, and were making for the little white village of Moville on our right. The low white houses, set in a background of green, made a lovely picture… and there was the tender waiting to take us to Derry, the city of the gallant Siege and of countless subsequent fights between Orangemen and Catholics…

'We steamed up Lough Foyle for nearly two hours in the twilight. And such a twilight! It was a "cead mille failthe" from an Irish sky. Its rich purple tints overhung the dark green hills, shedding everywhere a soft subdued light that disposed the mind to gratitude and repose… It faded away only when the lamps of Derry and Derry's Custom House came in sight.

'In the Derry Custom House, when, at last, the sleepy-looking officer comes and asks a few parrot questions, says "All right," and chalks up your baggage, you are left wondering why you had to wait at all. Except for an aching sensation of fatigue about the legs, you feel grateful to John Bull, who does not get his revenue by "taxing the foreigner," and who seldom minds what you have in your trunk, unless, perhaps, it is a roll of tobacco or a parcel of tea.

'There are several good, decent-looking hotels in Derry, and the charges are very moderate from an American standpoint. Good accommodation can be had for a dollar and a half a day. But the furniture is apt to be out of repair, and should be used with considerable caution at first. For the chairs are apt to have broken backs, and when you try to rest upon them they collapse and land you on the floor. And the coat-racks are equally treacherous. When you hang your coat the apparatus at once comes to the ground. The servant said these were only accidents. I do not agree with her. An accident is a deviation from the ordinary course of events, whereas these occurrences were not deviations, but examples of the ordinary course of events in Derry hotels, and the real accident would have been a chair that did not collapse, or a coat-rack that held your coat…'

Remarking on the local twang, the visitor wrote: 'The people of Derry speak with a peculiar brogue which I have heard nowhere else. They pronounce the word "hill" as if it were "hull." A strike of firemen and sailors happening to be on, I asked an unemployed fireman what wages he used to get. "Twunty-nine shullin's a week," he replied.'

12 JULY 1846

Charlotte Elizabeth Tonna was the daughter of Michael Browne, rector of St Giles's Church and minor canon of the Cathedral at Norwich, where she was born on 1 October 1790. She married in early life a Captain George Phelan of the 60th Rifle Corps, and spent two years with him while he served with his regiment in Nova Scotia. They then returned to Ireland, where Phelan owned a small estate near Kilkenny. The marriage was an unhappy one, and they separated about 1824. Mrs Phelan subsequently resided with her brother,

Captain John Browne, at Clifton. Later she moved to Sandhurst, and then to London. In 1837 Captain Phelan died in Dublin, freeing his widow from the legal bondage of matrimony, and in 1841 she married Lewis Hippolytus Joseph Tonna. She died at Ramsgate on 12 July 1846, and was buried there.

While in Ireland Mrs Tonna began to write, under her Christian names 'Charlotte Elizabeth', tracts for various religious societies. She was very hostile to the Catholic Church, and some of her publications are said to have been placed on the *Index Expurgatorius*. In 1837 she published an abridgment of Foxe's *Book of Martyrs*. She edited *The Protestant Annual* (1840), *The Christian Lady's Magazine* from 1836, and *The Protestant Magazine* from 1841 until her death. She also wrote poems, two of which, entitled respectively 'The Maiden City' and 'No Surrender', were composed specially for the Orange cause and were extremely vigorous and popular. She was also the author of the popular novel, *The Siege of Derry, a Tale of the Revolution of 1688*.

In August 1837, while in Londonderry, Charlotte Elizabeth was made an honorary member of the Apprentice Boys of Derry organisation, and described the experience in a letter written at the time in the Maiden City:

> You know the famous brotherhood of the famous Apprentice Boys of Derry, an association to which honorary members are admitted but sparingly, and none who are not considered firm in cherishing and upholding the sacred principles of 1688.
>
> The car that was to convey us from the Maiden City stood at the door and I was anticipating the pain of a farewell look at the old walls, when some young men of this formidable fraternity made their appearance, with a document that, at least, I shall know how to value better than I could ever deserve it—a simple, affectionate, beautifully written address, expressive of that unity of principle, which, I bless God, does indeed exist between us, and tendering a welcome to their ancient city, upon grounds that must appear passing strange, considering the awfully illiberal character supposed to belong to the club, as it is called.
>
> Their thanks are tendered for what they denominate exertions on behalf of their benighted countrymen...
>
> Now I am admitted an honorary member of the association, and, as such, I am entitled henceforth to bear the motto which, by Divine blessing, I will act up to, in its highest, holiest, purest, and most extended import—No Surrender.

13 JULY 1939

On 13 July 1939, the *Londonderry Sentinel* related to its readership that the 'heroine' of the previous day's 'Twelfth' in Derry was Miss Alice Smyth, a twenty-five-year-old factory worker, who, 'single-handed and unprompted', recovered the Governor Walker sash from possible destruction when it fell off the statue into the Bogside.

In the afternoon a wind had crept up and girls working in Messrs. Anderson's factory, Bishop Street, which overlooked the City Wall, saw the sash on the Walker Statue gradually falling down and in danger of blowing away. Seeing the danger, Miss Smyth left her work and ran to the Apprentice Boys' Hall, where the keys of the Walker Pillar were kept but could see nobody about. She then went in search of help to three places in London Street, but these were also closed. She tried the Synod Hall and then went to the Fire Brigade Station and told them the position.

On returning to her room at the factory she was just in time to hear a shout from the girls and to see the sash lifting in the wind, when the rope at the end became unloosed, and drop over ninety feet from the top of the pillar into the Bogside. Without taking time to go out by Bishop Street, Miss Smyth went down a ladder at the back of the factory from a second storey and ran on to the City Wall. Her first intention was to run round to Friel's Terrace where the 'large and valuable sash' had fallen on waste ground, but instead she went to the parapet and looked down to see the sash in possession of what she believed was a hostile crowd of men who were examining it.

Miss Smyth, who was alone on the wall, bluffed the men by calling out to several that she knew their names. 'That is our property,' she cried, 'give it back at once or there will be trouble.'

Miss Smyth, who said she was excited and determined to recover the sash at all costs, was successful, and one of the men threw it up to another man who had come on the scene. On returning to the factory with the sash wrapped round her, Miss Smyth was given a great ovation by the girls, who cheered her and afterwards tried on 'the sash which Walker wore'. Miss Smyth kept the sash and met the procession on its return to Londonderry from Coleraine. She then handed it over to a Grand Lodge officer. It was restored to its position by two volunteers, Messrs. C. Finlay and W. Ferguson, members of Britannia Loyal Orange Lodge 1912, on the 'Twelfth' night.

Miss Smyth had strong Orange family connections. She resided at 4 Moore Street with her father, a member of City of Derry Loyal Orange Lodge 433. Her brother Stephen was a member of Coronation Loyal Orange Lodge 1062.

The Belfast Naturalist Field Club (BNFC) was one of the organisations that sprang from the Belfast Society for Promoting Knowledge that had been founded in 1788. It also generated the excellent Linen Hall library and Belfast's first museum. The field club continued in existence for many years in the forefront of disinterested scientific and archaeological study. Their work gave a spur to the development of photography, natural history and early ecological considerations. On 14 July 1908 the club was eighty-seven years old and forty-five of the members travelled to Derry to visit the city museum housed then in what had been an institute for the education, clothing and maintenance of male orphans founded in 1840 on the bequest of John Gwyn, a linen merchant of the city.

The house and grounds had been bought by the Brooke Estate with aid from the Honourable the Irish Society and presented to the City Corporation in 1901. The house also held the Municipal Library, and the grounds became Brooke Park. The museum was characteristic of the time with lots of glass-fronted display cases holding stuffed birds, butterflies and eggs. There were authentic Zulu spears and shields and the prize exhibit was the actual coach, it was claimed, in which Mary Anne Knox had been mortally wounded by John McNaghten in 1761. He has lived on in infamy as 'Half-hanged' because at the first attempt at hanging him the rope broke.

There were of course no videos, no moving images and no special thematic exhibitions. Museums, except to amateur ornithologists, lepidopterists and geologists, were used as a type of metaphor for all that was dull, cut-and-dried and stuffed. The members of the BNFC were only too aware of this and like many other similar societies made many field trips to observe and record aspects of nature in the wild which they carefully recorded, with notes, sketches and photographs, and by this means played a useful part in increasing biological knowledge. The Derry trip was to a prime location with Brooke Park, looking its well-behaved summer best, and the institute with its plain Palladian façade in stark contrast. One of the group included an American academic called Praegar who was able to identify and name thirty species from the United States prior to their being exhibited in a special display case.

'The party, which included over a dozen ladies, were delighted with the collections of shells, butterflies, insects, birds, dried flowers, reptiles...' claimed the reporter for the *Derry Standard*, who went on to describe the bits of platinum from the Ural Mountains in Siberia and 'the still more sought after gold deposit transferred from the auriferous regions of the Rand'. Before they left the BNFC members paid tribute to the work of the curator D.C. Campbell and hoped that the museum would be used educationally by the Derry public. Only five hundred people, a very small part of the city's population, had visited it.

Stressing that his remarks were by no means intended as a censure on Londonderry Corporation—they could not be everywhere—the City Coroner, C.A. Milligan, said at an inquest on Wednesday, 15 July 1959: 'It is just too bad the Corporation lorries did not light this bonfire before the accident happened.' He was speaking after the jury had returned a verdict of accidental death at the inquest on a three-year-old child, Eugene Pacelli Callan, of Strabane Old Road, Waterside, who was smothered when material prepared for a bonfire collapsed on him.

Earlier he had described the boy's death as a 'shocking tragedy', and said, 'Perhaps a touch of irony is added because the Corporation have been lifting bonfires in the streets and, unfortunately, this one was not lifted.' He said the bonfire was prepared on waste ground behind Strabane Old Road and it must have been quite a structure because it was over ten feet high, and the boys had left an entrance in it for the purpose of using it as a hut. Unfortunately the child must have got into it somehow and it was not clear that the little boy was inside when the pile collapsed.

Head Constable Michael Finn, in associating himself with the Coroner's expression of sympathy, said parents very often considered that their children were safe when they were on waste ground, but it was regrettable that one of those things should happen. Dr J.R. McClean of the City and County Hospital said when the child was admitted artificial respiration was carried out immediately but there was no response. Death had taken place some time previously.

Evidence was given by a number of boys who lived in Strabane Old Road about preparing the bonfire. William George Cairns said they had timber built for a bonfire and at 4.30 on Monday the pile of sticks was standing upright, but at 4.50 he saw the branches lying down flat; the bonfire had collapsed. He had set off with other boys collecting more wood and they came back with some branches later. At 5.30 they decided to rebuild the bonfire and started to carry the branches away. They had nearly all of them away when he saw Frank Shields carrying something. He did not remember seeing the deceased about at any time.

Frank Shields said they had the branches piled up and they went to gather more wood. When they saw the timbers had collapsed, they decided to take them to another position and started to carry them away. 'I had shifted some branches and came back for another when I saw Eugene Callan lying on the ground under the branches and there were a lot of branches on top of him. We pulled the branches away and got Eugene out. He was unconscious and we carried him to his home.'

16 JULY 1969

In the spring of 1969 the campaign for civil rights was growing in intensity. Each fresh demo was greeted with ever greater violence by the Royal Ulster Constabulary (RUC) whose leadership seemed to have no other means of dealing with legitimate protest except by ordering their lower ranks to use batons, CS Gas, rubber bullets and water cannon to quell the 'civil disorder'. On Saturday, 19 April, a banned Northern Ireland Civil Rights Association (NICRA) march clashed with opponents and riots ensued. The main area of conflict was the intersection where William and Rossville streets met by the base of the huge complex known as the Rossville flats. When the British army were mobilised and became a constant presence on Derry streets the area became known to them as 'Aggro Corner'.

The march had followed the day after Bernadette Devlin was elected as Westminster MP for mid-Derry and there was a considerable euphoria among Derry Nationalists. Most of the demonstrators went home but a hard core remained to carry on running battles with the RUC. William Street was a mixed residential area with, on the right-hand side going down, a large bakery, a shirt factory and some private houses. In one of these lived Samuel Devenney, a forty-two-year-old married Catholic with nine children who worked as an undertaker. He was standing at his doorway chatting with a neighbour when a group of young people in flight from the police ran up William Street, some taking refuge in the Devenney house. Nine still unidentified RUC officers broke the door down and batoned members of the family. Samuel was the main recipient of their attentions, sustaining multiple injuries, a possible skull fracture, and damage to the eyes and mouth. He also suffered a severe heart attack. Released from hospital after three days, he was recalled on 22 April and kept in until 19 May. He died of cardiac problems less than two months later, on 16 July. The inquest attributed cause of death to natural causes.

By the autumn the RUC had a new chief, Sir Arthur Young, and he was anxious to have the Devenney case thoroughly investigated. He was, however, met with 'a conspiracy of silence' and no one was ever charged with the murderous assault. The family and those neighbours also assaulted were compensated. Violence continued intermittently throughout the summer until the extreme violence of August in Belfast and Derry led to considerable structural damage and the beginnings of political reforms. The shirt factory close to the Devenney home was destroyed and the collapsing masonry shattered their house. The reputation of the RUC among Derry nationalists, never very great, sank to zero because of the Devenney incident. It was one of the events that, badly mishandled, contributed to the decades-long violence that followed. On 19 April 1999, the thirtieth anniversary of the original assault, a public meeting was held to mark the occasion.

17 JULY 1879

Rifleman John Boyd, Royal Irish Rifles, was born on 17 July 1879, and died at Edmonton Hospital, London, from wounds received in action, on 6 October 1915. He was a member of Ebrington Presbyterian Church, and his name is commemorated on Derry's Diamond War Memorial. Rifleman Boyd was the eldest son of James and Mary (née Reid) Boyd of 12 Nassau Street in the city; the son-in-law of Robert Gray Anderson; and the husband of Isabella (later Evans) Boyd, whom he married on 13 August 1908.

Rifleman Boyd worked in Messrs. Hogg & Mitchell's factory, and was at the outbreak of the First World War called up as a reservist. Around September–October 1914, he wrote home to his father from a hospital in a French town, where he was lying wounded, giving a very lucid account of his experiences in the firing line:

> Just a few lines to let you know I am alive. I was wounded on the chin by a shell, and will be in hospital for some time, and will have a scar to show that I was in the fight. Colonel Bird DSO got struck with a piece of the same shell, and had his leg shattered. So I am fortunate to be alive. I have been in it all. Our regiment has given a good account of itself. I was at Mons, Cambrai, and Rheims. That is the place where the Germans got the good positions. There were old French forts there, and our artillery could not get them out. But had we got plenty of artillery we could have beaten the Germans with sticks. We have about three officers left. We crossed a bridge here, which consisted of only one plank, the Germans shelling it all the time. They had blown it up on their retreat. So our engineers got one

plank, an old boat, and a dead horse or two, and made a bridge—you can guess what it was like…

Boyd was home on sick furlough at the end of 1914 and, on his recovery, re-joined his regiment at the Front, but was again wounded, his injuries this time extending over the chest, face, and neck. His body was brought to Derry the day after his death at Edmonton Hospital. A comrade of Boyd, Rifleman T. Hillis, Royal Irish Rifles, wrote to his widow stating that in a great charge, in which their company suffered very severely, he last saw John Boyd, who was a bomb thrower, in his place on the flank of the company, and expressed the sympathy of his comrades with Mrs Boyd. 'Your husband,' he concluded, 'was a true soldier and a man, and I trust you will bear your great loss like a soldier's wife.' Rifleman Boyd was buried in the City Cemetery. His funeral took place on 9 October 1915 with military honours. The band and pipers of the Royal Inniskilling Fusiliers attended, and the same regiment supplied the firing party.

18 JULY 1933

'The date will be written in letters of gold, even in the crowded history of Londonderry, for the events which took place on it were memorable. It was a day of pomp and pageantry, a day of holiday and rejoicing, a day of giving and receiving, a day of dedication and commemoration, and, to crown it all, a day of glorious weather, with the sun shining down in benediction upon the happy proceedings of the day, which, with solemn and sacred appropriateness, culminated in the impressive service in the Cathedral commemorating the Tercentenary of its founding by the Honourable the Irish Society.'

That is how the *Londonderry Sentinel* began its coverage of the events of Tuesday, 18 July 1933. The above, and the opening and naming of the new Craigavon Bridge across the Foyle, were the central events of the day. In attendance were the Lord Mayor of London, Alderman Sir Percy Walter Greenaway, and the Sheriffs of London, complete with their State coaches; Lord Craigavon, Prime Minister of Northern Ireland, and other heads of the State; the Governor, Deputy Governor, and members of the Honourable the Irish Society; and the representatives of the great Livery Companies of London, as well as many distinguished people from all parts of Ulster.

The Lord Mayor of London had a busy ten hours in the Maiden City and participated in all the events of the day, which included: the Lord Mayor's State procession from Ebrington Barracks to the city side of the Bridge; the handing over of the Bridge by Viscount Craigavon to the citizens; the acceptance of it by Alderman Captain J.M. Wilton, Chairman of the Bridge Committee; the presentation of a dagger to the Lord Mayor, who subsequently opened and named the new edifice 'Craigavon Bridge'; the laying of a wreath on the City War Memorial by the Lord Mayor; the conferring of the Freedom of Londonderry on the Lord Mayor, and the presentation to him of a silver casket containing the certificate; the luncheon in the Guildhall by the Honourable the Irish Society in celebration of the opening of Craigavon Bridge; the garden party in Brooke Park by the Mayor and Mayoress in honour of the Lord Mayor and the Sheriffs of London; the opening of the hand-wrought iron gates at the London Street entrance to Derry Cathedral by the Governor of the Honourable the Irish Society, Alderman Sir Charles Batho, and the dedication of them by the Lord Bishop of Derry and Raphoe, the Right Reverend Dr Peacocke; and the service in the Cathedral in commemoration of the Tercentenary of its founding at which the Lord Mayor and Governor read the Lessons.

Schoolchildren and members of youth organisations were given a prominent place in the day's proceedings, particularly the opening of the Bridge, which cost £255,000, and which was the gift of the Northern Government to the people of Londonderry for the benefit of the city.

19 JULY 1895

Albert Chevalier—the actor and music hall entertainer known as the 'Costers' Laureate' because of his songs in Cockney dialect on London common life (a 'coster' is a cart peddler)—was born in the Royal Crescent in London's Notting Hill on 21 March 1861. His brother, Auguste, who went under the pseudonym of 'Charles Ingle', served as his manager and occasional partner, and was known as a composer of music hall classics.

In 1869, Albert premiered as Mark Antony in an amateur production of *Julius Caesar* at the local Cornwall Hall. He then joined the Roscius Dramatic Club at the age of fourteen, adopting the stage name Albert Knight. An actor from 1877, he played legitimate roles in the Royal Court Theatre, Sloane Square, and elsewhere for almost a decade and a half. He made his music hall debut in 1891 at the London Pavillion, where he was an immediate hit, singing such songs as 'The Coster's Serenade' and 'It's the Nasty Way 'E Sez It', and in 1896 he embarked on a successful tour of the United States.

In 1895, on Friday, 19 July, Chevalier had performed for two hours before an audience in Derry's City Hall. Commenting succinctly but favourably on the evening, the *Derry Standard* wrote: 'As a delineator of coster life in London, or rather the brighter side of it, Mr Chevalier seems to be unrivalled. His character sketches are highly artistic and by no means caricatures, but it would require a larger acquaintance with the Cockney dialect to enable an audience fully to appreciate many of his songs. Knowing this, no doubt, he presented some of his more attractive sketches, which were highly appreciated. His rendering of "My Old Dutch" (the words being a pet appellation for a wife), given with inimitable pathos, was well-received by all. "Tick Tock" was another fine delineation of an old man, surrounded by all the accessories of a humble home, who sings contentedly of his happiness until he falls asleep.' Bringing its brief critical appraisal to a close, the *Standard* wrote: '*Our Bazaar* was one of his best sketches, and was loudly applauded. Mr Chevalier was assisted by a clever conjuror, an eminent pianist, and a lady who sang very pleasingly some choice songs.'

From 1920 Chevalier acted in the play *My Old Dutch*, written by himself and Arthur Shirley. Chevalier had actually invented the term 'old Dutch', and was once asked to explain the source of the phrase. He said that his wife's face reminded him of a beautiful little Dutch clock they kept on their mantelpiece. He died on 10 July 1923, and is interred with his son and father-in-law at Abney Park Cemetery, Stoke Newington, London. Their grave is cared for by the Music Hall Guild of Great Britain and America. As he refused to include obscenity in his act, Chevalier is credited with improving the general respectability of music halls.

20 JULY 1909

The success of the Williamite forces at the Boyne in 1690 is celebrated, as most people know, on 12 July each year. It has not the same air of tension in Derry as in other parts of the province. *Its* day comes later when the ending of the Siege of 1689 is commemorated as the 'Relief of Derry'. In 1909, with the distant prospect of Home Rule preoccupying people's minds, tensions increased.

At a special court in Bishop Street on Tuesday, 20 July of that year, Thomas Heaney of Dungiven Road, Waterside, was examined on a charge of the unlawful killing of William McKeever of Ballyshaskey on 12 July. The account of the magistrate's examination of the case was given in full the following day in the *Derry Journal*. The purpose of the hearing was to determine whether there was a case to answer. The original charge was assault but that was changed swiftly to murder when McKeever died on the morning of the fifteenth.

The trouble started on the late afternoon of the big day in a public house at Ardnabrocky owned by a Mr Kerr and managed by Hugh Quigg. McKeever had come into the pub, stated Quigg, between five and six and drank a bottle of stout. An hour later a crowd entered, described by Quigg as the Killaloo Band. Sometime later Heaney and a few companions joined the crowd, now numbering about thirty, and the scene was set for confrontation. McKeever was seen to take off his coat and announced that he could beat every Orangeman in the place. It was Heaney who took up the challenge but the first blow was struck by McKeever. After a while McKeever fell to the floor, and before he could be stopped, Heaney began to kick him where he lay. As he rose to his feet Heaney struck him again, and at that point Thomas Campbell separated them and helped McKeever into his coat. He left by the front door but was later found in an ill condition in one of the outhouses. He was eventually taken to the Infirmary in Derry, reaching there about 9 p.m.

The autopsy performed on 15 July revealed that the cause of death was peritonitis caused by a rupture of the small intestine of nearly two inches in length. The *Journal* used much column space to give the full cross-questioning of the many witnesses by counsel; but in spite of alternative suggestions as to the cause of the rupture there was at least a *prima facie* case that Heaney was responsible and the case was sent for jury trial at the County Assizes.

21 JULY 1926

The telephone was invented in 1875 by Alexander Graham Bell, a Scot born in Edinburgh who had emigrated to Boston. By 1879 London opened its first exchange and by the end of the Great War it had become a universal, if still slightly cumbersome, means of communication. In the 1920s there were not many private domestic receivers; the majority depended on the bright red kiosks that were to be found at nearly every street end, a mushroom growth generated as a 'nice little earner' by the Post Office. Derry's turn came in 1926 when the local telephone manager wrote to the town clerk for permission 'to erect and maintain telephone street kiosks in a suitable position in the city'.

The letter was read at a Corporation meeting on 19 July and an account of the rather stormy meeting was given in the *Derry Journal* two days later on Wednesday, 21 July. The Post Office's chosen first location was at a point between the north side of Butcher Street and the northeast corner of the Diamond. Councillor Greenway proposed and Councillor Bradley seconded a motion that 'so far as the Corporation were concerned and had the power to do so, they would grant permission...' They also suggested that a call office be erected and maintained in the Guildhall. Councillor Gilliland proposed an amendment that really had little to do with the Post Office but much to do with the Diamond, at the centre of which, space had been assigned to the Derry Committee for the building of a war memorial.

Slightly bewildered, Mayor John Gilbert Magee ruled the amendment out of order but Gilliland persisted in his complaint that the centre of the Diamond (once the site of the Council House and then given over to seats and flower beds) had been chosen as the space in which to erect the memorial and nothing appeared to have been done about it. Magee reiterated that discussion of the memorial had nothing to do with telephone kiosks. Things became quite heated as Gilliland objected to being 'hammered down' and Magee denied the charge, suggesting that Gilliland put down a notice of motion rescinding the resolution about the war memorial and then propose his amendment. Gilliland said he just wanted to galvanise the War Memorial Committee into action but Magee sternly rebuffed him, saying, 'You are out of order. Keep to the telephone kiosks.'

Gilliland, a veteran of the trenches, persisted in attacking the Memorial Committee, saying that it had taken so long to use the site for which it was granted that it should be forfeited to the Corporation. Magee, his patience now visibly ebbing, thundered, 'Are you not going to obey the Chair?' while Gilliland, with mock innocence, asked, 'Am I not in order?' and had the last word despite the mayor's exasperated cry: 'We are dealing with telephone kiosks!' Greenway's original motion was passed and Derry got its red boxes, and, in time, its war memorial in the Diamond.

22 JULY 1946

On 22 July 1946 the King David Hotel in Jerusalem was bombed in an attack carried out by the militant Jewish underground organization, Irgun. Ninety-one people of various nationalities were killed and forty-six were injured. Among the fatalities was Derry man, George Thompson Farley, son of Professor W.J. Farley, formerly of McCrea Magee College in the city.

News that George Farley was missing was reported in the *Derry Standard* on Wednesday, 24 July. The newspaper stated that Farley had had a distinguished career at Campbell College, Belfast, and Trinity College, Dublin. At Campbell he was a scholar, head prefect, and Company Sergeant-Major of the Officers' Training Corps. He captained the rifle team in 1930, and had been on the team that won distinctions at Bisley the previous year. He gained a Senior Exhibition at Trinity in 1932, was a scholar in 1934, and a first class Moderator and Gold Medallist in Philosophy. He became a Cadet in the Colonial Civil Service in 1935.

On 31 July 1946, the *Standard* announced with regret the news of Farley's death. He had flown to London in May on official government business and again early in July. Before returning to Palestine on 7 July he was appointed a Principal in the Colonial Office, Whitehall, where he expected to begin work in October. He had been married in Jerusalem in 1937 to Doreen Gertrude, and had two sons.

The King David Hotel contained the central offices of the British Mandatory Authorities of Palestine, primarily the Secretariat of the Government of Palestine and the Headquarters of the British Forces in Palestine and Transjordan. The attack, which originally had the endorsement of the Haganah (the chief Jewish paramilitary group in Palestine), was the deadliest directed at the British during the Mandate era (1920–1948).

Irgunists planted a bomb in the basement of the main building of the hotel, under the wing that lodged the Mandate Secretariat and several offices of the British military headquarters. Warnings were relayed by telephone, including one to the hotel's own switchboard, which the hotel staff decided to disregard, but none directly to the British authorities. A likely reason why the warning was disregarded was that hoax bomb warnings were rife at the time, and a bomb search had already been carried out, probably due to another hoax call or tip-off received by the hotel earlier in the day. Later telephone calls from a worried Palestine staff member and the police caused growing anxiety and the hotel manager was informed. In the closing minutes prior to the explosion, he called an unknown British officer, but, for whatever reason, no evacuation was ordered. The ensuing explosion caused the collapse of the western half of the hotel's southern wing. Some of the deaths and injuries occurred in the road outside the hotel and in neighbouring buildings.

23 JULY 1898

The St Columb's Total Abstinence Society was the creation of Derry's own 'apostle of temperance', Fr Walter Elliott, who had been inspired by the success of the charismatic Fr Mathew in Cork. As a priest in the city he had seen the depredations that over-indulgence in drink could wreak and decided that total abstinence was the only solution. His society was founded in 1873 and had remarkable success. He died seven years after its founding but his work was continued by others and the society's numbers grew each year. Many of its members had never tasted alcohol and joined as a kind of personal sacrifice, but the chief purpose was rehabilitation—giving those who made an effort to 'go dry' the support and companionship they needed.

In 1898 the spiritual director was Fr Hugh McMenamin and it was he who led the society's annual excursion on 23 July which was reported on in full detail in the following day's edition of *Derry Journal*. The outing that year was to Omagh and not the usual venue of Moville, which with its lough-edge location and public park might have seemed a better choice. The reporter suggested that the 'many facilities afforded by modern progress have so placed it within the reach of the humblest of our city to enjoy a day's recreation amid sylvan glades or by the "shores of the sounding sea" that the announcement of an excursion does not evoke the enthusiasm which it formerly created'.

The members assembled in the grounds of St Columb's College at 7.30 a.m. and marched in procession up Bishop Street, along Ferryquay Street, down Carlisle Road and John Street to the Great Northern terminus. They carried five banners and were led the by now locally famous St Columb's TA Brass and Reed Band. The banners had pictures of St Columba, Fr Elliott, Fr Mathew, and Daniel O'Connell, the Emancipist. St Eugene's Fife and Drum Band from the Waterside came next and the rear position was given to the St Columb's Flute Band.

At Omagh they were met by cheering townspeople led, like the excursionists, by local priests. A local man, George Murnaghan, had made his demesne at Lisnally available for the fête and there were facilities for all kinds of sporting competitions. The members were summoned to lunch by a bugle and after a day of unusually good weather the sight of many balloons rising into the summer sky was the signal that it was time to return on the homeward train. All agreed that 'the charm of the ocean was entirely forgotten in the greater charm of a thoroughly Irish welcome'.

24 JULY 1951

The special Children's Court held on Tuesday, 24 July 1951 had a long list of juvenile malefactors and G.C. Lynn, the Resident Magistrate, seemed determined to avoid delays or adjournments. A thirteen-year-old girl pleaded guilty to stealing a purse containing five shillings and a weekly bus ticket, the property of Enid White of St Johnston, and to have 'received' the article,

233

knowing it to have been stolen. She was discharged on paying costs. Two fifteen-year-old boys were charged with disorderly behaviour in Butcher Street on 15 June. They were 'shouting and hammering doors along the street'. Both denied the charge, admitting to nothing more heinous than singing. Costs were set at three shillings but there was no fine.

Also presented before Mr Lynn was the case of two schoolboys, aged fourteen-and-a-half, who threw stones at the corrugated iron gate belonging to D.C.G. Craig of Northland Road, one of their teachers at Foyle College. They were both from very respectable families, said Patrick Maxwell, their solicitor—the parents could clearly afford legal services— and had gone round to apologise. The parents paid the cost and the boys were admonished but not fined. Two others were not so lucky. Aged fifteen and thirteen, they admitted the larceny of the wheels and springs of a bath chair valued at £1 10s, the property of Thomas Cooke, Caw House. They had come across the wheels on the main Derry–Limavady Road, near the main Gransha gate, and assumed they had been dumped by the owner. Nevertheless, the RM fined each boy five shillings with costs.

A similar case involved the theft of four pram wheels and springs, valued at £3, the property of Edward Molloy of 17 Bann Drive. He had just moved into the house and was in the process of decorating it, shifting some of his possessions outside during the operation. The unnamed culprit, on seeing the gear, wheeled it away, but was charged five shillings costs and placed under the care of the probation officer for twelve months for his troubles. This involved home visits and reporting weekly to the officer.

The most serious charge was that of breaking and entering by a fourteen-year-old boy who had a key that fitted the lock of John Curran's office in Union Hall Place. The pickings were small—tenpence—but the principle was serious. He was fined £1.

25 JULY 1966

On 24 March 1966 Henry Martin Doherty, a little boy aged five, was killed by a bin lorry as it reversed slowly up the mews lane off Violet Street at the foot of Chapel Road, Waterside. Dennis McClelland, the thirty-two-year-old driver, was summoned for alleged dangerous driving. The hearing took place on 25 July at Derry Petty Sessions in front of J.M. Shearer, the Resident Magistrate, with McClelland represented by D. Clarke.

The first witness was Constable Crane who simply recounted the defendant's original statement. The refuse team consisted of six operatives, four of whom collected the bins and dumped the contents into the lorry. In the days before wheelie-bins it meant carrying the odorous containers as short a distance as possible before banging them against the edge of the lorry to knock out the foul-smelling mixture of coal ash, organic matter, newspapers and plastic that constituted household waste in the days before recycling. The effect of the battering to empty the last of the waste meant that, quite soon, the bin's rim was knocked so much out of shape that the lids did not fit.

McClelland had said that he had reversed slowly in from Violet Street, checking by looking back out of his window as he went that the way was clear. His other driver did not check his side nor was there anyone covering the back of the appliance, the rest of the team being further down the lane readying the bins on both sides. Having gone a short distance he felt 'a slight bump'. As far as McClelland could see, there were no children playing in the rain and all his mates were accounted for. However, one of the collectors said that a child had burst out of a side lane and been knocked down, but added that the lorry 'was hardly travelling at one or two miles an hour'.

Clarke made it clear to the court that there was no precise safety protocol; there was no assistant driver or any official safety first officer whose job it would have been to reassure the driver that it was safe to proceed. Here the RM intervened to comment and suggest that the system should be tightened up. He had come to the conclusion that since McClelland had by his own admission been reversing half-blindly and 'was driving to a large extent into the unknown', he was 'guilty of dangerous driving'. He fined him £20, a sum with the buying power of £277 today.

26 JULY 1689

By the end of July 1689, in the last days of the Siege, conditions in the city were desperate. The Reverend George Walker, who had made himself governor, recorded in his *A True Account of the Siege of London-Derry* published at the end of 1689, just how serious things had become by 27 July. He was not an impartial observer, tending to downplay the contribution that the large Presbyterian minority had made to the defence of the Maiden City, but his account of privation in the final hours makes cheerfully grisly reading:

> The garrison is reduced to 4,456 men, and under the greatest extremity for want of Provision, which does appear by this Account taken by a Gentleman in the Garrison of the price of our food:

	l. s. d.
Horse flesh sold for	0-1-8
A Quarter of a Dog	0-5-6
A Dog's Head	0-2-6
A Cat	0-4-6
A Rat	0-1-0
A Mouse	0-0-6

Per pound fatned by eating the Bodies of the slain Irish.

One of the other accounts kept of the Siege was that of Captain Thomas Ash, who, having had some military experience, had come to defend Derry against the army of James II. His account of a rather strange 'experiment' that took place on 26 July 1689 seems quite cruel to modern eyes but was unremarkable at the time:

> An experiment was tried on a cow at Ship-quay. She was tied and smeared with tar, and tow stuck to it, which was set on fire to make her roar, thinking that the enemy's cows which were grazing in the orchard would come to her. But she was not tied fast enough for when the tow took fire and was blazing about her, she made off, and was going to the orchard. But our men shot from the wall and killed her; she belonged to Mr Graves.

Observers could see a fleet at Culmore unable to reach the city because of the floating barricade devised by Jean-Bernard Desjean, *Sieur de Pointis*, the French Chief of Artillery, and did not realise that in a few days this boom would be broken. Next day Ash recorded another necessary bloodbath:

> This day the cows and horses, sixteen of the first, and twelve of the last, were slaughtered, the blood of the cows was sold a fourpence per quart, and that of the horses at twopence. Two of our men were killed at Butcher's-gate from the orchard. The soldiers got one pound of meat mixed with Dutch flour, and next morning one pound and a half of horsemeat per man. There is not a dog to be seen, they are all killed and eaten.

On the 28th, Ash was delighted to record that 'on this day we were delivered from famine and slavery'.

In the Edwardian era one of the more popular public entertainments was an open-air concert by a military band. With the death of the old queen in January 1901 and the coming to the throne of her sporty sixty-year-old son the Victorian Age was seen to be over and the emphasis was on pleasure. Things were still uneasy in Ireland but with national politics fairly quiescent there was no overt antagonism towards the armed forces. Regimental bands were highly polished and the programme they offered showed great variety, with specially composed marches, selections from the London theatre musicals including those by Gilbert and Sullivan and Lionel Monckton, and classical overtures. In Brooke Park or the Guildhall Square in their dress uniforms they used to provide a pleasant background for an evening's promenade.

On the afternoon of Saturday, 27 July 1901, the band of the Irish Guards marched to the Brandywell showgrounds on their first visit to Derry. It could well have been one of their first visits anywhere since the foot regiment had been established only at the beginning of that year. The concert was covered by a reporter for the *Derry Journal* who was disappointed by the turnout: 'In so far as the effect it had of arousing general local interest or attracting the public the visit of the Irish Guards to Derry may be written down as a dismal failure. Two performances were given by the band in Brandywell Road grounds on Saturday afternoon and evening, and if the attendance at the first was unsatisfactory the attendance in the evening was still worse.'

There was not even the excuse of Derry's usual rainy summer: 'Probably at seven o'clock the second programme was started in ideal weather.' The journalist deplored the sight of fifty expert musicians 'all the way from London discoursing from one of the finest operas before less than half their number of hearers'. Things improved slightly after an hour but the 'house' never reached a hundred. Some visitors 'from a distance' talked aloud of the situation, asking with deliberate irony whether it was not true that 'some folk living in the North were fond of bands' and wondered about the 'present blankness'. Was it because there was a 'lack of a big drum'? Meanwhile the Guards were getting steadily through their programme, 'guided by G.H. Hassall, of music by Wagner, Weber, Verdi and Suppé'.

In the hope of greater enthusiasm and frequent encores, apparatus for flare illuminants had been positioned around the bandstand 'but these were not lighted'. Owing to the poor attendance the intervals between items lasted only a few minutes and the whole programme was finished well before nine o'clock. The Guards quickly packed up their instruments, marched rapidly by 'the nearest route for the great Northern terminus and left Derry by the half-past nine train for Dublin'. The city's reputation for musical appreciation had taken a bit of blow.

Popular account has always associated Captain Browning and his Derry merchant ship, the *Mountjoy*, with the breaking of the boom across the Foyle when the city was besieged in 1689. Contemporary writers whose works gained wide publicity told only the story of Browning's deed and of his small victuallers. The respected nineteenth-century historian Lord Macaulay used the same emphasis, with the upshot that for generations the distinction of breaking the boom has gone solely to Browning, his crew and his ship, while others who arguably played a much more pivotal role in the episode still remain largely forgotten.

On 28 July 1689 a small squadron escorted the victuallers who were bringing aid to the besieged city of Derry. The flotilla included the man-of-war *Dartmouth* and HM frigate *Swallow*. The squadron weighed anchor and stood towards Culmore, the *Dartmouth*—which led the way—being first at the Fort. She was under the command of Captain Leake, afterwards Sir John Leake, and of his behaviour, the *London Gazette* commented:

> Captain Leake behaved himself very bravely and prudently in this action, neither firing great or small shot (though he was plied very hard with both) till he came on the wind of the Castle, and there beginning to batter, that the victuallers might pass under the shelter of his guns, he lay between the Castle and them and within musket shot and came to anchor.

The boom, however, had yet to be reached and breached.

The *Mountjoy*, under Browning, passed the Culmore fort, together with the longboat of the *Swallow*, which, in the words of the *Gazette*, was 'well-barricaded and armed with seamen to cut the boome'. That they fulfilled their task admirably is also clear from the records. The captain of the *Swallow* (Wolfran Cornewall) gave each man a guinea at the time, but the amount was afterwards brought up to a total of £10. The navy treasurer's accounts for the period contain an entry of the reward to nine of the crew in the boat, with the words, 'they being the boat's crew that cut the boom at the carrying the victualling ships to the relief of Londonderry'. It also preserves the names of these nine men.

There were, however, *ten* persons in the boat. The name of the tenth is preserved elsewhere. He was the boatswain's mate of the frigate *Swallow*, and it was he who was in command of the longboat. He was injured by a wood splinter while he and his crew were cutting the 'boome' with axes in order to open a passage for the *Mountjoy* and the *Phoenix*. In *Life of Sir George Saville, First Marquis of Halifax* it is recorded that William III told Saville 'that he would remember Shelly, who cut the Boom chain at Londonderry'.

The names of those in the *Swallow's* longboat were: Boatswain's Mate Shelly; Robt. Kells; Jeremy Vincent; Jas. Jamison; John Young; Alex. Hunter; Hen. Bremen; Wm. Welcome; John Field; and Miles Tonge.

29 JULY 1903

Edward VII was born in 1841 but had to wait fifty-nine years before becoming king. Victoria had never thought of abdicating but considering her firstborn's reputation for gambling, drinking and sex, it would have seemed to her unthinkable that he should become monarch a minute earlier than was necessary. Now, with a marked German accent which was a legacy from an education imposed upon him by his unloving, unloved father, he became a very popular king. His long-suffering, chronically deaf Danish queen, Alexandra, helped with the *rapprochement*, and Edward's short reign of nine years saw Britain peaceful, prosperous, and showing the beginnings of the Welfare State.

A tour of home territories usually follows royal succession but a scheduled trip to Ireland in March 1902 was postponed until July 1903 due to Nationalist unwillingness to offer the monarch an address of welcome. The Reverend Daniel Mannix, President of Maynooth, a noted nationalist, avoided an awkward situation by flying the king's racing colours instead of the Union Flag. The tour took nine days, and 29 July found them in the Maiden City, when the king in an after-dinner speech noted that since his last visit, 'your ancient city has prospered'. He went on:

> In the distant days of the great missionary of the West, St Columba, this city was a famous home of learning, and I rejoice to find it true in this respect, to its traditions. In particular the Queen and myself are glad to learn that much has been done here for the higher education of women, which is so happy a feature of our time.

Both the city bishops, Dr O'Doherty and Dr Chadwick, were then presented to the royal couple.

There followed a tour of the heavily bedecked city. Shipquay Gate was made to represent a Norman drawbridge. On Waterloo Square there was 'a splendid display of bunting and the fountain in the centre of the square was shown off to perfection'. The Infirmary and the nearby Brooke Park were on the itinerary and, according to the *Derry Journal*, 'Amid the music of the various bands stationed at intervals, the chime of the bells of St Eugene's Cathedral, the passage from the Guildhall to the Derry City and County Infirmary was one long triumphal march.' Later the cortege came down Clarendon Street and it was greeted with a tremendous outburst of cheering that increased in volume as it passed the Strand Presbyterian Church where the Union choir, massed on a platform, sang 'Come Back to Erin', and not surprisingly, 'God Save the King'.

Immediately after this demonstration of affection the royal party boarded the train for their next visit, this time to Buncrana. Three days later, on 1 August, the king and queen sailed from the Cove of Cork, then known as Queenstown, an earlier tribute to the old queen.

30 JULY 1941

The Northern Ireland Road Transport Board (NIRTB) was the semi-state body that ran all the bus services in the north except for Belfast in the 1940s. Its coverage was adequate, when one considers that petrol was rationed, new parts hard to come by because of the war, and new rolling stock out of the question. Breakdowns, if not frequent, were not unexpected and so when, on 30 July 1941, the morning bus from Park to Derry broke down it was no great surprise. When James McCloskey, the driver, eventually got through on the telephone, using at least three operators, to report that his vehicle had broken down, Albert Brown, a twenty-three-year-old mechanic was sent out to deal with the problem.

He repaired the bus and drove it back to Derry. He came down Dungiven Road and turned the corner into Spencer Road, and just opposite Victoria Hall, at the top of Distillery Lane, pulled out carefully to pass a stationary bus from the city service. He was going deliberately slowly—a witness thought at about fifteen to twenty mph and in second gear—when the rear of the vehicle developed a slight skid to the near side. Brown managed to control it but a few yards further along, where the road has a slight bend to the right, the bus went into a much more serious rear skid, mounting the pavement and smashing the back into the wall of a house. In doing so it hit fifty-year-old Margaret Wilkinson, who lived on Chapel Road close by. Her lifeless body lay across the pavement with blood streaming from her head and mouth. A few yards away her sixty-eight-year-old sister Anna Wilkinson lay with blood pouring from a head wound and her arm twisted behind her back.

Robert Dunn, an aircraft tester home on leave, realised that Margaret was dead but with help from some onlookers carried Anna across to Victoria Hall and sent for Dr Kelly, whose surgery was close by on Clooney Terrace. He attended to her wounds and reassured himself that her arm was not broken. He sent for an ambulance and then examined the body of the dead woman. At the inquest held in the City and County Hospital the next morning he testified that she had sustained multiple injuries and was bleeding internally. In his opinion death had been instantaneous, caused by shock and haemorrhage. Evidence was heard from six other witnesses, including the driver and Constable Mageean, assistant inspector of vehicles. He confirmed that the brakes, steering, screen-wiper and horn were in good working order. He had examined the scene carefully and found no sign of skid marks, but the road surface was wet and there was a slight camber.

Captain J.T.E. Millar, the City Coroner, brought in a verdict in accordance with the medical evidence. He said the accident was due to the state of the road and that there was no negligence on the part of the driver.

31 JULY 1924

The sub-headline printed in the Friday edition of the *Derry Journal* in its coverage of the Derry Petty Sessions of 31 July 1924 was the unusually enigmatic: 'A Tip on the Shoulder.' What might it mean?

Mary Anne Campbell and Ellen Horan were cousins and lived opposite each other in Orchard Street. James Horan, Ellen's husband, was a co-defendant in an alleged assault case that took place during an auction of furniture in his home that Campbell, the complainant, attended. She had placed herself by a table where a number of people were gathered and Horan, she said, had caught her by the shoulder and pushed her away. When he relinquished the physical contact, his wife took her by the shoulder and moved her out of the house. Campbell insisted that had they asked her to leave she would have done so without resistance. Scott, the Horans' solicitor, during cross-questioning, got her to admit that she was not on good terms with her cousin and that her sister had occupied their house some time ago. He further put it to her that she had caused the Horans a great deal of trouble. He reminded her that she had been put under a rule of bail for her conduct to them and that she had been so dismissive of the court's authority that she went to jail rather than submit to bail.

Mrs McManus, a witness, said that Campbell had caused no disturbance on the day in question; nor had she done anything to justify her ejection from the Horan household. Scott revealed that the trouble had begun when the house was purchased by the Horans, and it was never established legally whether it had been Campbell or her sister who had actually owned the house before the Horans moved in. Scott went on to suggest that because of Campbell's previous actions the Horans believed that she was going to cause trouble at the auction. Humphrey Babington, who spoke for Campbell, suggested to Horan that she was annoyed at seeing her cousin in the house, but she swiftly replied, 'I felt very much annoyed, and if anyone else had endured from her tongue for the last two years, they would feel annoyed too.'

The bench consulted together for a few moments and Mr Jones, the RM, announced their decision: a technical assault had been committed by Mrs Horan and they would fine her one shilling with court costs.

AUGUST

1 AUGUST 1718

On 1 August 1718 William Nicolson, the newly appointed Bishop of Derry, held his 'first and second' service to celebrate the anniversary of the end of the great siege—the 'Relief of Derry' as it has been since known. Nicolson had made his primary visitation after his appointment on 5 July. He recorded his first impressions in his diary for that day:

> Going (with the Dean & Mayor of Derry etc) to dine at Fawn, we took our way by the Top of Greanan-Gormely whence we could see the Outlets of the two great Loghs of Foyle and Suilly. The word signifies the place where (Queen) Gormely basked herself in the sun... Here are Remains of a Fort of Stones, like that of Maiden-Castle upon Stanemore, around which are Cavities or Lusking-Holes.
>
> NB. The mountain of Sleaver-Snaght (ie Snowdon) is the highest in Inchowen; on the Top whereof, saies Mr McManus, there are beds of Shells (of Oysters, Cockles ad Mussels) which have laid there since Noah's Flood, and have always a moisture n 'em at High-water. The Isle of Inch in Logh Suilly is in the parish of Temple-Moor. The Oysters here as good as at Colchester.

On the day of the celebration, as he records:

> Col. Michelburn's Bloody Flag being hoisted the first time on the steeple p.m. Great Guns & Volleys. Even'. Splendid Treat in the Tolset [tholsel], Fireworks & Illuminations.

243

It was just twenty-nine years since the dramatic breaking by the *Mountjoy* of the boom across the Foyle narrows and the Maiden City with its Derry crimson banners was *en fête*. Nicolson had to follow the received wisdom of the period that the siege heroes were all members of the Church of Ireland, with no great credit given to the equally heroic stance of the Presbyterians. The myth of Anglican supremacy had been advanced by George Walker and it was his version of the story that was the accepted one.

Like most bishops of the time Nicolson was not Irish; he was born in Cumberland in 1655 and after a stellar career in the Church was appointed Bishop of Carlisle in 1702. Of all the Irish dioceses Derry was the prize and he accepted the post gladly in 1718. Rich as the diocese was there was terrible poverty among the ordinary people and, in some years, actual famine. In a diary entry for 1721 he records how, on the accidental death of one of his coach horses in a field near his house, fifty or sixty cottagers suddenly appeared with axes and cleavers 'and immediately divided the carcase: Every man carrying home his proper dividend for food to their respective families.' Nicolson stayed in the Northern See until his appointment as Archbishop of Cashel on 28 January 1726, but died three weeks later in Derry and was buried in the cathedral.

2 AUGUST 1924

When in the post-war general election of 1945 Clement Attlee's Labour party had a landslide victory, it was no surprise that the forceful Ernest Bevin was appointed Foreign Secretary. He once said that in the Foreign Office the only post he was qualified to take was that of Foreign Secretary or janitor. In fact he became one of Britain's finest.

He was illegitimate, had left school at twelve and subsisted on casual work. He had great drive, intelligence and ambition, and by the age of thirty was an official of the dockers' union. In 1922 he was one of the founders of the Amalgamated Transport and General Workers Union (ATGWU) which became Britain's largest union; he was its secretary from 1922 until 1940, when he became an MP. He served in Churchill's wartime coalition government as Minister of Labour and after 1945 could have ousted Attlee at any time because of his TUC support, but served him faithfully till his death.

In August 1924, having served two years as ATGWU's general secretary, he visited Derry to address the local members in the Guildhall. It was quite a coup, for even then the forty-three-year-old was clearly a coming man. He had spoken the previous night in the Ulster Hall in Belfast where 'he had witnessed one of the most remarkable labour demonstrations that had ever been witnessed in the North of Ireland'. He reminded his Derry audience that the standard of living, inadequate as it was, would have been much worse 'had it not been for the great and powerful influence of the labour movement'. He went on to say that he felt 'the only way to protect the interests of the people was to unite in one great organisation all the workers that they could possibly get hold of'. It pleased him that the 'workers of Derry were in favour of the unifying of the movement'.

Already with hindsight we can see that he had begun the process that led to the General Strike of 1926 and the surge to political power of the unions that was such a feature of British politics from 1945 until 1980. He observed that if the workers abused the inevitable power that would become characteristic of their movement, they would bring about their own destruction. It is unfortunate that subsequent less balanced TUC leaders had not remembered this piece of advice. If they had, the whole history of industrial relations in the 1980s might have been different and less destructive of a noble movement.

Bevin's finish was oddly prophetic:

> I said in the last dockers inquiry when our men were on strike that I have denied the right to directors to take the accumulated reserves of industry and give them away to shareholders. I did so because finance is only entitled—assuming you admit its rights at all—to the return of what it invests.

There was prolonged applause as he sat down.

3 AUGUST 1910

In Derry before the Great War responsibility for civic fire-fighting was undertaken logically enough by the Water and Fire Brigade Committee of the Corporation. A report in the *Derry Journal* for 3 August 1910 gave an account of how difficult it was for the committee to get much-needed funding for a vital service. That committee had come in for a great deal of criticism over its poor attempt at saving the Guildhall when it went on fire two years previously, but the city fathers, especially John McFarland, the mayor, do not seem to have learnt a necessary lesson.

Alderman Anderson, chairman of the committee, and Trimble, the Fire Suprintendent, reported that they felt it their duty to point out that the Fire Brigade was not properly equipped for saving life:

The hand ladders at the station cannot be relied upon for the speedy and effective service, which is absolutely essential. It is scarcely necessary for us to say that the first duty of a fire brigade is to save life and it is a principle that the first machine sent out in answer to a call should be a fire escape.

The report went on to say that the provision of a motor fire escape was a matter of the utmost urgency. The machine could carry hose and other appliances and the pumping engine could be held in reserve; the heavy expense of its upkeep, amounting to £45 per annum (£3,500 today), could be avoided. At this point the mayor interjected with 'This is another motor', a mild pun that got the laugh he expected. Anderson, having joined dutifully in the laughter at the mayor's witty remark, began a further impassioned if rather sententious speech:

Human life was their first consideration in regard to a fire. Property might be destroyed but it could be replaced. Once human life was gone it could not be replaced… The time had come when some provision should be made in the way of providing a proper fire escape. If they did not do so they might wake up some day to find out it was too late and the citizens would say, 'That's the Corporation for you; they have made no accommodation for escape and—'

At this the mayor interrupted with 'And hang the mayor', and he got a laugh again. Momentarily serious he asked if there was not a proper fire escape at present, and when told that all the service had was a ladder, he suggested that if it had never been found deficient in the past thirty or forty years there did not seem any point in changing. In spite of this mayoral lack of co-operation the matter went to a vote, the mayor the only dissenter. Before the meeting finished the Water Superintendent stated that the details of the last analysis of the city's supply by Professor Leebody of Magee had been the purest for many years.

4 AUGUST 1901

When Cecil Frances Alexander, the famous hymnist, died on 12 October 1895, her husband William, Bishop of Derry, was seventy-one. He had never been as well-known or as popular as his famous wife but was happy to remain until his retirement in his palace in Bishop Street, his main non-ecclesiastic purpose the editing of his wife's poems. He was not to stay there for much longer, for the Primate Archbishop Gregg died a few months later and William was appointed

Archbishop of Armagh and Primate of All Ireland. His daughter Eleanor (known as 'Nell') went with him, acting as his hostess, until his retirement to Torquay in 1911. He died there later that year, not long after he had been presented with Grand Cross of the Victorian Order.

On Sunday, 4 August 1901, while on a visit to Derry he preached to a crowded congregation in St Columb's Cathedral. He and Nell were guests of Captain and Mrs Macky of Belmont. Among the distinguished members of the congregation were the Governor of the Irish Society, Sir George Faudel Phillips, Lady Phillips, and the members of the Visitation. The seventy-seven-year-old archbishop needed assistance to dismount from his carriage and he used two sticks to aid his progress. Macky had driven his carriage to the western door and, as Alexander descended, the bells rang out to welcome him back. The procession moved slowly up the main aisle, His Grace showing evidence of great emotion. The same depth of feeling prevented his beginning the sermon for some moments, but when he spoke the text from Isaiah, 'The voice said: "Cry", and he said: "What shall I cry? All flesh is grass and all the goodliness thereof is as the flower of the field. The grass withereth, the flower fadeth but the word of our God shall stand forever"', his voice was strong and clear.

As his text indicated he began first to consider the state of Biblical studies and noted that the ancient classics might not form part of the curriculum of the new universities: 'Many might be forced to think, perhaps with a sigh, that their sons would live to see the poet Virgil abolished from schools and universities.' He was not quite right about that—it took two generations finally to wipe Latin out; but he was absolutely wrong in his next statement: 'Whatever came, Greek was sure to be spared, because it was pre-eminently the language of the New Testament.' He indicated a dislike of thundering sermons: 'A moaning, groaning, atrabilious tone about human life was not the tone of the New Testament.' The peroration clearly pleased the capacity congregation and there was general mute satisfaction when he spoke the closing text: 'The word of our God shall stand for ever.'

5 AUGUST 1955

Early in 1942 the United States Marine Corps sent for the 'Fighting Seabees', the military Construction Battalion (CB) to build them a camp at Springtown in Derry as a staging post for the then remote Second Front—the re-invasion of Fortress Europe. They worked quickly and well, and soon had a mini-township with streets, community hall and shops, Post Exchanges or PXs, as they succinctly called them. There was no lack of material or quality because millions of dollars were spent on the 'war effort' and nothing was too good for the 'leathernecks', as the marines were called, since they were the elite fighting force.

When peace broke out there was a surfeit of equipment that the Americans had no intention of shipping back home. Included were hundreds of bicycles that were offered to the City Corporation, but in a mixture of superiority and red tape the people's representatives refused to accept them, so the commandant set tractors against a pile of them and buried them in pieces in the various camps. The Quonset huts were there to stay and they were soon requisitioned freelance by many Derry families who lived in miserable billets in the older parts of the city—families sometimes subsisting in a single tenement room. Here were sturdy dwellings, properly plumbed, and compared with their usual habitations, palatial.

Ten years after the end of the war, on 5 August 1955, the camp had begun to show signs of deterioration, not so much of fabric but rather of community relations. And where better to discover the extent of strife than in the Petty Sessions Court. There were fourteen summonses to be dealt with by J.M. Shearer, the Resident Magistrate, on that day, all arising out of 'trouble between residents'.

Hugh Carlin and his wife, Isabel, brought an action against John Brennan, his son James, Margaret Brennan and Margaret McNutt, all of 141 Springtown Camp, for alleged abusive and threatening language on 14 July past. All of these were dismissed on the merits. A further case brought against the Brennans by the Carlins for another assault on 31 July caused them each to be fined £1 and bound over for twelve months. The Carlins also complained against Margaret Brennan, and Margaret and John Nutt. The cross actions between the three families got so complicated that, at times, the RM showed his confusion. Patrick Maxwell for the Carlins, and Cecil Milligan for the Brennans and McNutts, also had difficulty in disentangling the various charges and counter-charges. A brief moment of drama occurred when a witness claimed that Mrs Margaret Brennan had been struck by a milk bottle. She was introduced to the court by her husband and a WPC because she was in a highly nervous state. In consideration of her physical condition, the RM decided not to ask for her evidence and the case ended with minimal fines and all parties bound over.

On Tuesday, 6 August 1901, the foundation stone of Carlisle Road Methodist Church was laid. The ceremony was performed by Her Grace the Duchess of Abercorn (who was accompanied by Lady Gladys Hamilton) in the presence of a large crowd of people. The proceedings were due to begin at three o'clock but long before that hour almost every point of vantage from which a view could be obtained was occupied by people of all creeds and classes.

A number of flags and banners had been erected on the new schoolhouse behind the church and on the hoarding and scaffolding of the latter. At one end, just on the line of Carlisle Road, a platform had been erected, covered with carpet and furnished with chairs and couches for the accommodation of the Duchess of Abercorn and other leading figures. This was approached by a sloping and carpeted passage from the street, and at the upper end the foundation stone was held by a block and tackle suspended from a trestle.

The Building Committee, having secured the site with considerable difficulty, decided to invite competitive designs from architects in Derry and Belfast, knowing the problems the difficult shape of the site and the conditions of the ground might cause. Several architects forwarded their designs and that of Mr Alfred A. Forman of Londonderry, having clearly overcome all the difficulties, was accepted by the committee as being generally the best design. The style of architecture was perpendicular English Gothic, and the whole of the works were under one contract, to be carried out by Mr Robert Colhoun, builder, from Strand Road in the city.

The duchess and Lady Gladys arrived shortly after three o'clock and were escorted to seats on the platform, where a little girl, Miss Eileen Mee, presented Her Grace with a beautiful bouquet which she was pleased to accept and acknowledged in gracious terms. At this time there were on the platform, in addition to the duchess, a large number of ladies and gentlemen, and a considerable attendance of Methodist ministers including the Reverend C.H. Crookshank of East Wall Methodist congregation, which was erecting the new church.

The proceedings were commenced by praise, prayer and the reading of a portion of Holy Scripture after which the Reverend Crookshank bid all present a very cordial welcome on behalf of the committee and members of the Church at East Wall, and expressed the gratification which they all felt in seeing so many persons who, by their presence, expressed their sympathy with the great work in which they were engaged. The Mayor of Londonderry, also addressing the assembly, said it gave him very great pleasure to be present on that auspicious occasion of the laying of the foundation stone of what he hoped would prove a most beautiful church, a credit to the Methodist community and a credit to the city.

By the Bank Holiday Act of 1871 a number of days became *ipso facto* public holidays enjoyed by many who had never been in a bank in their lives. One of the most popular of these was the first Monday in August because the thousands, whose only break in the relentless working week was Sunday, had now an official summer holiday to spend at the nearest beach. It was changed in 1965 to the last Monday in the month and lost its full appeal. On the cusp of the new twentieth century it was *the* big day and properly celebrated with seaside trips, funny hats, and the new treat, ice cream, made popular and available thanks to refrigeration.

Anticipation was high and the *Derry Journal* of 2 August 1899 shared in the enthusiasm, anxious in those more leisurely days to give plenty of column inches to muse upon the event, and to supplement the advertisements of the travel companies. The coming Monday, 7 August, had the reporter's total approval: '[It] has won a broadly fixed popularity and gained the sanction of almost every community as a suitable day for outdoor pleasure. Being a bank holiday gives it a sort of official standing as a "play-day for the public".' He continued by pointing out that it 'has the advantage of being preceded by Sunday—a fact that allows to many a grateful extension of the recreation period'.

The piece went on to advise the readership that the Great Northern Railway had made special arrangements for a trip to the 'Irish metropolis': 'As almost everyone knows Dublin is not only famed for fine public buildings and beautiful parks but it also possesses—what some other big cities cannot lay claim to—a genial good-natured population, who yield to none in kindness and courtesy to visitors.' Other excursions offered were to Belfast, to Enniskillen ('for Erne lake scenery'), Bundoran ('by special and ordinary trains'), and 'the following stations on the Donegal line—Donegal, Mountcharles, Killybegs and Glenties'. The Northern Counties line had excursion tickets for many stations along the way including Belfast, Ballymena, Ballycastle, Castlerock, Dungiven and Magherafelt. Ballymena was to be the venue for 'an interesting military tournament' involving the 3rd Dragoon Guards with the performance of a full military band to 'enliven the proceedings'.

Not to be outdone, the line closest to the people's hearts, the Derry, Lough Swilly and Letterkenny, offered to take trippers to Fahan and Buncrana, where 'good sea bathing can be had'. For the adventurous there were Foyle river trips to Moville on the *Earl of Dunraven* steamer. 'Taken all round there is no lack of accommodation and variety for the numbers who will avail themselves of the privileges for outings... within their reach.'

The history of Ireland in the 1640s was one of extreme complication. As always the events in Britain strongly affected the colony. Charles I, having tried to run the country without parliament, had been forced to recall it but was so wrongheaded that he found himself in a bloody civil war with Scots Presbyterians and the Roundheads, who under the brilliant generalship of Oliver Cromwell eventually defeated the Royalist army and set in train the events that led to the beheading of the king on 30 January 1649.

For most of the decade Ireland was a maelstrom of shifting loyalties, and Derry was a pattern of this confusion. It was garrisoned with troops loyal to the English parliament under the command of Sir Charles Coote. By now the rest of west Ulster was full of planters who, though Presbyterian, still owed allegiance to the king—or realistically his heir, Charles Stuart. They disapproved of the extreme stance of the 'republicans' who had murdered the king, especially since, having undergone his execution with great and patient dignity, he was beginning to assume martyr status.

Derry was about to suffer its first siege, a dry run for the Great Siege that would convulse it in 1689. Presbyterian royalists (almost an oxymoron) began to advance north and west to the 'republican' stronghold that had been a place of refuge for Protestants eight years earlier, when, in October, some of the dispossessed in the six plantation counties rose against the foreign 'usurpers'. They surrounded the city in March and began the process of starving the besieged out by cutting all food supplies. There were occasional forays during April and May in which Coote was victorious, exchanging prisoners captured at Carrigans, four miles to the south in the fertile Laggan, for badly needed food.

Coote, who was a seasoned commander, laid a *cordon sanitaire* all around the walls and made preparations for a long war of attrition. It lasted twenty weeks and was brought to a conclusion by the unlikely intervention of one of the leading Catholic generals, Eoghan Rua (Owen Roe) O'Neill, who had won fame with the overwhelming defeat of Scots Presbyterians at the battle of Thistle Hill, Benburb, County Tyrone in 1646. With the usual courtesy of the time he was anxious to parley rather than engage in murderous slaughter but he must have sensed that Ireland was heading for a new darkness, at least as far as Catholics were concerned. Coote did not hesitate to treat with O'Neill, who was as politically acute as his uncle, the great Earl of Tyrone. He eased his Puritan conscience by insisting that God sometimes 'made use of wicked instruments to bring about good design'.

O'Neill arrived in the northwest following the handiest route up through the Foyle basin, and with three hundred cavalry and 4,000 infantry, soon scattered the besiegers on 8 August 1649. It was the last action in which O'Neill took part; he died three months later of tetanus.

9 AUGUST 1966

At the Derry Petty Sessions court on 9 August 1966 Hugh Vincent Kelly, aged fifty-eight, was charged with driving while unfit due to drink. He was perfectly reasonable about the matter, confiding in the policeman who interviewed him in the early hours of 17 March, the day the offence took place, 'I think anyone who drives when they are drunk should be jailed.' He was represented by Patrick Maxwell, a well-known local solicitor, who elicited in cross-questioning that the intake had been for medicinal purposes because he had flu. Evidence of incapability was given by Dr Bernard Shiels, who had examined the accused at 2.15 a.m., and said that Kelly had told him that he had had five hot whiskeys and five beers. A blood test had proved positive.

Constable McAlernan had been on night patrol near the foot of Bishop Street at 1.40 a.m. when he heard the sound of a car being driven very fast along Foyle Road. Four pedestrians had to jump clear as it sped past but it stopped when McAlernan motioned it to do so. Kelly behaved 'in a very helpful and friendly manner', explained that his fiancée was in the vehicle, and 'on the way to the station... talked incessantly but quite clearly'. Once there, Kelly announced again, this time to Sergeant McAlinden, that he was very much against drunken drivers but insisted that *he* was not drunk: 'I had five halves and five beers and that's the first drink I had since Christmas.' The sergeant was at pains to emphasise that while in custody Kelly was well behaved and a perfect gentleman.

The forensic report, taking a concentration of alcohol as anything above 150 to be *de facto* dangerous, found that the defendant had a count of 200. Kelly testified that he had left home about 10.30 p.m. on 16 March and drove to the Halfway House, where he had two hot whiskeys and two beers; these he took because he had the flu. He left the pub at 12.45 a.m., driving without lights because the beams were not working. When he reached the foot of Bishop Street, he was not going very fast and was not expecting to find people crossing the road at that hour of the morning, but he had no difficulty in avoiding them, being perfectly capable of driving. When he received half of the blood sample he'd provided from the RUC, he sent it to the public analyst in Manchester, and *his* report gave the reading as 150.

Head Constable Sterritt asked again if he had drunk 'five halves and five beers'; Kelly assented but said they had been spread out over the evening between 7 and 11.30. When J.M. Shearer, the Resident Magistrate, said that there must be a conviction, Sterritt put in a plea for leniency, saying that the defendant was leaving for America that night. Shearer imposed a fine of £25 with extra costs of £13 19s, and said he had no alternative but to suspend Kelly's driving licence for a year.

10 AUGUST 1910

It was a fine day in Derry on Wednesday, 10 August 1910, when new gardens—which replaced the old Town Hall in the Diamond—were formally opened. The proceedings began at noon, the arrival of the Honourable the Irish Society and the members of the Londonderry Corporation being heralded by the band of the Hants. Regiment. After the ceremony the band took up a position in the new gardens and delighted the citizens and visitors with a select programme of music. The members of the Corporation, in their robes of office, were met at the Bishop Street entrance to the gardens by Sir Alfred Newton, Governor of the Irish Society, Lady Newton and members of the Visitation.

Lady Newton severed the cords, and her husband, who was received with loud cheers, said it afforded the Honourable the Irish Society the very liveliest satisfaction to meet the Mayor, aldermen, and burgesses of that ancient city. They were assembled on a spot which teemed with historical and civic associations. It was upon that site, in 1616, that the first Town House or Exchange was erected by the Irish Society at the modest outlay of £500. That building appeared to have partaken of a semi-military and civic character. According to a very interesting account given in Colonel Colby's ordnance survey, accompanied by a wood cut, the building was of a Moorish type, with a block-house in the centre some five storeys high. Midway up there was a balcony on which was planted cannon. The balcony was supported by fourteen pillars, and the ground floor formed an ambulatory which was used either as a market house or exchange.

That building served the purposes of the citizens until 1688–9, when during the Siege of Derry it was destroyed. About four years elapsed before the new building was erected. It appeared to Colby that in those days, as in the present, the Corporation of the city went to work very carefully. No doubt plans were prepared for the new building, but they evidently did not meet the requirements of the citizens of those days. But ultimately a very costly building was erected, also at the cost of the Irish Society. That building performed the service required of it for about two hundred years, when in 1823, it was renovated at an outlay of £6,000, serving the citizenry up to within a few years before. When the Guildhall was destroyed as the result of the disastrous fire of two years previously, it occurred to the Society that this old building should be removed, and they suggested to the Corporation the clearing of the site. That suggestion was accepted with the result that the city had now this open space. He ventured to claim that it opened up a picturesque view of the river, with a charming background of delightful woodland scenery, which very few cities possessed, and, in his judgement, none excelled.

11 AUGUST 1908

Until the coming of partition Derry was one of the most prosperous and go-ahead towns in Ireland and its port was one of the busiest. There was often crowding at certain parts of the docks, especially where, between the Harbour Board offices and Boating House Lane, there was set a line of heavy-lifting cranes. The SS *Woodburn*, captained by George Skimin, had just reached the north coast of Ireland by 11 August 1908 but was not able to finally dock at Derry quay until the evening of the twelfth. Skimin was known for his fierce temper and was not pleased when, right on his stern, he was aware of a vessel carrying grain, making for the same part of the docks. The *Woodburn* came right in and anchored expertly at the quay while the rival stood a bit off, anxious to tie up close to a crane. Its master contacted William Hamilton, the harbourmaster, who ordered Skimin to shift the *Woodburn* twenty feet astern to make room for the other ship.

He was greeted with a total refusal and a barrage of vituperative language. On the morning of 13 August he arrived with a formal notice to Skimin, using the authority of the Harbour Docks and Piers Clauses Act. He was met with the same volley of insult and an eventual if reluctant compliance with the order. It was not enough for the harbourmaster who had been humiliated in front of two of his Harbour-Constables, Graham and Edwards, who could testify to the nature of the language used. Captain Skimin's ship was impounded and he was summoned to appear at Derry Petty Sessions on Tuesday, 18 August on a charge of having obstructed Hamilton in the execution of his duty, and using threatening and abusive language.

Skimin was defended by a local solicitor, Charles O'Doherty, while Dr Reid made the case for the prosecution. The panel of magistrates was led by William

Austin, RM. Reid began by saying that the prosecution did not intend to go with the first count since the order to move the *Woodburn* was in fact carried out, but would continue with the language charge. O'Doherty said that Hamilton ordered the mate to let go the bow rope and the vessel swung round. The movement brought the captain on deck; he was in a rage and shouted, 'Hold on forrard.' He had to order the action known in naval parlance as a 'back sling' to prevent his ship fouling the grain boat. His solicitor described his manner as 'a bit ruffled' and suggested that his client 'used some hasty language, as any seaman would do in the circumstances'. James McGriffin, the *Woodburn*'s mate, and William Ross, one of the crew, supported O'Doherty's statement. In spite of this Reid asked the magistrates for a substantial penalty, saying that it would be impossible to maintain order if the harbourmaster's instructions were ignored. Skimin was fined 10s 6d with 14s 6d costs.

12 AUGUST 1936

The foundation stone of the new Apprentice Boys' Memorial Hall was laid on Wednesday, 12 August 1936, by the mayor of the city at that time, Senator Captain James McElmunn Wilton. Speakers at the ceremony were the Attorney General Right Honourable A.B. Babington, Sir Ronald Ross, MP for Londonderry City and County in the Westminster Parliament, and Matthew Kerr, the Governor of the Apprentice Boys at that time. The thousands who had assembled in the precincts of the new Memorial Hall raised cheer after cheer as the foundation stone was laid. Hundreds of people, who were unable to obtain a view of the ceremony, visited the hall and admired the stone with its clear inscription, and were impressed with the dimensions of the new building.

Scenes of animation were witnessed elsewhere during the day. More than 20,000 Apprentice Boys participated in the procession on the walls and thoroughfares of the city. Reporting specially on the stone-laying ceremony, the *Derry Standard* stated: 'All streets in the city, as it were, seemed to lead to Mall Wall and its surroundings at 4 o'clock in the evening for what was rightly regarded as the principal item on the programme for the day—the laying of the foundation stone of the new Apprentice Boys' Memorial Hall.

'Many people came to the city specially for this memorable event and they must have carried away with them very pleasant recollections of the time spent while the ceremony was being performed. It is worthy of note that Viscountess Craigavon is to make an appeal on behalf of the Apprentice Boys so that the new headquarters may be opened free of debt next year.

'It was fitting that the foundation stone should be laid by Captain Wilton, Mayor of the city, a Derryman, three generations of whose family have filled the office of president of the Apprentice Boys of Derry Club, and one of the gallant Apprentice Boys who answered the call to arms and served King and country in the Great War, where he distinguished himself on the battlefield and won the Military Cross.

'Brother E.S. Murphy KC, who walked at the head of the procession, took the chair on a specially-constructed platform at the main entrance, outside which the stone was laid. A place has been reserved for the laying of a foundation stone by the Orange Order later.

'The scene was a brilliant one and an inspiration to everyone in the great multitude, which was representative of the people of Ulster. Every vantage point near the hall, the historic Walls, and the roof-tops was thronged with Loyalists intent on witnessing a ceremony which means so much to every lover of the Maiden City…'

13 AUGUST 1895

On Tuesday, 13 August 1895 the *Londonderry Sentinel* reported that a gloom had been cast over the previous day's Relief of Derry commemorations by the death of sixteen-year-old John Alexander Holland. The boy had been walking to his own house, 99 Fountain Street, at twenty past five on the morning of the Twelfth, when he was struck on the head by a wooden plug from an improvised mortar and killed instantly.

Young Holland, who was employed by Messrs. T. Young & Sons Ltd., was particularly clever in the designing and making of arches. He and some other boys had constructed three most elaborate arches to span Fountain Street. The work of swinging the emblems into position began at four in the morning and the lad, having finished, was going into the house for early tea before starting out for work. The fatality occurred only a few yards from his front door.

It appeared that at the head of Victoria Street a crowd was occupied in saluting the Relief anniversary by discharging a powder-filled axle-box. It was customary for these cannon to be exploded sitting on their end so that the plug went harmlessly into the air. On this occasion, however, by some means the fuse was lighted while the tube was lying on its side. The result was that the ignition of the powder blew the plug down Fountain Street. Thus, young Holland was killed over thirty yards from the scene of an explosion with which he had absolutely nothing to do. The effects of the blow were dreadful: striking him on the head, the missile completely shattered the side of the skull. The poor young fellow, on being struck, reeled and fell. His father, John, who witnessed the terrible event, having gone to the door to tell the boy that his tea was ready, ran forward, as also did a Mr Daniel Wilton.

Doctors Browne and James Craig were quickly sent for and the lad taken home, but he was beyond all hope. Young Holland's companions touchingly conveyed an expression of their grief by draping in crape the arch he had just completed. The flagstaffs and marshals-poles of the Mitchelburne Club of Apprentice Boys, to which he belonged, were also draped.

14 AUGUST 1898

The *Derry Journal*, the second oldest newspaper in Ireland, was the northwest's chief nationalist voice ever since its support for Catholic emancipation in 1829. It had always a kind of dilemma when reporting the twice-yearly events associated with the Apprentice Boys of Derry, founded about the same time, but as a counterblast to O'Connellism. The sectarianism and violence associated with the 'relief' of the city, that had seen the ending of the Siege on 12 August 1689, was never quite as severe as that generated in Belfast on 12 July but it was always a time of increased tension with the rival tribes stepping up to a metaphorical line in the sand.

The reaction of the paper's editorial staff tended to be in keeping with the prevailing politics. If things were relatively quiet the events of the day were reported with a fairly straight face, reserving any serious condemnation for occasions when there was a positive chance of violence, injury and destruction of property. The Apprentice Boys 'relief' celebrations in 1898 were really peaceful and the paper's edition of 14 August told the story with some irony. The outdoor parade was, in the *Journal*'s opinion, 'spiritless' and 'lacking in novelty'. It also noted that 'the vast majority taking part in Saturday's demonstration were strangers to the city'. Special trains on the Belfast and Northern Counties and Great Northern lines 'brought contingents from Belfast, Portadown, Armagh, Lurgan and other places'. The reporter did not think to mention that Derry was a kind of Protestant Mecca, the Maiden City, for which in tribute to the place's bloody past, collarettes of 'Derry crimson' were worn. He did faintly mock the robust recurring declarations of 'maintaining the Union' and 'unabated devotion to the glorious principles of civil and religious liberty', conscious of the hollowness with which these pieties resounded to nationalist ears, already exalted by the celebrations of the centenary of the United Irishmen's rising of 1798.

The paper's report did not fail to note that there was a great deal of drunkenness observable. The formal proceedings had finished by four o'clock, several hours before the excursion trains were due to leave: 'During that period many of the excursionists imbibed freely... At the railway termini there was a good deal of disorderly conduct but the officials managed to get off the trains without much loss of time.'

15 AUGUST 1917

Private Greer Wilson, 8th Battalion Canadian Infantry (Manitoba Regiment), was killed in action in France on 15 August 1917, aged 26. He was the son of Samuel and Mary Wilson, of 2 Rock Villas, Strand Road, Londonderry. Educated at Foyle College, his name is recorded on the Vimy Memorial, Pas de Calais, France, and on Christ Church World War I Memorial, Londonderry; it is also commemorated on the city's Diamond War Memorial.

Greer Wilson held an educational post in Canada, and joined up after the declaration of war. He had been previously wounded. His name was read out during a memorial service held on Sunday, 4 November 1917 for the members of the congregation of Christ Church who had given their lives in battle during the previous year. His name was also among a list of the Great War dead associated with Foyle College read aloud during that college's annual prize-giving ceremony held on Thursday, 19 December 1918.

Greer Wilson's eldest brother was Captain Charles Wilson, Shropshire Regiment, who before the Great War held an important position in the Indian Civil Service, and was later a judge in Malaya. His youngest brother, Robert, was for many years manager of the Rock Mills. Robert was educated at the Londonderry Model School and Foyle College. He was an apprentice in the Londonderry shipyard when the Great War erupted; he immediately volunteered for service and joined the North Irish Horse. He went to France as a sergeant in 1915 and received his commission in 1918. He went to India in that year, and after taking part in the frontier campaign, remained in the Indian army in the 1st Cavalry (Skinner's Horse).

He was a fine horseman and won the Duke of Connaught's Cup for horsemanship when passing through the Cavalry School at Sagru. He became adjutant of his regiment, and of the Cavalry School, and retired from the Indian army in 1935. In 1938 he went into the RAF Volunteer Reserves, attaining the rank of Wing Commander. Robert was a Staff Officer for Training, and died on active service in Aldershot in November 1943.

The father of the three brothers, Samuel, died at the age of 82, on Saturday, 7 September 1935. For the long period of fifty-nine years, he was associated with the firm of Messrs. Samuel Gilliland & Sons Ltd., millers, and was entrusted with the responsible and important position of general manager and secretary of the company. He had also, for many years, been closely associated with Christ Church in various capacities. He had served on the select vestry and had been a churchwarden, a synodsman, and a parochial nominator. He took a keen interest in education, and was a member of the school committee, while also a governor of Foyle College.

16 AUGUST 1917

Second Lieutenant Joseph Hamilton Miller Andrews, 11th Battalion Royal Irish Rifles, was born in June 1896, and died from wounds received fighting in Belgium on Thursday, 16 August 1917. He was the son of James and Martha Hamilton Andrews, of 'Glenmont', Templemore Park in Derry. Lieutenant Andrews's remains are interred in Ypres Reservoir Cemetery, Belgium, and his name is commemorated on Derry's Diamond War Memorial.

Andrews was previously twice wounded in July 1916, and was invalided home for several months. Sympathetic reference was made to his death at morning service in Carlisle Road Presbyterian Church by the Reverend John Huey on Sunday, 23 September 1917. At the time of his death, his brother, Stewart, was in France serving with the Canadian Field Artillery. His father was born at Crossroads in 1847, and had come to Londonderry at the age of seventeen, starting employment with Robert Sinclair & Company. Around 1880 he moved to work for Welch, Margetson & Company, and remained with them as manager of their shirt department until he became local representative of several Manchester houses. During all his life in Londonderry he was a devoted member of Carlisle Road Presbyterian Church, and for a greater portion of that period, he was a ruling elder in the church. For many years, he carried on a Bible Class for young men, and was superintendent of the Sabbath School for a considerable period. He was also secretary of the Presbyterian City Mission, always taking a deep interest in the moral and spiritual life of the city, being a generous helper of every good cause. He was a liberal supporter of the church's activities, and in business was a man of uprightness and integrity; his sterling character won for him the admiration of all who knew him. In 1884 he married Miss Martha Hamilton, daughter of Mr Joseph Hamilton, Three Trees, Quigley's Point. She died on 20 November 1950.

James Andrews predeceased his wife, dying on 14 March 1927, and his funeral took place from his residence to the City Cemetery two days later. A large cortege, including many local businessmen and friends of the deceased, heard the Reverend David Hay remark that it could be said of James what Dr Johnson had said of Oliver Goldsdmith: 'He touched nothing that he did not adorn.'

17 AUGUST 1952

In August 1952 the *Londonderry Sentinel* reported that a stone from Derry's historic walls was making its way to Chicago. It was being taken out by Edmund Warnock, Northern Ireland's Attorney General, to Colonel Robert McCormick, proprietor of the *Chicago Tribune*. Mr Warnock and Colonel McCormick were close friends, and when the latter, who had a collection of more than a hundred stones from famous battlefields and places of historical interest, expressed a desire to have a stone of Derry's walls, Mr Warnock promised him he would do his best to meet his wish.

Ways and means were found to this end and Mr Warnock took the precious stone with him as he left Derry on 17 August 1952 on the first stage of his journey. While removing stones from Derry's walls was by no means encouraged, the circumstances in this case, opined the *Sentinel*, were exceptional. It was to be exhibited with other stones in Colonel McCormick's notable collection and would help to rouse interest in Derry's story of the Siege. Each stone, as Colonel McCormick received it, was built into the wall of the *Tribune* building in the Windy City.

Colonel McCormick's interest in Derry's walls was not unexpected, for an ancestor of his was one of the defenders of the city in 1689. When McCormick had visited this side of the Atlantic, his London editor got in touch with C.D. Milligan, the editor of the *Sentinel*, and author of *The Siege of Londonderry* and *The Walls of Derry*, who supplied him with some biographical notes on Captain James McCormick, a participant in the Siege. Hailing from Lisburn, Captain McCormick had held a commission in Colonel Arthur Upton's County Antrim Regiment and served with Sir Arthur Rowdon's force, with which he came as it retired to Derry. During the Siege he served as a Captain in Colonel Mitchelburne's Regiment. Captain McCormick was one of the leaders of the numerous sorties by the defenders of Londonderry against the besiegers. Referring to these sallies in May, Mackenzie, the famous Siege diarist, said that few days passed without Captain James McCormick and other officers going out with small parties, and they 'seldom returned without doing some execution on the enemy or bringing in some small prey'. Captain McCormick was one of the signatories to the address to King William after the Relief. He served with Mitchelburne's Regiment at the Boyne and figured in the subsequent campaign.

Before his departure for Chicago, Mr Warnock said: 'I thought, since Colonel McCormick's forbears came from County Londonderry, that I would take him a stone from the Walls of Derry. I managed to secure one which I am taking with me. Several McCormicks played a considerable part in the events of the Siege. One was an officer in the besieged garrison, and two more were attainted by James's Dublin Parliament for their work in the Williamite cause. This is the reason for Colonel McCormick's interest.'

18 AUGUST 1856

On 18 August 1856 the foundation stone was laid for Magee College on a rural site on what would later be called Northland Road. The necessary sanction had been issued by the Lord Chancellor in 1852 and now the new college that had caused some controversy at its inception could come into being. It was Maria Martha Magee whose benefaction had made the project possible. She had been born Maria Stewart in Lurgan, and suffered the early deaths of her husband, in 1800, and of her two sons in early manhood. She acquired a fortune as the only relict of her two rich brothers and moved to Dublin. When she died on 22 June 1846 she bequeathed her estate of £60,000 to various charitable causes, including £20,000 to trustees in Derry to build a Presbyterian College, where arts and divinity would be taught to both men and women—a very advanced idea at the time.

Presbyterianism had come through a stormy period; the New Light faction, accused of Arianism and led by Hugh Montgomery, had been routed by Henry Cooke, and it was with his approval that another divinity college should be established. He had already established that Assembly College, built near the new Queen's College, should be the leading Presbyterian divinity school for Ireland.

One of the main speakers, the Reverend John Brown of Agahadowey, signalled that the new college would be a non-denominational:

No surly janitor shall stand at the gate and say to men of any denomination, 'Here is a fountain of science and piety at which you may not drink.' On the contrary, man of every creed and no creed, if they conform to the laws of order and decency, may attend its lectures and share its literary distinction.

It was also the first college to grant equal status to women as well as men but, since it had no licence to grant degrees, later studies had to be taken in other institutions, such as Queen's in Belfast and the Royal University and Trinity College in Dublin.

Though the occasion was a solemn one, with readings from the 132nd Psalm, which has the appropriate sub-title of 'A Song of Degrees', there was room for some local versifiers to celebrated the event:

> Bright was the morn, unclouded was the sky,
> When Presbyterians with their heads on high,
> Repaired beyond the Maiden City's walls
> To found a College with its lofty halls
> And stately domes, that all the world might see
> The princely bounty of defunct Magee.

The 'defunct Magee' was not the only benefactor of the college. Basil McCrea, one of the trustees, provided £7,000 in 1909 to set up a chair in natural philosophy. His will left a further £70,000 subject to his sister's life interest, and when she left £5,000 to the college in 1911, it became known for some years as McCrea-Magee. It is now a constituent college of the University of Ulster.

19 AUGUST 1935

'An old Foyle boy; an old Derryman; and a great Irishman' was how the *Derry Standard*, on Monday, 19 August 1935, announced the death of the Right Hon. Sir John Ross, Ireland's last Lord Chancellor. Sir John had passed away two days earlier at his residence, Dunmoyle, Sixmilecross, County Tyrone, after an illness of several weeks. He had contracted bronchial pneumonia about a month before his death, and while at one time he seemed to have thrown off its effects despite his eighty-two years, he had a relapse from which he did not recover. He inherited Dunmoyle through his wife, who was the only daughter of Colonel Deane Mann. Both she and his only daughter, Mrs Saunders, predeceased him. His granddaughter, Miss Saunders, also lived at Dunmoyle.

Sir John was born in December 1854, in Derry, and was the eldest son of the Reverend Robert Ross, minister of Carlisle Road Presbyterian Church, and a former Moderator of the General Assembly. His mother was also a Derry woman, being the daughter of Stuart Christie.

Sir John was educated at Foyle College, and in later life was elected the first President of the Old Boys' Association of that school. After leaving Foyle he entered Trinity College, Dublin, where he had a brilliant scholastic career. In 1876 he was First Classical Scholar and in the same year was President of the University Philosophic Society. A year later he was elected auditor of the College Historical Society. Taking up law as a career Sir John followed this pursuit with marked success. In 1879 he was called to the Irish Bar and in the short time of two years he became a KC and a Bencher of the King's Inns. He had the honour, in 1892, of being elected a Member of Parliament for his native city, Derry, representing it until 1895.

He was appointed as Judge of the High Court of Justice in Ireland in 1896 and held that position until 1921, when he attained the highest peak in his career by his appointment as Lord Chancellor, relinquishing the position following the creation of the Irish Free State. In 1919 his services were recognised by George V, and he was created a Baronet. He was also a member of the Privy Council of Ireland and a Knight of Grace of the Grand Priory of St John of Jerusalem.

Although he was kept busy with the duties of his career, Sir John found time to take an eager practical interest in charitable and philanthropic organisations. In 1898 he was appointed a Commissioner of Charitable Institutions and Bequests. A keen literary man, he was deeply interested in education and from 1905 until his retirement he rendered valuable service on the Board of National Education in Dublin. Sir John published three books: *The Years of My Pilgrimage*, *Pilgrim Scrip* and *Essays and Addresses*, and frequently contributed to leading magazines. *Pilgrim Scrip* gives a humorous account of a schoolfellow at Foyle, Percy French.

20 AUGUST 1888

J.F. Warden, the dedicated proprietor and manager of the Royal Opera House in Carlisle Road, announced early in the summer of 1888 that a week of Italian opera should begin on Monday, 20 August. Now in its sixth year the Opera House had grown in prestige, if not exactly in profit, but considering the popularity of the programme he hoped to do well. The company, led by Madame

Evelina Servid from the Theatre Royal, St Petersburg, included Mlle Carolina Mosianji from Turin; Signor Battista Baldini, the Apollo Theatre, Rome; Signor Vittorio Bellati, St Petersburg; and Signor Paolo de Benghardi from Paris. The conductor was Signor A. de Gabrielle of the Theatre Royal, Naples.

They were to open with the most popular opera of the time, Verdi's *Il Trovatore* on the Monday, do *Rigoletto* on the Tuesday, Gounod's *Faust* on Wednesday, Verdi again on Thursday and Friday with *Ernani* and the great tear-jerker *La Traviata*. Warden was taking a risk but thought it worthwhile, and he was applauded for his courage and showmanship by the local papers. The *Derry Journal* of Wednesday, 22 August gave fifteen precious square inches to a leader that was partly review and partly strong encouragement to Warden and his staff:

> The local public are indebted to the lessee of the Opera House for the many superior entertainments he has placed within their reach. Some of these, having regard to the comparatively limited community of local theatregoers, are brought to Derry at a hazard.

The writer was gratified that Warden had deemed Derry worthy of sharing in the best attractions which he offered in Belfast: 'On these grounds alone we would hope the Italian Opera will have a spirited support whilst among us.' He went on to reassure those who had not yet attended any of the performances that, judging by the success of *Il Trovatore* on Monday and *Rigoletto* the following night, 'the company is deserving of warm support of those who appreciate operatic music'.

There was nothing elitist about that appreciation. People took the chief arias as part of the common treasure of popular song. When the Cork Opera House hosted an opera season at the time the seats in the 'gods' were full at least an hour before the curtain by people singing the chief arias from that evening's offerings. In Derry, too, 'Home to Our Mountains' from *Il Trovatore*, 'The Soldiers' Chorus' from *Faust*, 'La Donna è Mobile' from *Rigoletto*, and 'Bibiamo' from *La Traviata* were unselfconsciously whistled and sung by 'street urchins' who had never seen the inside of any theatre. The *Journal* leader writer made much of his own personal restraint in forbearing to give summaries of the plots. Of *Il Trovatore* he wrote:

> It will not be necessary to give a description of so well-known a composition, and such would be no more in place than an explanatory sketch of a Shakespeare play.

On Monday, 21 August 1899, there called at the *Sentinel* office (then situated in Pump Street) an old gentleman, Robert Miller of Sydney, New South Wales, who had left Derry as a lad in 1841, made a fortune in the land of the Southern Cross, and had returned with his family to see the Maiden City. Mr Miller was a native of Lettermire, near Cumber, Claudy. He had visited the old homestead and found the home still standing, and on the previous day had worshipped in Brackfield Church.

'Yes,' he observed, 'I find that Derry has grown a bit—a good bit—since I left. The railways have made a difference. When I entered the city first as a lad going to serve my time with Mr Henry Thompson, of Goshaden, I came in down the Old Hill and over the old wooden bridge. Bridge Street was then in its heyday—the wealthy quarter. Mr Thompson's grocery was at the head of Bridge Street.

'How did I come to go out? Well, the late Alderman McArthur came back to Derry with such a glowing account of Australia that Mr Thompson went out. I was his apprentice and decided to go too, and I have never regretted it. He started business as a wholesale grocer in Sydney, and I became his partner. He died in 1861, and I bought out his share.' The business prospered mightily, the firm having a large English and Continental connection.

Mr Miller recalled with pleasure some interesting incidents of old Derry. He was at the election of Sir Robert Ferguson, initially a Whig and then a Liberal politician, who represented the city in Parliament for thirty years (1830–60) and resided at The Farm, Derry. A monument to Ferguson, known as 'The Black Man', now stands in Brooke Park. 'Those were the days,' Mr Miller said. 'After his return Sir Robert was carried down in triumph from the Courthouse. In front of him went a man carrying a large bag of silver, out of which, as he walked, he sent showers of coins among the crowd. The sport of watching the rougher men wildly scrambling for the money was greatly enjoyed.' Mr Miller remembered when there were no houses outside the walls at the front of Shipquay Street, and when the tide ebbed and flowed over the site of the Ulster Hotel where he was staying. Asked about politics in New South Wales, he exclaimed: 'For heaven's sake don't pay your members. We do, and the arrangement has not provided the best man. They get £300 a year, and are only windbags.' He considered Australia a fine field for mechanics, but no clerks need apply.

'Yes,' he said in conclusion. 'I am right glad to see the old city and neighbourhood advancing so well. You are nearer to us than when I sailed from Plymouth fifty-eight years ago. The voyage took four months and some days.'

Sir Robert Stephenson Smyth Baden-Powell was born in London in 1857, educated at Charterhouse, and after failing to gain a place at Oxford, joined the Indian army. His defence of Mafeking during the South African War brought him worldwide fame. Rising out of this experience he founded the Boy Scout movement, which he began in 1907 with a camp for twenty boys on Brownsea Island, Poole Harbour, Dorset. He published *Scouting for Boys* the following year and about thirty other books throughout his life. With his sister Agnes he founded the Girl Guides in 1910.

Sir Robert and his wife Lady Baden-Powell visited Derry during the weekend 21–22 August 1915, and inspected and addressed the city troops of Boy Scouts and also the then recently organised St Augustine's Company of Girl Guides.

The address was given at a service in St Augustine's Church on Sunday, 22 August. Baden-Powell spoke from the front of the chancel rails, saying: 'I want you to think of the motto which guides all of us in our work as scouts and as guides—both have the same motto, and that is "Be Prepared". It means, as you probably know, that you should always be prepared to do your duty at whatever cost it may be to yourself; your duty comes first, and you have to prepare... by training yourselves in all the different points laid down in your regulations. That is part of your duty, and it actually comes within the scope of the promise you made when you first became a scout or a guide. The promise is threefold— first, to honour God and the King (that is, to do your duty for God and your King); second, to obey the Scout law or the Guide law (which is the same thing); and third, to do a good turn to somebody every day (which means your duty to your neighbour). The great point is that you must be prepared to do your duty, and once you are thoroughly realising that object you are living a right and proper life. You are learning how to live and how to die, because if you have done your duty, although you may be quite a youngster, you have done all you can, and if suddenly called on to die you are prepared to die, and your life has not been wasted. There is a chance for each of you to make the most of your life, and make it useful: by always doing your duty to the best of your ability...'

Subsequently, the Baden-Powells were escorted round part of Derry's Walls, and then visited the Guildhall where they were conducted through the municipal hall, which they inspected with pleasure. Sir Robert took a keen interest in the stained-glass windows, particularly in the one presented by the Mercers' Company, of which he had been Master the previous year. Afterwards they visited St Columb's Cathedral, and were shown around the historic building. Before leaving, Baden-Powell signed his name in the visitors' book.

Lieutenant Daniel Kerr, Cheshire Regiment, was killed in action at the Dardanelles on 6 July 1915, aged twenty-three. He was the son of Mr S.J. Kerr of Craignamaddy, Bushmills, and his name is recorded on the Helles Memorial in Turkey. A student for the Irish Presbyterian ministry, Kerr offered himself early in the Great War for service with the cavalry, but there being no vacancy in that department he was given a commission in the Cheshires. After a course of training, Lieutenant Kerr embarked with his regiment and reached Egypt early in June 1915. On 2 July 1915, he landed in the Gallipoli peninsula, where four days later he was to lay down his life.

Kerr graduated from Queen's University, Belfast in 1912, and proceeded to Princeton Theological Seminary in America for the winter of 1912–13. During the summer of 1913 he engaged in the active work of the ministry, having charge of a mission station in Canada for five months. The remaining part of his theological course was taken at McCrea-Magee College in Derry.

A Catholic namesake of Kerr's, Lance Corporal Daniel Kerr, 6th Battalion Royal Irish Regiment, was killed in action in France on 20 August 1916, aged twenty-two. He was the eldest son of Michael and Laura Ellen Kerr of 18 Deanery Street in Derry, and his remains lie interred in St Patrick's Cemetery, Loos. His name is commemorated on Derry's Diamond War Memorial. Lance Corporal Kerr joined the colours at the beginning of the Great War. Captain A.D. Place, writing to Lance Corporal Kerr's father on 23 August 1916, said: 'I must write to you to sympathise with you and your family on the death of your son, Lance-Corpl Kerr. He was killed in action gallantly doing his duty. His death is a great loss to the company, as we always found him a most willing and keen soldier. He was killed on the night of the 20th, and was buried by the priest here in a little graveyard on the night of the 21st. I can't tell you how I feel for you. Your son was one of a party who were carrying bombs over to the German trenches. He had already gone over, and had come back for more when he was killed. The other officers of this company also ask me to send you their sympathy.'

Lance Corporal Kerr had been a very popular member of the Derry Wolfe Tone Band from its formation, and at a meeting of the band in the Wolfe Tone Hall on the Brandywell Road on Wednesday, 30 August 1916, Mr James Taggart (president) stated that the band had given up to thirty members to the colours. The majority of them had been wounded in action, and as fighters in the field they had all maintained the best traditions of Derry's Columbcille.

'The Town I Loved So Well' is a well-known song by Phil Coulter which recounts his childhood in Derry. Part of the song recollects:

> In the early morning the shirt factory horn
> Called women from the Creggan, the Moor, and the Bog
> While the men on the dole played a mother's role
> Fed the children and then walked the dog.

A similar observation on the Maiden City's reversal of then traditional gender roles was noted many years before, by William E. Curtis, the special correspondent of the Chicago *Record-Herald*, in an article on Derry, dated 24 August 1908. Concluding the piece, Mr Curtis wrote:

> Londonderry is unique for another reason. The ordinary relations of husband and wife and their domestic responsibilities are reversed here. The women work in the shirt factories and the men stay at home, keep the house, do the cooking and washing, and take care of the children, because there is nothing else for them to do.
> There is a large excess of women in the population. They number two to one man, which is not due to natural causes, but because women are attracted here from the neighbouring towns and counties to obtain work in the factories, and the young men have to leave Londonderry and go elsewhere to find employment. Many of them go to the United States and Canada.

Extracts of Curtis's article were reproduced in the *Londonderry Sentinel* on 10 October 1908, with the newspaper stating that, although 'interesting enough throughout', the piece was 'a curious mixture of accuracy and error—most snapshot articles generally are. Some things that are quite separate are jumbled together in a quite funny way, but on the whole Mr Curtis tries to do justice to the city.'

'Londonderry,' wrote Curtis, 'is unique in several respects among all the cities of the earth. It does not look like an Irish city at all. It resembles Plymouth, England, and if you were dropped down here from a balloon you might easily imagine yourself in that ancient seaport, which is perfectly natural, because everything here is English, and there is no sympathy with the rest of Ireland…'

Writing on the city's vibrant shirt industry, Curtis commented: 'The principal business of Londonderry is to make shirts, collars, and cuffs, which are shipped to Australia, South Africa, India, and other British colonies. There are several large factories, which employ about 2,000 men to do the heavy work and 20,000 women, who do the stitching and laundering by old-fashioned methods. An American buyer I met in Belfast the other day spoke rather contemptuously of the Londonderry shirt factories, which he declared, "are not in it for a minute" with those of the United States. He insists that a single shirt factory in Troy makes more shirts and collars than all the factories in Londonderry combined, and that by their modern machinery and processes the Troy factories can make and finish half-a-dozen shirts while they are making one here.'

25 AUGUST 1947

The tragic story of the deaths of two Derry lads who lost their lives while bathing at Downhill on the afternoon of Sunday, 24 August 1947, was related to an inquest in Castlerock the following day when the jury returned a verdict of accidental death from drowning. The deceased were Leonard Simpson, a sixteen-year-old apprentice electrician from Ashcroft Place, Waterside, and twenty-year-old John Taylor, a bakery employee from Fountain Hill, also in the Waterside.

Sixteen-year-old Myra Dinsmore said that she and Simpson, her boyfriend, were staying with her aunt, Mrs Lyttle, at Downhill. They met John Taylor, a good friend of Simpson's, at Downhill station on Sunday afternoon, and the two males bathed from the strand at a point about a quarter of a mile towards Magilligan. After playing about the beach for some time they again entered the water at the same place at 4.30 to wash the sand off themselves. Dinsmore waited for them at the edge of the water, guarding their clothes and towels, and watching them jump the waves and play with a ball; she did not believe them to be out of their depth. Suddenly, Taylor and Simpson disappeared from view, and suspecting that there was something wrong, Dinsmore ran first to the railway embankment to see better, then to her aunt's house. She didn't witness any struggle in the water or hear any call for help, and thought at first that the two were playing a trick on her by keeping out of sight. She could not say if they had disappeared together, but stated they were only in the water up to their waists.

J. Millen, a juror, observed: 'It was evident that no alarm was given, or other bathers in the vicinity would have heard it.' And District Inspector Kerr added: 'At first Miss Dinsmore did not realise what had happened. She thought that while she was not looking they might have left the water and hidden in the sandhills.' A Constable Loughrey said that Taylor's body was washed ashore at 8 p.m., with Simpson's remains coming ashore at the same spot thirty minutes later. The tide was beginning to come in at that time. Kerr had inspected the beach and found it quite flat and free from holes. Other bathers, he remarked, had made no complaint of an undercurrent or the state of the beach.

26 AUGUST 1909

Life in Derry was essentially quiet in the early years of the last century except during the summer marching season that reached a climax on 12 August each year as the Apprentice Boys celebrated the anniversary of the ending of the Great Siege of 1689. At this time some normally law-abiding citizens, spurred on by the atavistic emotion that replaces history in most Irish people, could tend towards violence. As in July in East Ulster, some overly enthusiastic participants have found themselves in court, 'up before the beak', as their Cockney brothers might put it.

On 26 August 1909, James Quigley of Fahan Street was charged with 'assaulting an unknown visitor on the occasion of the Orange demonstration in Derry on the 12th inst', as the *Derry Journal* reporter put it in the following day's edition. It was not strictly an 'Orange' demonstration, rather the local 'Derry Crimson' affair, but the leading nationalist paper had no time for such niceties.

One of the 'excursionists' had wandered into Rossville Street, a nationalist area, and soon realising he was not welcome, asked Constable Coleman, one of the RIC officers on duty, for directions. As Coleman later stated in court, he decided to accompany him to Strand Road and they were subject on that short journey to shouting and booing from a crowd of children. At this point Mr Tracy, Quigley's counsel, objected on the grounds of relevance. He repeated his objection, even when admonished by William Austin, the presiding magistrate. Coleman continued with his evidence: a crowd collected, Quigley ran forward from it and assaulted the man accompanying Coleman with his closed fist 'and staggered him to the ground'. Coleman had to force the man into a house in Rossville Street for safety.

Tracy in rebuttal told a different tale. The unknown man—his name was never given—had, according to the defence, cursed the pope, and though Coleman had not heard him utter the incendiary words, he could not deny that he might have said them before he arrived on the scene. Mr X was clearly drunk, said Tracy, and in his confused state had wandered about the Derry streets, provoking 'hostility by cursing the pope and other aggravating epithets'. Tracy and Austin themselves showed great mutual hostility and, in one instance, when told to sit down and hold his tongue, Tracy refused the bench's order.

Fined 10s 6d and costs Quigley was granted, on Tracy's insistence, three days to pay the amount.

27 AUGUST 1973

On 18 December 1825 a meeting of the Apprentice Boys and other citizens was held for the purpose of commencing subscriptions towards the erection of a monument to George Walker, joint Governor of Derry, during the Siege of 1689. Just over four months later, on 24 April 1826, another meeting was held at which it was resolved 'that the ancient cannon should be provided with carriages and placed on the Royal Bastion, which should be enclosed with a handsome stone work and iron palisades and that a testimonial should be erected in its centre, whereon the city flags should be hoisted on each anniversaries of the Shutting of the Gates and the Relief of Derry'.

The first stone was laid on 7 December 1826 by the Mayor of Londonderry, Major Richard Young, and was completed in 1828. The entire expenses were £4,200, which included £100 for the statue. The column was of Portland stone and the diameter was 6 feet and 9 inches, while the height was eighty-one feet, of which the pedestal measured fifteen, including the steps. It was ascended by a spiral staircase of 110 steps, which measured 3 feet 5 inches in diameter. The statue itself was nine feet high.

The inscriptions, in marble tablets, on the four sides of the base, as well as including the names of the siege heroes, also included the following inscription: 'This monument was erected to perpetuate the memory of Rev. George Walker who, aided by the garrison and brave inhabitants of this city, most gallantly defended through a protracted siege, from the 7th December 1688 to the 1st August following, against an arbitrary and bigoted monarch, heading an army of upwards of 20,000 men, many of whom were foreign mercenaries, and by such valiant conduct in numerous sorties and by patiently enduring extreme privations and sufferings, successfully resisted the besiegers and preserved for their posterity the blessings of civil and religious liberty.'

The governor's likeness was procured from an old painting. He was represented in the clerical costume of the day, and in his right hand he held a Bible while his left, pointing towards the spot where the boom was laid, indicated the approach of the vessels sent for the relief of the city.

On 11 August 1828 the statue was elevated to its station and, on the following day, which was the anniversary of the opening of the gates, the procession halted at the testimonial, when the crimson flag of the city was hoisted on a staff beside the statue amid the discharge of twenty-three field pieces. Just over 145 years later, a bomb detonated just a few minutes after midnight on 27 August 1973, destroyed the monument. The explosion, which was heard over a wide area of the city, ripped the pillar from its base and left only a nine-foot stump standing.

28 AUGUST 1951

It was said of the short story writer 'O. Henry' (William Sydney Porter) that he got most of his stories while working as a reporter at the night courts in New York. Derry might not have been so rich a source but reports of children's courts make clear that some criminal careers start early. At the special juvenile court held in Derry on 28 August 1951 there were eight young people, ranging in age from nine years to sixteen-and-a-half. No names were given but the legal procedures were identical to those of an adult court.

The first case concerned a twelve-year-old boy who had broken into the house of Lieutenant Commander R. Mitchell of Clooney Park West and stolen a ladies wristlet watch valued at £10 3s 6d and playing cards that cost 12s. He was fined 10s and a further £1 for the earlier offence of stealing a rug from Mrs Mitchell. He was placed under the care of the Probation Officer for twelve months, who was also required to take under his probationary wing two boys aged ten-and-a-half and twelve who removed a wire guard from the window of Patrick Gallagher's house at Foyle Hill, Lone Moor Road, and stole one tin of condensed milk, six boxes of matches, eight sheets of personal points (wartime rationing was still in force), one toy motor car, part of a toy doll and a tennis ball, the lot valued at around £1 5s.

A fifteen-year-old boy had stolen an envelope containing £15 belonging to Mary Ferry of Dunlewey in County Donegal. He claimed he had found it and went to Buncrana where he spent all but 4s 6d of the money. He was sent to an industrial school. The Probation Act was not applied in his case; he may already have had a criminal record. The only females before the court were in their mid-teens and pleaded guilty to stealing a coat worth £6 from the cloakroom of a local (unnamed) dancehall. The older girl put on the coat and both walked away, later pawning it for ten shillings, which was the amount that each was fined, the catwalk model placed in probationary care.

Ten shillings was also the fine imposed on a nine-year-old who had stolen sweets from a younger boy—or rather he recovered his own sweets that he had exchanged for some marbles. He decided it had been a 'bad swap' and having thrown away the marbles chased after the boy to reclaim the sweets. The row that followed caught the attention of a policeman on his beat and both were taken to the barracks, no doubt to the extreme pleasure of the desk sergeant. Finally, a thirteen-year-old who had stolen three cabbages from a garden was also released on probation.

29 AUGUST 1838

On 29 August 1838 Dr Peter McLaughlin, Bishop of Derry from 1824, laid the foundation stone of St Columb's Church on the site in Chapel Road that he had obtained from the local MP and Master of the Rolls, Sir Robert Alexander Ferguson, who had represented the city at that point for twenty-nine years. The Waterside parish priest was known as Archdeacon McCarron, even though the Cathedral chapter had become obsolete many years before. There were reckoned to be 105 Catholic dwellings in the city part of Glendermott parish, which had a total population of 666. Religious services were held in the coach house of a Dr White but, with a site available, it was appropriate to begin building Derry's second post-Reformation church.

Dr McLaughlin, who was born in Donaghmore, Castlefin, had also been Bishop of Raphoe (1802–19), and was noted for his physical strength and energy. He attended the Irish College in Paris and bore witness to the storming of the Bastille in that city on 14 July 1789, the first event in the French Revolution, and helped defend the small college from the mob. The city had one other church, St Columba's, Long Tower, completed in 1786. Dr McLaughlin had two ambitions: to provide what was then judiciously called a 'chapel' for his flock in Glendermott parish, and the more remote possibility of achieving a cathedral for the diocese, to be built on the west bank of the Foyle.

In fact both projects came to splendid fruition but the bishop did not live to see either wish fulfilled. He died on 18 August 1840 but had already set in motion the systems that would eventually realise his ecclesiastical ambitions. The bishop had had every right to hope that he might live to bless the finished church but there were difficulties. Whether he clashed with the contractor or whether the contractor, accused by local historians of being 'churlish', was the uncooperative party, it is no longer possible to determine but the building was not ready for use until 1841, at a cost of more than £2,000. A local critic may or may not have pleased J.J. McCarthy, the architect, when he wrote: 'The edifice is a plain rectangular building, which, if it does not possess very comfortable accommodation within, has some claim to a few neat architectural features without.'

That same autumn, shortly after the placing of the first stone, Dr McLaughlin summoned the preliminary meeting that would result eventually in a cathedral for Derry, though it would be thirteen years before the first sod was cut, on 26 July 1851, by Bishop Francis Kelly. It was left to John McLaughlin, who succeeded his uncle as bishop, to bless St Columb's at its official opening.

30 AUGUST 1916

Second Lieutenant Eric Erichsen Craig, Royal Irish Rifles, was killed in action on 30 August 1916. He was the fourth son of Dr James and Matilda (Tillie) Spence Craig of 2 Carlisle Terrace, Derry. His remains are interred in St Quentin Cabaret Military Cemetery, Heuvelland, Belgium, and his name is commemorated on Derry's Diamond War Memorial.

Lieutenant Craig was educated at Foyle College and Queen's University, Belfast, where he was a medical student when the Great War broke out. He joined the Officers' Training Corps and in December 1915 received his commission in the Royal Irish Rifles. He went out to France on 18 July 1916. An officer in the Rifles, writing to his father, stated that Craig was killed instantaneously by a German trench mortar. At that time, Eric Craig's brother, Lieutenant F.W. Craig, medical superintendent officer of health for Londonderry, was at the Front with the Royal Army Medical Corps, while another brother, Lieutenant Alexander Craig, RAMC, had served for a year on the Western Front.

His father died at his residence on 15 May 1923, at the age of sixty-two. His funeral to the City Cemetery took place two days later. Many people lined the funeral route: Carlisle Square, Carlisle Bridge, Abercorn Road, and Carlisle Road were crowded with sorrowing mourners, while a long line formed up between John Street and Abercorn Road. Prior to the removal of the remains a short service was conducted at the house by the Reverend R. Craig from Ballymena and the Reverend David Hay, minister of Carlisle Road Presbyterian Church, of which Dr Craig was a member. When the coffin, which was of panelled oak with massive brass mountings, was removed to the hearse the members of the Session and Committee of Carlisle Road Presbyterian Church formed up in line behind the chief mourners. These included Dr Craig's four sons: Dr Alexander Nelson Craig, Dr Fred William Craig, Matthew Nelson

Craig, and James Craig; and two brothers, Dr Frederick A. Craig and David Craig. All along the way to the cemetery groups of people assembled to view the solemn cortege, which was fully three quarters of a mile in length, a large number of vehicles bringing up the rear. One of the most outstanding features of the funeral was the immense wealth of wreaths and floral tributes. They numbered almost one hundred and were rich in colour and design.

Speaking at the graveside, the Reverend Mr Hay said: 'Few of us have ever seen so large a funeral because few of us have ever known so good a man. Truly it could be said of him as it was said of his Master, "He came not to be ministered unto but to minister." Like his Master, his activities were not confined to any particular class or creed. His sympathies did not run in any narrow sectarian channel but were at the disposal of all in need.'

31 AUGUST 1849

The nineteenth-century essayist and historian, Thomas Babington Macaulay, was born in 1800 in Rothley Temple, Leicestershire, England. He was educated privately and at Cambridge. At the age of twenty-six he was called to the bar, but had no fondness for this profession, and turned his attention to literature. He also became a Member of Parliament in 1830. After a spell in Bengal, he became secretary of war, and penned the extremely popular *Lays of Ancient Rome*. His major work, the *History of England from the Accession of James II*, was published between 1848 and 1861, the fifth volume unfinished.

Researching his *History of England* brought Macaulay to Derry in 1849, where he spent two days. He recorded his impressions of the city, extracts of which were published by his nephew, George Otto Trevelyan, in his *Life and Letters of Lord Macaulay*, which was published in two volumes in 1876:

> *August 31, 1849.* I left a card for Captain Leach, of the Ordnance Survey, and then wandered round the walls, and saw the Cathedral. It has been spoiled by architects who tried to imitate the Gothic style without knowing what they were about. The choir, however, is neat and interesting. Leach came, a sensible amiable young officer, as far as I could judge. I went again round the walls with him. The circuit is a short one. It may be performed, I should say, in twenty minutes. Then we got into a car, crossed the wooden bridge, and took a view of the city from the opposite bank of the river. Walker's pillar is well placed, and is not contemptible. The honest divine, in his canonicals, is at the top, and makes a tolerable figure at some distance. Then we crossed again, and drove to Boom Hall, so called from the memorable boom. The mistress of the house, a very civil lady, came out and

acted as cicerone. We walked down to the very spot where the boom was fastened. It was secured by a chain which passed through the earth of the bank, and was attached to a huge stone...

On the second day of his stay, Macaulay noted:

Saturday, September 1. As soon as I had breakfasted, Sir R. Ferguson came, and walked round the walls with me. Then he took me to the reading room, where I met Mr Leach, and a Mr Gilmour, a great man here. They walked with me round the walls, which I have thus gone over four times. The bastions are planted as gardens. The old pieces of ordnance lie among the flowers and shrubs: strange antique guns of the time of Elizabeth and Charles the First: Roaring Meg, a present of the Fishmongers, with the date of 1642: another piece of the same date given by the Vintners; and another by the Merchant Tailors. The citizens are to the last degree jealous as to the integrity of these walls. No improvement which would deface them would be proposed without raising a storm...

SEPTEMBER

1 (?) SEPTEMBER 1617

By the time Elizabeth I had been queen for twelve years it was clear that two parts of the world were ripe for colonisation: Virginia (called after her) and Ireland, equally full of potential and equally dangerous because of their endemic warlike natives. The queen, more intellectual than most on the English throne, had certain governing characteristics: a strong will, a sense of legality, and a hatred of waste. She had great respect for learning and knew how important it was that the children of her colonists should have the same educational opportunities as their cousins at home. For this purpose she caused to be passed in the Dublin parliament a series of measures, an important one of which required the establishment of 'a free school in every diocese of Ireland... the schoolmaster shall be an Englishman of English birth of this realm'. The act had no practical application outside of the Pale, the 'loyal' part of the country, then consisting of lands fifty miles north and thirty miles west of Dublin.

In 1608, as part of the Plantation of Ulster, James I, her successor, ordered: 'There shall be one Free School, at least, appointed in Every County for the education of Youth and learning and religion.' Royal schools were established in the counties of Cavan, Armagh, Tyrone, Donegal and Fermanagh. The new 'Londonderry', essentially owned by the London guilds, was initially intended to be included but somehow never received the royal charter. The county did get its 'Free School' but it was built in 1617 by a philanthropic individual: Matthias Springham, 'Master of the Guild of Merchant Taylors', at his own expense. Alone among the established schools of the Plantation it had no royal charter and survived thereafter with no endowments apart from the '20 Markes stipend yearly' donated by the Honourable the Irish Society, which had been established by the guilds.

The building, 67 feet long and 25 feet broad, was a storey and a half in height. On the ground floor were a schoolroom, hall and parlour, and in the dormer were the sleeping quarters for the master, the usher and the boarders. On a stone above the door was inscribed:

> Mathias Springham, AR
> Ad honorem Dei et bonarum
> Literarum propagationem.
> Hanc scholam fundavit
> Anno salutis MDCXVII

which translated as 'Mathias Springham Ar(miger) [Esquire] founded this school to the honour of God and the for the purpose of the dissemination of the classics in the year of salvation: 1617.'

It was built close to the Augustinian church in what is now called in tribute Society Street. During the Siege the scholars were sent home and the building was used as a mill to grind corn to alleviate the hunger of the besieged. It was badly damaged by Jacobite cannonballs and had to be completely rebuilt after the relief of the city. The date of its opening is not recorded; the suggested date follows the practice of English schools.

2 SEPTEMBER 1955

On Wednesday, 31 August 1955 a little girl ran out from a group of her friends at Laburnum Terrace and was hit by a city bus travelling on the Lone Moor route towards Stanley's Walk. The inquest was held two days later by the city coroner Cecil Milligan. The girl was Kathleen O'Donnell from 37 Melmore Gardens, and her age was given as six. Patrick Maxwell appeared on behalf of the parents, Head Constable Finn represented the RUC, and M.C. Feeny and Son, the Ulster Transport Authority (UTA), the body responsible for all public transport systems in Northern Ireland.

After the jury had been sworn a number of witnesses were called. Patricia McGuinness from nearby West End Park stated that at around 3.35 p.m., she noticed a number of children walking towards Stanley's Walk. A girl ran out from the group into the path of the bus that swerved unsuccessfully to avoid her. McGuinness ran across the street to find the child's body lying face down in the roadway. Ernest Fleming, the conductor of the bus, said that the vehicle was going at about twenty miles per hour; the bus was empty and he was too busy with his report to notice what was happening, but became suddenly aware that something was wrong when he heard a scream and felt the shock of the emergency stop.

One of the witnesses called was a nine-year-old schoolgirl, Kathleen McCay, who stated that there were 'two big girls and two wee girls walking on the footpath. One of the wee girls ran out in front of the bus that turned its wheels and went on to the footpath.' William Bond, the driver, gave the same estimate of speed as the conductor and said little Kathleen was about five or six yards from the bus when she ran out. Constable Shaw from the motoring division testified that the brakes were in good condition and his colleague, Constable Hartop, who had been on duty at Laburnum Terrace, described how, on hearing the hysterical scream of children and the noise of braking, he ran to the scene to find Kathleen under the vehicle. He told the conductor to phone for an ambulance as he extricated the body: 'The child gave a little moan and appeared to die almost immediately.' This corroborated the evidence of Dr Kevin Breslin, who said that death had been instantaneous.

When the little girl's father had given evidence of identification Milligan asked the jury for their verdict and concurred when they found that death was due to multiple injuries and added a rider exonerating the driver from blame. He, the jury foreman and Head Constable Finn used the opportunity to express sympathy with the O'Donnell parents and with the driver. Patrick Maxwell thanked on behalf of the parents all those who had done everything they could in a sad occurrence.

3 SEPTEMBER 1782

The *London-Derry Journal* in its edition of 3 September 1782 reported that on the previous Saturday 'the Rev. Dr McDavitt, the Roman Catholic Bishop of the diocese of Derry, appeared before the Honourable Mr Justice Lill in open court and took and subscribed the Oath of Allegiance as prescribed by the late Act of Parliament for that purpose'.

Dr Philip McDevitt was born at Crislagh in 1724, near Burnfoot, County Donegal, and was ordained priest in Paris in 1752, after study in the Irish College there. He graduated Doctor of Divinity from the Sorbonne and ministered in his native diocese from about the early 1760s as a peripatetic priest with a base at Ballybrack, just outside Moville.

The Carey family who owned much of the land in that part of Inishowen made it practically impossible for him to carry on his pastoral work there and he found it advisable to move to Clady, on the banks of the river Finn between Tyrone and Donegal. Conscious of the need for more diocesan priests and with the hope of an educated laity he established a small seminary there. Appointed bishop on 14 January 1766 he was the first as such to take up residence in Derry City for more than 150 years—since the murder of Réamonn Ó Gallachair in 1601. This initiative he postponed until 1780, by which time the more extreme of the Popery Acts of Queen Anne had been repealed. During his episcopacy at least eighteen churches were built in places as far apart as Garvagh, Kilrea, Buncrana, Limavady and Omagh.

Making it his mission to build up the strength of the Church after the long century of submerged practice, McDevitt was prepared to acquiesce in the conditions of the oath. He was sternly against the rising spirit of radicalism and frequently admonished his flock 'never to forget the many obligations you are under to your Protestant brethren, who have generously stood forward as your advocates and protectors'. He remained as firmly against the revolutionary doctrines coming later out of Paris as John Troy, the Archbishop of Dublin, who dubbed such ideas as the 'French Disease'. Derry, at the time of his residence, had very few Catholics not regarded as a political threat. Most were poor and illiterate but McDevitt persevered in attempting to restore the city to its former ecclesiastical supremacy.

One of the eight other priests named in the newspaper story was John Lynch, who had been born c.1750 at Balteagh, near Limavady. He had been given the unenviable task of tending to Derry's small Catholic flock without even a church in which to hold services. A reliable tradition records that Mass was offered under a hawthorn tree outside the city walls to the north 'from 1595 to 1784' when Lynch succeeded in having a partial edifice built. He did not live long enough to see the intended quite finished but his Requiem Mass on 24 December 1786 was offered in a substantial building already known as the Long Tower church, the city's first in post-Penal times. By 1797, when Bishop McDevitt died, the church was the centre of a vigorous and growing parish.

Upwards of 20,000 people—including almost 5,000 who travelled in special buses from Belfast and district—met on Craigavon Bridge in Derry on Saturday, 4 September 1976, and recited the Declaration of the Peace People, which began: 'We have a simple message for the world from this movement of peace. We want to live and love and build a just and peaceful society...' The movement had been launched the previous month in Belfast after three children had been hit and killed by a car careering out of control, the IRA driver having been shot dead at the wheel by the army.

Men were well outnumbered in the huge crowds, which converged from both the city side and the Waterside ends of the bridge. The attendance was representative of nearly all shades of opinion, and religious and political outlook. There were tears of emotion in many eyes as women from Protestant and Catholic areas in Londonderry and Belfast met on the bridge. When the founders of the peace movement in Belfast, Mrs Betty Williams and Miss Mairead Corrigan, and the Derry organisers, Mrs Margaret Doherty and Mrs Joyce Kelly, addressed the huge crowd, they referred to the 'people of Derry—and Londonderry'.

During the rally eighteen-year-old Fiona Molloy sang 'Peace', a song composed by an SDLP member of Londonderry City Council, Mr Daniel Feeney, and Mr James O'Hagan. In addition to reciting the Declaration, the crowd joined in singing 'The Lord Is My Shepherd', 'When Irish Eyes Are Smiling' and 'Danny Boy', and in repeating the Lord's Prayer. Betty Williams was warmly applauded when she told the huge crowd: 'We are going to work very hard to get this peace movement going, but, when I see so many people standing here on this bridge, there is no reason why we cannot stop violence.' With tears in her eyes, she added: 'It is like a dream come true to be at such a rally.' At the conclusion of the rally Mrs Williams said: 'Our message for the peace people is come together on this bridge, get to know each other, and seek to see the other person's point of view.'

Mairead Corrigan said her happiness at addressing such a large crowd was tinged with sorrow: 'For so long I stood back and watched so many fine men and women die on the streets and did nothing about it. I am sad because I stood back and condemned people whose motives and reasons I did not understand.'

The Anglican Bishop of Derry and Raphoe, the Right Reverend Dr Robert Eames, who was unable to be present at the rally, but was represented, had earlier pledged his full support for the demonstration. The Catholic Bishop of Derry, Most Reverend Dr Edward Daly, did attend and chatted with people at Wapping Lane, an entrance to the predominantly Protestant Fountain.

The *Londonderry Sentinel* for 5 September 1925 carried a rather sad tale of marital incompatibility and the demon drink. At the Petty Sessions court on Friday, 4 September, John Canney, of no fixed abode, was summoned for neglecting his children. The case had been brought by the National Society for the Prevention of Cruelty to Children (NSPCC) and their case was made by Captain Julian Miller of the law firm, Miller and Babington. Inspector Bell of the NSPCC stated that, on 8 May, Canney had given him six shillings to pass on to his wife, part of the twenty-four shillings weekly he was drawing as unemployment benefit. A week later, having received £1 from the Labour Exchange, he disappeared leaving nothing for his wife and family. She had to go to her mother's house with her four children, aged three to fourteen.

Mrs Canney confirmed that she had been married for fifteen years and, since she had last received money in May, she was dependent upon her mother. She had been laid low with pneumonia for five weeks and 'had it not been for her mother's care she would have died and her children would have starved'. When H.W. Porter, the chairman of the magistrates' bench, asked, 'Was he good to the children when he was at home?', Mrs Canney replied, 'I cannot complain that he was bad to the children'; nor, she admitted, was he abusive to her.

Canney then spoke, asking his wife to tell the court whether it was not a fact that between ten and eleven o'clock he had come to her mother's house to give her money, and her mother had put him out on the street. 'Yes,' she replied, 'for being drunk!' Canney insisted that he had left quietly but his wife claimed that he had given her mother a lot of abuse, and was also under the influence of methylated spirits. The bench asked for an 'anything known' report on the defendant and Sergeant McCartney of the RUC said that a similar case brought against Canney previously had been withdrawn. Miller added that, on the occasion referred to, the case had been adjourned because the defendant's conduct had been improving.

This revelation did not soften the magistrates' attitude. The sentence of three months with hard labour seems disproportionate. In those years, before the establishment of the Welfare State, magistrates were unlikely to ask for a psychologist's profile. It was a case of a 'meth-drinking ne'er-do-well' who let his children starve. So, in spite of evident alcohol addiction, Canney was given an exemplary sentence.

Jimmy O'Dea was the finest Irish comedian-actor of the twentieth century. He started as an amateur actor specialising in Ibsen and Chekhov until he met writer Harry O'Donovan in the early 1920s; their creative partnership was to provide top quality entertainment in the form of Christmas pantomimes and summer shows which had Dublin audiences rolling in the aisles between 1924 and '65.

O'Dea often took to the stage in drag: sometimes he was a sharp if slightly bewildered Dublin housewife trying to buy herrings, or tangling with authority while trying to elude the Customs and Excise officers as she crossed the border into Northern Ireland; but it was as the widowed Biddy Mulligan, the 'Pride of the Coombe', that O'Dea really made his name. He was a brilliant actor with precise timing and a striking pair of dark eyes, with a tenor voice that rarely lost its innate refinement. Though he played people whose 'palace consists of one room' he was not from working-class Dublin. Known as 'Mr O'Dea' to the company or 'Guv'nor' to the stars, he could be a martinet backstage.

His first visit to Derry was on Monday, 6 September 1932, when the variety programme *Laugh Now* opened in St Columb's Hall. One Derry critic reacting to the show's title observed that it made some people 'be disposed otherwise but long before the end of the show even the most staid had found irresistible the sparkling witticisms and humour that adorned the programme in profusion'. One of the most successful sketches was about the misery of facing two sets of customs officers at the border, which displayed O'Donovan's adeptness at comedy that, however sharply topical, was not vicious. Also on the programme were Noel Purcell who would afterwards find fame as a rival pantomime dame (grotesque as only a man of 6ft 4in in skirts could be) and a distinguished film actor, and Eileen Marmion, a petite fifteen-year-old star who sang, danced and acted in sketches. Noel and Eileen married nine years later; as Purcell put it: 'She waited for me to grow up!'

As well as more than a hundred O'Dea-O'Donovan productions, O'Dea made three silent films, went on to do two Ealing Studio comedies in 1938–9, and was memorable as the engine-driver in *One Minute Way* (1957) and as the King of the Fairies in *Darby O'Gill and the Little People* (1959). In later years his comic foil was Maureen Potter, like himself a brilliant actor rather than a joke-teller, who carried on the tradition after his death. Her impersonations of such worthies as Ian Paisley were nearly as funny as O'Dea's Queen Victoria or the ineffable Biddy Mulligan.

The Apprentice Boys' parade on 12 August 1936 had passed off almost without incident. On 7 September that year, however, two men—Maurice Reid of 9 Victoria Road and Stanley Cinnamond of 36 Carlisle Road—appeared before P.S. Bell, the Derry RM, charged with throwing fireworks and causing damage to the clothing of a woman walking along Carlisle Road. May Warden and her friend Sadie Millar were passing an ice cream restaurant on the day of the parade when a squib coming from the window of the shop landed on her coat, burning it. When she complained to Constable Gillanders, indicating Reid as the culprit, he denied it; she admitted that she had not seen him throw the rocket, but had seen him in the window when it was thrown.

When asked to reveal the contents of their pockets Reid and Cinnamond both had squibs, and Cinnamond pleaded guilty to throwing squibs. One of them had burned a hole as big as a person's hand in Warden's coat, damaging the dress underneath. Also present in the restaurant was David Walker from the Waterside, who took no part in the episode and had no fireworks in his possession, but who insisted that squibs were being let off all over the street. One of the magistrates, Mr Lynn, asked if the visitors' trains had not all left by then and Walker, who seemed to have side-lined T.C. Wylie as the defendants' counsel, said the fun was only just starting. When asked how he thought the girls must have felt, he answered that rockets were always thrown on Twelfth nights.

May Warden claimed that the coat had cost £1 17s 6d and that the frock was ruined. Bell, the chairman of the bench, said it was fortunate that the girl had not lost an eye, reminded the pair that there was no licence for discharging fireworks in the streets on the 12th of August or any other night, and adjourned the case until the defendants paid each 12s 6d to May Warden. When Wylie said that Reid was innocent, H.E. Scott of the Crown Prosecution Service replied, 'The court says otherwise.' Bell's reaction, though perfectly proper, displayed a hint of 'Apprentice Boys will be boys' in his demeanour: 'I am trying to do rough justice here. Technically Reid is entitled to a dismissal. If the two of them get their heads together there will be nothing more about the case. The police have enough trouble without this.'

Later in the morning Wylie returned with the money and Bell discharged the defendants without proceeding to a conviction. It really had been a quiet Twelfth.

On Tuesday, 8 September 1908, Derry and its surrounding district were hit by a heavy flood which continued for more than one hour. While it lasted traffic was almost entirely suspended and the city was virtually under water. Large areas became impassable due to flooding and the *Londonderry Sentinel* reported two days later that Derry had looked more like Venice.

The worst disaster of the day was the destruction of the upper reservoir at Creggan. The reservoir, capable of holding twenty million gallons of water, was the oldest in the city side of the Foyle. Before its construction in 1851 by Richard Hassard, the city had been supplied from the old reservoir at Waterside. When the rain began falling that Tuesday morning the caretaker at Creggan, seeing that the by-wash was not sufficient to vent the quantity rushing down from the high ground, telephoned Mr Findlay, the water superintendent, to inform him he feared there would be a disaster.

Mr Findlay hurried up to witness a remarkable spectacle. The torrent dashing down from the mountain had just succeeded in bursting through the bank separating the upper from the middle (or main) reservoir. The bank was 25 feet high. Once an inroad was made in it the whole of the enormous mass of earth and stone gave way, and was washed into the reservoir below; a 25-foot gap was formed in the bank, through which the contents of the reservoir dashed with a roar, sending showers of spray high into the air.

For a time it seemed doubtful whether the bank of the middle basin would be strong enough to stand the strain. Luckily, the rain did not lead to a storm, and the chief storage source of the city escaped in consequence. Also the Corporation had strengthened and raised the bank the previous year, a move which had almost certainly prevented matters from being worse. When the last readings at Creggan had been taken the week before, the upper basin contained ten million gallons, the middle basin seventy-two million gallons, and the lower basin twenty million gallons.

The *Sentinel* stated that, by Tuesday afternoon, five hours after the rainstorm, a torrent was finding its way into the bed of the emptied basin. Additionally, there was a heavy flow down a by-wash alongside. This was carefully conducted past the middle reservoir and down into the lower basin, which at this time was not a quarter full. Over the sill of the overflow from the middle basin water was rushing in a 'miniature Niagara'; the water in both middle and lower basins was greatly discoloured, and the newspaper speculated that the work of rebuilding the embankment would be very costly.

9 SEPTEMBER 1916

Private Edward Friel, 6th Battalion Royal Irish Regiment, was killed in action at Ginchy, seven miles east of Albert and two miles northwest of Combles, France, on Saturday, 9 September 1916. The forty-year-old's name is recorded on the Thiepval Memorial to the Missing, Somme, France, and is also commemorated on Derry's Diamond War Memorial.

Friel was by trade a compositor and had served his apprenticeship at the *Derry Journal*, where he later found employment before enlisting. Friel, whose brother John had fought with the Grenadier Guards in the Boer War, left behind a wife and three children to mourn his loss.

Ginchy was one of the strongest defended of all the fortified villages on the German line, positioned as it was on high ground. On 9 September it was stormed with such zeal that neither the intense German artillery barrage nor machine gun fire, while inflicting dreadful casualties, could hold up the assault. Indeed, some of the attacking troops had to be restrained from pursuing the fleeing enemy, so that they could dig in and consolidate the gain.

Shortly after Friel's death, his wife received a letter from John Hasty, who had served with her husband, in which he wrote: 'I knew your husband very well. I was constantly in his company when he was in Fermoy, Kilworth and Blackdown, and also out here in France. You need have no fear for his spiritual welfare, as he was a very devoted Catholic, and never neglected his duty. It may be some little consolation to you to know that he is greatly regretted by all the officers and men of the battalion.'

Then, on Tuesday, 19 September, a letter arrived from Friel to his father in which Edward vividly related how the Irish Brigade gallantly captured Guillemont, a village situated five miles east of Albert, on 3 September: 'Each company had two pipers playing behind them as they advanced. They played "A Nation Once Again", "'98", and several other tunes... We captured 800 prisoners and a lot of machine guns. Our victory was great, and we have won a name for ourselves, but I see by the papers that they are classifying us as British troops, not Irish, but the truth will soon come out, and then it will be—All hail to the Irish.'

10 SEPTEMBER 1899

On Monday, 11 September 1899, an inquest was held in the licensed premises of John Connor, Strand Road, concerning William McGonagle, Jnr., who had died the previous day at his father's house in Great James Street. The coroner Thomas Lindsay presided and a jury with chairman, Andrew McClintock, was sworn in. Sergeant Mills of the Royal Irish Constabulary attended on behalf of the Crown.

The boy's father, having given notice of identifying the body, said in evidence that he had last seen his son between nine and ten p.m. on Saturday, 9 September, but he had been away from home on the Sunday when the death took place. His son had complained about a cut on his head sustained when he had fallen from one of the vans at the Post Office, where he worked. He had taken a little drink but nothing significant.

Sarah Doherty, the deceased's sister, said her brother had come to the Great James Street house at about 11 a.m. on Sunday and said he was going to bed. About ten or fifteen minutes later she went upstairs to check on him and found him lying as if asleep. Twenty minutes later a noise brought her back up. She found William lying on the floor where he had fallen out of bed. This had happened to him in the past when he had drink taken, but he had been perfectly sober when he'd gone upstairs and had had no access to liquor since. She managed to help him back into bed; he recognised her and spoke her name but afterwards seemed to become very nervous and stretched out his arms to her. Some instinct led her to send for a priest though he did not complain of being sick.

Dr O'Kane arrived after the priest, and in his evidence, stated that he found William in bed; he breathed only once or twice in the doctor's presence before his breathing finally stopped. O'Kane found a small scalp wound on his back of his head; his pupils were widely dilated but there was no smell of alcohol. In his opinion the injury to the head had caused congestion of the brain but he could not be sure without an autopsy.

Hugh Hegarty, another witness, said that he had seen William fall in the Post Office yard. He had been attempting to climb up into the van and had put his hand on the rump of the horse to steady himself. The horse moved forward and he fell on his back, cracking his head on the ground.

In light of the medical evidence the jury decided that William had died from heart failure following an effusion of blood to the brain. The foreman joined with the coroner in offering condolences to the family.

Hugh Culling Eardley Childers was born in London, the son of the Reverend Eardley Childers. He received his early education at Cheam School and subsequently at Oxford and Cambridge. He then decided to seek a career in Australia and in October 1850 arrived in Melbourne along with his wife, Emily Walker. After seven years, Childers returned to Britain, entering Parliament in 1860 as the Liberal member for Pontefract, and serving in a minor capacity in the government of Lord Palmerston. With the election of Gladstone's government in December 1868, he rose to greater prominence, serving as First Lord of the Admiralty. He resigned through ill health in March 1871, but after spending some months on the continent, recovered sufficiently to take office in 1872 as Chancellor of the Duchy of Lancaster.

His cousin, the novelist and politician Erskine Childers, is much better known as an historical figure. Born in London in 1870 and raised in Ireland, he served in the British army during the Boer War and in 1903 published *The Riddle of the Sands*, a widely read thriller warning against a possible German invasion which influenced public attitudes towards naval re-armament. A convert to the struggle for Irish Home Rule, in 1914 he was involved in smuggling guns to the Irish Volunteers in his yacht *Asgard*. He served in the British forces in World War I, but after the failure of attempts at a settlement between Home Rulers and Unionists his opinions became more extreme, and during the Anglo-Irish War he played a leading part in Sinn Féin publicity and propaganda. Childers advised the delegation which negotiated the Anglo-Irish Treaty, but rejected the final document and became one of its most virulent opponents. Blamed by many Treaty supporters for the Irish Civil War of 1922–23, he was court-martialled and executed by the pro-Treaty Government.

Childers had not always been such a vigorous defender of Home Rule. In his college years he'd spoken vehemently against the policy, even though he greatly admired his cousin who was a member of Gladstone's Liberal Cabinet and an early advocate of Home Rule. When the Liberals regained power in 1880, Hugh Childers was appointed Secretary of War on 28 April. Less than five months later he entered on his governmental commission personally to visit the reported distressed districts in Donegal and adjacent counties. Accompanied by his second wife, Katherine Anne, and daughter, he travelled from England to Ireland via Stranraer, and arrived in Derry on the evening of Saturday, 11 September 1880. The distinguished party, who were received at the Northern Counties Railway station by a Royal Irish Constabulary guard of honour, drove to the Imperial Hotel.

The following day being Sunday, the Childers attended Divine service in St

Columb's Cathedral, and were afterwards entertained to lunch by the Anglican Lord Bishop. During their brief stay a visit was made to the walls and other places of historic interest in the city.

12 SEPTEMBER 1603

The Nine Years' War ended with the Treaty of Mellifont in March 1603 and the long-prepared plans for the 'civility' of Ulster were put unstoppably into effect. The 'planting' of the County Coleraine was handed by James I to the unwilling Livery Companies of the city of London as a patriotic duty and a profitable enterprise. James was aware of the strategic significance of 'Londonderry', as he would call it, placed nicely between the unruly O'Donnells, O'Dohertys and Ó Catháins, and a place he intended to develop both as a garrison and Ulster's chief city. His man in Derry was Sir Henry Docwra who had begun to fortify the city towards the end of the war with Hugh O'Neill, and who was now its virtual owner.

At the war's end many of James's troops were able to return home and Docwra was confirmed in his royal position as the ruler of the Maiden City. One of his protégés was the young O'Doherty chieftain, Cahir, Lord of Inishowen, who was one of the jurymen who condemned O'Neill. It was he who described the settlement: 'It lies in the form of a bow bent, whereof the bog is the string and the river the bow.' To show his royal appreciation, on 12 September 1603, James I granted to

Sir Henry Dowcra, Knt. Governor of Lough Foyle and Privy Councillor the right to hold two markets, on Wednesday and Saturday, and a fair for six days viz.—on Vigil, day and morrow of St Lawrence [9, 10 and 11 August] and for three days following, at Derrie every year with horse races, there to be held during the same markets and fairs, together with the issues, profits, emoluments, belonging and appertaining to the said markets and fairs: rent 2s 6d.

Ten months later, on 11 July 1604, Docwra's services were further awarded by the king, not entirely altruistically, with the presentation of a liberal charter for the incorporation of the city. It described the place in glowing terms:

The town or borough of Derrie is, by reason of the natural seat and situation thereof, a place very convenient to be made both a town of war and a town of merchandize, and so might many ways prove serviceable for the crown and profitable for the subject, if the same were not only walled, entrenched and

289

inhabited but also incorporated and endowed with convenient liberties, privileges and immunities.

The document goes on to praise the 'extraordinary valour and industry' of Docwra. So did the city of Londonderry come into existence, the capital prefix a gesture to the source of its investment. Docwra later published *A Narration of the Services... under the Leading of Me, Sir Henry Docwra, Knight*, in which he complained that he had been badly treated and unappreciated by the king. In 1606 he obtained permission to sell his property interests in the city he had virtually created to George Paulett, whose quarrelsome nature led to rebellion and the devastation of 'Londonderrie'.

13 SEPTEMBER 1948

The year 1948 was the 150th anniversary of the rising of 1798. The centenary in 1898 had produced a number of excellent ballads including 'Boolavogue', 'The Boys of Wexford', 'The Memory of the Dead' and 'The Croppy Boy'. Local tributes took the form of a *'98 Cantata* with text and lyrics by Thomas Mullan and music by local composer Edward Conaghan, and part of the 1948 celebration was a revival by local artistes of such local favourites as 'Tone Is Coming Back Again' and 'Bonfires on the Antrim Hills'. It was conveniently forgotten that in Ulster the rising was almost entirely Presbyterian in membership and that Derry and the northwest had played little or no part.

Since the insurrection had had four distinct outbreaks in different parts of the country, from May until August, a date of commemoration, 12 September, was finally agreed for the 150th anniversary celebrations. A rally was held in St Columb's Hall, and the *Derry Journal*, then as now the chief voice of nationalism in the northwest, gave blanket coverage to the event in its edition of Monday, 13 September 1948. The chief speaker was Senator Denis Ireland, the Belfast Protestant journalist who had deplored the severing of the six counties of Northern Ireland from the rest of the country. He noted that since permission to use the Ulster Hall for the Belfast celebration had been refused, they would meet that night on Cave Hill where Tone, McCracken, Neilson and Russell had taken their oath never to rest until Ireland was free from the British yoke. Later he observed that, in spite of world conditions then, the futile arguments of Stormont were exactly the same as they had been thirty or forty years before. More in hope than expectation he predicted that soon Emmet's epitaph might be written and that the doctrines of the man who had landed 150 years before on the shores of the Swilly would soon be justified for all time.

The rally had an extra edge, as the chairman, Dr Denis Kavanagh, a popular local GP, pointed out. The Taoiseach John Costello was about to declare a republic and 'in a very short time the last symbol of submission to the British Crown would be removed from three-fourths of their country'. Kavanagh added that the Irish would never be content until there was freedom for the whole country. The general euphoric tenor of the rally was maintained by Eddie McAteer, the local MP, when he said: 'In my belief we are on a rising tide of Nationalism at the present moment. The best tribute we can pay to the men of '98 is to copy their persistence, their courage and their teachings. Before freedom is attained we must weather the dark hour that comes before the dawn.' Finally the *Journal* reminded its readers that a special train would leave the Great Northern station for the final '98 ceremony in Belfast on Sunday, 20 September at 8.30 a.m.

14 SEPTEMBER 1951

On Wednesday, 12 September 1951, Andy Cole, a well-known Derry publican from Strand Road, and Patrick Kelly, a friend from nearby Barry Street, set sail from Derry Quay and headed roughly northeast for Greencastle, Inishowen Head and the open sea in a twenty-seven foot sailing boat without an engine. Their intention was to sail her round Inishowen to Buncrana where an engine was to be installed. In those days there was not the same preoccupation with safety devices such as flares, precise local weather forecasts and life-jackets as are required today. They were regarded as unnecessary, especially for a coast-hugging trip of less than eighty miles.

Once out in the Sea of Moyle, a notoriously choppy stretch of water, especially around the time of the autumn equinox, they ran into a strong souwester that made their progress west extremely difficult. By Thursday morning they had made it as far as Inishtrahull Sound, the band of water between the island of Inishtrahull that lay north and east of Malin Head, the most northerly point of the Irish mainland, and the outer bastion of Lough Swilly. They were being driven so far off course that they found it necessary to strike the mainsail and some of the rest of the canvas. In spite of this extreme measure the current drove them steadily to the northeast, eventually carrying them to the Inner Hebrides. Late on the Thursday evening they worked out that they had come into a stretch of water between two landmarks they identified as Rathlin Island to the south and the Rhinns of Islay north-north-west.

It was at this point that the boat began to ship water and they had to keep feverishly bailing to prevent their vessel from capsizing. They fell silent, saving all their energies for the labour of bailing, and then Cole saw smoke at the Mull of Kintyre, the tip of the long finger that ends only five miles from Fair Head in County Antrim. It came from the funnels of HMS *Pincher*, a minesweeper of the Royal Navy, on routine patrol. They got very excited when they realised that the ship was coming nearer. In spite of the wind and the water sloshing about their knees they managed to hoist sail, the better to be seen.

It was with great relief that, when the warship grew close, they were able to tie a tow on their boat and be slung on board. Cole's right foot was crushed as he landed on the *Pincher's* deck, and when the ship docked at Campbeltown on the Friday morning, 14 September 1951, he was taken to the Cottage Hospital to have his foot X-rayed. That night he was stated to be comfortable but was kept in for observation. By then he had come to terms with the fact that his boat had capsized soon after the *Pincher* moved off again. Kelly, though suffering a little from exposure, was able to start for home on the Saturday.

15 SEPTEMBER 1927

On Thursday, 15 September 1927, a fire occurred in the Butcher Street premises of Alexander Byrne, resulting in the elimination of almost two families and involving the loss of seven lives, including two babies. The oldest victim of the terrible tragedy was Mrs Annie Cowley, aged 38. Her children Edward (11), Veronica (7), James (4) and Isabella (12 months) also perished. Mrs Mary McCourt (19) and her infant child Lily (10 months) died too.

The two families lived in apartments on the third storey above the shop of Byrne's, a ladies' outfitters. Mrs Cowley's husband, Patrick, an ex-serviceman, was undergoing treatment in the Galwally Branch of the UVF Hospital in Belfast at the time of the tragedy. He'd had his leg amputated some time previously as a result of war wounds, and a week prior to the fire was ordered back to the institution to have removed some nerves that were troubling him. Naturally, the news of the tragedy came as a terrible shock to him. Mrs McCourt's husband, John, was out at the time of the fire, while Mr and Mrs Cowley's sole surviving child, nine-year-old Hannah, had been sent on an errand. Reverend Joseph Byrne, the son of the proprietor and a Catholic priest who was currently serving in a Scottish parish, but was home on holiday ill with tonsillitis, occupied a room over the other portion of the premises on the same floor as those who perished. He was rescued dressed only in his pyjamas and taken to the house of a Mr W.P. O'Doherty a few doors away.

The fire was discovered shortly after four o'clock. Captain Michael J. Baker, who had a cycle shop in Butcher Street, saw a girl gazing up at Byrne's premises, and attracted by this, went to where she was and saw the hall and staircase ablaze. He raised the alarm and, returning, saw a woman, believed to be Mrs Cowley, looking out of one of the top windows. He shouted to her to break the window, which she did, and told her she would have to jump. He went and fetched some blankets which he and several others held out for the building's occupants to jump into. Mrs Cowley was told to jump out, and someone also shouted to throw the babies out, but she disappeared. She was seen coming back with a baby in her arms and approaching the other window, but from the condition in which her body was afterwards found, it was surmised that she quickly suffocated.

The fire brigade, on getting the alarm, were unfortunately prevented from travelling directly to the scene, along Magazine Street or Ferryquay Street, due to these thoroughfares being impassable because of repair work being carried out.

16 SEPTEMBER 1961

'Hurricane Debbie', which claimed the lives of at least eleven people in Ireland, including five in Ulster, hit Derry on the afternoon of Saturday, 16 September 1961. It left in its wake serious material damage, a few nervous breakdowns and a large number of bodily injuries. Beginning approximately at one o'clock, the storm screeched mercilessly for four hours. Initially it was only a 'capful' of wind, but it quickly gained momentum and by two o'clock it was raging with hurricane force.

The precursor to 'Debbie' was a tropical wave that moved off the coast of Africa. It became 'Tropical Storm Debbie' on 6 September, but reached hurricane strength the following day. It moved north-westward, reaching a peak intensity of 120 miles per hour on 11 September, but a trough of low pressure pushed Debbie north-eastward towards unfavourable conditions. As she raced north-eastward, she maintained tropical characteristics until 16 September, when she became extra-tropical just southwest of Ireland.

There were regular lulls of short duration in the Derry storm, which proved deceptive. When they occurred it was optimistically thought that tranquillity had returned, but the wind was merely resting before gathering itself into another colossal mass, angrier than the last. Inexplicably, people who could well have afforded to stay indoors returned outside without any seeming regard for their safety. Men and women could be seen here and there rushing to a corner for shelter and being irresistibly propelled by the wind. Similarly, some pedestrians, caught off step in the full force of a blast, were observed gripping supports like house railings or telegraph poles until there was a brief decrease in the storm's strength.

Fortunately, in Derry at least, most of the reported injuries were relatively minor. Flying slates were the primary source of danger and in some parts they littered the footpaths and streets. Branches of trees and pieces of wood were also tossed about the thoroughfares, and showers of small stones and dust were driven before the gale. The entrance to St Columb's Park was almost completely blocked by fallen trees and branches. Brooke Park suffered less but was also storm-damaged. Clondermott Intermediate School, opened seven years previously, was seriously damaged and had one of its roofs hurled aggressively to the ground, while Templemore School had also been battered, bruised and partly unroofed.

The spray from the turbulent River Foyle rose in columns so high that at one stage it reached the parapet of Craigavon Bridge and passers-by felt it upon their faces. And so the mayhem continued until approximately five o'clock when the wind began abating.

17 SEPTEMBER 1900

On Tuesday, 18 September 1900, the crime reporter of the *Londonderry Sentinel* gave an account of the previous day's events at the petty sessions. On that Monday morning the magistrates' panel consisted of Messrs. McCay, Anderson, Doherty and McCartney, with Alderman Bell presiding, and the first item was a charge of vagrancy brought by Constable Mason against James Doherty, who had been found sleeping in the Ballantine's brickyard. Doherty claimed he did not know what he was doing as he was 'on the beer'. The constable had found him there after a complaint had been made. His accommodation problems were solved at least temporarily by the panel, who ordered him to be imprisoned for seven days.

Next up was Kate Nixon, also a vagrant and possessing a considerable ability in vituperation. Constable Quinlivan made three charges against her: vagrancy, assaulting him by striking him on the face, and using obscene and profane language. Because of her record of previous convictions she was sentenced to two-and-a-half months' imprisonment. It is not clear just what happened next; the *Sentinel* reporter merely said: 'After the decision of the Court had been pronounced the conduct of the prisoner became so bad that she had to be removed...' Maggie Ryan, the next prisoner, also on a vagrancy charge, received her sentence of seven days with much less fuss.

The real criminals came next. Constables Little, Sweeny and Johnston summoned a number of boys for wheeling little carts on the footpath. It was, apparently, a new form of summer amusement and had resulted in a number of complaints to the police. In spite of urgings by District Inspector McHugh, Bell said that because it was a first offence he would impose a fine of only 2s 6d but warned that a further offence would result in a more severe penalty.

John Ward was fined five shillings for leaving his horse unsecured at the Lough Swilly station. He said in defence that he'd had toothache and had gone to the dentist, leaving a boy in charge.

Finally the court heard a renewed application for an exemption from the licensing laws for Robert Duddy's public house in Ferryquay Street to accommodate the theatrical companies and those employed in the Opera House after the ordinary closing hours. The police still urged refusal despite the new management, with DI McHugh saying his objection 'was precisely that same' as before. In this case the majority of the panel of magistrates allowed the late licence.

18 SEPTEMBER 1924

The Derry Petty Sessions was for many years the scene of much local drama as witnesses, plaintiffs and defendants gave not necessarily consistent accounts of past events under the usually patient eyes of the bench of magistrates. On 18 September 1924 a case involving a 'brawl between neighbours', as the local press headlined it, and to which the *Derry Journal* gave the slightly mysterious sub-head 'A Club or a Beetle', was heard before Patrick Breslin, presiding, Mrs Semple, Captain J.M. Wilton, H.W. Porter and James Hamilton. The case was not so much a 'domestic' as an 'inter-domestic', involving two families in Orchard Row (now disappeared), off Ferguson's Lane that ran from Bishop Street to Foyle Road. William Jackson took a case against William Dunn and his wife Ellen, while the Dunns made a counter-charge against the Jacksons.

Jackson said that, on Saturday, 13 September, Dunn had come to his door to accuse him of having insulted his wife the previous evening. Jackson denied having even seen Dunn's wife. The men began to wrestle with blows to the chest and threats of 'breaking necks'. Ellen Dunn appeared on the scene with an Indian club that she threw at Jackson. When it fell on the street she picked it up and inflicted a wound an inch and a half long above one of his eyes. The Dunns' solicitor, T.E. Conaghan, put it to Jackson that he had drink taken, which Jackson denied. The latter then accused Dunn of 'nagging at him' ever since he began living beside them and said that Ellen had fought 'with the whole street'.

The next witness was a neighbour, Mrs Large, subpoenaed by both parties and 'therefore neutral'. She said that she was visiting the Dunn house because Ellen was ill but when the row started she ran out and the two of them began to attack Jackson. Mary Lee, another neighbour, became aware that things had livened up when she heard shouts of 'That's not fair; that's too many for one.' She ran to Jackson's assistance and saw Mrs Dunn lift a club with which she struck Jackson on the head. She thought that Ellen Dunn's appearance had aggravated the situation and stated that it did not take much to upset the people of Orchard Row. Asked about the club she said she thought it was a 'beetle'. [This was a heavy wooden instrument for literally beating the dirt out of washing in the days before detergents.] There was predictable laughter at another remark from Wilton on the bench that 'you would hardly imagine that Mrs Dunn was practising Indian club exercises' [a popular keep-fit programme of the time].

A majority of the bench bound over the warring parties to keep the peace in personal bail of £5 and two sureties of £2 10s each. And so a kind of calm descended once more upon Orchard Row.

19 SEPTEMBER 1829

The *Londonderry Sentinel* has its provenance in the opposition to the call for Catholic emancipation in the late 1820s. The call occasioned a major change in policy of the local newspaper, the *Londonderry Journal*. From its formation in 1772 by Scotsman, George Douglas, who ran a stationery business in the Diamond, the *Journal* had had a robustly Protestant and conservative editorial policy.

In 1829, however, its new owners decided to back the call for Catholic emancipation. The editor, William Wallen, fervently disagreed and left the *Journal* to found his own newspaper with a number of like-minded associates.

The *Londonderry Sentinel and North-West Advertiser* was initially published on 19 September 1829, six months after the Catholic Relief Act became law.

The decision to establish the *Sentinel* at that particular period appears on hindsight a courageous one. The *Journal*, which had been in existence for over half a century, was the only newspaper in the northwest, was well-established and presented itself as a formidable rival. Those factors aside, the times were highly unfavourable for a newspaper enterprise. Not only had a two-penny revenue stamp to appear on each sheet of newsprint sold, but a duty of half-a-crown was exacted in respect of each advertisement. In addition, the reading and writing constituency among whom the paper could potentially secure a circulation were limited in number. Londonderry at the time had only 12,000 inhabitants and there was no assurance that the city would grow: the manufacture of linen, the staple industry at the time, was slowly declining; there was no indication that the fledgling shirt industry would grow to the extent it eventually did; and the great impetus of trade, afterwards given by the owners of a fleet of ocean-going merchant ships, had not begun to be felt.

It is not known how the founders of the *Londonderry Sentinel* got together, but an original list shows that the newspaper's supporters were drawn from Fermanagh, Tyrone, and Donegal, as well as Derry, and embraced leading men in those districts. It is also not clear how long the preparation period was before the appearance of the *Sentinel*'s first number. It was small in size, a matter of twenty-four columns. The headings were of uniform size, irrespective of the importance of the subject dealt with. 'Display' advertisements were not the rule. The type was clear and the issue entirely free from the 'literals'—as the wrong letters were called. The first impression was produced on a Columbian press by hand-power at the rate of 150 copies per hour. Advertisers rallied with enthusiasm to the new paper, confident that its declared principles would ensure for it large acceptance by the reading public.

The *Sentinel* of 1829, and for well up to half-a-century afterwards, was produced on the ground floor and basement of a house in Pump Street, later forming part of the Mercy convent.

20 SEPTEMBER 1932

The annual meeting of the Derry Philharmonic Society took place in the Northern Counties Hotel on Tuesday, 20 September 1932, with the Reverend J.C. Greer presiding. In his opening address he expressed the view that the society exercised a cultural influence without which Derry would descend to the level of the ordinary provincial town or village. There were counter-attractions now that were not in existence twenty years ago, he continued, and as the senior members of their Philharmonic chorus died out it was difficult to get others to take their place.

It was a tale often heard before, and would be repeated many times in the future. In the case of the Philharmonic in 1932 economics played their dreaded part. Admission prices to concerts had been kept at pre-war levels, except for the new entertainment tax that all such events had to pay, but the cost of productions had doubled. James Blair, the honorary secretary, was much more upbeat in his report, commending the excellence of the two concerts that had been given during the previous year:

> If the success of the work done last year and the two concerts given are to be accurately gauged by the measure of approbation given by the Press and the public, the society would appear to have reached a high-water mark last season. Under the capable direction of Mr A.J. Cunningham a high standard of artistic achievement was attained on both occasions… As a conductor and interpreter of classical music his powers remain unimpaired and the committee realise that it would be a great tragedy if he was unable to carry on the good work. They sincerely hope that the specialised treatment which he purposes undergoing will restore his eyesight considerably and enable him to take up his usual place at the conductor's dais again.

Blair was also anxious to express the committee's gratitude to the ladies who had organised a successful dance in aid of society funds; to the local gentlemen, who so kindly and efficiently acted as stewards at the concerts; to H.B. Phillips, who took care of bookings and did not charge; and to the management of the Northern Counties Hotel for the free use of rooms for committee meetings.

After the submission of the report by the treasurer, Robert Platt, T.G. Lewis, the honorary auditor-elect, strongly criticised the imposition of an entertainment tax on a society like the Philharmonic, the object of which was educational. He was chided by F.J. Simmons for being not exactly patriotic, attacking 'the poor government about the £40, which is really divided over the 400 members and paid by them'. When Mrs McGuinness, the vice chairman, moved that a chartered accountant be asked to audit the accounts as a matter of prestige, Lewis immediately resigned. The Reverend Greer, as chairman, did his best to smooth things over, reminding him that he had just been elected. When Lewis insisted, he said they would let the matter stand in the meantime.

It looked like an open-and-shut case: on the evening of 18 August a crowd of circus-goers had cut the guy-ropes of the 'big top' and destroyed a 'cinematograph machine'. Further they attacked the circus band and their instruments. The events of the night were recalled in the Recorders Court on 21 September 1904 as Mrs Davies, the owner, sought £140 in compensation.

Having told the plaintiff's version of events Patrick Maxwell, acting for the appellant, called as first witness Robert Davies, son of the applicant. Davies listed the rolling stock and equipment: twenty-three horses and seven vans. The tent was less than six months old, had a diameter of 95 feet and a seating capacity of up to 500. The evening performance had not been able to take place because of the trouble, and when Maxwell prompted him with 'You had a good number of admissions', Davies replied, 'More than we got money from.' This caused a certain amount of laughter in court. Davies went on to describe how the crowd had hooted down a woman tight-rope walker and assaulted her as she descended. The ringmaster brought on the performing horses but the crowd, now in a state of ugly excitement, shouted, 'Take them away.' As a last resort a cinematograph machine was brought out to show films on a screen but the darkness merely increased the tension.

Some rougher elements in the crowd jumped into the ring, tore down the screen and overturned the projector. Then, with support ropes cut inside and out, the tent fell down and members of the audience cut large holes in the canvas wall. Damage was caused to musical instruments, the projector and the screen, and the tent was left in sore need of repair. There were clearly many who had slipped in without paying. Michael Fitzgerald, the circus clown, said in evidence that in one part of the tent there were four large holes cut and seven of the stay ropes severed, in another section eight holes and three ropes cut, in a third part seven holes and seven ropes cut, and the remaining quarter so badly attacked as to make it a total wreck.

It became clear that the tent held more than twice the number people it was constructed for, whether of paying customers or not. Fear of injury and airlessness had added to the growing hysteria. There were some of the audience who were out to make trouble, and they had not been isolated and brought under control. When it was suggested to Sergeant Quinlivan, a police witness, that it was circus people who had felled the tent as a crude but effective means of crowd control, he heartily concurred. It seemed to convince Judge Overend, the Recorder, who found that the damage was not malicious and that the owners had oversold the tickets. He therefore refused the application and required them to pay costs.

On 22 September 1976 the *Sentinel* published an interview with 78-year-old Mrs Nellie Jarvis of 218 Fountain Estate, who recalled many features about days gone by in the Maiden City. Born in Fountain Street where four generations of her family lived, Mrs Jarvis, whose father was Mr William McGahey, said it was a really great place to live: 'We were all neighbours together, your troubles were everybody's troubles, when a mother was having a baby all the neighbours rallied round, looking after the other children and bringing big bowls of gruel to give the mother strength—it was all breastfeeding in those days.'

The eldest of a family of ten—six daughters and four sons—Nellie had to do her share of the housework: 'In the evening it was my task to brush and plait my sisters' hair and clean their shoes in readiness for the morning. Of course there were no bathrooms in those days—we took hip baths by the fire. But those were happy family times. As well as saying our prayers each evening before going to bed, we did our party piece at our mother's knee.'

What was Christmas like in those days? 'It was great,' she said, 'but of course very different from now. We didn't get anything like the children of today get; you got a stocking with an orange, an apple and a slice of your mother's sultana cake. I remember once getting a doll which had cost 2s 11d, but I wasn't allowed to play with it—it was considered too good and I was made to hang it upon the wall as an ornament.

'One of the highlights of my Christmas was being taken to the pantomime in the Opera House. No matter how poor a family was, they always seemed to manage to take their children to the pantomime and, of course, another highlight for me was the children's Christmas party, which was held in the Cathedral School. The Christmas tree was always loaded with presents which had been supplied by local people and the teachers in the school, and very good presents they were.'

Nellie Jarvis had led a busy life as a housewife, mother and business woman. For forty-six years she and her husband, Tommy, ran a news agency at the corner of Hawkin Street and Carlisle Road. 'I loved the news agency business,' she said. 'We made so many friends and I always enjoyed meeting the country people who came in every weekend for their newspapers. We worked long hours, opening for business at 6.45 every morning and not closing until 11 o'clock at night. We did a great business when the Opera House was open— people would call in after the show to buy sweets to take home to their children.

'Of course in days gone by Carlisle Road was a great street; it was really a parade ground for all the young people in the evenings...'

Translations is a three-act play by Brian Friel which was premiered at Derry's Guildhall on Tuesday, 23 September 1980. It is set in *Baile Beag* (Ballybeg), a small village at the heart of 1830s agricultural Ireland when the new English language National Schools are about to commence, and the British army is carrying out the first Ordnance Survey of the area. This involves finding English translations or phonetic equivalent for local place names.

The main characters, English and Irish, stand at a moment of cultural transition, and the play explores their response to this crisis in their personal lives and in the historical life of the community. Friel has said that *Translations* is 'a play about language and only about language', but it deals with a wide range of issues, stretching from language and communication to Irish history and cultural imperialism. Despite the 1833 setting, there are clear similarities between *Baile Beag* and today's world.

More than three months before the premiere—on Wednesday, 4 June— the *Londonderry Sentinel* announced on its front page that *Translations* was to have its 'world premiere in Londonderry—in the Assembly Hall of the Guildhall'. The decision had been confirmed at a press conference held the previous day by Friel, who said that after the opening production the play would be transferred to the Grand Opera House in Belfast, which was then being refurbished; after a week's run there it would make a short tour of Northern Ireland. A tour of Southern Ireland was at the time being negotiated.

The play would be presented by the new Field Day Theatre Company which had been established by Friel and Stephen Rea, and the rehearsals would take place in Derry. Field Day was an independent theatre group and a spokesperson said they 'gratefully acknowledged the generous sponsorship of the Arts Council of Northern Ireland' and stated that private sponsorship was also being sought.

Welcoming the announcement of the world premiere presentation in Londonderry, the Deputy Mayor, Marlene Jefferson, said she was particularly glad that the production had provided the City Council with the opportunity to bring back theatre to the Guildhall. Commenting that council officials were trying to carry out certain modifications and purchase some equipment to enable the Assembly Hall to be more adaptable for theatre productions, the Deputy Mayor added: 'I hope that this world premiere and the extended visit by a professional company will encourage local amateur dramatic organisations to consider again using the Guildhall as a major venue for their productions.'

Emphasising that the council was 'still earnestly progressing the development of a permanent purpose-built civic theatre', the Deputy Mayor continued: 'The use of the Guildhall as an interim measure should make it possible to build up audiences and encourage more theatre-goers in the Council area. The adaptations planned for the next few months should enable the Guildhall to be used by all local amateur groups. In addition, it should make it more attractive to other major professional touring companies.'

William King, a 49-year-old man, was dead on arrival at Altnagelvin Hospital on the night of Wednesday, 24 September 1969, following an attack on him in London Street during a sudden and unexpected flare-up of sectarian violence in the city centre. Mr King, a widower with a family of four, resided at Fountain Place. A native of County Donegal and one of a family of fourteen, he was a security officer at the Du Pont works at Maydown and had served in the army during the Second World War.

The origin of the disturbance which resulted in his death was not immediately obvious. One account of what happened was that Mr King's son, Stewart, was injured during the confrontation between rival factions near the London Street–Bishop Street junction and that Mr King was injured after going to assist his son. Stones and bottles had been thrown and the trouble, which lasted about a couple of hours, abated when reinforcements of military arrived and pushed the crowds out of sight of each other. The military, who were armed, donned steel helmets and carried batons but did not use them.

On Thursday, 25 September, an army spokesman said five soldiers, including one officer, Major Michael Reynolds, were injured in the disturbance having been struck by missiles, but all were on duty again that day. He said there had been no delay in going to Mr King's aid. Quoted in the *Londonderry Sentinel* he said: 'I am told that, as soon as they saw this man on the ground, they went straight to the crowd near him and, in fact, fought them back in order to rescue him. He was taken away by friends who could not get near him until then. Some of the soldiers were actually injured in rescuing Mr King.' He also said that reinforcements came from other detachments within ten minutes of a signal being sent but he did not know at what stage the request for extra men was made.

More details of the disturbances emerged at an inquest into the death of Mr King, held on Thursday, 20 November. The State Pathologist, Dr T.K. Marshall, described head, face and body injuries to Mr King that could have been sustained during an attack in which King was kicked, or perhaps, struck by hard objects. Moderate force was used, he said. There was nothing to indicate that the injuries could have caused death. After giving evidence of coronary disease, sufficient to have caused a heart attack at any time, and saying that such a heart attack could have been precipitated by the events of the moment, he said in his opinion the cause of death was atheroma.

25 SEPTEMBER 1947

One of the complicated side issues arising from the setting up of the Northern Ireland state was where the border could legally be said to lie on the River Foyle and the lough. When the original apportioning of escheated land to the London livery companies at the start of the seventeenth century was determined the Honourable the Irish Society insisted on the inclusion of O'Doherty land on the west bank of the river and an equivalent bite out of McDonnell territory on the east bank of the Bann so that it would control the ports of Coleraine and the new Londonderry. It was hoped that the Boundary Commission of 1923–25 would restore the west bank of the Foyle to Donegal but the commission made no substantial proposals and it was abandoned.

The problem of fishing rights remained and it was to provide matter for the courts for many years to come. Another aspect of the problem was to surface during the Second World War when Derry was the most westerly Allied seaport and submarine base. How close to the Inishowen shore could a destroyer sail without infringing Éire's neutrality? The Foyle Fishery regularly brought trespassing cases against individual anglers, especially unlicensed ones, when its bailiffs thought they had had some proof of misdemeanour. The notional 'border' could be said to stretch for at least fifteen miles south to Strabane where the confluence with the River Finn marked the Donegal border.

On 25 September 1947 at Derry Petty Sessions court a fisherman from Culmore called James Thompson was summoned by John Patterson, a fishery inspector from Bready, just over the county border of Tyrone. There were six boats at Dunalong a few miles south of Bready where the river is quite narrow, and one, while retaining the net on the Donegal side, shot it in Northern Ireland grounds. The defending solicitor Walter Murnaghan was a well-known Nationalist and he used the technique, as often before, of mockery which the magistrate, Captain P.S. Bell, was happy to share. The defendant had worked for Foyle Fishery, and Bell suggested that 'This is a case not of a poacher turning gamekeeper but of a gamekeeper turned poacher.'

Murnaghan wondered if the accused had been guilty of 'invading Northern Ireland' and asked his adversary if he believed that there was some invisible dividing line in the middle of the river. More soberly he insisted that his client had been doing what others had been doing and they were not interfered with, citing a number of cases in Donemana where there had been no conviction. It struck a raw nerve with Bell: 'Are you seriously asking me to take as precedent the decision of some Resident Magistrate junior to myself?' Murnaghan hastily assured him he was not and was happy to acquiesce when he imposed a fine of £5 with £1 5s costs on each of the three summonses against Thompson.

26 SEPTEMBER 1829

Annually, around mid-September, members of the Murray and Mitchelburne Parent Clubs of the Apprentice Boys of Derry attend the graves of Colonel Adam Murray and Colonel John Mitchelburne, who rest side by side at Old Glendermott Churchyard. Both clubs are named after Murray and Mitchelburne, who were notable figures in the 1689 Siege of Derry drama. Murray was a local farmer from County Londonderry who proved to be an inspiring leader and soldier. He led a cavalry unit with considerable distinction and was a popular choice for the governorship of the city but refused it. He received no reward for services during the Siege and the date of his death is unknown.

Mitchelburne was an Englishman, born in Sussex in 1648, who had considerable military experience by the time of the Siege. Following the death of Henry Baker, who had been Joint-Governor with Reverend George Walker, Mitchelburne replaced him. His wife and children died during the Siege. He remarried, and passed away on 1 October 1721. Following his death a well on his land at Prehen became a site of veneration for local people, both Catholic and Protestant. In 1829, a person who made an autumnal visit to the graves wrote the following account using the pseudonym 'Alpha', which appeared in a very early issue of the *Londonderry Sentinel*, dated 26 September 1829:

> In the bottom of a deep glen of considerable length, whose banks though far extended, are gradually precipitous; and at the distance of two miles and a half over a sloping green ridge in a south easterly direction from the Testimonial lately erected to the gallant Walker... lie the venerable remains of the valiant Colonel John Mitchelburne... On the arrival of the visitor he is directed to a plain coarse slab of whitish grey, nearly in the middle of the enclosure, without any other ornament attached to it, than that of an inscription, rudely engraved, and evidently undergoing, like the mortal remains of its possessor, the unavoidable ravage of time... Across the slab, obliquely, as if from the left shoulder to the

middle of the right side, is a crack or opening, like a military belt, and so wide that it dishevels some of the letters so as to render them illegible. Here the beholder may picture to himself the great resemblance which exists between the opening in the slab, and the wound of a sabre across the naked breast of a soldier, ere he reads the unostentatious epitaph over him who was Commander-in-Chief of the Garrison, in the ever memorable Siege of the interesting city of Londonderry... Mouldering near the same spot lie the bones of his fellow-soldier, the courageous Colonel Murray. The slab which covers him is nearly the same as that which is placed over Mitchelburne. The inscription on it is so defaced with moss, etc., that it is quite unintelligible. Waving over his head are a rugged thistle and a bunch of nettles, indicative, as it were, of his inflexible attachment and determined bravery...

27 SEPTEMBER 1912

The most important single day in the Unionist struggle against the Home Rule bill was Covenant Day, Saturday, 28 September 1912, when an unprecedented rejection of the very limited devolution on offer signalled a possible break from the Westminster parliament and the threat of a civil war. On that day 471,414 men and women signed a Solemn League and Covenant (one man, Colonel Fred Crawford, extravagantly in his own blood), a document deliberately couched in emotional and apocalyptic language, borrowing the title of an agreement made in 1643 by Scots Presbyterians and English parliamentary opposition to Charles I. It was devised by Thomas Sinclair, a Belfast merchant, and approved by James Craig and Edward Carson as a means of maintaining the exaltation of their followers while increasing their inner cohesion.

In Derry in the build-up to that important Saturday the local papers carried the news in characteristic fashion. *The Derry Journal* all but ignored the event until the following Monday when in a series of 12-point sub-headlines it more or less dismissed it as of little significance: 'ULSTER' DAY: IGNORED IN LONDON; UNNOTICED IN DUBLIN; TAME IN DERRY; QUIET EVEN IN BELFAST. The *Londonderry Sentinel* and *Derry Standard* printed the wording of the Oath in their anticipatory editions on 27 September:

> Being convinced in our consciences that Home Rule would be disastrous to the material well-being of Ulster as well as of the whole of Ireland, subversive of our civil and religious freedom, destructive of our citizenship, and perilous to the unity of the Empire, we, whose names are underwritten, men of Ulster, loyal subjects of His Gracious Majesty King George V, humbly relying on the God

whom our fathers in days of stress and trial confidently trusted, do hereby pledge ourselves in solemn Covenant, throughout this our time of threatened calamity, to stand by one another in defending, for ourselves and our children, our cherished position of equal citizenship in the United Kingdom, and in using all means which may be found necessary to defeat the present conspiracy to set up a Home Rule Parliament in Ireland. And in the event of such a Parliament being forced upon us, we further solemnly and mutually pledge ourselves to refuse to recognize its authority. In sure confidence that God will defend the right, we hereto subscribe our names.

They carried details of religious services that would be held in anticipation of the signing in a promiscuous mixture of Anglican and Presbyterian: St Columb's Cathedral, First Derry, Christ Church, St Augustine's, Carlisle Road, Clooney Hall and All Saints. The main venue for men to sign was the Guildhall while for the women, who had a shorter, ancillary declaration to sign, there were the Synod Hall and Craig Memorial. In the Waterside both men and women could sign in the Hall Bond's Hill. Orangemen and Apprentice Boys were to meet on the Mall Wall at 2.30 wearing regalia. Finally a general display of Union Jacks was requested.

28 SEPTEMBER 1880

John Sims Reeves, the foremost English operatic, oratorio and ballad tenor vocalist of the mid-Victorian era, was born at Woolwich and received his musical education from his father, a musician in the Royal Artillery. At the age of fourteen he had progressed so far as to be appointed organist of North Cray church. He seems to have studied medicine for a year, but changed his mind when he gained his adult voice. It was at first a baritone, and he made his earliest appearance at Newcastle in 1838 or 1839 in various baritone parts. He studied with Hobbs and T. Cooke, and, his voice having become tenor, he appeared under William Charles Macready's management at Drury Lane.

Four years were spent studying on the continent under Marco Bordogni in Paris and Alberto Mazzucato in Milan, and his debut in Italian opera was made at La Scala. He reappeared in London in May 1847 at a benefit concert. His career on the English operatic stage began at Drury Lane in December 1847, under the conductorship of the famous French Romantic composer Hector Berlioz. In 1848 he went to Her Majesty's Theatre, and in the autumn of that year, at the Norwich Festival, was a great sensation. From his first appearance at the Sacred Harmonic Society in the following November he was recognized as the leading English tenor.

His retirement from public life, at first announced to take place in 1882, did not in fact happen until 1891 when a farewell concert for his benefit was given at the Albert Hall. His savings were invested in unlucky speculation, and he was forced to reappear in public for a number of years. He died at Worthing on 25 October 1900.

Twenty years earlier, on 29 September 1880, the *Londonderry Sentinel* reported to its readers that Mr Sims Reeves's long talked-about farewell concert in Derry was given the previous night in the Opera House, 'before a most numerous and brilliant auditory'. The 'magnetic influence', the newspaper continued, 'which the name of the eminent English tenor has long exercised on the musical public had, doubtless, considerable effect in drawing together so large an assembly, and the fact that it would be his last public appearance in this city no doubt attracted many persons who would not otherwise have been present.' The demand for tickets had been so great that 'in addition to the boxes, a large part of the pit was portioned off for reserve seats. On the score of attendance the concert was, hence, a decided success.'

Among the artists appearing with Sims Reeves was his son, Herbert Reeves. The latter, who was warmly welcomed, made his first appearance with Schubert's *Ave Maria*. Herbert, opined the *Sentinel*, was 'in physical aspect, to speak in semi-vulgar parlance, a real chip of the old block', but his voice lacked 'the richness, fullness, and truthfulness possessed by his father'. It was, however, 'perfect in tone, is well-trained, and time may give it mellowness and strength'.

29 SEPTEMBER 1932

At Derry Petty Sessions on 29 September 1932, Patrick McColgan of 6 Waterloo Street was charged with reckless driving, using a motorcycle without the permission of the owner, not having an insurance certificate and disobeying the traffic regulations. R.W. Glass, the presiding Resident Magistrate, heard first from Sergeant Briggs of the RUC, who stated that McColgan had entered Waterloo Place on the wrong side, turned suddenly to the left and crashed through the plate-glass window in Smylies' shop. In the Infirmary, to which he was taken by ambulance, it was found that one of his eyes had been almost cut out and his arm also severely lacerated. Other injuries were later discovered. As usual in police court cases much of the work of prosecution was done by a high-ranking officer of the RUC, in this case Head Constable Fallon, who elicited from his sergeant the further information that McColgan's speed at the time of the crash was 40 mph and that he had smelt strongly of drink in the hospital.

McColgan's solicitor was Patrick Maxwell, later a magistrate himself and an abstentionist Nationalist MP. He had the reputation of obtaining some mitigation of sentence in what seemed like an open-and-shut case. His first question to Briggs was deliberately distracting: 'Did he fall off the bicycle or throw himself off?' Briggs wisely made no attempt to answer Maxwell's impossible question, merely stating: 'He shot over the handles of the bicycle clean through the window.' John Jackson, the owner of the cycle, said that he had parked it outside a garage on Foyle Road and when he emerged from the building he saw the accused ride away on it without permission. Mrs Curran, who was standing outside the shop, was struck on the side and knocked on her back, sustaining bruises and an injured thumb. Her husband testified that he had just managed to sweep his two children out of the way.

When Maxwell began his defence things looked grim for McColgan; yet he quickly established that McColgan had been the mechanic who regularly serviced and repaired the bike. He also claimed that he had been told by several people, including Daniel McSwine, that there was something wrong with the machine. He had driven off merely to take a test run of a few yards, having being given a push by McSwine and others. The machine had got stuck in top gear, the handgrip had jammed, and he could not stop it. He was forced to keep on through the traffic straight to Guildhall Square and into Waterloo Place. He decided to use the kerb outside Smylies as a brake, which would explain his sharp turn to the left. The ploy did not work; he was pitched through the window and had to spend a month in hospital. It was at least a coherent defence.

Glass, while showing some wry appreciation of it and sympathising with McColgan, felt he had to impose a severe sentence, fining him £13, but since it was a first offence, allowing him to keep his licence.

30 SEPTEMBER 1929

In 1929 the song-writing partnership of Buddy de Sylva, Lew Brown and Ray Henderson wrote the following lyric:

> If I had a talking picture of you-oo,
> I would run it ev'ry time I felt blu-oo.
> I would sit there in the gloom

Of my lonely little room
And applaud each time you whispered. 'I love you!
Love you!'

It could not have been more topical since talking pictures, or 'talkies' as they were soon to be called, had arrived. Warner Brothers' studios, ignoring the dismissal of the new 'fad' that would never take on, had produced in 1927 *The Jazz Singer*, a film in which the exuberant singer and vaudeville star Al Jolson sang and briefly spoke. He was born Asa Yoelson, the son of a Jewish cantor and was brought to USA by his parents in 1893. The early films in which he appeared were achingly sentimental but had the magic of sound. It changed the whole nature of cinema and finished the careers of many 'stars' whose voices could not match their appearances. It also meant a golden opportunity for stage actors who could speak.

When American audiences heard Jolson actually *say*, 'You ain't heard nothing yet!' they went wild. His second talkie *The Singing Fool* reached Europe in 1929, coming to Derry that autumn. Strangely it remained in Derry people's memories as 'Sonny Boy' because of a tearjerker sung by Jolson to his baby son. It had been written as a joke by Brown and Henderson but Jolson took it quite seriously, added a few lines and claimed some of the royalties.

Strangely it was the Midland, Derry's smallest cinema and the only one in the Waterside, which would be the venue for the new attraction. Taking its name from the LMS station a few yards away, it showed mainly re-runs but was a pioneer in the cinema revolution. It charged extra for the week of *The Singing Fool* and had full houses. On the first night, Monday, 30 September 1929, about halfway through the film Jolson suddenly began to speak. In fact it was hard to hear what he was saying or singing because the audience burst into excited conversation: 'Jolson's talking! Is that what he sounds like? The young usherette had to shine her torch at the loudest groups so that the rest might hear. There was no doubt; the talkies had arrived and were here to stay.

Midland advertisements in the local papers used an icon, a cross made of the two words 'see' and 'hear' intersecting at the letter 'e', and a fortnight later it was showing—with full sound—*The Donovan Affair* with Jack Holt.

OCTOBER

Gladys Aylward, the famous missionary, was born in 1902. The child of nonconformist parents, she worked as a parlourmaid but never doubted that God had other plans for her. In 1930 she travelled to China where she joined an elderly Scottish missionary in establishing the Inn of the Sixth Happiness in the remote outpost of Yangzheng in Shanxi province in order to convert the population to Christianity.

Aylward worked in China until 1949, becoming a Chinese citizen in 1931. In 1940, she led 100 children from Shanxi, then occupied by the Japanese, across mountainous territory to safety, an act of bravery that was to be commemorated in the 1958 biopic, *The Inn of the Sixth Happiness*. The mountains of north Wales doubled for China in the 1930s and '40s in the film which starred Ingrid Bergman as the missionary who carried the Christian faith to regions dominated by warlords and converted a mandarin, played by Robert Donat. Curt Jurgens was cast as the Chinese soldier with whom Bergman fell in love, only to leave him when the party of children had to be led to safety over the mountains.

Four years prior to the release of the film, back in October 1954, Aylward visited Derry at the invitation of the Worldwide Missionary Convention Committee. On the first day of that month, a Friday night, she spoke to an enthralled congregation for over an hour in the Londonderry Baptist Church. Miss Aylward said that they had gathered that night in the hope that they would leave the church determined to catch 'fish' to serve God. 'May they have

310

power to catch men and women and make them disciples for Jesus Christ,' she continued. Telling of her early call, she said that she read an article in a magazine about China and, as she was saved, she felt that God had called her to go there. She had no education and no knowledge of mission fields at the time.

She went to South Wales and began to read the Bible more often. She related how she had bought a third-class ticket and travelled across Europe and Asia by the Trans-Siberian Railway to reach the Far East. She told of many thrilling moments in her journey. She spoke of how God Almighty had guided her through trials and distresses, and went on to explain how God had sent her to a place where there was only one missionary, and where the Gospel had never been heard. They lived together in a single room and in a place where there were numerous inns where evil men congregated. She went on to tell how God had told them to open an inn amongst the others and how they got their first converts into it.

The following night, Miss Aylward continued her story in the Baptist Church, and concluded her visit when she addressed a gathering in the Assembly Hall of the Guildhall on 3 October.

2 OCTOBER 1944

The *Derry Journal* of 2 October 1944 contained an item discussing the report on the running of the City and County Hospital for 1943. It also covered a recent monthly meeting of the hospital board of management. The Second World War had reached a point when it seemed clear that the Allies would finally defeat the Axis forces but the tenacity of the Wehrmacht was keeping the combined powers from penetrating German territory. At home in Derry, safe from Hitler's last aerial weapons, the V1 and V2 flying bombs, the blackout had become the 'dim-out' but there were many scarcities, including paper. Newspapers, magazines and published books all showed signs of austerity, the periodicals reduced to skeletons of their former selves with many being totally unavailable.

The opening paragraph commended R. McCarter, the hospital secretary, who wrote the report, that though 'paper restrictions have compelled [him] to abridge the details, the pages of the report make interesting reading, affording as they do an interesting insight into the exacting nature of the work that goes on intermittently, day and night, within the walls of the institution—work that has increased ten-fold, if not more, as a result of the war'. A list of benefactors was included, 'the better to impress on the minds of the readers how absolutely indispensable is every phase of the hospital's activities if the interests of the community are to be fully served'.

This was several years before the establishment of the National Health Service by the post-war Attlee government. Mention was made of a contemporary form of health insurance, the Hospital Weekly Contributory Scheme, organised voluntarily by local firms for their workers. The weekly amounts were small: the members associated with the hospital had contributed £2,870 for the year at two pence a week. This indicated a membership of 6,360, and since members and their dependents were entitled to free hospital treatment, the service was available to at least twice that number. The target for 1943 had been £3,000 but it was hoped that with the addition of a few new firms that target might be reached in 1944. The selling slogan, 'So much for so little', seemed just in the circumstances.

At the monthly meeting of the hospital board of management, the Mayor (Senator F.J. Simmons) congratulated McCarter on how splendidly turned out the report was and expressed his bewilderment as to how he had found time to produce so valuable, interesting and complete a record. Another member of the board, J. Anderson Piggot, supported Simmons in his praise of the report. The City and County Hospital continued as the chief northwest hospital until the larger inclusive building at Altnagelvin on the east end of the city was completed in the spring of 1960. The old west bank site, that had a commanding view of the Foyle, and the buildings were used for some time as a centre for those with special needs but later became an apartment complex.

3 OCTOBER 1925

Nowadays as one walks boldly into a well-lit, comfortably heated betting shop to pick up a freely available ball-point pen before reading the racing pages of all the sporting dailies, it's hard to imagine the nature of the 'hole-in-the-corner' hovels that used to cater for the 'fancy'. The 'commission agents', as the back-street bookies used to call themselves, were geared to purpose: consultation, whispered bets, money passed through a little window, and a sweat on the 2.30 at Haydock. Even being present in one of these 'shops' was illegal. As with all 'moral' legislation, it was impossible to apply, so from time to time cases were brought and exemplary sentences imposed.

On 3 October 1925 the *Londonderry Sentinel* reported that Thomas Murray was prosecuted 'for using an office in Orchard Street for the purpose of horse-betting'. A number of defendants found on the premises were also summoned.

Murray's defence was handled by John Tracy who maintained a light touch throughout the proceedings. When Head Constable Newman deposed to entering the premises at 2.15 p.m. on 9 September and finding a number of betting slips and a copy of the *Sporting Chronicle* relative to a race that was being run that day, he was asked by Tracy if he knew anything whatever about racing. When Newman replied in the negative Tracy caused laughter in the court by observing: 'Maybe it is as well for you.'

He offered a plea of 'Guilty' on his client's behalf but went on to attack the legislation that, seventy years before, could not be discussed on the scheduled day by the House of Lords because the session had been adjourned due to it being Derby Day! He continued in this wry way pointing out the inconsistency of the law's approach to different strata of society, ending with a damning peroration:

> If a man wants to put his hand in the fire or indulge in speculation it is his own affair. Betting prosecutions were brought for the purpose of satisfying Mrs Grundy. When it was legal for a peer of the realm to indulge in betting it was not fair that working men be deprived of the same privilege.

[In Thomas Morton's 1798 play *Speed the Plough* Mrs Grundy was the righteous neighbour of Farmer Ashfield whose approval Ashfield's wife was overly concerned to have; Mrs Ashfield repeatedly asked: 'What will Mrs Grundy say?'] Murray was fined £5 and each of the twenty-four other defendants, whose names and addresses were printed in the paper, 2s 6d.

4 OCTOBER 1932

John McCormack, possibly Ireland's greatest ever tenor, admitted that he could not act very well and after some initial success in opera preferred the concert platform to exercise his talent. His singing of 'Il Mio Tesoro' from *Don Giovanni* was spectacular but he was a poor Don Ottavio. Nobody in Derry cared; they were so entranced by his singing, they did not mind when the rather beefy hereditary Papal Count tended to finish his concerts with 'The Old House' and the inappropriate line, 'Why stand I here like a ghost or a shadow?'

He paid his third visit to Derry on 4 October 1932 when he was forty-eight and at the height of his powers, and after the recital confided in the *Derry Journal* reporter: 'I got a thrill tonight. That audience was the finest I've had in years.' By chance or design, as he sang his twenty-two songs in the Guildhall, the film *Song o' My Heart* was being screened 100 yards away in St Columb's

Hall. The earliest Irish 'talkie', its outdoor scenes were shot near Bray in County Wicklow and the tenor received $50,000 a week for the ten weeks he worked on it. It featured the Irish actress Maureen O'Sullivan as the daughter of a family that is saved from ruin when McCormack raises money by a song recital. O'Sullivan later played Jane to Johnny Weissmuller's Tarzan.

McCormack's previous visit had been on 14 October 1909, when he gave a recital in St Columb's Hall, and 'Now,' he smiled and said, 'they are showing my film there.' His programme consisted of material which included three songs from the film, one of which, 'Just for Today', was hugely popular. When the audience heard Edwin Schneider, the accompanist, play the introduction to the 'Derry Air' they began to applaud so loudly that he had to begin again. However, the words were not those of Fred Weatherly's well-known 'Danny Boy' but ones McCormack had written himself, beginning, 'Oh, Mary dear…' For most of the audience the encore songs, 'The Rose of Tralee', Johnny Patterson's 'The Garden Where the Praties Grow', 'Bless This House' and 'The Last Rose of Summer', were the highlights of the show. Rachmaninov, the great Russian composer, had once said to McCormack: 'John, you sing a good song well; you sing a bad song magnificently!'

For one of these encores he turned his back to the audience and sang to those who, unable to get seats in the hall, were allowed to sit on the bank of tiered seats behind him. When 'Where thy mates of the garden lie scentless and dead', the last line of Tom Moore's 'Last Rose of Summer', was sung the applause grew deafening but the singer raised his arms in a gesture to show that the evening had come to an end. 'No more!' he said and left the stage.

5 OCTOBER 1968

Future historians of the Troubles that characterised Northern Ireland for the last three decades of the twentieth century will have to decide when and how they began. Each apparent nucleus can be seen to have an earlier cause and the sequence soon has the amateur historian back in the seventeenth century and the Ulster Plantation. In spite of this proper academic caution, the march that was brutally stalled in Duke Street in Derry on 5 October 1968 must be regarded as a significant event in the story. It was not all that unusual; other confrontations between the Stormont regime and the nationalist opposition had met with the same kind of police reaction, but on this occasion, probably for the first time, television viewers all over the world were given a graphic pictorial account of how Northern Ireland dealt with its internal affairs.

The march was arranged by the Northern Ireland Civil Rights Association (NICRA), a blanket organisation founded in 1967 that included a number of reform groups including the Dungannon-based Campaign for Social Justice, the Nationalist Party and a radical student group, People's Democracy. NICRA's aims were a reform of the static system that kept the Unionist party in power in Stormont and in a great majority of local councils. Sectarianism in job and housing allocation was rife on both sides and Derry was a prime example of clear malpractice both in local government employment and accommodation. A significant majority of non-Unionists were not able to have political power because of ward-rigging and multiple franchise.

The city, then, was an obvious place to protest, but the march was banned by William Craig, the Minister of Home Affairs, as 'provocative' and likely to clash with a hastily organised 'traditional' march by the Apprentice Boys. NICRA wanted to accede to Craig's edict but the local organisers, the Derry Housing Action Committeee (DHAC), persuaded the rest to ignore the ban. The crowd was met in Duke Street with the usual peace-keeping methods of the RUC and the B-Specials, naked of identifying badges: baton charges (in which Gerry Fitt and Eddie McAteer, both MPs, were injured on head and groin) and water cannon were deployed widely in what seemed like another aborted protest in the murky history of the province. This time, however, the eyes of the world were upon Duke Street, and some fellow MPs of the ruling Wilson Westminster government were actually present to see for themselves.

The rioting and looting that ensued was the worst since 1920, and it was to be repeated many times. Unlike the situation in 1920 there was nothing the bishop or other local clergy could do to influence events. NICRA quite soon achieved its limited aims—Derry was granted a ruling commission that established an equitable system of local government—but darker forces were gathering and the heady spring of reform was soon to be eclipsed by many winters of discontent.

6 OCTOBER 1566

Anyone acquainted with the map of Ireland cannot help but notice the tactical significance of Derry's geographical location. Sited exactly between Donegal and Coleraine, as the first counties were named, it was both buffer and outlet. Even before the shiring its position between O'Cahan country to the east, O'Donnell territory to the west and O'Neill land to the south made it a desirable piece of property to be in possession of. Hundreds of years earlier the wide bay of Lough Foyle was a handy base for invading ships, as the Vikings realised, and the many navigable rivers—the Foyle, Mourne, Derg, Finn, Strule and Drumragh—provided access for their shallow draft vessels allowing them to penetrate nearly to the headwaters of the Shannon. Each of the intermittently warring tribes desired it as a garrison and an outlet to the sea, at a time when roads were something of a luxury and things went swifter by water.

Elizabeth I decided to turn the distressful country—'the land of Ire', as Sir Robert Cecil, her minister of home security, called it—to profit but there was great need of 'pacification', especially in the rugged northern province. She was its legal sovereign as surviving heir of her father Henry VIII who had himself declared king in Dublin in 1541. Early in September 1566, in the eighth year of the her reign, she dispatched Colonel Edward Randolph with 1,000 foot soldiers and fifty cavalry from Bristol as part of an expedition against Shane O'Neill, known as *Seán an Díomais* (Shane the Proud), who though originally accepted as 'The O'Neill', had been declared an outlaw after his territorial ambitions caused the English of the Pale too much grief.

Randolph's force was sent into Lough Foyle on 6 October 1566 to attack O'Neill from the rear while the forces of the lord deputy Sir Henry Sidney pushed up from the south. Randolph turned the derelict monastic settlement of Doire Columcille into an armed garrison, committing the ultimate sacrilege of using the hallowed Tempull Mór, once the largest ecclesiastic edifice in Ireland, as an arsenal. Persistent rain had a deleterious effect on the cavalry, with a quarter of them succumbing to illness. The fever was regarded by believers as the patron saint's revenge on the heretical, iconoclastic English. On 15 November 1566, however, O'Neill's men were roundly defeated at Muff, five miles from the city, in Donegal, by Randolph's better disciplined forces, which contained some O'Dohertys from Inishowen, Shane's old enemies. The colonel himself was killed in an ambush and the command passed to Colonel St Low. The Tempull Mór and most of the town were obliterated the following April when a fire caused the gunpowder to explode, and the site was abandoned as untenable.

Shane himself barely escaped with his life on 8 May 1567 when he tried to defeat an army of the O'Donnells at Farsetmore outside Letterkenny on the tidal plain of Lough Swilly, his men caught by the swift incoming tide.

Emmeline Goulden was born in Manchester in 1858. Her father was a successful businessman with radical political beliefs and her mother was a passionate feminist. In 1879, Emmeline wed Richard Pankhurst, a lawyer and supporter of the women's suffrage movement. He was the author of the Married Women's Property Acts of 1870 and 1882, which permitted women to retain earnings or property obtained before and after marriage. His death in 1898 was a tremendous shock to Emmeline.

In 1889, Emmeline established the Women's Franchise League, which campaigned to permit married women to vote in local elections, and on the Friday night of 7 October 1910, she addressed a large audience of all classes in Derry's St Columb's Hall, held under the auspices of the Irish wing of that organisation. 'The spacious platform was very tastefully arranged for the occasion,' noted the *Derry Standard* three days later in its lengthy coverage of the event, 'the floral decorations being on a lavish scale. The air was laden with the aroma of sweet-smelling flowers, and through tall variegated pot-plants and autumn-tinted leaves half-concealed lights shed a soft radiance around the speakers and others on the platform.'

Mrs Pankhurst, whose speech was regularly greeted with cries of 'hear, hear', applause and laughter, began by saying that she wanted to express her gratitude to the people of Ireland, both in Londonderry and elsewhere, for the particularly keen interest taken in the women's suffrage movement, and for showing that they were ready and willing to hear all that was to be said about it, and give the movement a courteous reception.

It was necessary to explain, continued the noted campaigner, how this movement for votes for women had come about. Unless they could realise the urgency of the need for women's enfranchisement it was impossible to understand the real force behind the movement. She asked them to consider whether women would have done all that was reported of them across the channel, gone out into the streets, faced thousands of police, and gone into crowded meetings unless there were many real grievances which had made matters intolerable for them. The movement was not a new one, continued Pankhurst, as women had been putting forward demands for the vote for the past fifty years. Up to 1832 there was nothing against women having a vote, but the Reform Act was passed which opened the door to so many male voters and shut it in the face of the women.

Further acts had conferred still greater extensions of the franchise, and all this time women had been trying in vain to secure some rights. Men had been able to find means of bringing pressure to bear on the government of the time to force them to grant extension of the franchise, and the women of 'today', said Mrs Pankhurst, sought to convince the government that it was politically dangerous to neglect women's claims any longer, and politically expedient to grant them.

8 OCTOBER 1606

The first decade of the seventeenth century started badly for the Gaelic lordship with the defeat of the O'Neill–O'Donnell alliance at Kinsale in 1601. This was followed by a 'scorched earth' policy that forced O'Neill to the not disadvantageous peace of Mellifont. The departure of O'Neill, O'Donnell and Maguire allowed Arthur Chichester to push ahead with his plans for the Ulster plantation. The see of Derry had been vacant since the killing of the last Catholic bishop Réamonn Ó Gallachair and would remain so until 1720, with the appointment of Terence O'Donnelly, but it was not until 1780 that any Catholic bishop felt confident enough to reside in the city.

James I was determined to bring 'civility' to the province and, as the decade wore on, developed intricate plans for the future of the city and the County Coleraine, which became the new County Londonderry. With his logical bureaucratic mind he disliked disorder and long before plantation details were finalised had appointed George Montgomery to the vacant see. Derry *juxta* Raphoe and Clogher would be the first Ulster see for the newly established Church of Ireland. It was entirely typical that James should appoint a Scot, even though a majority of the loyal people of his native land were Presbyterian. Montgomery was born in 1569 in Ayrshire but was rector of a parish in Somerset when James VI became James I of England and Scotland. While Elizabeth I lived, Montgomery had acted as a kind of intelligence officer for the future king and now he was rewarded with the benefices of a tract of land that was effectively the whole of west and south Ulster. His wife Susan was naturally pleased though vague about her future home. As she wrote to friends: 'The king has bestowed… three Irish bishoprics, the names of which I cannot remember, they are so strange, except one, which is Derry.'

Susan and George did not begin their journey to their new home until 21 August 1606, nearly two years after the original appointment, and with the hope that 'we shall not stay long in Ireland'. On 8 October she wrote with relief to the same friends that they were settled in Derry:

I like it indifferent well thus far… We have our fat cattle and fat sheep brought in by our tenants as fast as we can use them... I find Derry a better place than we thought it would, for there are many of our country folk, both gentlemen and gentlewoman, and as brave they go in their apparel as in England... If my cousin William does dispraise the country believe him not, for truly it is a fine country.

George did not have the same benevolence towards the place as his wife. His purpose, approved by the king, was essentially to establish his triple diocese as the established church for the region and to extirpate Roman Catholicism with its treasonable attitude to Rome as taking priority over the temporal kingdom. That secondary goal was not achieved by the time of his death in 1621 because a structure had been established that would succeed in holding Catholic congregations in place until the Popery Acts were nothing but a distant, if painful, memory.

9 OCTOBER 1928

Among the seasonal entertainments that the people of Derry anticipated most were the visits of the circus. The best known of these was the guaranteed Irish Duffy's Circus that tended to stay for a week in Derry but could offer mere 'one-night-only' stands in smaller towns, thus giving rise to the slang term for a brief amorous dalliance as a 'Duffy's Circus'. The owner of Carmo's World-famed Circus and Menagerie were sure enough of their quality to book the 'show ground' for a two-week period in the autumn of 1928.

The opening on 8 October had been eagerly looked forward to but it was never made clear who the 'great Harry Carmo' actually was. Mention was made of a Henry Houston as general manager and of the publicity manager Dan Derry, who the *Derry Journal* claimed was 'a native of the city'. The picture printed in the paper shows a man respectably dressed in black suit, highly polished shoes, neat collar and tie and a Trilby hat, the only slightly racy element of which was an ornamental band.

The *Journal*'s man saw the show on the Tuesday night, the fourth to be given of the twice-daily performances at 3 p.m. and 8 p.m. He had written an anticipatory essay on the previous Friday, noting whimsically that 'the most feeble effort at marquee entertainment' is 'invariably labelled "the greatest performance the world has ever seen"'. After seeing the show, he was able to reassure his readers:

Beneath the gigantic waterproof erected at the Northwest of Ireland Agricultural Show Grounds there is provided a wonderful feast of delightful entertainment. If the audience is not being dazzled with astonishing feats of human or animal skill, its members are being treated to comic interludes which set them rollicking with laughter.

He was especially impressed by the lion tamer, 'a powerfully built and magnificently garbed Oriental, wearing Eastern garb' who, carrying only a whip, entered a specially constructed cage in the middle of the ring followed by six ferocious-looking lions. He had been working with them for only four weeks but put them through various clever tricks, including a big finish in which the lions form a circle around one of their number and the tamer sits on its back. Finally he ordered them back to their own cage. All but one of the noble creatures obeyed; the tamer tossed aside his whip, lifted the recalcitrant cat and carried him on his shoulders out of the enclosure. As the reporter put it: 'It is a truly extraordinary display of man's complete mastery over the king of beasts.' It was also the answer to the question he posed at the beginning of his piece: 'Does a circus hold more than a juvenile appeal?'

10 OCTOBER 1880

On Sunday, 10 October 1880, First Derry Presbyterian Church was re-opened after undergoing internal improvement. The church is believed to have been on the site of an earlier meeting place erected circa 1690, which gave way to a larger edifice created around 1777, and opened by the Reverend David Harvey on 24 June 1780. All the documents relating to its earlier history were destroyed by fire, but the cost was known to have been in the region of £4,000.

Repairs were carried out in 1828 at an outlay of £700, and its external appearance was then greatly improved. Other alterations took place at a later period, the most important being the re-pewing and repainting of the whole building in 1862–63 at an expense of between £1,200 and £1,500. Suitable buildings in the rear of the church were also constructed, and in 1854 a hall for lectures and meetings was erected. As part of the 1862–63 improvements considerable addition had been made to the pew accommodation and the external appearance of the building was greatly enhanced a decade later when, through the munificence of a Mr Robert Alexander, massive ornamental iron railings which enclosed the area in front of the church were erected.

The 1880 improvements took about four months to complete. The outside of the building, the lecture hall, the male school, and the railings in front, were all painted. The inside of the church underwent a complete change. The expansive ceiling was struck out in panels and brought out in oil in imitation of rich plaster decorations. The guilloche ornaments, the beams with their intersections, the centre flowers, mouldings, and other foliage were beautifully executed. The walls were painted in a stone colour, in harmony with the tints of the ceiling. The gallery fronts and wainscoting of the walls were also brought out in delicate tints; while the columns supporting the gallery were entirely remodelled and enriched with foliated capitals, picked out in white and gold.

The pews were finished in a rich shade of medium oak and panelling was introduced around the sides, giving them a chaste appearance. An addition was made to each pew in the way of umbrella brackets and trays, and all pews were numbered with brass figures. The pulpit was made to resemble walnut, while a shaded niche behind it gave striking effect to the new embossed margin panes on the southern end of the church. The railings of the stairs leading to the pulpit were in white and gold, while the building was lit by three large ceiling lights, and the wall and upright brackets with tripod burners. The aisles in the body of the church were covered with linoleum, and the pulpit platform and space reserved for the choir and precentor were laid with carpet.

The designs for the improvements were furnished by Mr John Guy Ferguson, and the painting by Messrs. A. & W. Shannon, Bishop Street. During the time the improvements were being carried out, the church members worshipped in the Union Hall, Shipquay Gate.

11 OCTOBER 1397

Between the years 1394 and 1398 Derry was without a bishop in residence, though Eoin Ó Mocháin had been appointed to the post on 16 September 1394. It was a time of confusion and conflict between the English administration in Dublin and the older local chieftain and clan system. This conflict also affected the Church as the rivalry between the older monastic system clashed with the Episcopal one more favoured by the Plantagenet kings. John Colton, Archbishop of Armagh, as head of the Church in Ireland, decided to settle the confusion personally by making an official archiepiscopal visit to the diocese. He had served previously as justiciar, the official representative of Richard II in the country, and was a man of considerable wealth and political power.

The visiting party, consisting of fifteen senior clerics, with members of both Gaelic Irish and Anglo-Normans, essentially constituted the Irish establishment and had both ecclesiastical and political power to impose the king's will (as interpreted by them) on the diocese, using excommunication, in the tightly knit society of the time implying virtual loss of identity. They had many attendants who needed billets as well as their masters, so it was a relief when after travelling up the almost trackless Foyle basin, they arrived in Derry late in the evening of Wednesday, 10 October 1397. They found accommodation at the monastery known as the *Dub Regles* (Black Abbey), where as the travelling clerical scribe, Richard Kenmore, recorded: 'The dean... caused provisions in abundance to be supplied for the... Lord Primate and his retinue, and for their horses, free and without expense, to the said Archbishop until the following Saturday.' The abbey was founded by the Canons Regular, also called Augustinians from their patron whose rule they followed. St Augustine's Chapel of Ease now stands on the same site.

Colton began the day of Thursday, 11 October with two Masses, 'one solemnly sung, and another without singing', and then the main tribunal began. Colton sat in the choir and asked for reports on diocesan matters, especially those relating to the *Dub Regles*. He was told that, after the resignation of Abbot Reginald O'Doherty, the monks had appointed Hugh MacGillibride O'Doherty as guardian of the monastery. He had taken into his personal possession the seal of the monastery which previously had been kept 'under the custody of three keys'—the responsibility for its safekeeping lying with three different people. The guardian had to acquiesce when Colton demanded its return.

A series of other reports confirmed the suspicions of the outsiders that not all the monks led utterly exemplary lives. Concubinage was commonly practised; indeed Simon, a Dominican who was Bishop of Derry from 1349 to 1380, was excommunicated (and later reinstated) for adultery and concubinage. At the request of the monks Colton drew up a set of more stringent rules for the house which he published at a church at Banagher, near Dungiven.

12 OCTOBER 1895

Just after six o'clock in the evening of Saturday, 12 October 1895, the bell of St Columb's Cathedral began to toll with the single repeated note that could only mean one thing: Cecil Frances, the wife of Bishop Alexander, who had been ill for more than a month, had died. They had been married for forty-five years and seemed to have been supremely happy. 'C.F.A.', as she was universally known, was born in Dublin in 1818, the daughter of Major John Humphreys of Wicklow, who on appointment as land agent to the Marquis of Abercorn, brought his family to live in Milltown House in Strabane. Alexander bore cheerfully the twin embarrassments of have being 'cradle-snatched' by a wife who was six years his elder and who remained the more famous for all of their lives.

As befitting one of her class and sex she taught in Sunday school and, in an enlightened way for the time, strove to make the catechetical year more interesting by writing seasonal verse. She published *Hymns for Little Children* in 1848 and by some mysterious alchemy three of the pieces were set to tunes so appropriate that they became world famous. These were 'All Things Bright and Beautiful', 'There Is a Green Hill Far Away' and 'Once in Royal David's City', hymns that are celebrated by a stained-glass triptych window in the baptistery of St Columb's Cathedral, just across the street from the Bishop's House where she died. Her complete works would fill a fairly thick volume. 'The Siege of Derry', a long poem describing the successful resistance of the city to the Jacobite army in 1689, was praised by Lord Macaulay, the classical historian of the period, and her imitation border ballad 'The Legend of Stumpie's Brae', set in a district across the river from her girlhood home in County Tyrone, is a brilliant pastiche. It describes the fate of a pair who kill a pedlar and are forced to cut off his legs to help dispose of the body until his spirit curses them:

> 'Ye think ye've laid me snugly here
>   And none shall know my station;
> But I'll hant ye far and I'll hant ye near,
> Father and son, wi' terror and fear
>   To the nineteenth generation.'

A pall of gloom was cast over the city by the death. She was mourned equally by rich and poor, Catholic and Protestant. Blinds were drawn out of respect in the homes of poor Catholics in the immediate neighbourhood of Nailors Row, just beneath the city walls that marked the edge of the episcopal gardens, and in Walker's Place and Palace Street. She was buried on Friday, 18 October. As the funeral moved from the cathedral out through Bishop's Gate the streets of shuttered shops were crowded with mourners. Her hymn 'There is a Green Hill Far Away' was partly inspired by the hill of Creggan seen from the back garden of the palace. She was buried on another green hill in the city cemetery, the first Protestant grave to be marked by a cross.

At the outbreak of the Great War, the 1st Battalion King's Own Scottish Borderers was stationed at Lucknow, India, and the 2nd at Dublin. The latter went to France in August 1914, being one of the four battalions of the 13th Brigade. In the Battle of Mons, fought on 22 August, the Borderers lay along the Conde Canal. It was there that the army got the directive to retreat, and with the other regiments of the division, the Borderers fell back some five miles on the morning of Monday, 24 August.

The battalion was in tremendous spirits and had only lost a few men, but in the retreat it had a dreadful time. Of the half-dozen brigades the 13th was in the rear, and accordingly it felt the full force of the German assault. At Fromeries on the Monday, and again at Le Cateau on the Wednesday, it was involved in some desperate combat, and on those days the battalion was almost annihilated.

The Borderers soon recovered from this punishment, but when the army was commanded to 'make good the Aisne', they were again put in a position of danger. They were ordered to traverse the river opposite Missy, and all through Sunday, 13 September, they struggled on, but the ground over which they had to move was quite open, and when night came they were still on the wrong side of the Aisne. Their efforts, however, had assisted the other brigades of the 5th division to cross, and these in their turn assisted the Borderers and their comrades of the 13th who crossed on 14 September. The Borderers were next found at Cuinchy, where the 2nd Corps was fighting hard to repel the Germans from Lille.

On 13 October they were in the thick of a slow advance, and 23-year-old Lance Corporal Andrew Gentle lost his life. Born in Falkirk, Stirlingshire, he lived in Londonderry for sixteen years before enlisting in Glasgow. He was a member of Second Derry (Strand Road) Presbyterian Church, and resided at 117 Foyle Road. His name is recorded on the Le Touret Memorial, Pas de Calais, France, and on Derry's Diamond War Memorial.

Tribute was paid to Gentle at the Second Derry Boys' Brigade Annual Display held on Thursday, 1 April 1915, by the Mayor of Londonderry, Robert Newton Anderson, who remarked that twenty-five of the old boys of the company were at present serving their king and country, while one, Andrew Gentle, had died on the battlefield.

Andrew's brother, Private Neil Gentle, Black Watch (Royal Highlanders), was later killed in action in France on 14 November 1916. His name is also commemorated on Derry's Diamond War Memorial, and on the Thiepval Memorial to the Missing, Somme, France. Neil, who had formerly been employed by Mr J.P. Thompson, Ferryquay Street, joined the colours over fifteen months before his death and had been at the Front for nearly twelve months.

In 1915 Derry had four railway stations: the Londonderry and Lough Swilly (L&LSR); the London Midland and Scottish (Northern Counties Committee), known locally as LMS; the County Donegal Railway (CDR); and the Great Northern (GNR). It was the golden age of steam and, though not the most convenient, railways were certainly the best for speed and heavy transport. At the Quarter Sessions held in the Derry courthouse in Bishop Street before Judge Todd on 14 October 1915, judgments were delivered in two cases involving railway companies.

The one against the GNR concerned the missing of an important mart at Trillick by two cattle farmers, the brothers William and Terence McManus, because of the lack of a promised 'special' to convey their stock to the fair. Judge Todd awarded £11 against the company due to the McManuses' loss of earnings.

The second case involved the delay in transit of goods from Clonmany to Dublin, and in the overly elaborate judicial summary it became clear that some aspects of the workings of the 'Lough Swilly', as it was conveniently known, were less that efficient. The complaint was originated by the Dublin firm of Richard Dickeson that claimed £7 15s 8d for equipment allegedly lost or damaged during transit from Clonmany Military Camp to Dublin. The Lough Swilly would have transported the equipment to Derry where it would have been taken from Pennyburn to Foyle Road to be loaded on to the Dublin GNR train. Clonmany, like several other places in Donegal, was used as a preliminary training ground for the soldiers, as a kind of alternative holiday camp. It was closed two months after the outbreak of the war on 4 August 1914. With the great increase in recruit numbers much larger camps were required, and so Finner and Dunree were used instead. The dismantling of the site meant that equipment surplus to need was sold off or returned from hire.

The goods in question undoubtedly reached Clonmany Station on 1 October 1914 and were given into the care of Mr Friel, the stationmaster, where they remained, as witnessed by an employee of Messrs. Dickeson, still unprocessed on 8 October. As Todd observed, this constituted a breach of the company's contractual obligation to deliver goods 'within a reasonable time'. He rejected Friel's claim that the missing goods were pilfered since there was not the slightest corroboration of the charge. The judge was quite scathing in his reminding the representatives of the company that it took twelve days for the stuff to travel the twenty-four miles from Clonmany to Derry and only two days to do the more than 150 miles from Derry to Dublin. The delay did lend itself to interference by pilferers and the Lough Swilly had a duty of care while the material was in their possession. He had therefore no hesitation in awarding Dickeson £6 18s with £1 8s in expenses and the usual costs.

For the eight days between the death of Cecil Frances Alexander, the hymnist and wife of Bishop Alexander, and her funeral, the city of Derry was in universal mourning. The funeral, set for Friday, 18 October, would be a large one with many visiting clerical and lay dignitaries in attendance. As part of the preparations the cathedral bells were tested; they had recently been refurbished and a firm of bell-founders had come from London to tune them. It was decided that the great bell, weighing 0.85 tons, which would play such an important part in the solemnity sounding during the procession to the cathedral and later to the cemetery, did not sound quite right. The tolling to announce Alexander's death on the previous Saturday had sounded curiously muffled. There was not sufficient time to summon the official tuner from London so Joseph McDermott, a local builder, whose men were working elsewhere about the cathedral, said that he could fix it in a minute if his men followed his instructions.

On 15 October, the clapper was tied and three men upended the bell by main force. James Ross, the verger of the cathedral, and another of McDermott's men remained in the bell-ringers' room holding the rope while McDermott climbed up into the belfry. He extended the wire by five inches and declared himself satisfied with the work on the bell. He then said he would signal the instruction to turn the bell by pulling both rope and wire. Nothing happened for five minutes and then they saw the wire being moved and the rope shuddered. The men in the ringing-chamber took this to be their signal and pulled the cable to turn the bell. They pulled hard on the rope but it would not move; something was jamming it and they went immediately to investigate. They found McDermott's lifeless body crushed between the big bell and the framework, his head and upper body out of sight inside the bell. It was presumed that death was instantaneous.

It took eleven men to raise the heavy bell enough to extricate McDermott's body. The grisly business of carrying the body down the spiral stairway was eventually achieved. An extra poignancy was lent to the fatality by the fact that when the crushed corpse was being conveyed away to the mortuary on a cart, the deceased's three children, pupils of the Deanery School beside the cathedral, came running out excitedly to find out why a crowd had gathered. Frederick

James Clark, the Dean of Derry, had made his way to the belfry before arrangements had been made to remove the body and he was deeply traumatised by the sight. An inquest was held in the home of P. McMonagle in Butcher Street on Friday, 18 October. John Coleman, foreman of the jury, was soon able announce the verdict that the deceased was crushed by the overturning of one of the cathedral bells.

16 OCTOBER 1899

Nazareth House, the orphanage and old people's home run by the Sisters of Nazareth in Bishop Street, was first opened in 1892. They depended mainly on charity though they did receive some diocesan help. Members of the order took turns to knock on the doors of Derry houses, irrespective of creed, and the progress of these mendicants in their blue, white and black habits was a common sight in the city up to the end of the 1960s when government support was formalised. By 1899 they had begun to find the going tough and were pleased when the *Derry Journal* gave them more than 40 square inches of space to appeal 'to all who love God's poor'.

It was an 'unpleasant duty' but a necessary one and 'one that will gladden the hearts of their many friends'. Apart from the simple appeal for funds the sisters used the opportunity to describe the work they did and to emphasise that, with their vow of poverty, none of the cash collected was for their personal use but went towards the general good of their charges. The urgency of the appeal was based on the requirement to pay off a heavy debt incurred by 'providing additional, and absolutely necessary, recreational and building grounds for the inmates of the home, and thus make the lives of the aged and infirm, the little boys and girls, and the tiny infants, more healthy and more happy'.

The 'home', as it was universally known, had at the time of the appeal 270 inmates and 'many and pressing' were 'the demands for admissions pouring in from all quarters'. Part of the service provided was a primary school, and the Ministry of Education had informed the Reverend Mother through the local inspector of National Schools that a much larger schoolroom for the children and infants was required. The sisters' response was to commission the building of an 'entire and spacious new wing for the children' that would leave ample room for the aged in the present building and 'place both them and the little ones in surroundings more roomy and more healthy'.

It is not clear whether the text of the appeal originated with the sisters or if the *Derry Journal* reporter collaborated in its writing. Apart from the inevitable pieties and the dilatation upon charity as the greatest of virtues, it was an effective piece of pleading. There was no doubt about the deserving nature of the cause or the sincerity of the promise that 'the prayers of the community will be offered for all benefactors thrice daily and the Holy Sacrifice will be offered for the same intention'. The piece continued: 'Subscriptions may be sent to the *Derry Journal* office, Shipquay Street, or the Sister Superior, Nazareth House, Londonderry, and will be duly acknowledged in the Press.' In a case of emergency like this, the problem of the city name was judiciously ignored.

17 OCTOBER 1942

At different times during the Second World War there were rallies for what was then known as the 'war effort'. They were partly for the imparting of information about the state of hostilities—in as much as the War Office censors permitted its release—and partly to raise awareness and money among civilians. Wastepaper and cans were assiduously collected, railing removed from gardens and gates, and people urged not to spend money foolishly. There were competitions for patriotic slogans with prizes for such mottos as 'Save for Victory', 'Tanks a lot!' and 'You Can't Spell Vic ory with an Absent "T".' One such event was held in Derry on Saturday, 17 October 1942, a few weeks before the defeat of Rommel at El Alamein that was the turning point of the war in the west. It was called 'Tanks for Attack' and it took place in the Guildhall Square.

The city had been transformed by the coming of the Americans, who, as civilian technicians, even before Pearl Harbor, had turned the sleepy port into a naval base with submarine training school and graving dock. The torpor of the 1930s was banished and the slightly bewildered citizens enjoyed the lashings of chewing gum, cigarettes and cigars, and candy, of which there seemed to be an endless supply. The American bases, too, provided employment for a town where there was virtually no work for men. By the autumn of 1942 many families had regular 'Yankee' visitors who could even provide the magical nylons for the grateful mothers and daughters. It was appropriate then that some input from the US servicemen should be part of the event. The main speaker at the rally had been well briefed. He was Lieutenant P.V. Dabbiere, United States Naval Reserve, and his speech made reference to Derry's older history:

Standing here in sight of those famous Derry walls, which your forefathers helped to build, we are called upon today to build another wall—a wall of tanks, which will move forward against the enemy. I personally love freedom and I know that you also like freedom. I would rather suffer the pangs of hell than be in the clutches of that monster in Germany... We in America cherish our homes, and I am quite certain that you in Ireland—having the same feelings as we have and having so much in common with us—cherish your homes as we do. We love that free way of living and that is why so many of us have left our homes and have given up so much to come over here in the cause of liberty, and to endure that we will maintain that freedom, that sanctity of our homes.

After the exhortations to buy savings certificates that would not only help the war effort but provide for their future, the huge crowd was entertained by a march past of American forces led by the regimental band.

18 OCTOBER 1879

The edition of the *Derry Standard* dated 18 October 1879 carried as prominently as the small font and rigid layout of the papers of the time permitted the following advertisement:

> St Columbkille's Church and Derry Diocesan Seminary
> At Casino, Londonderry
> Under the immediate direction of the Most Reverend Francis Kelly DD, Bishop of Derry.
> In this college students will be prepared for Maynooth and other Ecclesiastical Colleges; also for the Civil Service Examinations and also for the Intermediate Examinations.
> The Ordinary classes will be in Latin, Greek, French, English and Mathematics. German and Italian will be taught if required.
> Special teaching, suited to age and previous education, will be provided for those intended for mercantile pursuits.
> The College will be open for boarders on Monday 3 November.
> The Classes for Day Scholars at the same date.
> President: The Rev Edward O'Brien, lately Professor of Rhetoric in Maynooth College.

The seminary's primary purpose was the provision of education for students for the priesthood—hence the term Junior Seminary. Several attempts had been made by previous bishops from the time when the Popery Acts began to be mitigated in the 1770s to establish a seminary for the diocese and there were short-lived schools in existence at Clady, near Strabane, in Ferguson's Lane, not far from St Columb's at the Casino in Bishop Street, and in Pump Street, in a house later given as a convent to the Sisters of Mercy, who had been invited to the city by Bishop Edward Maginn in 1848.

Thanks to the efforts of Bishop Kelly, in 1869 there was land to build upon and space to develop in a park surrounding the little casino built as an amenity by the rich and eccentric but philanthropic Earl Bishop Frederick Hervey. The word 'casino' then had no gaming connotation but was used by Hervey to describe his summer lodge. Since it was less than half a mile from the episcopal palace and hardly ever used by him, because of his regular absences, it became the home of the school that Catholic Derry urgently wished for and needed. Work could not begin until Friday, 11 May 1877, and not much more than two years later the school that, during its history, would see two of its pupils win Nobel prizes and contribute greatly to the fields of art, music, science and literature, finally opened its doors.

The school moved to a split site in September 1973, with the senior school accommodated in Buncrana Road. With the opening of the co-educational Lumen Christi College on the Casino site in 1997 the two branches of St Columb's College were united.

19 OCTOBER 1772

A remarkable letter written by a Derry merchant in 1772 was brought back to the city by an American lawyer who arrived at Moville on Sunday, 24 June 1928. The letter, which the lawyer in question, Mr James M. Hepbron, managing director of the Baltimore Criminal Justice Commission, picked up at a bookstall in Baltimore, Maryland, where it was on sale with other archaic documents, actually described the shipment from Derry to Baltimore of two convicts who were to be sold and their price returned in the form of flour or flaxseed.

The commission was concerned with the study of the best methods for dealing with criminals. Hepbron had visited England and the continent the previous year, and attended Londonderry Police Court on 25 June 1928, expressing great interest in the proceedings. 'I was greatly pleased,' he told a *Londonderry Sentinel* representative, 'to find how remarkably small is your criminal record—only thirty-five cases of assault last year...'

The 1772 letter was incorporated in an article which Mr Hepbron was forwarding for publication in the Baltimore *Evening Star*. It was printed in the *Londonderry Sentinel* on 26 June 1928:

They say here in Ireland that a sight of the Walls of Derry (Londonderry) will make your heart beat faster… To-day this ancient city has little in common with Baltimore. Little business is carried on between the two ports. Londonderry receives an occasional shipload of grain from Baltimore, and in return sends wool. It was not always so, however. A hundred and fifty years ago there was considerable commerce between Baltimore Town and Derry. In some respects it was a strange business, as the following letter will attest:

Londonderry, 19th October, 1772.

Messrs. Samuel & Robert Purviance merchants, Baltimore Town, c/o the *Pitt* Captain McShane.

Sirs—Inclosed you have two transport warrants for James Adams and Jos. McCaffry for seven years, both of which are shipped on board the *Pitt*, Captain McShane, and now to you addressed. We request you'll receive and dispose of them to best advantage for our acct., and send the proceeds in best common flour, provided it does not exceed 16/6; but, if higher, we would chuse it in flaxseed. Hope they'll arrive in good time to have the proceeds by the Prince of Wales, but if otherwise beg you may not neglect to send it by the *Pitt*. We beg leave to observe these transports are fresh; sturdy fellows, one of them an excellent white smith and the other a weaver, and as servants were so lately in demand with you we flatter ourselves they'll arrive to a good market. Doubt not you'll use your uppermost endeavour for our interest. We are of opinion if these servants were dressed and clean on arrival it would promote the sale of them, but in these matters you are the best judges, and with compliments to your Mr. R. P. – Gentlemen, your most obedient servant,

John McConnell

20 OCTOBER 1926

On 20 October 1926, Nancy Convery, a sixty-eight-year-old woman from Coolderry, Coleraine, died of injuries received on 6 August that year. The charge brought against Archibald Henry, her neighbour and assailant, was then changed from GBH to murder. It was the most sombre case to be heard at the Winter Assizes in Derry, before William Moore, Lord Chief Justice of Northern Ireland, in December 1926. M.D. Begley led for the Crown, with William Lowry as second chair, while John Long defended Henry. Both assailant and victim were described by Begley as belonging to 'the poor labouring class and next door neighbours'; it was clear the relations between the parties were strained.

Continuing with his opening remarks, Begley informed the jury that, between seven and eight o'clock on the evening of 6 August, a man called James O'Neill had become involved in an altercation with Henry, whom he accused of being drunk.

Nancy Convery had interfered on O'Neill's behalf and Henry had struck at her with a billhook where she lay on the floor. The implement left a wound two and a half inches long over her left ear and fractured her skull. She lingered for more than two months before finally dying. Sergeant Brown of the RUC produced a map of the scene, and statements by Robert Curry, David Campbell and Maggie Convery, the victim's sister, corroborated Begley's presentation. Maggie Convery insisted that, having knocked Nancy down, Henry then 'went for the billhook'. Taking the stand Henry said that the deceased had called him 'a liar, a thief and a rogue'. After further provocation he pushed her and she fell. He then ran into his own house to arm himself with a walking stick, and not knowing he 'had got hold of the billhook', gave her 'a few touches' with it. He claimed he had no intention of doing her any harm.

O'Neill, when questioned, denied that the victim had called Henry any of the names he claimed she did. There being no further evidence, or much rebuttal from Henry's defence counsel, the jury were asked to retire. The details were pretty damning and they were not out for long, returning with a verdict of 'guilty as charged'. They had no authority to change the charge but they did make a recommendation to mercy. The judge noted the recommendation but produced the piece of silk that was called the 'black cap' and sentenced Henry to be hanged on 5 January 1927.

21 OCTOBER 1932

On Friday, 21 October 1932, the body of Hugh Sheppard, a twenty-one-year-old Derry man from 28 Albert Street, off the Fountain (a street now disappeared), was discovered lying in a burn in Prehen Wood. An inquest was held the following morning in the city infirmary (also disappeared) by Dr M.F. Leslie, the coroner for the Liberties. A jury was sworn in and Head Constable Neely held a watching brief for the RUC.

Dr Hugh Graham, the house surgeon, said that Sheppard was dead on arrival at the infirmary. An examination revealed no evidence of violent trauma and the doctor concluded that death was due to asphyxia that could have been caused by the position in which the body had been found. It had been established that Sheppard was an epileptic and probably had had a seizure, though Dr

Graham could not yet be absolutely certain. If the man had a fit and fell into the water, it could have been a contributory factor of death.

The remains were identified by Sheppard's brother, David, who confirmed that Hugh did suffer from epilepsy for which he had occasional medication, but was otherwise in good health. He had had a seizure a week before in his own house and the attacks were liable to return without warning. He had been working for John McBrine, who had a butcher's shop at 19 Spencer Road, and had told him that he had two or three pigs that he needed to slaughter up at the Bolies, a section of Prehen Wood through which the Bolies stream flowed. When Sheppard did not return after half an hour, McBrine went up to the Bolies but failed to find him. He noticed a single pig crossing the stream near the piggery and when he went closer found the body lying face down in the water, which was no more than two or three inches deep. Tracks of footsteps and other marks made it clear that Sheppard had slipped over the 'brow' of the bank. With help from some other men the body was lifted from the stream; attempts were made at artificial respiration, but without success. A bucket of pig meat was present in the stream beside the body, and Robert McNaul of Prehen Road said that he had seen Sheppard standing at the door of the piggery.

He was well known in the district and people were aware of his illness. One witness, William Wilson, said he'd had to go to his assistance several times in the past. Sergeant G. Kennedy stated that he and Constable Kane had gone to Prehen and tried further resuscitation without success. The jury assented to Dr Leslie's statement that the deceased had fallen into the stream because of a fit and had drowned.

22 OCTOBER 1951

One of the disastrous side effects of partition for Derry was the cutting off of the city's hinterland of Donegal and Sligo. The effects became alarmingly clear before the 1920s were over, and the decade that followed was aptly named the 'Hungry Thirties' as far as the city was concerned. The one bright economic spot was its reputation as the world's greatest supplier of shirts, a reputation that persisted throughout the war and for a few decades afterwards.

By the start of the 1950s Derry's 'staple industry' began to falter slightly before the influx of Asian products all but killed it. One aspect of the loss of Donegal was that a number of the expert stitchers, side-seamers, patent-turners and finishers came from that county, and by a stern Ministry of Labour injunction they could not work in Derry without permits that could be withdrawn without notice. This was one of the features of a story in the *Derry Journal* on Monday, 22 October 1951, which announced that, on the previous Friday, 250 workers in the industry had been paid off, bringing the recent total of redundancies to more than 1,000. Many others still in employment were on short-hour engagements and, as the *Journal* reporter soberly put it, 'the industry faces its grimmest outlook for years'.

The *Journal* was still true to its early subtitle 'Northwest Advertiser' and at least half of its readership, especially of the Friday edition, came from across the border in the 'State', as it was then imprecisely described. By the time the story appeared only a few of the permits for Donegal workers had been revoked but it was inevitable that if there were more workers than jobs, preference would be given to those employees who lived in Northern Ireland. The Donegal workers had an excellent reputation for industry and efficiency, and the local employers would have preferred to keep them.

An ironic aspect of the lay-off was that even at this time of shedding workers two of the leading city factories, not named but easily guessed at, had had to take on a few extra hands, while the rest worked overtime because of a number of 'specials'—rush orders that the factories took pride in filling very promptly. Derry was used to bad news but the idea that shirt-making, too, would crumble was almost unthinkable. The news was bound to affect trade in the town though it had not yet been felt by the retailers. Sales *were* lower than normal for the time of year but local drapers tended to blame the unseasonably good weather for the lack of purchases of the recently arrived, new winter stock.

23 OCTOBER 1911

Born into a theatrical family in Coventry in 1847, Ellen Terry made her debut at the age of nine. In 1864 she gave up the stage to marry the artist G.F. Watts, but the marriage failed within a year and she returned to acting. Terry left the stage again to live with architect and theatrical designer Edward Godwin, with whom she had two children. The couple parted and Terry returned to the stage once more to support her children. In 1877 she married actor Charles Kelly but they separated in 1881. A woman of striking beauty Terry began her lengthy stage association with actor Henry Irving in 1878 but, wilful as ever, married the US actor James Carew in 1907, remaining with him until 1910. Acting less, she lectured on Shakespeare in the years 1910–11, and gave one of these lecture recitals in Derry on 23 October 1911.

The following day the *Londonderry Sentinel*, commenting ebulliently on the recital, wrote: 'The crowded state of St Columb's Hall last night showed that the name of Miss Ellen Terry, even when associated with a lecture recital, possesses the magnetic power of attracting a large audience. Much had been expected of her performance—of her wonderful personality, her methods, and her peculiar faculty for visualizing character which have gone to make her the most talked of and written about actress of the past half century. These expectations were fully realised.'

The newspaper continued excitedly: 'From the moment Miss Ellen Terry appeared on the platform and was accorded an enthusiastic welcome until she said "Good-night" she exhibited much of that grace and ingenuity, charm and freshness which have rendered her so dramatic a figure in drama. The audience were enchanted by her beautiful voice and the emotional feeling which she displayed as she brought in rapid review before them most of the women Shakespeare had created, and how distinct is her intonation and how flexible her voice, the vividness with which each character stood out bore ample testimony.'

Remarking on the first and second parts of the programme the *Sentinel* wrote: 'Her presentation of first Viola, then Desdemona and Emilia, and finally of Juliet, which made up the first part of the programme, were charming, and she delivered her several speeches, especially those of Juliet, in convincing style. In the second part of the programme she covered a wide range, and dealt in a racy and instructive manner with Katherine, Lady Anne, Helena, Julia, Constance, Cordelia, Cleopatra, Katherine of Aragon, Hermione, Imogen, Cressida, Lady Macbeth, Ophelia, and Portia.'

The newspaper concluded its positive review thus: 'Her most virile interpretation was possibly that of Portia, one of the noblest and most lovable of Shakespeare's women. "The quality of mercy" appeal came with special emphasis and force and was received with loud applause. The "Mad Scene" in *Hamlet* was most touching and effective, while Lady Macbeth was represented with tragic force and intensity. The devotion of Cleopatra also found adequate treatment, and altogether the recital, which lasted almost two hours, was followed with rapt attention and considerable profit.'

24 OCTOBER 1786

Kitty Wilkinson, 'the originator of baths and washhouses for the poor' and 'Saint of the Slums', was born Catherine Seaward in Derry on 24 October 1786. In 1794 her parents left for Liverpool. At the mouth of the Mersey their ship struck the Hoyle Bank and her father and sister were drowned. Aged twelve, she went to work in a cotton mill in Caton, near Lancaster, and as an apprentice had some privileges, one being given the chance to improve her education. She left the mill and went into service for a few years, then wed a sailor. Soon afterwards he was lost at sea, and she found herself a widow with two young children. Additionally, she had to care for her mother who was blind and insane, but with characteristic hospitality opened her door to anyone who needed assistance.

After her mother's death she returned to Liverpool where conditions were much worse than at Caton, and she took in washing to earn a little money. She also took in three motherless children who, when their father died, she brought up as her own. She married Tom Wilkinson, whom she had met at Caton, and they settled down in her house in Denison Street. Tom was a hospitable man, so their home became a centre of good works and kindly acts.

In 1832, when cholera broke out in Liverpool, Kitty was foremost amongst the devoted workers. Her scullery housed the only boiler in the street, so she offered the use of it to her neighbours to wash affected clothes and bed linen. They accepted the offer so willingly that she had to fit her cellar as a washhouse, and this doubled as a disinfecting room for clothes from the cholera homes and for those who had not yet been infected by the outbreak. She managed it so well that not one of her workers became infected. It was then that she had the idea of a public washhouse, and the first one was opened in May 1842, in Upper Frederick Street, Liverpool. She and her husband were the first superintendents.

Tom died in 1848, but Kitty outlived him by twelve years, dying on 11 November 1860. The epitaph on her grave in St James' Cemetery, Liverpool, reads: 'Indefatigable and self-sacrificing, she was the widow's friend, the support of the orphan, the fearless and unwearied nurse of the sick, the originator of baths and washhouses for the poor.' A stained-glass window in the 'Lady Chapel' of Liverpool's Anglican Cathedral, built around 1910, also commemorates the life of Kitty Wilkinson.

More recently, it was announced that Mrs Wilkinson was to be the first woman commemorated by a statue in Liverpool's St George's Hall. The statue was to be carved in Italian marble, and would cost in the region of £150,000.

One of the finest houses in Derry was Thornhill, the home of the Watt family who owned one of the world's greatest distilleries. It is still possible in more modern pubs to find mirrors celebrating the Tyrconnell and Inishowen malts, often showing jockeys guiding their mounts over jumps in steeplechases. The tall chimney of the distillery in Abbey Street was as well-known a landmark as the spires of the two cathedrals and the Guildhall. The plant that took up most of the south side of William Street made grain whiskey while the branch in Spencer Road made the connoisseur's single malt. Over 300 men were employed in the enterprise, including coopers, carpenters and office staff.

The owner, Andrew Alexander Watt, known to his workers (behind his back) as 'A.A.', was sixty-eight in 1921, and with his sharp features and military moustache was not a man to clash with. He had built up a whiskey empire that was internationally famous and worked harder than any of his operatives— and when his workforce decided to strike, he did the unthinkable.

Conditions were deplorable: noisy, dark and dangerous. The multi-storied granaries were the size of football pitches, the mixing vessels were twenty feet deep and there was danger of drowning in the 50,000 gallon tank. There was a strong case for better wages and conditions, but from A.A.'s point of view, business was cut-throat and it was only by innovation and new technologies that he was able to keep ahead of the competition.

The strike took the form of locking out the owner, who arrived from Thornhill in his Rolls to find his own gates shut fast against him. He climbed on to one of his own whiskey barrels and, in a menacing voice, said: 'Well, men, I put it to you like this... what is it to be? Will you open the gates?' The answer was equally stern: 'The gates stay shut!' 'Very well!' exclaimed A.A. 'Shut they are and shut they shall remain.'

It proved to be one of Derry's darkest days, all the more deleterious in that her economic life was heading for eclipse as the border deprived her of her hinterland. The dramatic moment passed but some weeks later, on 25 October 1921, a notice was posted on all the gates that the distillery would shut permanently in one week's time.

The closure affected many others besides the distillery employees; carters, railway workers and dockers were all in danger of losing their jobs. Why, it was wondered, did the man act so precipitately? Like many others of his ilk he could not predict the effects of partition on the local economy. Perhaps he was just tired of the strain of keeping ahead of the opposition. He moved to Easton Hall in Lincolnshire where he died seven years later. His action removed from Derry its main source of male employment and the spiral into recess continued remorselessly. Thornhill became a convent and then a grammar school.

26 OCTOBER 1917

Private William Maurice Davin, Canadian Infantry, was born in April 1893, and killed in France on 26 October 1917. His name is listed on the Ypres Menin Gate Memorial in Belgium as well as being recorded on the St Augustine's Church of Ireland First World War Memorial and the Diamond War Memorial in Londonderry.

Davin went to Canada before the Great War erupted, but joined up immediately, and from that time until his death saw extensive active service. He was wounded by shell splinters in November 1916; on returning to the Front after his recovery he had a lucky escape when a bullet was prevented from causing him serious injury when it struck his cigarette case.

Davin's father, who had founded the successful box manufacturing firm Messrs. George Davin & Sons Ltd. in Aubrey Street, Derry, received a letter informing him of William's death by a military colleague of his son's, Private W.E. Wiltshire: 'It is with the deepest regret that I pen these few lines, telling you what little I am able regarding the death of your son William, who fell so nobly in action during a recent engagement by our battalion. As he was one of my greatest pals, I feel that what is your loss is also mine. Billy was not in the same company as I am, so it was not until we returned to billets that I became known of the sad news. I then learned from a corporal who was near him at the time that William had been struck in the head by a piece of flying shrapnel, death resulting immediately, so he suffered no pain...'

Davin's brother, Second Class Air Mechanic Fred G. Davin, Royal Flying Corps, was wounded in both thighs during aerial operations on the Western Front in 1917, and was named by Sir Douglas Haig in despatches as deserving of special mention. Fred had also been in Canada at the time of the outbreak of hostilities but returned to Londonderry to join the North Irish Horse before transferring to the Flying Corps. Another brother, Arthur J. Davin, enlisted with the 10th Battalion Royal Inniskilling Fusiliers (Derry Volunteers); during fighting in May 1916 he was wounded and taken prisoner, but was released after the signing of the Armistice.

Derry's Catholic/Nationalist voters, though in the majority since the mid-nineteenth century, were virtually disenfranchised because of electoral boundary manipulation. This imposed powerlessness lasted until the Troubles and the electoral reforms of 1973, but municipal sectarianism in such matters as housing allocation and job appointments meant years of frustration for nationalist representatives. They were not actually powerless since membership of important committees gave them access to a limited influence.

The tensions caused by the situation increased after the setting-up of the Northern Ireland state, when more than 500,000 Catholics, mainly in Belfast, Derry and Newry, and in counties Tyrone and Fermanagh, found themselves—largely against their will—in a situation of non-compliance. Unionist awareness of this potential dangerous resentment made them deaf to any suggestion of reform. When the convergence of a number of sociological elements produced the discontent of the late 1960s the main spur to protest was the sense of 'second-class citizenship' felt more and more keenly by a much better educated population, thanks to general welfare reform in the United Kingdom.

A typically angry confrontation in the council chamber occurred on 27 October 1955 when anti-Partitionist aldermen and councillors rated the majority for obvious partiality in appointments to council posts. Alderman James Hegarty had evidence that an employee, who had been urged to join the Orange Order, was advised that he had been spending too much time in the company of Catholics. When he refused, saying that he would choose his own company, he was told he would be dismissed. Hegarty made an impassioned plea for a rational, unbiased system to be adopted for the allocation of posts: 'It is about time that everybody got a fair crack of the whip. Let appointments be made on merits and not on religion or on what Order one belongs to.'

Sometimes stung by the effective barrage of accusation Unionists would respond by insisting if the boot were on the other foot nationalists would behave in exactly the same way; they cited council appointments in Newry where there was a nationalist majority. Alderman McAteer said he regarded such practices by any party as unjust and positively immoral, and called into question the worth of any candidate whose appointment was approved under anything other than impartial standards. He pointed out that it was vain for the mayor to call for a greater degree of civic spirit in Derry: 'How can people feel any civic pride if you Unionists, the self-elected administrators of the city, are going to engage in this ugly, squalid anti-Catholic plotting?' A motion asking that a recent appointment be referred back to the Health Committee was defeated by twelve Unionist to seven anti-Partitionist votes.

It was in the summer of 1848 that six sisters of the Mercy Order arrived in Derry from their house in Tullamore, County Offaly, or King's County, as it was then known. They had been invited by Bishop Edward Maginn, who died not long afterwards of the typhus that, during the Great Famine, killed as many Irish as starvation. Their mission was to the poor of the city, many of whom had crowded into the Protestant citadel, driven there by hunger and disease. They continued to play a vitally important role in female education until the twenty-first century. The sisters provided a day school in Pump Street until their Thornhill premises on the Culmore Road, bought from the Watt family, were opened in 1932; they also ran two primary schools.

The centenary of their arrival in Derry was commemorated by High Mass on 28 October 1948. Every priest in the diocese was present in the cathedral that morning to take part in the ceremony that was celebrated in the presence of the Most Reverend Dr Neil Farren, Bishop of Derry. The celebrant was the Right Reverend Monsignor Joseph O'Doherty, late president of St Columb's College. The singing of the '*Te Deum*' gave the *Journal* reporter a heaven-sent opportunity for a piece of lyrical description:

> It was an inspiring scene during the singing of the '*Te Deum*'. Golden sunshine from a cloudless sky streamed through the stained-glass windows of the Cathedral over the heads of the clergy, nuns and laity as they stood before the golden tabernacle to give thanks for a golden century.

Monsignor John McShane, once also president of St Columb's College, was chosen to preach the centenary sermon, and he pulled no punches:

> We have come to celebrate the centenary of the establishment of a religious community of sisters, who in response to the appeal of the illustrious Bishop Maginn, came to make a breach in the City Walls and to help in the re-building of the edifice of religion that had been desecrated and well-nigh overthrown through centuries of persecution. The year of their arrival, 1848, was a year of sad but glorious memories of the story of our land. The Penal Laws, no doubt, had failed in their purpose for in spite of 'dungeon, fire and sword' our people had clung to the faith of Patrick. But then came the awful visitation of the Famine...

There was more of what seems to modern ears a slightly irrelevant political slant to the sermon. It is unlikely that the six originals were in any way conscious of other than educational and social motives for their mission. The beginning of the sermon was characteristic of its more polemical time but, after the nationalist *obbligato*, the rest most eloquently summed up the Order's worthy achievements in the city.

29 OCTOBER 1924

The Irish Civil War between those who accepted the 1921 Treaty terms and the anti-Treaty IRA ended in 1923, and most of the IRA internees had been released by the Free State government by the end of 1924. Eamon de Valera, who had announced the end of the conflict, was still regarded as a dangerous figure by both governments and was liable for arrest in Northern Ireland. It was a time of several by-elections, both north and south, and he risked imprisonment by coming to Derry to speak on behalf of the Sinn Féin candidate. Though marginalised during the civil war he was clearly leader of a growing opposition to the Free State regime of William Cosgrave that, in time, would claim its parliamentary place as the party of government.

The *Derry Journal* of 29 October 1924 gave a detailed account of de Valera's movements during the previous week, tracking him from Sligo on Saturday, 25 October, to his arrest on the Sunday night and his incarceration in Belfast's Crumlin Road Jail on the Monday. It was later revealed that de Valera and his associates were searched and all their luggage ransacked by Free State troops in Sligo, and as they neared the border it became clear that the RUC were determined that he should not enter the North. All the roads leading from Donegal into Derry were patrolled by the police and even the fields on both sides of the boundary were kept under careful watch. He might have reached Derry earlier but that both the cars in his group had broken down at Carrigans, four miles from the city on the main Sligo Road, and he was forced to walk the remaining distance.

He managed to evade the patrols until he reached St Columb's Hall, where the rally was to be held. It was there that the future taoiseach was arrested, hustled into a police car and taken to Victoria Barracks on Strand Road. He was not put in a cell but spent the night in a comfortable room with a large armchair. Ever conscious of the need for vigilance he had at some stage found it necessary to make his way through fields, for by the Monday morning his shoes were still thick with mud. A friendly RUC constable offered to clean them for him in Victoria Barracks but 'Dev' happily bent to use the brushes and polish himself. He was then taken by District Inspector Cahill by car to the Midland station and put on the 7.15 a.m. train—in a third-class carriage.

He spent some time in Crumlin Road Jail until the election results were declared. Two Sinn Féin candidates were, in fact, elected.

30 OCTOBER 1901

Prize-giving day had a special significance in Derry's schools over a hundred years ago. It was an opportunity to make modest boasts, and to engender pride among students and parents of both the school and its achievements. These halls of learning tended to be fairly grim places, especially for boarders, with strict discipline and not much in the way of entertainment to be had. The boys were encouraged to exhaust themselves at games, by then mainly Gaelic football in St Columb's, although rugby and cricket had been played when the school first opened in 1879. By 30 October 1901 it had completed almost twenty years as a diocesan seminary and when the staff, pupils and distinguished visitors gathered in the assembly hall, there was an air of deserved attainment.

The guest speaker was the Most Reverend Dr John Keys O'Doherty, who was the only bishop of the diocese to have been born in Derry, and was the first to have been consecrated in St Eugene's Cathedral (in 1890). He had published a volume of occasional writings, including poetry, called *Derriana* (1902), so it was no surprise that his address should have several literary allusions, including a quotation from Goldsmith's *The Deserted Village*, giving a slightly sanitised version of current teaching methods:

> That as a bird with fond endearment tries
> To tempt its new fledged offspring to the skies…

The platform party was impressive, including the school president Dr McHugh and his deputy Dr O'Kane, both of whom later became bishops of the diocese. The remaining clerical teachers were named, but the rest were consigned to a single sentence by the *Derry Journal* scribe who reported on the occasion: 'The lay teachers in the several departments were also present.' The paper's readers were not going to be allowed to forget that St Columb's was an official junior seminary, the original and primary purpose of which was to provide the scholastic foundation that pupils would require at the senior seminary, Maynooth. The provision of an educated laity, though clearly included in the school's ethos, was always relegated, at least in public, to second place.

The president announced that he would not deprive the boys of a very pleasant day and would have the bishop distribute the awards as quickly as possible. These were provided by the Intermediate Examinations Board, as was the practice of the time, and amounted in that year to an impressive £451. This was done expeditiously to continuing cheers, and the prospect of 'a very pleasant day' came nearer; but the students still had to listen to many wise words about temperance, truthfulness and the avoidance of bad company before they were finally released on their free day at the bishop's command.

31 OCTOBER 1666

More than two-thirds of the city of London was destroyed by a conflagration that raged for five days, from 2 to 6 September 1666. Many important buildings, including the old St Paul's Cathedral and eighty-nine other churches, the Royal Exchange, the Customs House and 13,200 dwellings were destroyed. Of particular concern to the citizens of the new model town on the Foyle was the loss of forty-four livery halls and their headquarters, the Guildhall, the home of the Honourable the Irish Society, the company of merchant tailors who owned much of the land in Londonderry, a name that a majority of the citizens deemed a badge of honour.

To show solidarity and fraternal sympathy a number of the burghers sent £250 'towards Releife of the poore distressed of the late dreadfull ffire' accompanied by a letter that was read out at a meeting of the Common Council on 20 November 1666. The historian W.S. Ferguson, who published many scholarly essays on the early history of Foyle College, where he taught, had found the original manuscript among the records of the corporation of London. He reckoned that 31 October was the likely date of its dispatch, and published the letter preserving the original spelling and punctuation on 10 August 1950.

It begins:

> Sorrows soe smothers or expression, that we knowe not what to say much Lesse sufficiently to bewayle yor (nay, our own Dreadfull Losse) by those by those late repeated Direfull and astonishing judgemts it has pleased the Almightie to lay on you, of our Dear Mother City.

And concludes:

> We must consider ourselves phisitions of small value; But yet we hope that the warmeinge a Ragge, or Compassionat holding of the Head from such an Infant as wee are (especially at this tyme) Tendred so freely to you, or Honnored Mother, may possibly prove a greater cordiall than better compounded and more effectuall

medecyns from abler Helpers; Such as it is with all candor and Humility wee most freely offer, not out of constraint but with a willing mynd as a evidence of or Duety unto God and you, To whom that this together with the other more supplies from other of greater ability (ors being indeed but as small Gleanings of all the vintage of this or Israell) may be accepted to God and you, is the Hearty prayers of

> Honble Gent
> Yor really faithfull and obliged
> Servts

Their 'small Gleanings' of £250 would today have the buying power of £28,700. The letter was signed by local dignitaries, including the mayor, Thomas Moncrieff; George Holland, the Dean of Derry; Hugh Edwards and Robert Morrrison, city sheriffs; and Colonel John Gorges, the local agent of the Irish Society. The mother-city officials were sufficiently moved to have the letter 'fairly entred into the Journal to remain a Memorial hereof to Posterity and upon receipt of ye said money the hearty thanks of this Court be returned by letter to ye said city of Londonderry'.

NOVEMBER

1 NOVEMBER 1914

Thirty-one-year-old Sergeant Andrew Charles Glover Ferguson, 1st Battalion Irish Guards, was killed in action during the Great War on 1 November 1914. His name is recorded on the famous Ypres Menin Gate Memorial, Belgium, and commemorated on Derry's Diamond War Memorial. He was the son of John and Elizabeth Ferguson, George's Street, Londonderry, and was on the reserves when war broke out. Although not selected to go with the initial Expeditionary Force he volunteered to accompany them, and was thus included in the first contingent of the Guards sent to France. Sergeant Ferguson was a very popular instructor of the UVF in the Maiden City prior to the war, and was also gymnastic instructor in the YMCA. At the time of the Boer War he volunteered for the frontline, but was not in the mounted detachment of the Irish Guards selected for service in South Africa.

Accompanying the letter notifying Mrs Elizabeth Ferguson of the death of her son was the following communication: 'The King commands me to assure you of the true sympathy of his Majesty and the Queen in the loss of your son—(Signed) Kitchener.' Sergeant Ferguson died during the First Battle of Ypres (fought October–November 1914). The Irish Guards suffered severely on 1 November. A sergeant, returning home from the Front several months later, related the details of Ferguson's death: 'The Guards were in the trenches, and were being hard pressed by a superior force of the enemy, when they ran short of ammunition. Things looked bad, and the German sharpshooters were so busy that to put one's head above the trenches was risking almost certain death. The situation was becoming desperate, when Sergeant Ferguson decided to make a dash out of the trenches to bring up the much-needed ammunition. No sooner, however, had he left cover to make his dangerous run to the rear than a German bullet pierced his head and killed him.'

Sergeant Ferguson's father was, for twenty-eight years, a member of Londonderry Harbour Police, and a sergeant-in-charge for more than half that period. In early life, John Ferguson had joined the Royal Irish Constabulary, and saw considerable service, principally in Leitrim and Cork. He was stationed in Cork during the Fenian rising, and took part in many dramatic incidents. Some time after retiring from the RIC he was appointed to the house staff of the much-maligned William Clements, 3rd Earl of Leitrim, who was assassinated in Cratlagh Wood on 2 April 1878. John subsequently came to Derry and found employment as a guard on the Great Northern Railway before joining the harbour police. He died at the City and County Infirmary, Derry, in March 1908, after a brief but painful illness.

2 NOVEMBER 1926

The concept of ciné-variety was a kind of middle ground between the new aggressive popular entertainment of film and the older music hall. The silver screen was bound to win in the end because of its pre-packaged economy and no need for the complications of orchestra, backstage staff and temperamental artistes. A typical evening's entertainment would consist of a variety show with singers, dancers, comedians and specialty acts like acrobats and conjurers, followed by a 'moving picture'. The Derry Opera House maintained the concept in the 1930s and it was still possible to experience ciné-variety in Dublin until after the war.

On 2 November 1926 the audience at St Columb's Hall were treated to one of the most exciting special effects movies ever made, *The Thief of Bagdad*, made two years previously. Films took quite a while to trundle as far as Derry in those heavy-reel days. It was probably the finest picture that Douglas Fairbanks ever made; with his dazzling smile and regularly bared chest, he was famous for his athletic leaps, especially the trick of sliding down heavy curtains by cutting them with his dagger. He was a thrilling Zorro in 1920, D'Artagnan in 1921 and Robin Hood in 1922, but *Thief* with its magic rope, flying carpet, winged horse and cloak of invisibility was a sensation. Based upon the Arabian Nights tale of a poor Baghdad slum-dweller's adventures in the royal palace, the sea of lava, the valley of monsters and under the ocean, it pleased everyone—

including many who dismissed the genre—because of the special effects devised by William Cameron Menzies and the direction of Raoul Walsh. The addition of silent screen beauties Julanne Johnston and Anna May Wong didn't hurt its commercial chances either.

For the Derry screening, a specially augmented orchestra was hired under the direction of J.S. O'Brien. The evening's variety section had soprano Daisy Ronald and baritone Walter Kinniburgh singing the popular 'I Passed by Your Window'. The film only ran for four nights but the management of the 'Hall', as it was known, promised for Friday and Saturday *A Gilded Butterfly*, 'a romantic drama', and on stage *Songs of Italy* with such favourites as 'O Sole Mio', 'Santa Lucia', 'Ciribiribin', 'Funicui Funicula' and 'Donne Mobile'.

3 NOVEMBER 1915

Magee College began as a Presbyterian seminary with an Arts faculty, and it opened its doors to students in 1865, nine years after the foundation stone was laid. It was endowed by Martha Maria Magee who left a part of her considerable fortune for the purpose. Basil McCrea, one of the trustees, had donated £7,000 to set up a chair of natural philosophy, and in his will left £70,000 subject to his sister's life interest, who in turn left the college a further £5,000 in 1911. In recognition of this generosity it was known for a time as McCrea-Magee, and when the time came, on 3 November 1915, to celebrate its golden jubilee that was its title. By that time it also had a number of non-divinity students, including women, and was affiliated to Trinity College where degrees begun in Derry were completed in Dublin.

The occasion of the jubilee provided an opportunity for the Graduates Association to present to Professor J.R. Leebody, the sole survivor of the original staff, an illuminated album, and to inaugurate a mathematical scholarship known as the President Leebody prize. The platform party included the senior Magee academic staff and many Presbyterian ministers from around the province. Leebody's opening remarks were taken up with obituaries of Professor Graham, whose tenure of the chair of metaphysics and ethics had lasted thirty-four years, of Joseph Irwin, who had been a trustee, and of Dr Dickey, professor of Hebrew and Biblical criticism. He was therefore all the more relieved to welcome to the faculty Dr Strahan, 'a man pre-eminently fitted to carry on the high traditions of the chair'.

By 1915 the Great War in Europe had reached the stalemate of the trenches, and such a preoccupation could not be banished from the minds of those gathered. As Leebody voiced those feelings there was heartfelt applause: 'The question for many students at present was not: "What prizes and honour can I obtain?" but "What can I do to help my country in her hour of need?"'

The final business of the gathering was the delivery of a cheque by the Reverend J.A.H. Irvine, on behalf of the Graduates Association, to W.J. Hanna, Chairman of the Trustees, to begin the process of founding the new Leebody Prize for Mathematics. The professor acknowledged the compliment and assured the company that no tribute could have been more profoundly appreciated than to have his name associated with a college prize.

4 NOVEMBER 1943

With the rise of Nazism and the moral certainty of war with Germany from 1937 on, there was a notable recruitment drive in Derry for the Territorial Army (TA). Here the TA were directed to become artillery—not the light field artillery, but because of the certainty of attack from the air, a heavy anti-aircraft contingent. They were designated the 24th and 25th Heavy AA Batteries, known universally as 'Ack Ack' from the old international signalling code for AA. By early 1939 it was clear that the appeasement of Hitler over Czechoslovakia with the Munich agreement had not stopped his territorial ambitions, and no one was unduly surprised when the city's TA members were called up and put permanently into uniform.

The Royal Artillery had some differences of nomenclature from other army divisions. The 'other ranks' were called gunners, lance-bombardiers, and bombardiers instead of privates, lance-corporals and corporals. Ranks above that were as in the infantry, sergeant and staff sergeant. Officers began at 2nd Lieutenant and usually rose no higher than Major. The 25th Heavy AA Battery's senior officer was Captain Sir Basil McFarland, who was promoted to Major when the 25th were sent to Egypt in September 1939. By the autumn of 1943 they were part of the Allied combined forces that engaged in the slow war of attrition as they inched their way north from Naples. Early in November Major McFarland sent a cable that reached Derry on Thursday, the fourth of the month, to express sympathy with the relatives of four Derry men killed in action.

They were Lance-Sergeant James Gilmour of 20 Aubrey Street; Lance-Bombardier J.L. Douglas Mark from Limavady, the son of a former MP for North Derry; Lance-Bombardier William Stewart Peoples of 2 Gordon Place; and Gunner Robert Hamilton of Culmore. Gilmour was one of three brothers, all serving with the forces overseas, and had been a plumber with the Derry

Gaslight Company after education at Derry Cathedral School. Mark had been a student at Foyle College and played for the School XV and Limavady Rugby Club; he was remembered as 'a great comrade and a grand soldier' by McFarland. Twenty-six-year-old Peoples, who was married with a four-year-old daughter, was employed as a builder, like his father, by Messrs. Baxter & Co. Hamilton, had worked on the staff of Austin's Ltd., the department store in the Diamond, and had joined up with several other members of staff at the outbreak of war; his father had been head gardener in Thornhill, the home of the Watt family who owned the Derry distilleries.

It was a grim message for McFarland to have to send but at least he could add: 'All other Derrymen here are grand.'

5 NOVEMBER 1941

The date 5 November has had a special significance for St Columb's College throughout its history. It was the day of its opening in 1879, the day on which an important extension—including a new chapel—was started in 1939, and the day of its dedication in 1941. Since its founding it had had eight clerical presidents, three of whom—Bernard O'Kane, Charles McHugh and Neil Farren—had become bishops of the diocese, and the incumbent on that day was the Reverend Joseph O'Doherty. His four years in office (1939–43) were characterised by geniality and—uncommon in senior clergy—great skill as a ventriloquist and prestidigitator. It was a day of special celebration and also of some natural concern that everything should go well. Not only had the extension and the chapel to be blessed but a specially commissioned portrait of Neil Farren, the late president, now Bishop of Derry, was to be unveiled.

The college site had once been known as the Casino, established by the eccentric but philanthropic Frederick Hervey the Earl Bishop. He was a prodigious builder of roads, bridges and especially houses, great and small. Not content with his palatial house inside the city walls, in the appropriately named Bishop Street Within, he built a *casino*, a word then that had no gaming associations but simply meant 'little house'. With its façade of an Ionic temple it was preserved as the first chapel, a fact that would have pleased the mischievous Hervey, since its colloquial meaning was 'brothel'. In his address after the dedication the bishop said he regretted the eradication of the old chapel since it had had historical importance as the Earl Bishop's ballroom. A new chapel was essential because of increased numbers, and the old building had become structurally unsound.

The day began with High Mass said by the president in the presence of the bishop, who sat on a crimson throne with a canopy. Ninety priests were seated in the nave of the new chapel, described as 'built in early Gothic style with three beautiful stained-glass windows behind the altar', while Dr John McShane, a previous president, gave a dedicatory sermon. Afterwards at a dinner in the new refectory, the portrait of Dr Farren, showing him in his episcopal purple cassock and rochet, was unveiled by T. Coulter, the most senior member of the lay staff; the president declared that, if anyone deserved an honoured place on the walls of the college, Dr Farren certainly did. The portrait had been painted by George H. Collis from Carrickmacross, County Monaghan, who had studied in London and Paris, and was well-known as a portraitist and a deviser of interior designs for many Irish churches, including the Pro-Cathedral in Dublin.

For many years after the event the school was granted a half-holiday each 5 November.

6 NOVEMBER 1908

On the evening of Thursday, 5 November 1908, James Wray, a soldier in the Royal Artillery, stationed in Ebrington Barracks, was walking in Prehen near Derry when he saw a body in a deep quarry hole. It was removed to the city mortuary on the quay, where it was identified as being William Hayes, a forty-three-year-old bespoke tailor who had been missing since the previous Tuesday. The inquest held on the following Friday in the Police Court in Strand Road by Thomas Lindsay, the city coroner, gave rise to some controversy and confusion regarding the verdict, and a marked difference of opinion between the coroner and Sergeant Meehan of the RIC, who represented the Crown.

The first witness was the dead man's wife Annie Hayes who deposed that the last she'd seen of her husband was at 7.30 on Tuesday morning when he left their home at 8 Creggan Road to go to his shop. She said he had been complaining of pains in his heart and of shattered nerves. He was also 'peculiar in his demeanour', silent and withdrawn, and shunning all companionship. Meehan asked Mrs Hayes if her husband had ever been confined in any institution; there was a buzz of interest in the courtroom when, after instruction from the coroner, she admitted that he had spent ten months in the asylum in 1891.

James Martin, Hayes's assistant, said that his employer had arrived at the shop as usual on Tuesday morning but left to go for a walk when he found that the irons were not yet warm. He never returned. Questioned about Hayes's demeanour Martin said that 'he was very dull and never engaged in conversation inside the shop'. Dr Crosbie, who had performed the autopsy, said death was due to drowning but the presence of two cuts on the left hand side of the neck made him suspect that Hayes had attempted to commit suicide. When a member of the jury asked if they could not also have been caused by shelving rocks in the quarry, Dr Crosbie admitted that they could. Pinkerton, the foreman of the jury, wondered if perhaps they could have been caused accidentally while Hayes was shaving. Here the coroner intervened: 'I got cut that way this morning. There is no evidence of suicide in this case.' The sergeant and the doctor continued to insist that there was just such evidence, and an air of tension developed between the two sides.

In the end the unsatisfactory verdict 'Found drowned' was accepted, even though Sergeant Meehan asked that the verdict include the added words: 'The man drowned himself in a fit of lunacy.'

7 NOVEMBER 1977

What was believed to have been one of the largest whales ever to enter the Lough or River Foyle was spotted by hundreds of people off the Newbuildings area of Derry on the afternoon of Monday, 7 November 1977, nearly thirty miles from the Atlantic. The whale was seen by golfers on the Prehen links, overlooking a quiet stretch of the River Foyle south of the city. The whale had been observed passing along the river in front of the docks, surfacing from time to time. It dived under the anti-mine defence nets north and south of Craigavon Bridge and re-appeared off Prehen.

Robert Graham, an official of the Foyle Fisheries Commission, went out in a motor boat in an attempt to identify what species it was and had the unnerving experience of the whale surfacing close to his craft. 'I was standing up in the boat at the time,' Mr Graham told a *Londonderry Sentinel* reporter, 'and the whale came to the surface almost alongside. It was then that I realised just how large it was—its dorsal was as tall as myself and it was about twenty-two feet long. It dived under the boat, circled around, and then passed under the boat a second time.'

On Wednesday, 16 November, nine days after its first appearance, the *Sentinel* reported that the killer whale, which had become the centre of attraction for thousands of people, 'vanished as silently and mysteriously as it had arrived'. During that week, officers of the Fisheries Commission, led by the Chief Executive Officer, Gerald Hadoke, assisted at times by river craft of the Royal

Marines, endeavoured to encourage the mammal to swim back underneath Craigavon Bridge and return to the open sea, twenty-five miles to the north.

The whale showed no difficulty in swimming under the anti-mine nets on both sides of the bridge designed as protection against IRA attacks. During the week it had repeatedly appeared at first inside the nets and, seconds later, on the other side, as it rolled and showed its five foot high dorsal fin and occasionally spouting jets of water into the air. One of the last men to see the whale was Hadoke, who had been consulting with experts in London on how best to lure it back to the Atlantic. On the afternoon of Saturday, 12 November, Hadoke watched the whale negotiate the Crook at Ross's Bay and then enter the Narrows, the two mile straight stretch of river leading to Culmore Point and the entrance to Lough Foyle. Then, at the last moment—at Madam's Bank—the whale stopped, turned back, and as dusk fell, was sporting itself once more, this time at Ross's Bay. And that was the last it was seen.

8 NOVEMBER 1938

St Columba was undoubtedly one of the most important and influential figures the islands of Britain and Ireland has produced. He is generally thought of as the father of Scottish Christianity; as the evangelist of the Picts; as one of the patriarchs of the early 'Celtic' Church; and as the founder of a Christian establishment on Iona, the chief of a network of monasteries which for many years would play an important role in the spread of Christianity throughout Ireland, Scotland and the north of England.

Due to his strong association with Derry—he allegedly founded a monastery here in AD 546—there have been proposals to erect a monument in his memory in the city. Such a suggestion is not new, however. Speaking at the weekly luncheon of Derry Rotary Club on Tuesday, 8 November 1938, Commander Frank Gilliland, Royal Naval Volunteer Reserve, expressed the hope that one day something would be done in Derry to preserve the saint's memory in stone. Commander Gilliland said that when he'd visited Iona the previous summer, he bought a small handbook written by a Congregational minister in which the story was related that when St Columba was about to build his monastery in Derry, he found that to do so, he would have to cut down two oak trees. Rather than kill the trees, Columba found another way of erecting the edifice.

Commander Gilliland was addressing the Rotary Club members on the commercial timbers of the world, and was dealing with oak which, he said, was one of the most durable of all materials. Derry meant 'a place of oaks', and from the very earliest days it was found that oaks grew here very well. He had travelled a great deal over England, Scotland and Ireland, and had never seen any better oak trees than those planted at Brookhall in 1770.

In dealing with native trees, Commander Gilliland said the place of honour must be given to the oak. He stressed the importance of cutting the oak down at the proper season of the year, and said that oak properly cut had a durability to which there was no limit. It had been an extremely valuable timber before the introduction of steam and iron ships. In the days of wooden ships oak had been very extensively used but the handicraft of wooden shipbuilding was now entirely confined to yachts. He mentioned this because he'd had wooden yachts for over thirty years. He pointed out that teak was also used in shipbuilding but was at that present time used largely for decks only.

9 NOVEMBER 1948

When Derry had an opera house and such companies as Carl Rosa came they offered Verdi, Puccini and Rossini; but most popular of all, preferred even to *The Barber of Seville* and *Il Trovatore*, were the 'Irish' trio, *The Lily of Killarney* (by Julius Benedict), *Maritana* (by William Wallace) and *The Bohemian Girl* (by Michael Balfe). The last of these had the perennial aria 'I Dreamt I Dwelt in Marble Halls' and such parlour favourites as 'When Other Lips' and 'The Heart Bowed Down', and was composed by 'Signor Balfo', as his enthusiastic Italian public called him, who had been born in Dublin in 1808. The words for the opera were by Alfred Bunn who also supplied the libretto for *Maritana* (1845). His 'Let Me Like a Soldier Fall', 'Scenes that are Brightest' and 'There is a Flower' were nearly as popular as the hits of *The Bohemian Girl*.

The *Bohemian Girl's* plot of an heiress kidnapped, an aristocrat exiled and lots of dangerous gypsies, was unimportant; it was the songs that mattered. The gaudy Zigeuner costumes, especially that worn by the leader Devilshoof, started a rage for gypsy garb and large earrings. It reassured British and Irish entrepreneurs that they had a composer who was a match for the triumphant Italians and Germans. The songs had always been popular as party pieces and concert items, but when the Derry Parochial Players performed the opera in November 1948, in aid of the Derry Catholic Building Fund, it was the first time it had been seen for twelve years. The reporter for the *Derry Journal* was disappointed with the opening night's (9 November) house. It was a notable occasion for three reasons: the coming back of grand opera to the city, it was an opera by an Irish composer, and 'Derry showed its appreciation of the notable occasion by a half-empty house.' Tuesday night was better, 'crowded but for precisely a mere half-dozen rows in the rear of the floor...'

In fact the named players—Norah O'Leary, Edward Mount, Sean O'Leary, Michael Cutliffe, Mary Frances Gillespie and James McCafferty as Devilshoof—were all part of a tradition of musicality that continues to this day. The 1936 production had had John McCabe as musical director and it was fitting that he should also supervise this latest production. The headlines, 'Grand Opera in Derry' and '*Bohemian Girl* Triumph', were eventually lived up to.

10 NOVEMBER 1942

Mrs Eleanor Roosevelt, wife of Franklin Delano Roosevelt, President of the USA, began a two-day visit to Derry on Tuesday, 10 November 1942. She seemed to enjoy every minute of her stay as the guest of Captain V.L. Kirkman, Commandant of the US Naval Base, at his house on the outskirts of the city. She arrived at about 5.30 p.m. and was driven through the streets to the base camp by Robert McCarter, who had his driving license autographed by the famous lady. Mrs Roosevelt had flown from Belfast, where she spent four hours, during which she had tea at Government House and visited an American General Hospital and the American Red Cross Centre.

Her first call in Derry was about 9.30 p.m. at the American Red Cross Centre, Waterloo Place, where the band played 'When Johnny Comes Marching Home'. A soldier asked her for a dance, and Mrs Roosevelt answered, 'I don't think you would enjoy it very much.' The First Lady spoke to the boys in the dance band. Most of them were from the midwest, and some from other orchestras in the United States. For her benefit they staged a floor show.

Mrs Roosevelt also looked in at the Royal Navy Hall (before and after the Apprentice Boys' Hall), where an American Marines dance was in progress, and she cut a 167th birthday cake for the Corps and told the Marines to remember their great traditions. She said she had sons in all the US services. The following morning she stepped on to Derry's walls at the Governor Walker Memorial and spent a few minutes studying the view. She asked questions about the Walker Pillar and 'Roaring Meg'. It being 11 November, Mrs Roosevelt advanced to the War Memorial in the Diamond to lay America's tribute to the honoured dead of World War I. Lady Montgomery, mother of General Bernard Montgomery, was also there and received as much attention as the First Lady. She left a wreath on the memorial for the Women's Section of the British Legion. The two ladies met and Mrs Roosevelt, on shaking Lady

354

Montgomery's hand, said, 'I am so proud to meet General Montgomery's mother. I congratulate you on having such a son as I am very proud of my menfolk.'

Lady Montgomery replied that she was proud of the general and all her sons and added, 'The President and Mr Churchill are two of the greatest men in the world in my opinion, and the third may be either my son or Hitler.' Afterwards Mrs Roosevelt was officially received by the Mayor and Corporation at the Guildhall, and left the following message for the people of Ulster: 'I have been very much interested to hear of and see how happy the United States forces have been made here, and I am very grateful to the people of Northern Ireland for their hospitality both to the Army and Navy…'

11 NOVEMBER 1761

Prehen House is an elegant stone building about one-and-a-half miles from Craigavon Bridge, the oldest of the three bridges that span the River Foyle in Derry. It dates from 1745 and its architect, Michael Priestley, incised on an attic beam the initials 'M.P.' Built by Andrew Tomkins it passed into the keeping of the Knox family of Rathmullen and Moneymore after the marriage of his daughter Honoria to Andrew Knox. Their only daughter was born in 1740 and the new house was her home from early childhood. It was also the scene of the inquest into her death on 11 November 1761. The verdict of wilful murder perpetrated by John McNaghten and his band of armed ruffians would not have stood today; his purpose in attacking the 'travelling chariot', as the Knox ultra-modern conveyance was called, was heiress abduction and not killing. Nowadays he might have got off with manslaughter but there was no doubt that the heiress (worth £840,000 in today's money) had died of pistol wounds after four hours of agony in a farmhouse at Cloughcor, three miles from Strabane.

Her killer was about eighteen years older than she was and hopelessly addicted to gambling. Heir to Benvarden in County Antrim, an estate that netted him a handy £500 a year, he soon sold half of his property and mortgaged the rest to feed his addiction to 'play'. His father dead, he should have been his uncle's heir but that worthy so disapproved of his vice that he disinherited him and the young master of Benvarden was forced to use considerable charm and a way with the ladies to survive. His first wife, a Miss Daniel, who had brought a considerable dowry, had married him on his solemn promise that he would never 'play' again. She died, heavily pregnant, when debt collectors stormed their house.

When Andrew Knox offered him hospitality at Prehen he turned his attention to the Knox heiress and succeeded to the point that they went through a ritual form of marriage in Derry; but Mary Anne, though susceptible to his undoubted charm, would proceed no further in the business without her father's approval. The only resource left open to him was abduction, rape and a church marriage. In spite of his reputation he was allowed to escort her to visit some friends at Ards in County Donegal and, during an overnight stay in Strabane, failed in his attempt at rape. He was banished from the house and her company, and after claims in newspapers that she was his legal wife failed he laid the plan that went so badly wrong on 10 November 1761. During the attack at Cloughcor, on what was essentially an armed wagon train with outriders at front and rear, many shots were fired but only Mary Anne was hit, five times in all, by three balls in the upper body.

12 NOVEMBER 1934

Armistice Day, 11 November 1934, fell on a Sunday and was covered by the newspapers the following days. The anniversary of the 'eleventh hour of the eleventh day of the eleventh month', the end of 'the war to end all wars' required an extra press effort. Few guessed that another hideous world war was only five years away. The *Derry Journal*, the only nationalist paper in the northwest, reported the ceremonies on Monday, 12 November, and its coverage, it felt, had to contain an element of exculpation for the nationalist 'corporators' who did not attend. The Great War had affected most people in these islands and the paper was anxious not to belittle the sacrifices made by them but as one of the constant critical voices against the Stormont regime, now more than ever remote in its new gleaming white palace in Dundonald, it felt it had a duty to comment.

Among those who took part were ex-servicemen from Derry's old hinterland, Free State Donegal: Major Myles, who was a TD in the Dáil, Captain Wagentrieber, and Sergeant James Duffy of the Inniskillings, who had been bestowed with the highest British military honour, the Victoria Cross—awarded rarely 'for valour'—as a consequence of the extreme bravery he'd displayed during Allenby's campaign in Palestine in 1917. Also present were local members of the Italian Fascisti and Paymaster-Commander H.J. Cooper, representing the Catholic officers and ex-servicemen of Ireland.

The Mayor (Senator Sir Dudley McCorkell) laid a wreath on behalf of the Corporation and the ceremony ended with the heart-breaking sound of buglers of the Leicestershire regiment playing 'The Last Post' and Elgar's 'Pomp and Circumstance'.

The *Journal* reporter observed that the non-participation by Derry Catholic veterans was the direct consequence of the manner and circumstances attending the local celebration: 'The position of those bereaved and broken ones in such a ceremony has been rendered impossible by the associations surrounding the display and the unnecessary Imperial complexion it annually assumes with the use of emblems, having in this area a definitely partisan significance, while patriotic native colours have been banned by Government edict and purely national commemorations hindered and suppressed.'

In the same item the reporter noted that the Reverend W.M. Kennedy, preaching in First Derry Presbyterian Church, drew attention to the fact that Benito Mussolini, the self-styled *Il Duce*, leader of Fascist Italy, had ordered that Italian children be trained in the use of arms. The respected Italian community in Derry were greatly impressed by Italy's economic resurgence under Mussolini and enjoyed the trappings of Rome's historical grandeur that his movement used so effectively. They had enjoyed the visit of Count Balbo's Air Armada in July 1933 but there was no suggestion of support for Mussolini's territorial claims.

13 NOVEMBER 1889

Derry's Opera House in Carlisle Road had since its opening in August 1877 presented more plays than operas. High drama, from Shakespeare and Ben Jonson, was supported but what the punters really preferred were good old-fashioned barnstorming melodramas. Some of these were based on books like *Uncle Tom's Cabin* from the anti-slavery novel written in 1852 by Harriet Beecher Stowe. Another incredibly popular melodrama was *East Lynne* (1863) by Mrs Henry Wood, in which Lady Isabel Carlyle runs off with an aristocratic cad who leaves her with an illegitimate child. She returns in disguise as a governess in her old home and has the exquisite misery of tending to the terminal illness of her own child. Her cry in the play has become a comic cliché: 'Dead! Dead! And never called me "Mother!"' Theatre then was the popular entertainment that film later became. Plots were occasionally purloined from actual happenings as, for example, with *Maria Martin or The Murder in the Red Barn*, which told the story of the murder in 1827 of the eponymous Maria when she becomes pregnant by her lover William Corder.

So popular had this 'sensation' theatre become that working authors began to write original plays instead of adaptations. One of these was George Robert Sims, a journalist and playwright, whose melodrama *The Lights o' London* was first produced on 10 September 1881 and ran for 286 performances in London and almost as many in New York. It was revived many times, running throughout the Great War and after the author's death. The plot is typically sensational: Harold Armytage and his sweetheart Bess Marks, she poor, he the son of a rich man, elope. The father disowns him and his evil brother Clifford plots with Seth Preen, a friend of his father, to frame him for a crime. Seth hopes that Clifford will marry his daughter Hetty but she not unexpectedly becomes his mistress. Harold escapes from prison and rescues Seth from drowning. Seth does the decent thing, confesses all, restores Harold to his father's good will and Clifford is disowned.

Derry audiences were given the opportunity of seeing the 'powerful and touching drama' when it ran for a week in November 1889. A short review appeared in the *Derry Journal* of Wednesday, 13 November: 'though it is almost invidious to single out any of Mr Arnold's company for special mention, a word must be said for the "Harold Armytage" of Mr F. Maxwell, which is a finished and capable portrayal of the much harassed but brave-hearted son of the master of Armytage Hall. Miss Lulu Du Cane as "Bess" acts with great cleverness, and shows an intimate acquaintance with and a correct conception of the character.' The unsigned piece advised that 'none should miss the opportunity of seeing one of the best pieces of the foremost author among the modern school of dramatists'.

14 NOVEMBER 1938

On 14 November 1938 William Butler, a thirty-one-year-old unemployed insurance agent, threw himself over a low wall in Derry Jail and died on impact with a sunken causeway. He had been awaiting trial for the murder of his wife, Jennie Fox, on 16 July that year. They had been married on 26 February. They took rooms in 7 Lower Nassau Street, a terrace house not far from Brooke Park, the main green area in the west bank of the city, occupying the front bedroom and the room below it, and had use of the scullery and yard.

The relationship seemed to have been problematic from the start. The landlady, Mrs Margaret Mary Coyle, testified that they were quarrelling within a fortnight and that these noisy disputes grew in volume and intensity by July. Asked about whether a third party was ever mentioned she answered that she had overheard Jennie say, 'There was nothing with the fellow. He is as good as you. It is just your bad mind.' On 13 July she heard her say, 'You are a dirty brute and nothing but a pig', and threatened to tell her mother about his 'carry-on'. Living conditions in essentially one room in a small house were not ideal. His lack of employment and constant presence in the house must have added to the strain.

One way the couple had of easing the sense of confinement was to take frequent walks. Their street led to open country to the northwest and though they never seemed to engage much in conversation on these outings they were regularly seen in the Lovers' Glen and other popular peripheral walks. The autopsy revealed that Jenny's body, discovered on a lane parallel to the main Buncrana Road, had three wounds on the back of the scalp, two star-shaped and one straight into the bone. A pair of Butler's shoes was examined and it was considered that they might well have caused the trauma by repeated kicking. Jenny was also four months pregnant and it was considered that much of the connubial conflict might have had its source in sexual incompatibility.

When the police came to the house in answer to a distress call from Mrs Coyle on 14 July they found Butler lying in his bed covered in blood, having attempted, unsuccessfully, to cut his throat with a safety razor. Eleven days later he was discharged from the City and County Hospital and returned to Derry Jail where he was noted for his customary, almost catatonic, silence. He was due to face the next assizes court on the charges of suicide, then a criminal offence, and of murdering his wife. At the inquest following his death, Captain Alfred Fryer, the prison governor, said that he was slow to answer questions but gave no indication of suicidal tendencies—an odd comment in light of his early attempt. After the 'dive' he never recovered consciousness and died at 3.20 p.m. that afternoon.

15 NOVEMBER 1880

On 10 April 1838 Theobald Mathew, a forty-eight-year-old Franciscan priest asked by clergy of other faiths to establish a temperance society in Cork, led the way by taking a pledge to abstain totally from every kind of alcohol. His words on the occasion, 'Here goes in the name of the Lord', became famous as a rallying cry for young adults throughout Ireland. Commercial liquor was cheap then and there was always plenty of home-distilled stuff available. In the next six years government revenue from liquor sales dropped from £1.4 million to £0.8 million, and there was a notable decrease in crime. The TA, as the temperance association was known, had a notable effect on the population; the description 'drunken Irish' became less appropriate.

In Derry, towards the end of the 1870s, a similar interdenominational project led to the foundation of the Londonderry Temperance Council. It set up a coffee stand on waste ground just outside the city wall where the Guildhall was later built. It was open from 5 a.m. until 8 p.m. with extra hours on a Saturday night. Later three other booths were set up, the one on the quays very popular with the Derry dockers.

Drunkenness remained a problem in the city but Derry got its own apostle of temperance. William Elliott had been born in the city in 1843 and was a curate in the Long Tower parish from 1870 until his death on 15 November 1880. At the time cheap drink was causing its usual spate of violence, poverty, ill-health, and terror to wives and children. Elliott spoke against its abuse frequently from the pulpit and in 1873 formed the St Columb's Total Abstinence Society. His eloquence and energy attracted many of his parishioners and soon the TA Society had more than 3,000 registered members. Conscious that an alternative to the public house was desirable as a social amenity he worked to build the capacious St Columb's Hall as a theatre, assembly-rooms, offices and even schoolrooms. It opened on 22 November 1888, and the music for the occasion was provided, appropriately enough, by the St Columb's Total Abstinence Brass and Reed Band, another of Fr Elliott's initiatives. Dr O'Donnell, later Ireland's fourth cardinal, paid tribute to the work of the priest when he officiated at the opening ceremony.

Elliott died on 15 November 1880 of typhus and was buried in the Long Tower North graveyard, the only consecrated ground for Catholic burial on the west bank of the city. His grave faces the main entrance of the Long Tower church and underneath a marble statue to 'Derry's Father Mathew' is a memorial stone with the following inscription:

Erected by the Members of
St Columb's Catholic Total Abstinence Society, Derry,
In loving memory of our Founder
Rev. W. M. Elliott
Who died 15th November 1880
Aged 37 years
R.I.P.

The Young Men's Christian Association (YMCA) was founded in June 1844 by a young draper called George Williams. He realised that young men brought into the towns and cities to service the great surge of industry had no leisure access except the tavern or the brothel. He aimed to provide a healthy alternative with encouragement for development of both body and mind. It soon spread all over the world becoming particularly popular in the United States, where the 'Y' (as it is known there) is an important feature of any sizable town.

Derry had the honour of having the second purpose-built amenity for YMCA activities in the world. It was erected on the site of the old Linen Hall in East Wall, where the Millennium Forum theatre now stands, but having caught fire in 1978 had to be demolished. J.G. Ferguson, the architect, designed a large two-storey, stucco-faced hall with a gable pediment and set head sculptures of such Reformation worthies as Luther, Calvin, Knox and Cranmer high in the entablature. The Lord-Lieutenant of Ireland, James Hamilton, 1st Duke of Abercorn, laid the foundation stone in October 1866 and the hall was declared open on 21 November 1867, quite appropriately with a breakfast, which many of the local dignitaries, bank managers, clergy, solicitors, doctors, representatives of Derry's burgeoning commercial prosperity, and members of local landing-owning families attended.

Most of the cost was found by the association, with some local assistance, but some of the money was raised by a grand bazaar held in the Town Hall in the Diamond on the previous Wednesday, 16 November. It was essentially a day when the ladies took charge. A list of nearly sixty names was printed in the *Journal*, seven of them from the aristocracy, led by the Marchioness of Abercorn, the wife of the lord-lieutenant, with a fair sprinkling of 'Hons' and lots of local wives. The bazaar proved satisfactory from a financial point of view. Entrance fees netted £50 (or £3,230 today) and there were great sales from the stalls. As the *Journal*'s starry-eyed reporter wrote: 'A great deal of very superior fancy work was exhibited and readily found purchasers, while saleable articles of more substantial make-up were not overlooked in the arrangement of the stalls. It will give some idea of the success of the bazaar, when we state that at any time of the two days the Hall was crowded to inconvenience.' Earlier he had noted that 'there was still a small debt, comparatively speaking, on the building, and for the purpose of clearing this away the bazaar was held and we have no doubt the proceeds will go far to answer the end in view'.

Though it was generally accepted during the 1960s that the preponderance of new industry in work-starved Northern Ireland was located east of the Bann, especially in Belfast or within a twenty-mile radius of the city, some firms were encouraged to open plants to the west. One of these was Monarch Electric, a company that had two factories in Derry. The trouble with industries created with a certain amount of artificiality is that they are essentially frail, too reliant upon government subsidy, and insufficiently prepared to deal with the real world of industrial economics. By the late autumn of 1966 Monarch had to announce a number of redundancies and this sent alarm signals to the Ministry of Commerce at Stormont who had persuaded the company to build there.

The minister, the dynamic and tireless Brian Faulkner, became immediately involved and arranged to meet management and representatives of the two main unions, the Amalgamated Engineering Union (AEU) and the Amalgamated Transport and General Workers Union (AT&GWU) on Thursday, 17 November 1966. It was essentially a crisis meeting because, a few weeks before, the firm had paid off 430 workers and 525 were due for dismissal on the Friday of the following week. One way out of the impasse was diversification, and if unions and management could agree, Faulkner promised 'to improve on its present agreement with Monarch'. The company intimated that it had three possible projects in mind, one of which would 'employ mainly male labour [Derry's greatest need] and have a stability unknown in the record-changing market'.

The idea of a record-changer, even of a record, sounds to twenty-first century ears as unbelievably ancient, not to say antediluvian. The electronic revolution during the last fifty years has seen such breathtaking advances in sound and vision reproduction systems that even DVDs are teetering on the brink of extinction. But back in 1966 the idea of a cradle to hold and deliver a series of LPs (then regarded as a significant advance) was magical. The head of the AEU in Ireland, Charles Hull, adverted to the fact that there had been no pay-offs in any of the company's factories in England and Scotland, any run-down having been dealt with by natural wastage. There was a general trade union concern for the future of the 800 employees who were still employed in the two plants.

Later on the evening of that Thursday it was announced that a protest march would be held on the morning of the coming Saturday, 19 November. The organisers appealed for support from all Monarch workers, both past and present, and appealed to the shirt-makers, especially those who were on short-time contracts, for their backing. The marchers were to assemble outside the main gate of the factory in Bligh's Lane and proceed from there to the Guildhall.

The Derry City branch of the Young Republican Association expressed support for the protest and called on 'all fellow citizens to come out in strength to lend their support not merely to those made redundant but to the many thousands unemployed in the city'.

18 NOVEMBER 1888

Derry and the northwest of Ireland have had more than their share of windstorms over the years. From Tuesday, 18 November 1888 to the following Saturday, the region was convulsed by relentless high winds that caused havoc on land. At sea, in the North Channel, there were hitherto unseen 'atmospheric phenomena', as the papers described it.

On Tuesday, as the SS *Azalea* was making its way from Glasgow to Derry, Captain Heatley, its master, beheld a remarkable sight. An intense black cloud had gathered about a hundred yards ahead that soon enveloped the steamer. It plunged the vessel into darkness so complete that it prevented him from seeing the steersman at the wheel though he was only yards away. When they had passed through it, Heatley was able to look back and see that the cloud was almost completely spherical and of unrelieved blackness; the *Azalea* was immediately subjected to powerful gusts of wind and mountainous waves that lasted only a few minutes until the cloud disappeared and the sea became comparatively calm again.

Wednesday was very windy but this was quite normal for the time of year. It was not until Thursday night that the hurricane struck with full force. All the captains of steamers from Scotland bound for Derry stated in their experience that the force and persistence of the storm was unique. One skipper, Captain Kerr of the *Ivy*, had nothing but praise for his vessel's performance. In spite of giant waves and blinding spray she withstood all the sea and winds could do to her, and was able to go to the rescue of a schooner that was riding at anchor a few miles off Inishowen Head and in serious danger of being ground to pieces on the reefs at the shore. This was the *Volunteer*, the owner of which, James McCandless, was an experienced mariner; he assented to Captain Jackson's suggestion that they try to return to Derry. As she came about she lost every inch of canvas and was running before the wind at the mercy of the turbulence.

The owner and crew had begun to prepare themselves for destruction when the *Ivy* was sighted through the spume, eerily lit by constant flashes of lightning. After two hours of failure and disappointment, Kerr was able to get a cable on board and have it made fast. By this means the steamer battled through the peak of the Friday night terror to tow the *Volunteer* safely into the harbour in Derry as the storm finally began to subside.

There were no fatalities in the city but in Belfast a woman was killed when a shutter she was trying to remove from a window crushed her skull.

19 NOVEMBER 1896

Derry in the 1890s was a prosperous, go-ahead city, the port and market centre for the whole northwest of Ireland. Its hinterland could be said to stretch from the River Bann in the east right to Sligo Bay in the west. One of the obvious outward signs of its commercial importance was the Guildhall, a striking civic edifice designed in red sandstone by John Guy Ferguson in 1887. Constructed on reclaimed slob land on the very edge of the River Foyle it was opened in 1890—and unfortunately succumbed to fire in 1908. One of its features was the magnificent organ, considered to be among the very best in Ireland, set at the northeast end of the great hall. The specifications are impressive even now, with its 3,076 pipes distributed as follows: great organ 915, swell 1,037, choir 427, solo 427, and pedal organ 270. It was expensive and regarded as an extra that could not be charged to the city ratepayers; £800 of debt still remained to be paid. In November 1896 it was decided to hold what was called an 'organ bazaar' to raise money.

The *Derry Journal* reporter began his coverage of the 'bazaar' in Friday, 20 November edition by defining the word, in a Derry context, as 'a highly decorated building wherein is found many gaily adorned stalls laden with pretty wares, which are dispensed with the view of benefiting some useful object by daintily attired maidens possessing a peculiarly persuasive power as vendors'. The reporter warming to his task lays the 'compliments' on with a trowel: 'To this central organisation it is usual to add several branch attractions, mainly of mystic and musical character. The undertaking in its modern aspect relies almost wholly on the ingenuity, taste, enterprise, and executive ability of the feminine division of the community.' It is the sort of tongue-in-cheek approval that would have the modern sisterhood foaming at the mouth but it went down like crème brulée then.

The 'daintly attired maidens' came into their own on Thursday, 19 November, the second day of the bizarre bazaar. The event was opened by Mrs Tillie, the wife of William Tillie, owner of the biggest shirt factory in the world and chatelaine of Duncreggan, the mansion at the top of what for many years after was called 'Tillie's Brae'. By mid-afternoon it was announced that £1,200 had been collected and Dr Jones, to celebrate, played the 'Shepherd's Dance' from Edward German's *Henry VIII*. The bazaar was declared by all, especially those whose names were printed in the paper, to have been an outstanding success.

20 NOVEMBER 1918

The ending of the Great War on 11 November 1918 was quickly followed by the calling of a long overdue general election, set for the fortnight 14–28 December. Ireland had seen the rise of the abstentionist Sinn Féin party while the old constitutionalist Irish Parliamentary Party (IPP) floundered without a charismatic leader since the death of John Redmond, who had won a measure of Home Rule from Britain. The 1916 Rising, the execution of the leaders, and the surge in Sinn Féin support, as indicated by their by-election successes, had changed the whole complexion of Irish politics. Many people regarded their policy of abstention as sterile and constitutional nationalists feared that many nationalist seats would be lost because of a split vote.

The Catholic Church is usually very circumspect about public involvement in politics, but with partition virtually certain, and the danger to many nationalist seats in Ulster a matter of concern, one cleric wrote to the *Derry Journal* with a possible method of saving them. This was the Bishop of Derry, Charles McHugh, who, with his opposite number in Down and Connor, Bishop Joseph McRory, had been most critical of Britain's intentions over conscription and the future governance of Ireland. His letter was published in the Friday, 20 November, edition of the *Journal*.

He suggested three conditions that all non-Unionist candidates should have to follow: i) '...the candidate selected shall give a written pledge that on all occasions and in every legitimate way he will support unrestricted Self-determination for Ireland and... offer ceaseless and unrelenting opposition to Partition in any shape'; ii) 'Let there be established in each constituency... from which the man of their choice, acting on the principle laid down in [i] shall take instructions in regard to his official acts... [a] committee to be two representatives of... the Irish Party, Sinn Féin and Labour with an independent chairman'; iii) 'That in all his actions... the member... be guided by the committee and that failing to do so he resign his seat.' It was an unusually public manifestation of pastoral care but the stakes were high, and for the next five years Ireland was in a state of bloody violence.

When the results were declared on 28 December it was found that Sinn

Féin had all but annihilated the IPP. They won seventy-three of Ireland's 105 seats while the IPP got six. The Unionist party won twenty-five, mostly in Ulster, but that did not matter. Sinn Féin set up its own independent Dáil and the way was cleared for the horrors of the Tan War, the brief, one-sided civil war in Northern Ireland, and the bloodier, eviscerating civil war in the newly-formed Free State. The IPP had one small moment of satisfaction: Eamon de Valera, the only surviving 1916 leader, with typical arrogance, stood in West Belfast against 'Wee Joe' Devlin and was defeated: 8,488 votes to 3,245.

21 NOVEMBER 1971

On Sunday, 21 November 1971, two members of Londonderry Fire Service—Leading Fireman Leonard McCartney, of Violet Street, Waterside, and Leading Fireman David Alexander Wylie, of Galliagh—lost their lives when a portion of the Melville on Foyle Street, Derry's oldest hotel, collapsed on them as they were fighting a fire that completely destroyed the building.

The hotel had been closed for the weekend and there were only four people in it when the fire broke out about 4 a.m.—the owner, Mr Tony Kearney, and his wife; Mrs Maureen Pegg, the manageress, and her husband Mercer. They were awoken by the crackle of flames and made their way downstairs to the main entrance where they met police who had seen fire erupting through the roof and raised the alarm. The reception area and the second and third floors were well alight at that time. When the Fire Service arrived they attacked the conflagration with jets.

One month before the fire, the *Londonderry Sentinel* announced in an advertising feature that the latest phase in the Melville's £50,000 refurbishment being a new banqueting hall, seating 200, a new ballroom, a new cocktail lounge and a tastefully laid-out garden, the perfect setting for wedding photographs. There was also the Copper Grill, where late evening meals were served, and the recently re-opened Irish Kitchen. The interior of the hotel had been completely modernised and the sixty bedrooms, half of which had private bathrooms, had been renovated. The 'excellent food' was served 'efficiently and courteously'.

Back in July 1912 the *Sentinel* had reported on an earlier Melville Hotel refurbishment, giving a little history of the building. 'Somewhere about three quarters of a century' previously, stated the newspaper, James McCrea, a wealthy merchant and owner of a fleet of 'smacks' which then formed the only regular means of communication between Londonderry and Glasgow, built a magnificent block of buildings in Foyle Street, easily the finest of its kind in the city of that day. Originally designed as opulent town mansions for the finest of the citizens, 'McCrea's Terrace' shared the characteristics of early Victorian architecture. Rising five storeys above the basement, it had 'splendid solidity of construction', big rooms, lofty ceilings, wide easy staircases, and roomy corridors. The *Sentinel* rekindled memories of the construction's association with the name of 'McCormick's Hotel'; later it became 'Jury's Hotel', but was taken over in 1912 by Mr John Watts-Manning, manager of the Earl of Leitrim's Hotel at Rosapenna, Donegal, and the Gweedore Hotel.

22 NOVEMBER 1888

On the evening of Wednesday, 22 November 1888 a large crowd assembled in the new temperance hall dedicated to St Columba, the city's patron saint. Called St Columb's, it was an eloquent and opulent testimony to the growing confidence of the Catholic population of Derry a mere forty years after the devastation of the Great Hunger. There already existed a fine cathedral, in use since 1873, though still without the spire that would be added in 1903, and now there was an assembly hall and many conference rooms, offices and eventually a national school (in the Orchard Street basement). Because of the sloping nature of the site the elaborate building has two storeys tilting into three. There was also a minor hall for smaller events. The building became an important part of Derry's social and artistic life. Many stage-shows were put on there and a series of pantomimes from the 1940s on were an important part of the city's Christmas entertainments. It became a cinema in the second decade of the twentieth century, showing its first 'flicker' (as movies were called then) on 24 March 1913.

That November evening the leading figure in the diocese, Bishop Francis Kelly, was absent from the mainly clerical platform party because of ill health—he died the following September. The guest of honour was the Most Reverend Dr O'Donnell, bishop of the neighbouring diocese of Raphoe, and among the laymen present were James Croom and Edward Toye, the architects. Their Baroque design was deliberately lush in keeping with the triumphal nature of the concept. They had commissioned three representative statues of Erin, Temperance and Vulcan, the Roman god of fire, and they were placed on top of the central attic pediment. Inside, above the stage in the Great Hall, was a picture of St Colum Cille leaving with twelve companion monks for exile in Iona.

Reverend Hugh McMenamin, soon to be the Administrator of the Long Tower church, took the chair and introduced the guest speaker. Patrick O'Donnell, recognised as one of Maynooth's most brilliant students, had been appointed professor of theology there as soon as he was ordained in 1880, and had been Bishop of Raphoe only a few months when he was called in to replace the aging Derry bishop. His talk was long but very clever and entertaining—he already had a countrywide reputation as a speaker. It was essentially an account of the history of Total Abstinence in Derry with special reference to Fr William Elliott who had founded the movement and had died exactly a week before of typhus. As Bishop O'Donnell put it, he had been called 'to enjoy a purer bliss'. The proceedings had begun with music, appropriately from the St Columb's Brass and Reed Total Abstinence Band, playing a march 'In Memoriam', specially commissioned in memory of that founder.

23 NOVEMBER 1938

By defeating Londoner Benny Caplan over fifteen rounds on 23 November 1938, James 'Spider' Kelly became the first Irishman to win a British and Empire Featherweight boxing title. Reflecting on his pugilistic career almost four decades after the Caplan fight, in a *Londonderry Sentinel* interview published on 15 September 1976, he said he never made much out of his long and distinguished career in the ring. His purse for the above bout in the King's Hall, Belfast, was £75, which led him to remark that he was 'born 30 years too late'. But he had no regrets: 'I was always terribly interested in boxing,' explained 'Spider' and he would have boxed for nothing, 'just to get in the ring with a pair of gloves'.

Born in 1911, 'Spider' Kelly was fighting from an early age—both outside and inside the ring. He was introduced to professional boxing by Dan Doherty in a cellar opposite the family home in Fahan Street. Shortly afterwards he travelled to Scotland at the invitation of Jack Dunn, and it was there that Kelly got his fighting name of 'Spider' because of the length and speed of his arms. Fighting in the Glasgow booths was a gruelling training ground for the future champion but it taught him all the craft and skill that was to make him such a feared opponent. 'The rings were so small that when you got up off your stool you found yourself standing in the middle of the ring,' he recalled. 'That's where I learnt my footwork—to get out of the road of the other fellow.'

He crossed to Scotland with no money—'I went on with the cattle and came off with the cattle'—and while he was there everything he did was controlled by Dunn. 'Spider' recalled that, shortly after he arrived, Dunn was 'able to afford a bowler hat and a smart suit'; 'Spider' got 'clothes, boots and minimal amount of money'. 'A lot of things happened to me in Glasgow,' said Kelly, who admitted that he never had enough money to afford his fare home. Eventually he got a passage out of Scotland through the kind offices of a 'friend on the boats'.

After his Scottish experience 'Spider' did most of his fighting in Belfast and London. 'Nobby Lynch was about the only sparring partner I had,' he commented. 'He was a hardy wee lad and no matter how hard you hit him he kept coming to you all the time.' Before a championship fight, 'Spider' put a great deal of faith in hill-training. 'The country air and walking did a power of good,' he explained, 'but when I went running around the fields, prancing in the air, people in Derry would just stand and look at me as though I was on my way to an asylum.'

24 NOVEMBER 1926

On Monday, 22 November 1926, at a curve in the Lough Swilly line not far from Fahan station, Samuel Brown Stevenson of Shipquay Street, Derry and the 'Look-Out', Fahan, was struck by the 6.20 p.m. train from the city. The *Derry Journal* on Wednesday, 24 November carried a full account of the accident and the inquest, which had been held on the previous day. The foreman of the jury, J. Gilbert Magee, was a well-known Derry estate agent and stockbroker who lived in Fahan and knew the deceased well. Dr O'Callaghan, coroner for North Donegal, presided at the inquest that was held in the station, with Superintendent Woods of the Civic Guards representing the Free State authorities.

David Hamilton, the dispensary doctor in Fahan, had identified the body as that of Stevenson, one of his patients whom he had last seen at Divine Service on the Sunday evening of 21 November when he was in good spirits and had exchanged some jocular remarks. At seven o'clock on Monday evening he had seen the deceased lying on the line; both legs had been severed, and the ribs and base of the skull had been fractured. Death was due to severe trauma. Hamilton had returned to the scene the following morning with two guards to examine it more thoroughly; he noted some imprints of shoes on the bank that suggested that Stevenson had been trying to climb up but had fallen back on to the track. He affirmed when asked by the coroner that he had never noticed anything mentally wrong with his patient.

Hedley Connell testified that he had driven the 6.20 from Derry and about sixty yards from Ferris's bridge on the Derry side he sounded the whistle as usual but felt a jolt as if he had hit something. He immediately slammed on the brakes and examined the engine but could see nothing in the dusk; when he stopped at Fahan station he could see that there were bloodstains on the left-hand side of the engine. He reported the matter to the stationmaster and heard later that Stevenson's body had been found on the track.

H.S. Robinson, appearing for the Stevenson family, begged that Mrs Stevenson not be called because she had enough grief to handle but revealed that her husband had been in the habit of walking from his home to the rectory and back by the line. He had asked his two children to come with him on Monday but the evening was so stormy and wet that he went alone. Dr O'Callaghan at this point intervened and said that he considered further evidence unnecessary. He had not had the pleasure of knowing Stevenson but from what he had heard the many tributes to him were well deserved. Magee, as foreman, associated himself with the coroner's remarks and said there was no man in Fahan who was held in higher regard.

25 NOVEMBER 1927

James A. Jamieson of Hollywood House, Eglinton, appeared at a special court in Derry on 25 November 1927 charged with having between 6 March and 27 September of that year obtained £45 by false pretences. The amount seems slight by today's currency but then it had the buying power of £2,080. Jamieson had created a business called Sellers Publicity Company and claimed to be the part-owner along with others including W.J. Williams of Pump Street and a builder, Mr Orr. He then went around various traders in the city announcing that he was producing a book that would promote the traders and their services country-wide. He had a mock-up of the intended publication to encourage his would-be clients to buy advertising space in it. The cost varied but there was a ceiling of £15. None of these advertisements ever appeared.

Since it was a police court the prosecution was led by a senior officer of the RUC, in this case District Inspector Cahill, who charged that Jamieson had claimed to represent a publicity company that, in fact, did not exist, an assertion that Mr A. Robb, Jamieson's solicitor, vigorously denied. Various witnesses told stories of the way the scam worked. Maurice Austin, a hairdresser of Carlisle Road, described how he had given Jamieson a cheque for £3 12s 6d, of which £3 was to pay for the advertisement and the rest to pay for the block (used in the printing). Following the usual practice the accused had with him the dummy copy of the book from which the client could choose a size of 'full-page' or 'half-page' and indicate where he wished the advertisement to be printed. This business-like approach was calculated to increase trust. Austin further testified that Jamieson had told him that the offices of Sellers Publicity would soon open in Pump Street, close to Austin's salon.

Other witnesses had similar stories demonstrating Jamieson's persuasiveness and fertility of imagination that would have served him well in honest dealings. These included Kathleen Reid and Alphonsus Brady, both hairdressers, M. Stewart, a furniture dealer who was told he could have an advertisement printed on the small pay envelopes for the many shirt factories in the city. Williams, whose name the accused had given as one of his partners, denied all knowledge of the affair. Sophie Bradley and Annie Duffy testified that they had rented rooms as offices but that the rental cheques had not been honoured.

For the confidence trick to work speed was of the essence; it was clearly Jamieson's intention to milk as many clients as quickly as he could and, having cashed their cheques, move rapidly on to fresh fields. He obviously had the charm and the spiel, but he lacked the lightning pace; in the words of the song, he had hung around this old town too long.

26 NOVEMBER 1931

Derry between the Wars was a city full of dancehalls, large and small, and very popular. One of the better ones was the Criterion, a term of excellence not appreciated by its usual clientele, who knew it as the 'Crate'. It was an upstairs hall in Foyle Street close to Guildhall Square, and later became the clubrooms of the friendly society, the Ancient Order of Hibernians (AOH). In 1931 it was a hotel and because of the strict licensing rules of the time the ballroom was in an anomalous position with the law.

Its owner, Sarah Reddy, was summoned to the Petty Sessions Court on 26 November to answer the charge of 'carrying on the business of dancing for profit in a portion of the premises having internal communication with licensed premises'. The resident magistrates R.W. Glass and P.S. Bell presided while District Inspector Lynn presented the prosecution case. He said that a club hired the ballroom and offered tickets on sale at the beginning of the season. This made it a business, he contended, in breach of the 1927 Act. Gerald Feeny for the defence agreed that dancing was carried on there for profit.

Head Constable Hueston said that, on 4 November, the bar within six feet of the ballroom was open. The lady in charge, Miss Larkin, testified that the hall was let to the 'Eight Club' and the 'Bohemian Dance Circle'. They paid a fixed sum and her duty was to see that they behaved properly. All the clients were members, their names listed in a book kept by her. Lynn immediately agreed that the place was well conducted and made no allegations other than the salient one that dancing there was illegal. Feeny swung into forensic action. There was a hall which complied in every way with the regulations but the police wished to prevent them from obtaining a public dancehall license. The dancing had begun there in 1927 and there had never been a prosecution. He showed that structurally it would have been extremely difficult to separate the bar from the ballroom.

Bell asked Feeny if he was arguing that dancing was part of the hotel business and he agreed, in spite of Lynn's counter that letting the hall in that way made it just the same as an ordinary public dancehall, and that could not be regarded as the ordinary business of a hotel. Bell referred him to the Northern Counties Hotel in Portrush; Feeny replied with some wit: 'I understand that the Public Health Amendment Act does not apply in Portrush.' Bell joined in the laughter, complimented Feeny on his handling of the case and dismissed the charge.

27 NOVEMBER 1936

For the three days of 25–27 November 1936 the city of Derry and Lough Foyle experienced the worst fog in the memory of even the older people of the city. There were already ominous signs on the Tuesday night when the *Lairdsrose*, one of the ships of the Burns Laird line that plied between Scotland and Derry, was preparing to leave Glasgow. She was due into Derry at seven o'clock on Wednesday morning but had to anchor off Inishowen Head, unable to proceed. The fog lifted a little late in the day and she advanced some miles into Lough Foyle but was forced again to anchor; Thursday, 26 November was spent at anchor while the passengers fretted about being marooned. They were not cheered by the estimated landfall of the morning of Friday the twenty-seventh.

Even then the city had to face its second day of Stygian gloom. Normal traffic was impossible and those brave souls who ventured out in cars had to crawl at walking pace, with many drivers so disoriented at the lack of familiar landmarks that they lost their way. Headlights were worse than useless because the beams merely made the dense curtain of foggy vapour seem as impenetrable as a wall. The city bus service was suspended and pedestrians literally bumped into each other. Sufferers from pulmonary troubles had a miserable time and those people with claustrophobia were in danger of hysteria at the feeling that the dark grey cloud was going to smother them. Those with any form of nervous complaint were urged to stay at home. Even indoors, with all lights on, the rooms assumed a kind of misty magic with distortion of vision so that furniture looked more distant and further away than it should. In fields and gardens trees seemed to tower and the known topography had been rendered alien and menacing.

On board the *Lairdsrose* there was an air of frustration, anger and complaint, mitigated a little by the need to show sympathy with those on-board who were conveying to Donegal the body of an eight-month-old baby for burial. All the arrangements for the funeral had been made but the ship was still seven miles from Derry, opposite Ture. With help from local boatmen from Quigley's Point, the corpse and the mourners were put ashore there. Several other steamers were held up in the lough; two, the *Clonlara* and the *Nordsen*, were out of Limerick and due to ship cargos of Derry potatoes to Algiers. During the Thursday a rumour reached Derry that the *Clonlara* had run aground at Ture but there was no truth in it. Another vessel self-immobilised was the *Dunmore Head*, a steamer specially designed to ship timber. A brief clearance on the Thursday afternoon gave two of the stranded vessels the chance to complete the passage up to Derry Quay. The *Lairdsbank*, out of Heysham, with some form of direction-finder, made it into harbour while the *Wheatcrop*, the appropriately named flour ship, followed in her wake.

28 NOVEMBER 1936

In Derry, for many years before the 1939–45 war, there were a number of useful thrift societies known as slate clubs. They provided funeral expenses insurance from a fund into which a small sum was paid each week in the name of a possible beneficiary. When the expenses of all funerals were paid the residue was divided among the remaining shareholders, the dividend providing a useful amount of spending money at Christmas, the pay-out being made on the Saturday before the feast. The work was voluntary and the scheme was one of a number of such arrangements that was characteristic of life here in the days before the Welfare State.

Alderman W.J. Bradley was secretary of the St Columba Slate Club that had offices in St Columb's Hall. On 28 November 1936 he had had a busy afternoon and evening because it was getting near Christmas and members in arrears had come to bring their accounts up to date so as to be eligible for the dividend; defaulters lost all their investment. Bradley left the office, and with two friends, Michael J. Roddy and Bernard McGinty, walked up Orchard Street, across Ferryquay Street to the Diamond, and then through Bishop Gate towards his home in Millar Street. At the top of the street where it leaves Bishop Street Without they parted company. He carried a bag containing £168 pounds in one pound notes, ten shilling notes, silver and copper plus one postal order for four shillings. Such a sum had had the buying power then of £8,600 today.

He had not gone far down the steep street when a car drove up and blocked his passage. A man with a handkerchief covering his face jumped out and demanded the bag. When Bradley refused he tried to snatch it from him and they began to struggle. All at once a second masked man hit him over the head and stunned him with was taken to be the butt of a revolver. Bradley was wearing a hat that helped soften the blow; otherwise the injury would have been even more serious. Bradley had a licensed gun in his overcoat pocket but he was unable to get it out during the fight. As the car sped off he fired one shot after it. The thieves returned fire, three shots in all. Bradley was treated by a local GP, Dr Watson, who inserted two sutures in his wound.

Afterwards, in an interview with the press, a heavily bandaged Bradley said that the bandits' accents betrayed them as Derry men, and they seemed to be in their twenties. The hold-up had all the marks of local knowledge; the significance of the date would not have escaped the criminals' notice since on no other night in the winter would the takings have been greater. Extra security was prepared for the slate club pay-out on 12 December.

29 NOVEMBER 1926

On Tuesday, 30 November 1926, John Tracy, the City Coroner, held an inquest into the death the previous evening of William Deehan, a five-year-old boy from Riverview Terrace in the Waterside. He 'met a tragic fate… through the upsetting of a cart, when he received injuries to which a short time he succumbed'. The sad story was told by the boy's grandfather, also William Deehan. He was a seller of logs as fuel, called 'blocks' in Derry, and was returning with his horse and cart after his day's work. The boy was sitting in the cart while his grandfather and another lad rode it standing. Riverview is a terrace on a steep hill and the terrain falls sharply below it. As the cart turned into the mews lane from Chapel Road it slipped sideways down the steep bank and toppled over to a place seven or eight feet below the lane. The grandfather and the older lad were thrown clear but young William was pinned beneath the cart.

The coroner began a series of pertinent questions: How wide was the mews lane? *Six-and-a-half feet.* Was there any protection? *There was once a fence but it had been destroyed by youngsters in recent years.* Deehan said that he had reported the condition of the lane to a Corporation official. He had in turn told the surveyor, who told him to drop it. Tracy asked if Deehan had ever seen children tearing away the fence and when he admitted that he had, he was asked why he had not told someone in authority. Deehan shrugged his shoulders with 'Why should I report a few children playing on a bank?' and got the response 'It is children playing on the bank that has led to this tragedy!'

Head Constable Wiseman asked why he had come that way and Deehan replied that he always used the lane since it brought him to the rear of his premises, but that he had made the turn in the dark and misjudged it. Dr M. Bryson, the family physician, gave evidence that he had been called to the Deehan household about 6.55 on Monday evening, 29 November, and found the little boy close to death. He was suffering from an abrasion on his right forehead and extreme shock. He was unable to speak and death soon followed. The jury found in accordance with the medical evidence, that death was due to shock, and added a rider: 'In view of the evidence given we are not sure that the Corporation is seriously at fault in not making a fence on this lane.' The coroner expressed sympathy with the relatives of the deceased and said it was a sad thing that a boy of his age should meet his death in such a way. The foreman, on behalf of the jury, and Wiseman, on behalf of the authorities, joined in the expression of sympathy.

30 NOVEMBER 1995

Guildhall Square in the centre of Derry had been the scene of several momentous occasions: the publication of the Saville Report, the hosting of Dana as winner of the Eurovision Song Contest, and on 30 November 1995, the visit of US President Bill Clinton and his wife Hilary Rodham to the city in a 'blaze of black limousines, American flags and high-pitched cheers'. The square and all the adjacent spaces were full of the people whose vocal chords were uttering those cheers. Clinton had been president for nearly three quite rocky years but his involvement in Irish affairs, especially in the Peace Process, was perfectly judged and handled with extreme political flair. His visit to the city where the whole rigmarole was judged to have begun was significant; he knew that and so did the thousands who gathered there to welcome him.

It was a chilly late autumn afternoon as two identical limousines with clouded glass in the motorcade went in different directions, the one with Bill and Hilary going counter-clockwise to park under the specially built security canopy to shield the couple from a potential marksman across the Foyle. Once inside the Guildhall the president dashed to the toilet; continuous public exposure has its strains. As the party moved to the platform at the front of the building they were overcome by the volume of the cheering that had penetrated the red sandstone of Derry's civic building. Clinton was just finishing one of the apples he had bought in a shop on the Shankill Road earlier in the day. Jim Lyons, one of his aides and a close friend, remarked that he mightn't get as big a reception at home in Arkansas, and Clinton agreed.

He took one look at the huge crowd and explained why he was there: 'I came here because you are making a home for peace to flourish and endure,' he said and the crowd in Guildhall Square went wild. There came what sounded like the flapping of the sails of some gigantic schooner running full before a force-9 gale and thousands of 'Old Glories' were waved in unison, the fabric equivalent of rhythmic clapping. The City Council had scoured Britain and Ireland for every available form of 'Stars and Stripes' but before they could distribute them the plastic pointed tips had to be broken off for security reasons. As someone remarked, they could not risk Clinton being stabbed with his own country's flag.

Later he said that he was honoured to share a dais with John Hume, and knew that the accolade was as much for the Derry man as for his American friends. The noise made it almost impossible to hear John Kerr, the mayor, give his speech of welcome. When he paused, the spectators chanted, 'We want Bill; we want Bill.' 'Bill', unused to the local accent, asked Hume why they wanted bull?

DECEMBER

1 DECEMBER 1948

The 150th anniversary of the insurrection of the United Irishmen in 1798 that had involved battles between the rebels and local militias in Dublin, East Ulster, Carlow, Wexford and Connacht, was celebrated at different times during the year. Though there had been little activity at the time of the rising in the northwest of Ireland for a number of reasons, Derry was determined to revive a musical work that had been written for the centenary, in 1898, by two Derry men: Edward Conaghan, who composed the music, and Thomas Francis Mullan, who wrote the lyrics and the narrative thread. The cream of Derry's considerable musical talent was assembled for the occasion, the Guildhall was hired, and for the two nights of 29 and 30 November, the cantata was staged to capacity houses.

The approach to the history was romantic rather than factual; there were massive cruelties perpetrated by both sides but particularly by the Yeomen, the local soldiery who helped out the British army, who remained a constant factor in Irish life until 1921. Thanks to such excellent ballads as John Kells Ingram's 'The Memory of the Dead' (more popularly known as 'Who Fears to Speak of Ninety-Eight?'), P.J. McCall's 'Kelly from Killane' and 'Boolavogue', Robert Dwyer Joyce's 'The Boys of Wexford', and William Mc Burney's 'The Croppy Boy', the short bloody episode became almost a part of shared Irish heritage. By 1948 it was part of Ireland's remote past and for a while its memory could be faced without angst.

The *Derry Journal* thoroughly approved of the occasion and, since as a tri-weekly it did not appear until the day after the second performance, it gave much space to its report in its edition of Wednesday, 1 December 1948. It quoted a paragraph from the souvenir programme recalling the original presentation in the Opera House when the orchestra had been conducted by the composer, and the chief accompanist and the soprano were the Misses MacDonald 'belonging to the Presbyterian section of the community'. (Considering that in Ulster the rising had been almost entirely Presbyterian, their association with the project had been quite appropriate.)

The 1948 performance was conducted by William H. Conaghan, the composer's son, and he had under his baton a chorus of 100 and an orchestra of twenty. The list of soloists: Dawson Noble, bass; Afric McGinley, contralto; John Kyle, tenor; Jose Hassan, soprano; and W.J. McDaid, baritone, represented the flower of contemporary Derry singers and they were supplemented by a guest artist, Michael O'Higgins, Professor of Singing at the Irish Academy of Music, who had just returned from a successful American tour and was preparing for a second concert season there in the spring of 1950. One of the songs from the cantata, 'Tone Is Coming Back Again', has passed into the great treasury of Irish songs.

2 DECEMBER 1921

Three IRA prisoners arrested before the Truce were due to be hanged in February 1922 in Derry Jail and instructions came from Republican headquarters that an attempt be made to free them. The escape that was carefully planned was fixed for two o'clock on the morning of Friday, 2 December 1921. A specially constructed rope-ladder with wooden steps was obtained and cars were waiting ready outside in Bennett Street which ran by the back wall of the prison. By chance two members of the constabulary, Special Constables Reid and Thompson, noticed a number of men at the head of the street where it met Bishop Street and opened fire. The men scattered just as a heavy rope was thrown over the jail wall. One constable made it fast while the other ran to the main entrance, calling out the military guard and rousing the prison governor, Captain Robeson.

More than a dozen prisoners, most of them barefoot, were found in the prison yard ready to climb the ladder. They were escorted back to their cells where in one of the corridors the bodies of two members of the Royal Irish Constabulary (RIC) were found dead. Constable Michael Gorman, a forty-five-year-old bachelor from Malin, had been tied up with rope and Special

Constable William Lyttle from Magherafelt, who had a head wound, was manacled by his own handcuffs. Some cotton wool and a bottle of liquid, thought to contain chloroform, were lying near them. Two of the prison warders were discovered tied up and gagged but when released seemed otherwise unhurt.

Three Ford cars parked at the foot of Lower Bennett Street on Foyle Road were impounded and three men, Joseph Lavery and James Campbell of Phillip Street, and Joseph McGuinness of Bishop Street, arrested. Raids were carried out in some nearby houses later that morning. By the time a special court could be arranged two further civilians, William O'Kane and John Callaghan, both of 13 Linenhall Street, were taken into custody. Also at the court that morning were two temporary warders, Michael Finnegan and Patrick Leonard, who had been part of the escape plan. It became clear that, as the two deceased constables and the two warders who had been found trussed and gagged in the passage way were on rounds, they were seized by prisoners who had already been released from their cells by Finnegan and Leonard. The policemen were knocked out with the chloroform applied by holding a saturated pad of cotton wool over their mouths and noses; the dose that was intended only to knock them out proved too strong with the unfortunate result that both men died.

Fifteen men, mostly prisoners, were arraigned for the killing of Gorman and Lyttle, and three were sentenced to be hanged. These sentences were later changed to manslaughter since it was clear that no lasting harm had been intended. They were released in the general amnesty that followed the Treaty.

3 DECEMBER 1848

On Thursday, 7 December 1848, the *Londonderry Sentinel* reported that the tranquillity which usually characterised the Sabbath in Derry was broken the previous Sunday morning by the intelligence that a steam vessel had arrived in the city's quay with a number of dead bodies on board. The newspaper further related that forty soldiers of the 95th Depot, then stationed in the city, were marched from the barracks before 10 a.m. to the yard of the Scotch Steam Packet Company, and together with the constabulary, under the direction of Mayor Alex Lindsay and some of the local magistrates, escorted a great number of persons from the Londonderry steamer to the Corporation Hall.

Alarming and contradictory reports began to circulate. It was stated that a large body of wealthy emigrants on the steam vessel were attacked and murdered during the night. Others claimed that the captain and crew, apprehending a mutiny on board the vessels, suffocated the passengers by fastening them down in the steerage and throwing Lucifer matches among them. The accounts respecting the number of dead also varied considerably. Some had it that thirty or forty individuals had lost their lives, others that as many as fifty or sixty had perished, while further statements put the figure at no more than fifteen or twenty. Shortly after eleven o'clock crowds were seen running to the wharf where the ill-fated ship was moored. Several groups assembled on the docks conversing anxiously about the event; in one of these groups was the commander of the vessel, who, in answer to the question 'How many were dead?' replied, 'Fifteen or twenty.'

Having gone on board a *Sentinel* reporter perceived the vessel to be in a filthy condition:

> Several bullocks were still on the deck, some of them dead, while many had been previously landed, and persons were engaged in getting those that were alive in the vessel on shore. On approaching the steerage cabin and looking down the companion the spectacle that presented itself was of the most appalling description. The floor resembled the hold of a slave ship, after its cargo of human beings had been deprived of life. There lay the bodies of the dead, literally piled upon each other, and corpses of men, women and children were strewed thickly on every spot, some stripped of their clothes, others having their features disfigured with wounds and contusions, the faces of others covered with froth, after having died in all the agonies of thirst and suffocation. In short, a more horrifying sight cannot be imagined. The effluvia was so intolerable that we could not venture to descend among the wretched victims.
>
> The bodies were subsequently brought on shore and examined by medical doctors, when it was discovered that the mortality was much greater than had been supposed, and that no fewer than seventy-two individuals had lost their lives, of whom twenty-three were men, thirty-one women and eighteen children.

4 DECEMBER 1911

Disaster overtook the Derry-owned steamer *Templemore*, which was driven into Murlough Bay, Ballycastle, during a gale on Monday night, 4 December 1911. The *Templemore* was due in Derry on Tuesday about one o'clock with a cargo of coal for Henry Lane & Co., the owners, but word was received that during the night the steamer had shipped heavy seas which flooded the engine room and extinguished the fires. The vessel was thus left at the mercy of wind and wave. The captain managed to manoeuvre the disabled steamer into the shelter of Murlough Bay, and the anchors having been dropped, assistance was sought. The crew got ashore in the ship's boat, and the tug *Earl of Dunraven* was immediately sent to give what aid was possible.

The owners consulted with Mr Maxton, the consulting engineer, asking him to proceed to the scene of the accident for the purpose of advising the captain what course ought to be adopted. Due to a previous engagement, however, Maxton was unable to accede to the request but advised the owners of the vessel to get in touch with his assistant, Charles K. Maude, who was on business in Derry.

Along with Mr McGuinness, one of the principals of the firm, Maude motored from Derry to Ballycastle. On reaching the seaside town Maude telephoned to say that they were proceeding on a small rowing boat to the tug, which had come from Moville to assist the *Templemore*. At eleven o'clock on Tuesday night Maxton despatched a wire to Maude, addressed to the Torr Head Signal Station, but received a reply the following morning which read: 'I cannot deliver your telegram to Mr Maude. *Templemore* broke adrift, and drifted northward around Fair Head 11.55 a.m. to-day.' Subsequently, McGuinness wired to Maxton as follows: 'Vessel took a sudden lurch, and we all jumped into the water, and Mr Maude and the fireman were below in getting the steam up.'

On Wednesday morning the drifting collier, which had broken away from her moorings, was sighted by the incoming Laird steamer *Brier*. Captain Beattie, of the *Brier*, changed a course in the direction of the apparent derelict and sent a boat to her, leaving one man on board. At this moment the *Earl of Dunraven* came in sight with some of the crew of the *Templemore* and other seamen. Under the superintendence of Maude, pumping was carried on with so much success that early in the day the fires were again lighted. Steam was got up in the main boiler, and with the help of the tug and her own steam the *Templemore* was worked towards Ballycastle.

Suddenly a huge sea swept the steamer from stem to stern and flooded the engine room, swamping the fires and carrying most of the crew overboard. Maude lost his life, as did a fireman, John Simms, a resident of Fountain Street, Derry.

5 DECEMBER 1928

Derry was one of the earliest towns in Ireland to have street lighting, an amenity it enjoyed while large sections of the city were still lit by gas. At a meeting of the Chamber of Commerce on 5 December 1928 its members began again to consider the possibility that those who had gone to the expense of having electricity installed were the only citizens who were being billed for street lighting, while *all* the population enjoyed the amenity. Most of the houses with power installed were subject to a rather alarming arrangement known as the 'limiter'. A special tariff was charged by which they paid for a minimum wattage and any increase in consumption, such as caused by too many lights swwitched on at once led to a dramatic flickering of all the lamps followed by a total loss of power.

H.W. Porter began the meeting by reminding the members that this was not the first time the matter was on the agenda. It was in fact a year since he drew the chamber's attention to the fact that consumers were paying £4,500 more than necessary and had required the secretary to write to the town clerk about the situation. W.G.S. Ballantine, the secretary, assured the meeting that he had written as directed to the town clerk but apart from an acknowledgement of receipt of the letter and a reassurance that the matter would receive attention, nothing further had been done.

Porter said that it was common knowledge that the cost of street lighting in future would be borne directly by the rates that had been increased for the purpose. He now needed to know what reduction individual consumers could expect since there had to be a sum of £4,500 no longer needed for the street lighting. He was aware that no such reduction had been made in the customers' bills and could draw but one conclusion: the consumers were paying twice for the amenity! Such a situation could not be allowed to persist. Captain Desmond, a local factory owner, insisted that the cost of street lighting should be borne by all since all benefited equally whether their homes were lit by gas or electricity. Councillor Magee of the Corporation, really crushing any hope of a rebate, claimed that if no reduction in the electricity tariff was forthcoming there was 'a solid reason' for it. A comparison of electrical charges in Derry with those in other places would prove to be greatly in Derry's favour.

It was agreed to find out precisely how the city actually compared with other places, and if the business community was being unfairly treated, a resolution could be passed asking for a reduction. The meeting ended when Ballantine, awaking as if from a dream, said he had written to the town clerk a few days ago about Mr Porter's motion and was still awaiting a reply. And so another exciting meeting of the Chamber of Commerce concluded.

At the Winter Assizes in Derry on 6 December 1924 a young man was charged for murdering his sweetheart, but with the help of the brilliant advocacy of C.L. Shiel, his defence council, the verdict was commuted to manslaughter. Both the accused and his victim were from Ballymoney, County Antrim, but the case was heard in Derry, a kind of neutral ground. Thomas Kennedy, who once had been a special constable and still had a rifle in his possession, had shot and killed his 'Matty', Martha Rodgers, who was employed as a servant girl by Mrs Hamilton of 'Ashleigh', Ballymoney.

The prosecution was led by the Attorney General, the Right Honourable Richard Best, who opened by describing the events of the previous 6 July. Kennedy and Rodgers had been keeping company, much to her parents' disapproval. So strongly did they object that they had already made plans for shipping her off to America. One last meeting was permitted on the first Sunday in July. They met outside Kennedy's home in Charlotte Street in the town and as they walked he was heard to plead with her to 'stick to him'. She gave the only possible answer—that they could not be together, but hoped that they might be friends. His response was chilling: 'I am going to kill myself, and you must be prepared to die too.' He ran off home, loaded his rifle with four rounds; then from a distance of six feet he aimed at her chest and fired.

He ran immediately to the police barracks and gave himself up. When the sergeant on duty reached the spot, Matty was still alive but dying of a wound in her left breast. Kennedy told the police that he intended to kill himself: 'If I had had time I would have done myself in.' There was no doubt about Kennedy's guilt, but was the crime murder or manslaughter? Shiel's defence was that Kennedy did not really intend to kill Matty, any more than himself. He was in such a non-caring state that he was clumsy, negligent and let the rifle go off unintentionally.

The Attorney General and the judge both congratulated Shiel on his very able defence and the latter admonished the jury as follows: If the prisoner fired at the girl knowing what he was doing, it was murder; if the shot went off accidentally and they considered him guilty of gross carelessness, they could find a verdict of manslaughter. On the other hand, if there was no gross carelessness, they could acquit the prisoner. The jury, after the briefest of intervals, found Kennedy guilty of manslaughter and he was sentenced to four years' penal servitude.

On 7 December 1900 a serious accident occurred in Derry's Bishop's Garden, Bishop Street Without, where part of a building that was being constructed suddenly collapsed, burying seven men in the debris, one of whom was brought out dead and the remaining six seriously injured. The operation was an extension being done for Messrs. Jones & Lowther, its purpose to provide a laundry for a neighbouring shirt factory. It was part of the back wall and a transverse section, both about twenty-five feet high, which fell with such ghastly results. The property, owned by the Church of Ireland diocese, had been obtained as a personal amenity by the notorious Earl Bishop, Frederick Augustus Hervey.

In the back wall there were large openings over which arches had been built, and it was believed that it was the collapse of one of the arches that brought down the wall at right angles to it, at which most or all of the injured men were working on scaffolds. There were two scaffolds, one higher than the other, labourers on the lower handing stones to the craftsmen above them. Those on the lower platform suffered more severely than the men on the higher one.

At about half-past one in the afternoon the walls fell with a tremendous crash, startling the people in the neighbourhood and the men at work at other parts of the building. It was later discovered that about twenty feet of the wall had fallen suddenly and without any premonitory shaking or warning whatever, burying the workmen among the masonry and broken timbers.

When the men were finally brought out one was found to be dead and the other six badly injured. These were removed immediately to the City and County Infirmary for treatment. The man who lost his life was John Anderson, a labourer who had formerly held a small farm at Bready, near Strabane, and was about fifty-five years old. John McFarland, also a labourer, who lived in Bennett Street, was the most severely injured of the others. He suffered from severe scalp lesions. John Freeman, originally from Portrush but who lived in Fountain Street, had a chest injury and several ribs broken. Charles Gallagher, an apprentice mason who also resided in Fountain Street, had sustained fractures of some of his ribs. Dominick Gallagher, a mason living at Hamilton Street, had a broken arm and bruises. Alexander Wright, Albert Street, had sustained a broken leg and some contusions. William Adams, an apprentice mason living in Fountain Street, had had his thighs contused but no bones broken.

One man, a mason named William Knobbs, from the Waterside, had a remarkable escape. He was on the very top of the wall when it collapsed, and went down with it, but strangely he was able to rise to his feet and found he had suffered no injury at all.

The Savoy operas, those comic masterpieces written between 1875 and 1896, became classics overnight. They were the result of a combative partnership between William Schwenk Gilbert and Arthur Sullivan, who supplied respectively the libretto and lyrics, and the unforgettable music. Rarely has a partnership of such equal talent managed to wed words and music so winningly. Not that either would have agreed, the second generation Irishman perpetually complaining that he had to reduce his music to a 'tee-tum, tee-tum' so that audiences could make out Gilbert's 'silly words', and Gilbert suggesting that all the tunes seemed the same. Sullivan was far more proud of his setting of 'The Lost Chord' and wished sincerely to write a grand opera while the irascible Gilbert, with less pretension, realised his limitations.

It was only four years after Gilbert's death that the Savoyards of Derry were given a week-long feast of that winning formula, and the *Derry Journal*, as enthusiastic as the capacity audiences, showed its appreciation. In its Wednesday, 8 December 1915 edition it praised the Derry Amateur Operatic Society productions being presented that week in the Opera House of *Trial by Jury*, *The Mikado* and *The Pirates of Penzance*. The first of these is quite short and was used as a curtain-raiser for the ever-popular *Pirates*.

The *Journal* critic wrote: 'They seem to be the only plays of their class that bear repetition without becoming stale. There is, for instance, a cheery freshness and engaging catchiness about the music to which the words of these works are wedded that soothes and entertains.' *The Mikado* with its charming fake orientalism and such songs as 'Tit Willow' and 'A Wandering Minstrel' was then, and probably still is, the favourite of all Gilbert and Sullivan's shows, especially now that the copyright so fiercely guarded by Bridget D'Oyly Carte (really Bridget Doyle McCarthy) has lapsed.

In 1915 the words and dances devised by Gilbert were sacrosanct and nobody minded. The cause was good, as readers were reminded: 'It only remains to be stated that the proceeds are in aid of the local War Relief Fund and anyone… who is in search of an opportunity to pass two or three hours away under most agreeable conditions can be cordially recommended a visit to the theatre this week.'

Derry has long had a reputation for excellence in music. There was music in the Derry air long before Phil Coulter had written about it or Dana had won the Eurovision Song Contest. The city seemed to have more than its fair share of fine singers. Long even before the Feis Doire Colmcille was established there was a great tradition of concerts, amateur and professional, that allowed its gifted artistes to show their quality to a very experienced critical audience.

A concert in St Columb's Hall on 9 December 1951 was typical of the wholesome entertainment available on a Sunday night when the local Corporation forbade a licence for films in the six cinemas in the city. The charity event, in aid of the Derry Catholic Building Fund, featured two priests on the bill. The first, Hugh Gallagher, had travelled from his curacy in Garvagh to entertain with such songs as 'Silent Worship', 'My Nancy' and 'When You and I Were Young, Maggie', all firm parlour favourites; and if it seemed a little odd that a priest should sing earnestly 'I did but see her passing by, yet will I love her till I die', no one seemed to mind.

The second performing priest was Bernard Chapman who was a skilled violinist and played a selection of Irish airs. When the soprano Nora O'Leary sang the '*Ave Maria*' he provided a violin obligato accompaniment. She and her sister Eva were regular performers in the yearly Christmas pantomime, playing usually principal boy and girl. There was one professional artist, known as Sergeant Eddie O'Doherty of the Mounties, who was one of the team of performers in the Big Bill Campbell radio show that was heard weekly on the BBC Light Programme, and was a popular item in seaside concerts in Blackpool and other resorts. He too had been a panto star before leaving Derry when he was known by his patronymic Edward Henry O'Doherty, or E.H. After 'Santa Lucia', sung by the O'Leary sisters, it was time for a kind of Irish ballet in a formal dance devised by Brendan De Glin who ran one of several Irish dance studios in the city. It was called the 'Tara Branch' and the dancers' elaborate steps recreated on the stage the chief elements of a famous piece of Celtic jewellery.

The final item was a performance which consisted almost entirely of people from Derry's other parish, St Columb's, Waterside. The St Columb's Choral Society, conducted by S.J. Burke, performed a special music fantasia written by the Derry composer Redmond Friel in tribute to the Very Reverend J.L. McGettigan, the late parish priest of the Waterside, who had been one of the founders of the Derry *feis*.

The chairman of the Norwegian Nobel Committee, in the presence of the King of Norway, on 10 December each year (the anniversary of Alfred Nobel's death) presents the Nobel Peace Prize. It is the only Nobel Prize not presented in Stockholm. The Nobel laureate receives a diploma, a medal and a document confirming the prize amount. The ceremony is held at the Oslo City Hall, followed the next day by the Nobel Peace Prize Concert, which is broadcast to more than 450 million households in over 150 countries around the world. In 1998 the joint recipient with David Trimble was John Hume, probably the man who had done most to bring peace to troubled Northern Ireland. It was a fitting culmination to a sterling career in public service, though in 2010 he would be named as 'Ireland's greatest' in an RTÉ survey. In the Oslo City Hall the sixty-seven-year-old statesman rose to the occasion with a speech, grave and fluent, that dwelt on his crusade for peace, and revealed that he was well fitted to receive the award.

After the usual formal acknowledgement of the gracious presence of the king and queen, the members of the committee and the distinguished guests, Hume expressed his gratitude for the hour bestowed upon him by the committee. His first tribute was to the 'ordinary people of Ireland, particularly those of the North who have lived and suffered the reality of our conflict'. He reviewed the previous thirty years, noting the many moments 'of deep depression and outright horror', and worried that, in Yeats's words, 'Too long a sacrifice can make a stone of the heart.' The Irish people 'endlessly gathered their strength to face another day and never stopped encouraging their leaders to find the courage to resolve this situation so that our children could look to the future with a smile of hope'. For this reason he insisted the award was indeed theirs and they would take strong encouragement from the day's significance that would strongly strengthen the peace process.

He used the opportunity to pay tribute to the many people who had contributed to the on-going process, including British Prime Minister Tony Blair, Taoiseach Bertie Ahern, US President Bill Clinton, the European President Jacques Delors, Jacques Santer, and the three men who so clearly facilitated the negotiations: Senator George Mitchell, former Leader of the Senate of the United States of America, Harri Holkerri of Finland, and General John de Chastelain of Canada. And, of course, to the outstanding Secretary of State, Mo Mowlam, who had died seven years later.

He finished with appropriate self-abnegation: 'I humbly accept this honour on behalf of a people who, after many years of strife, have finally made a commitment to a better future in harmony together. Our commitment is grounded in the very language and the very principles of the Universal Declaration itself. No greater honour could have been done me or the people I speak here for on no more fitting day.' His final words echoed the words of his 'great hero' Martin Luther King: 'We shall overcome.'

11 DECEMBER 1926

John Coyle, described in the local papers as an 'aged man' though he was only sixty-three, was knocked down and killed at 4.30 on the evening of Friday, 10 December 1926, while crossing Foyle Street. At that time the city's second main bus route, from Clooney to Messines Park, went by Duke Street and Strand Road. Coyle, who lived in Donegal Place, off Lecky Road, was a fish dealer and had parked his donkey and cart on the street while he crossed to pay a bill in offices opposite. It was on his return that he was struck by a bus coming from the direction of the Guildhall. The front and back wheels of the bus went over his head. Dr Keohane and James Trimble rendered what first aid they could until an ambulance arrived to take him to the City Infirmary, where he was declared dead on arrival. There was a great deal of blood at the scene of the accident but sawdust was used to cover up the evidence of the tragic affair.

It was in the infirmary that the inquest was held on the Saturday afternoon, 11 December, with John Tracy, the coroner, presiding. Humphrey Babington appeared for the driver of the bus, John McDevitt of 5 Nicholson Square, and A. Robb for the family of the deceased. Sir Henry Miller, City Solicitor, was also present, while Detective Inspector Cahill led the RUC team. A witness, Michael Doherty of 154 Lecky Road, said that while standing at a gateway on the same side as Coyle's donkey and cart he had seen him enter the roadway and head across to his side. Seeing the bus coming he'd hesitated but, instead of turning back, began to run intending to reach the other side safely. The driver had swerved to miss him but he was caught by the front near-side wheel. The bus, said Doherty, pulled up in about its own length and the driver jumped out of the cab and ran back to where Coyle's body lay.

Most of the police questioning concerned the traffic situation at the time. Was the bus going fast? Did Doherty hear a horn? Were there carts or lorries parked near or at the scene? It became clear that the deceased's hesitation may have been a contributory cause. It was also felt that the driver had done all he could, though one witness said that the bus was well into the middle of the road when Coyle saw it, having pulled out from behind a lorry. McDevitt had not been called but Constable Hughes, who had interviewed him, said the driver had seen the man cross in front of the bus and hesitate in the centre of the road. At that moment he turned to go back but he was struck by the left mudguard and knocked down. The jury agreed on a verdict of accidental death with no blame attached to the driver.

12 DECEMBER 1951

Since the days of Daniel O'Connell the *Londonderry Journal* (later the *Derry Journal*) was squarely on the side of nationalism. After the setting up of the Northern Ireland state it refused to use the word 'Ulster' except when referring to the historical nine-county province, and such titles as the 'Ulster' Transport Authority, 'Ulster' Special Constabulary and 'U'TV were never printed without the condemnatory quotation marks. The owners, editorial staff and its readers trusted it to attack the Stormont government at every opportunity, and what looked like a coup dropped into their laps when, at a public meeting in the Guildhall on 12 December 1951, J.J.L. Gibson, the Local Government auditor, criticised the amount of the expenditure incurred on three civic luncheons.

The *Journal* reporter was quick to point out that: 'All such functions are of an exclusively Unionist nature and the Unionist Corporators, who had no inkling of what Mr Gibson was going to say, got one of their biggest shocks when he commented adversely on details of the cost that included liquor, cigars and cigarettes.'

Nationalist members of the Corporation, led by E.G. 'Big Eddie' McAteer and Alderman Frank McCarroll, proprietor of the *Derry Journal*, were present, antennae quivering at the prospect of embarrassing their Unionist adversaries. They began with a general statement of disapproval at the extravagance in many aspects of city finances but subsequently broadened into a complaint about the way financial agreements were made. McAteer claimed that, in defiance of right practice, 'It is the customary method of Local Government here to appoint sub-committees with council powers and no one ever knows what is happening.'

There was further wrangling with C.S. Glover, the mayor, about dealings with local firms when the amounts in question were much in excess of £100. Gibson, who maintained throughout all the heated argument a detached and independent attitude, was at times heroically patient during the many attempts of officials to exculpate themselves from the charges of at least self-indulgence, if nothing more sinister. Gibson kept referring to the section of the relevant legislation permitting 'reasonable expenses'. He mentioned as an example the Armistice luncheon for thirty-nine people on 13 November 1950 in the Northern Counties Club that cost £49 5d in total. This meant that the charge for each person was £1 5s. Where, he asked was the 'reasonableness' there? Other lunches hosted by the Corporation worked out respectively at £3 1d and £2 1s 9d a head—again not 'reasonable'.

The meeting continued in this fashion with Gibson implacable but correct and various councillors trying to match his arguments with bluster. As an experienced civil servant, well used to the facts of public life in Northern Ireland, he probably knew that at the next presentation of his report he would have a similar tale to tell.

13 DECEMBER 1913

In the days before Children's Acts made it illegal to name an accused child in court proceedings their names were published freely along with their alleged crimes. On 13 December 1913 fifteen-year-old Thomas Kennedy of 140 Fahan Street, who had garnered quite a reputation as a cat burglar, was 'caught at last', to use the words of his captor, Sarah O'Kane, a grocer of 11 Argyle Terrace. He appeared at Derry Children's Court before Bernard Hannigan and G.R. O'Connor, RM, charged by District Inspector McHugh with breaking and entering O'Kane's house and stealing £2 10s. Michael, Sarah's husband, stated that on the morning of 21 November he discovered the back door open and his clothing 'tossed'. When he searched the pockets he found that £2 10s in gold was missing. On 4 December he discovered that the scullery window had been broken during the night and that cigarettes were missing. It was with some satisfaction that he heard his wife identify the culprit with her cry of recognition.

It is not quite clear why no attempt was made to have Kennedy arrested until 15 December. He had been employed as a message boy and knew the layout of the interior of the shop and house. In his statement to the police he admitted the three burglaries:

> About three weeks ago I went into O'Kane's yard and raised the window. I went into the kitchen and took £2 10s in gold out of a waistcoat pocket. I went another night and took some cigarettes—about three or four packets. I went another night after that. I had to break a pane of glass to open the catch and took two packets of cigarettes. I went in another morning to the scullery but could not get into the kitchen, as the door was bolted. I was going through the window this

morning when Mrs O'Kane called out through the window above, 'I have you now.'

The reported words seem somehow rehearsed and formal, not the sort of chat you would expect from a young tearaway.

Margaret Donaghey, one of the prosecution witnesses, who worked in McCready's salesrooms, testified that in November the defendant had bought a shirt from her and paid for it with half a gold sovereign. Later his father told the court that he would guarantee that the boy would never be guilty of this crime again and he would undertake to compensate Mr O'Kane for the loss. O'Kane replied that he did not wish to press the case against the boy; up till this affair he would have recommended him for a position. There still remained a mystery of a missing watch that O'Kane said had been in the kitchen. Kennedy admitted that he had seen it, picked it up and held it in his hand, but then claimed to return it.

The magistrates ordered the boy's father to pay a fine of 2s 6d, give £2 10s to Mr O'Kane and enter into bail for his son's good behaviour for three years.

14 DECEMBER 1948

At the Derry Children's Court on Tuesday, 14 December 1948, four young boys appeared before the Resident Magistrate, Major McLean, on a charge of stealing 'a quantity of pastries and biscuits' from a canteen belonging to the Red Shield Hostel in Pump Street, of value 30s. District Inspector Shillington of the RUC, prosecuting, said that eatables were missed on several occasions from a van that had been parked in Artillery Street each night. His colleague Constable McVeigh testified that following complaints he allowed himself to be locked in the van one night, and after ten minutes, heard the boys approaching. One inserted a piece of wire under the glass and released the hasp. The constable then got out and the boys made statements about being there on previous occasions. Patrick Maxwell, appearing for a number of the defendants, asked him if he would be surprised to learn that since that event a group of other boys had arrived and not only tried to steal pastries but the van itself.

The manager of the hostel said they did not wish the case to be pressed. The only reason that he had reported it was that one small boy who had got into the van had released the handbrake; but for the fact its progress was blocked by another van parked a little further down the street, there could have been a serious accident. The summons against the youngest malefactor, aged eight, was withdrawn and the rest were put under probation.

Other cases dealt with by the court concerned the theft of two comic books from William Irvine's shop in Foyle Street by two boys, aged twelve and thirteen, who could not be named because of their ages. They had stolen them while the assistant's back was turned, and ran off. One was also charged with purloining a pack of 'Snap cards'—then all the rage—from a city store. Claude Wilton, for one of the lads, said that his mother was a war widow and he had yielded to the temptation. He could have got the money from his mother if he had asked. Both boys were placed under the care of the probation officer.

In an adjourned case a fifteen-year-old boy was summoned for stealing a bicycle, valued at £4, belonging to John McFeeters, a bus conductor from Elagh. He had parked it outside the dry dock, and when he returned fifteen minutes later, it was gone. Wilton's defence case was that his client and a pal had thought the bike had been abandoned and they just rode it up the Strand. There was no criminal intent and they did not realise that, since the owner lived some miles away, they were causing him considerable disadvantage. The Probation Act was applied and the defendant's father paid £1 5s 6d costs and restitution.

15 DECEMBER 1761

There was something of a stir outside the courthouse in Strabane on the morning of 15 December 1761. The execution of the notorious John McNaghten for the murder of Mary Anne Knox of Prehen House, Derry, had been fixed for that morning but no carpenter in Strabane could be found to build the gallows. In spite of the guilty verdict, the career of the man with its elements of gallantry and romance—and the possibility that he had not fired the fateful shots—had given him something of reputation with 'the lower sort of people'. Enraged and in extreme frustration the Knoxes, father and sons, and their servants, built the scaffold themselves and now waited expectantly for justice to be done.

The prisoner, looking rather better than during the fourteen-hour trial when he had sported a month-old beard, was brought in chains from Lifford Jail, a fact that caused a further delay. It was unheard of for a man about to be hanged not to have his hands free. This odd legal practice gave rise to a further impasse: no blacksmith could be found to strike off the chains. One was finally summoned by an officer of the Light Horse and compelled under threat of his own incarceration to remove the fetters. The crowd, delighted with the entertainment, grew a little restive waiting for the executioner but none of the regulars would cooperate. They cheered, however, when the prisoner climbed to the top of the ladder, tightened the noose round his neck and threw himself off the platform with great force only to land on the ground, having broken the rope. He made no attempt to escape but climbed up again on to the platform, found a new rope and this time finished the job.

According to the legend his final words were that he did not wish to be known as 'a half-hanged man'. If the story is true he failed in his intention; since his story has been retold in every generation in the 250 years following his impulsive double leap, and he has always been referred to in Derry as 'Half-hanged McNaghten'. History has been kinder to him than his contemporaries; he is often seen as a lost romantic who dearly loved Mary Anne and wished her no ill. In the 1830s when the Ordnance Survey published their memoirs of the parish of Clondermot, they considered it appropriate to include an account of the 'death of Miss Knox'. As they noted, the event 'naturally excited much interest at the time, which length of years has but slightly abated'. They add that he was concealed from the law by different females of his acquaintance, and was discovered by some person who had observed a lady bringing food to an outhouse in which he was secreted. He remained a charmer right to the end.

16 DECEMBER 1955

There was a large gathering of Belfast and Derry citizens in the Mansion House, London, on 16 December 1955, to greet Sir Winston Churchill, upon whom the Honorary Freedoms of Belfast and Londonderry were conferred. It was the first occasion on which the freedom of any Northern Ireland city was conferred outside the country. The Londonderry Freedom Certificate was presented in a silver replica of 'Roaring Meg', the famous Siege gun, and the Town Clerk, R.H. Henderson, read the Council resolution conferring the freedom; Sir Winston took the ancient oath to be 'obedient, profitable and true to our Sovereign lady, Queen Elizabeth II, her heirs and successors and to the Mayor, Aldermen and Burgesses of the City of Londonderry'.

There was laughter when Sir Winston swore not to assent to or abet against the city 'nor any foreign goods concealed in merchandise, customs or any otherwise, and not to be retailed to any other man'. Then he held aloft the replica and signed the scroll. Just before this he had received the freedom of Belfast and with it a solid silver casket of Celtic design with the coloured enamel arms on the front and a cedar lining forming a cigar box. Lady Churchill was not forgotten, and from the Lady Mayoress of Belfast, Mrs Harcourt, and the Mayoress of Londonderry, Mrs Dowds, she received gifts of Irish linen.

Arriving at the Mansion House, Sir Winston and Lady Churchill were met by a guard detachment from four Irish regiments—the Irish Guards (under Second Lieutenant Lord Rideau, son of Field Marshal Earl Alexander of Tunis); the First Battalion, the Royal Inniskilling Fusiliers, under Captain J. Hassett (the party was composed entirely of Derry men); and then detachments of the Royal Ulster Rifles, and the London Irish Rifles. The saffron-kilted pipes and drums of the Inniskillings played traditional Ulster music as Sir Winston and Lady Churchill entered.

After a toast and speech by the Lord Mayor of Belfast, the Lord Mayor of Derry said he was privileged to offer a sincere welcome on behalf of the citizens of Londonderry to their new Freeman. 'You have heard his assent to our ancient Oath and you have witnessed him signing his name to our Roll of Honorary Freemen,' the Mayor continued. 'On that Roll are the signatures of many persons distinguished in statesmanship or arms dating back to 1690. Amongst those names are: The Right Honourable John Forster, Speaker of the House of Commons, 1786; the Right Honourable William Pitt, Earl of Chatham, 1788; Sir Arthur Wellesley, Duke of Wellington, 1807; Right Honourable Robert Peel, Speaker of the House of Commons, 1817; and General Ulysses Grant, President of the United States of America, 1879. Amongst the more recent distinguished men who are Freemen of our city are his late Majesty King George VI; HRH The Duke of Gloucester; Field Marshal Viscount Montgomery of Alamein; and Field Marshal Viscount Alexander of Tunis.'

17 DECEMBER 1813

By the end of the first decade of the nineteenth century Derry was becoming conscious of its municipal importance. It already had a cathedral, a jail, a grammar school and a Corporation Hall, and now felt the need of a courthouse. The first stone was laid on 17 December 1813 by John Curry, the mayor, and the Right Honourable Sir George Fitzgerald Hill Bart, and was ready for the sitting of the Assizes in 1816. It was completed by 1817 and regarded by Robert Simpson, writing thirty years later in *The Annals of Derry*, as 'the only building of which our city can boast, so far as architectural variety, chasteness of design and appearance, and execution are concerned'. His enthusiasm sprang from the fact that most of the other public buildings were nondescript. The Post

Office, for example, was run from a private house in Richmond Street: 'A new one is, we understand, in contemplation.'

The courthouse was built in Greek revival style on an empty site in Bishop Street Within and tends to block the view of St Columb's Cathedral. The architect was John Bowden who had just finished designing the Diocesan School at its new site on the Strand Road after the previous effort by Robert Elsam had proved 'too gloomy' and had to be knocked down. It was built of Dungiven sandstone with all the ornamental parts composed of whiter Portland stone. Simpson describes the front as 'exhibiting a tetrastyle portico, viz four columns with a flat overhead of the antique ionic order, modelled after the temple of Erectheus in the acropolis of Athens'. The royal coat of arms above the pediment, and the figures of Peace and Justice flanking it, are by Edward Smyth of Dublin. The builders, Messrs. Henry, Mullins and McMahon, also came from Dublin.

The interior followed the design of the Four Courts in Dublin, lit from above by ceiling domes. Other apartments included the Grand Jury's council room and their dining room, the County Treasurer's office, the Judges' room, the Record Office, and the offices of the Crown and the Peace. The total cost was £30,479 which, according to Simpson, was 'defrayed by the County'. It remains an elegant neo-classical building but because of its origins and British associations, it was a regular target for the IRA and required on-going refurbishment. One of these attacks caused collateral damage to the nearby cathedral, affecting the baptistry and the memorial stained-glass windows celebrating three of the hymns of the wife of a former bishop, 'C.F.A.' (Mrs Alexander): 'Once in Royal David's City', 'There Is a Green Hill Far Away' and 'The Golden Gates Are Lifted Up'. These have all been restored. Today, now nearly 200 years old, the courthouse remains one of Derry's finest pieces of architecture.

18 DECEMBER 1688

Amid the distractions of the struggle between the Catholic King James II and Protestant Prince William of Orange for possession of the Crown was the alleged plot of the Irish to massacre the Protestant population throughout Ireland, on 18 December 1688.

A letter containing a warning of this threatened massacre, and exhorting the Protestant citizens of Derry to refuse admission to the Catholic Tyrconnel's troops, was sent to George Canning of Garvagh. Canning forwarded this letter to Alderman Tompkins in Derry. A gentleman meeting with the messenger on the way to Tompkins was informed of the letter's contents, and he relayed the information to Colonel George Phillips of Limavady on 6 December, on which day the Earl of Antrim's new Irish regiment arrived at that place on its way to Derry. Colonel Phillips sent a messenger with this information at midnight to the city.

Next morning Phillips sent another messenger to Londonderry expressing his increased apprehension of suffering this regiment to enter the city. The messenger reported that he had passed some of the companies within two miles of the city. The aldermen, with the rest of the city's leading men, were in great confusion on receiving these accounts.

Alderman Tompkins consulted Reverend James Gordon, a Presbyterian minister, who advised the closing of the gates. Colonel Phillips himself arrived in Derry on that day and resumed the government of the city, which he had previously held. Alderman Norman and others in the meantime consulted the Anglican Bishop Ezekiel Hopkins, who rejected resistance. Many of the prominent citizens concurred with the bishop.

The Apprentice Boys muttered something about shutting the gates. They got some private encouragement to do so at first, but that was soon retracted, and the minds of all the men of authority wavered. In the meantime, the two companies of the Irish regiment arrived at the Waterside. John Buchanan, a deputy, had no objection to giving the regiment a most honourable reception, but Horace Kennedy, one of the sheriffs, had given the Apprentice Boys a secret hint during the preceding night, and they were at hand prepared to shut the gates against the Irish soldiers.

While consultations were proceeding within the walls the soldiers crossed the river and appeared at the landing place about three hundred yards from Ferry Gate. The young men of the city, observing this, ran to the main guard, seized the keys, and after a slight opposition, came to the Ferry Gate, drew up the bridge and locked the gate while some of Lord Antrim's soldiers were within sixty yards of it. They then ran to secure the other three gates, and having left guards at each, assembled in the market place. The names of the young men who shut the gates were Henry Campsie, Robert Morrison, William Crookshanks, Alexander Cunningham, Robert Sherrard, Samuel Hunt, Daniel Sherrard, James Spike, Alexander Irwin, John Coningham, James Stewart, William Cairns, and Samuel Harvey.

For many years the statue of Governor Walker on top of a column of fluted Portland stone was one of Derry's landmarks, until it was destroyed by an IRA bomb in 1973. It stood in the centre of the Royal Bastion and showed Walker, who had made himself sole governor of the besieged city after the flight of his joint governor, Robert Lundy. He portrayed himself as the hero of the Siege in his account completed before heading off to fight at the Boyne in 1690, where he was killed. There is no question about the soundness of his leadership or his charismatic motivational ability, but his strongly Anglican account effectively side-lined the strong Presbyterian contribution. His death while attempting to succour Marshal Schomberg completed the catalogue of his heroism and later history made him the icon of the struggle that rendered the city immortal after 'sufferings unparalleled in the history of British warfare', in one local historian's overstated account.

The idea for 'Walker's Testimonial' had been discussed for many years but it was not until 19 December 1826 that actual work began. The total height was of eighty-one feet, with a fifteen-foot pedestal. The pillar's diameter was six feet nine inches and inside was a spiral staircase of 110 steps, each three feet five inches in width. Walker's statue was nine feet high, the likeness taken from an old painting and showing him in canonical garb. In the right hand of the statue is a bible while the left is extended to point down river in the direction of the broken boom that enabled the relief ships bearing food to the garrison to reach the quay. On the day before, the 138th anniversary of the closing of the gates by the London apprentices, the first stone was put in place by the city mayor, Major Young, 'in the presence of the Corporation and a vast concourse of the citizens'. The work was completed in August 1928 at a cost of £4,200, including £100 for the statue. Among the subscribers the City Corporation donated £50 and the Honourable the Irish Society gave fifty guineas. The builders were Messrs. Henry Mullins and McMahon, and the statue was sculpted by John Smyth.

The left hand originally held a sword that disappeared during one of Derry's frequent storms, symbolically diverting attention from his military role and concentrating on his clerical career as Bishop of Derry, appointed by William III as a successor to Dr Ezekiel Hopkins, who left the city the day after the apprentices shut the gates. He did not survive to be consecrated and the post went to Dr William King. It remained a significant symbol for the 'Maiden City' and in early days a giant effigy of the 'traitor Lundy' was hung from the platform. After the statue's replacement in 1988, on the 300th anniversary of the Siege, it was placed in a monumental garden in Society Street.

There was a considerable buzz on 20 December 1840 for the staff and pupils of the Derry Diocesan School and Foyle College, now in Lawrence Hill, having long left its original site at Society Street, just inside the city wall. Not only were the delights of the Christmas holiday looming, but it was prize-giving day and his Lordship, the Right Reverend Richard Ponsonby, the Bishop of Derry, the patron of the school, was going to present the trophies, eight silver medals, that he himself provided. The allocation of prizes was significant of the attitudes of the time and gave a hint of what was to come in the future: five classical and three mercantile. Derry was growing fast and had already laid the foundations for what would make her by the end of the nineteenth century one of the busiest and most prosperous towns in the country. The clash between the classical mode and vocational need would lead to the establishment in 1868 of a separate school, the Londonderry Academical Institution, with a curriculum more appropriate to a 'town of merchandize', as James I ,who gave it its charter in 1613, first dubbed it.

In the 1840s proficiency in the ancient classics was still regarded as the most appropriate training to fit a boy for any future career. Besides, the school was a diocesan school and like its later Catholic equivalent, St Columb's College (founded in 1879), its perceived primary function was the early education of future clerics. About one o'clock the headmaster, the Reverend William Smyth, having seen his Lordship to his chair, accompanied by the Very Reverend Thomas Bunbury-Gough, the Dean of Derry, rose to call forward the prize-winners. Afterwards the bishop declared himself much gratified at presiding on the occasion and thus having an opportunity of rewarding well-directed industry and talent:

> I trust, my young friends, that the fair promise that you now give of future usefulness and eminence may be more than fully realised in your maturer years. I do hope that the honours you have now gained will excite in you a laudable zeal for prosecuting your respective duties with assiduity and care. Be assured that you will thus most effectually advance your own best interests and sustain the high character of this institution; for the credit and prosperity of which, all of us, as citizens and inhabitants of Derry ought to feel the most lively concern...

His Lordship was right to be concerned. Throughout the whole early history of the college it was dependent on financing from three sources: the City Corporation, the diocese and the Honourable the Irish Society and money was always most reluctantly granted by any of the three partners. A reporter covering the event revealed that an important member of the Irish Society, the Grocers' Company, had not only formally discontinued its annual subscription but had refused to pay in the years 1838–40.

21 DECEMBER 1933

On 21 December 1933 Foyle College held another prize day and this time the awards were distributed by the Duke of Abercorn, then Governor-General of Northern Ireland. It was quite a coup for Ernest Perceval Southby, the headmaster, to have His Grace of Baronscourt attend the event. The duke was welcomed to the Guildhall stage by J.R. Hastings, chairman of the board of governors. The duke began by apologising for the absence of his wife who was indisposed and claimed that he was more frightened at the prospect of addressing an audience of boys than older people 'because he was an old man, or as they would have termed it in his schooldays, "an old buffer". In those days elderly gentlemen used to utter a lot of platitudes to him but they went in one ear and out the other.'

It got the laugh he was angling for, that was dutifully repeated when he said that he had never believed, as he was frequently told, that schooldays were the happiest time of their lives, and would not do so now. What he did say was influenced by the world depression of the early Thirties that had deepened the economic slump in the city. His advice was practical, if not very original. He urged them to play the game and behave like gentlemen, and then things would come easily. They should make themselves as neat as possible; in seeking employment clothes made such a difference. With good old Derry courage they would carry through. He neatly overturned the old speech-day cliché by saying that, unlike most similar platform speakers, he had won prizes at school, 'two or three but still I did'. After the laughter and applause, he told them that 'As far as I remember, one was a treatise of the gospel of Luke.'

His next remark won him a volley of not unexpected applause. He said that his wife had asked him to secure with the headmaster's approval, of course, an extra week's holiday. 'I believe it rather lies with the Minister of Education but if I can put in a good word I shall do so.' Then he put his finger to his lips to let them share the secret. After the distribution of awards the duke accepted as a gift *The Charm of Birds* by Viscount Grey of Falloden. When the distinguished guests had said their pieces the headmaster announced that as far as results were concerned they had had a good year. He advised the pupils that the school governors had approved the new school uniform which would comprise black coat, black striped trousers, school tie and white collar. The proceedings concluded with 'God Save the King'.

22 DECEMBER 1942

Five people lost their lives on 22 December 1942 in broad daylight when a small tenement house at 138 Bogside was gutted shortly after eleven o'clock. But for the presence and heroism of seventy-four-year-old William J. McCrossan the death toll would possibly have been worse. It was believed the tragedy was caused by a bucket of tar catching fire whilst being heated in the kitchen for use on the roof of a piggery which was being erected by one of the victims.

There had been eight people in the house, with the names of the dead being: Michael Mallett, aged 25; his two children, Michael, aged four, and Emma, aged two; and Mrs Mary Ann McCrossan and her brother, William John Diver, both old age pensioners. The three survivors were the aforementioned William J. McCrossan, formerly a dock labourer; his son, Leo, aged 37; and Mrs Greta Mallett, husband of the deceased Michael. Greta, who was rescued from the flames, was taken to the Londonderry City and County Hospital in a state of severe shock, having sustained serious burns to her face, arms and head. The news of her husband and children's demise was broken to her by the Reverend J. McNally.

Once the fire was spotted, the alarm had been quickly raised and the neighbours who hurried to the scene were soon joined by workers from the city abattoir, a short distance away. Under the direction of Mr A.M. Logue, the abattoir superintendent, they formed a human chain relaying buckets of water to try to quell the flames. Some of the men attempted to enter the house but were beaten back by the heat and smoke which soon consumed the entire building. The fire brigade were quickly on the scene and entered the house after a half-hour struggle with the fire to discover the bodies of those who had perished.

Next door, in Harry Killen's house, William J. Crossan sat dazed. He had been having breakfast when he noticed the smoke. He ran upstairs and warned his son, Leo, who was an invalid, and Diver. The Crossans found the front door blocked by flames, so they went to the backyard, believing that Mrs Crossan had vacated the premises. From the back of the house he smashed a small window and pulled Mrs Mallett through it, but he could do nothing for Michael Mallett, whom he saw standing in the room with a child in each arm.

At a meeting of Londonderry Corporation, held on the same day, it was alleged there was a shortage of water. However, an inquest the following day heard that the water supply had been quite ample.

On 16 December 1966 John O'Leary, a fifty-six-year-old member of the travelling community, left his home, a tent that he had pitched at Dundrain, near Bridgend, across the border in Donegal, and began the four mile trek to Derry. There were a number of itinerant families living there, mostly travellers, and known to each other. At a court hearing in Carndonagh on 23 December, O'Leary described what happened next. Richard Valley was walking in the opposite direction accompanied by Teresa Millar, a girl from another camp family. By way of greeting O'Leary made some fairly joking remark about whether Teresa should be out in such company, at which Valley attacked him. O'Leary, still swathed in bandages, did not make clear what he meant by the remark, which may not have been intended as malicious, but reported instead that 'I was kicked on the ground and was all blood.' He went to a farmhouse about forty yards away for aid, and the owner did what he could but eventually sent for an ambulance. 'I was taken to hospital and had nine stitches put in my head.' The salient point was that he knew Teresa, who was just sixteen-and-a-half, and whose mother, also resident at Dundrain, was properly concerned about her welfare.

He continued his evidence, saying that he had left the hospital that morning because he feared that someone would steal his possessions: 'I could not stay any longer because if I did my stuff at the tent would be gone.' Valley, though not professionally represented, was granted permission to question the witness and accused him of producing a weapon and preparing to strike back. At a later stage Valley stated that he intended to marry Miss Millar and asked her to tell what actually happened when, having met her in Derry, he walked with her back to the Bridgend camp. She claimed that O'Leary was the first to attack Valley. 'He made a wind at him with an iron bar and later they were in grips. O'Leary fell to the ground but Valley did not kick him.' Valley continued, saying that the only reason he had attacked O'Leary was that he had a weapon in his hand.

Asked by Mr Justice Larkin as to whether Valley, whose address was given as 10 Eden Place in Derry—one of the 'disappeared' streets that once led from Chamberlain Street to Rossville Street—had any criminal record,

401

Superintendent Mullins of the Garda Síochána replied the he had had a record in 1958 but was clean since 1962. The judge said he was going to impose a sentence of four months with hard labour at Mountjoy Jail in Dublin but would suspend it if Valley would enter into a bond to keep the peace for three years.

24 DECEMBER 1934

The Strand Picture House, Derry, opened on 24 December 1934. Four days previously, the *Londonderry Sentinel* reported that the opening of the second largest cinema in Northern Ireland was 'eagerly awaited'. Over the entrance would be an 18-foot-long canopy with opalescent glass, neon tubular lighting and a neon electric sign.

The lobby, which gave access to the auditorium through three entrances, was approached by a flight of Sicilian marble steps with oak panelling and a frieze of plastic painting finished in imitation stone blocks and gold columns, and illuminated with tubular lighting on either side of the foyer. The foyer was symmetrically planned with twin staircases leading to the balcony. Facing the entrance was a clock, and overhead in the auditorium lobby was a large octagonal electric light. There were two main aisles in the balcony, along the back of which was a wide promenade. The colouring of the walls was in pastel shades with a bright red dado.

The balcony lounge had been designed so that part of it could be used as a café. There were five exits in all from the auditorium. The proscenium was carried out in fluted columns with illuminated wall brackets and frets of plastic painting. The cinema seats gave ample leg-room and were 'staggered' to afford an uninterrupted view from any area. The internal painting, which the *Sentinel* said was 'beautiful and gives a restful and pleasing effect', was mainly in pastel and soft rose pink and orange shades. The general illumination was by means of 'flush… ceiling lights' which gave 'a soft, diffused amber light'.

There was central heating provided by a system of low-pressure hot water radiators, and ventilation came from three electric fans. The newspaper commented that the cinema's acoustics were 'ideal, and the latest type of talkie apparatus has been installed'. The entire painting and decorative work had been carried out by the local firm of W.A. Dickie, Great James Street, and the architect was W.E. Taylor of the firm Messrs. Taylor and Lynch in Castle Street.

On 22 December the *Sentinel* notified its readers that the main feature would be *Here Comes the Navy* starring James Cagney, Gloria Stuart, and Pat O'Brien. There would be a continuous programme from 2.30 to 10.30 p.m. and, except on Bank Holidays, admission charges would be halved for the 'Bargain Hours' of 2.30 to 4.30 p.m. A children's matinee would be screened on Saturdays at 2.30 p.m. The cinema was managed by Mr W.L. James, who had been responsible for the success of the Waterside's Midland Cinema.

25 DECEMBER 1942

The first Christmas that the American forces spent in Ulster was, as they would have put it, 'something else!' The city had been tingling with the excitement of these exotic generous aliens, the kids eating Baby Ruth and Hershey candy bars, and the fathers and mothers in a haze of carcinogenic tobacco smoke from un-tipped Lucky Strike, Philip Morris and Camel cigarettes. And now there was Christmas, American style. One of the Christmas cards of the time had a verse that read:

> There'll always be a Christmas;
> Our flag is here to stay!
> So go ahead and celebrate
> In the real American way.

Christmas Day was relatively quiet. There was an 'At Home' in the American Red Cross Club when the sailors and marines were permitted to bring to the club 'the sort of girl you would bring to your home'. It was properly folksy but may not have been exactly what the servicemen had in mind for their entertainment. Dancing was the main attraction from three till six p.m. and it was followed by a movie show, confined to US servicemen. The dinner was the traditional one of turkey, followed by ice cream and free cigars, courtesy of Uncle Sam. That evening the officers' messes were hosts to fellow British officers and civilian friends.

There were four camps and children's parties were held in each, three on Christmas Eve and the fourth on the afternoon of Christmas Day. To these venues a total of 800 children were taken by bus for the most exciting party of their young lives. Until the coming of the 'Yanks' (a title which bewildered men from the Deep South) there were but poor pickings, with rationing, sweets on points that limited their accessibility, and two ounces of butter per adult per week. Now their wildest dreams were coming true, in Disney fashion: at the party there was an endless supply of ice cream, candy, cake and 'pop'. Each child was handed a bag of candy from the Christmas tree that also contained a chit for twelve shillings to be spent in local clothing stores—enough to buy them a good pair of trousers or a warm coat and, perhaps most important, a sound pair of boots.

These gifts were handed out by Santa Claus himself, looking exactly as Thomas Nast had drawn him seventy years earlier for *Harper's Magazine*, with red fur-trimmed coat and cap, breeches, and snow-boots. This Santa was Harry Harper and he hailed, not inappropriately, from Juneu, Alaska; he completed the magical effect by wearing rimless spectacles above his ruddy cheeks. To add icing on the cake there was a little entertainment by local artistes followed by cartoons featuring Donald Duck and other Disney favourites. The yuletide festivities were organised by Captain Van Leer Kirkman USN, with, of course, the real work being done by his Executive Officer, Commander E.R. Sperry USN.

26 DECEMBER 1862

On Tuesday, 3 December 1940, the *Londonderry Sentinel* reported that a sycamore tree which was on the Derry Walls between Butcher's Gate and Castle Gate had been blown down during a great storm that raged on the morning of 21 November. It was the last of fourteen sycamore trees planted on the western side of the walls, probably during the first half of the eighteenth century, in memory of the thirteen apprentice boys and James Morrison, who in 1688, had shouted 'Bring the great gun here' from the walls at Lord Antrim's men who had reached Ferryquay Gate, resulting in the flight of the Redshanks.

A Corporation minute of February 1752, which probably relates to these trees, orders Mr Nat Alexander to cut down the sycamore trees on the Mall Wall, dispose of them to the best advantage and give the amounts 'to Reverend John Torrens, Reverend Francis Huston, Alderman William Lecky and Mr William Kennedy, or either of them, which gentlemen were ordered to oversee the beautifying and improving the Mall Wall'. In August 1776, the Corporation directed the expenditure of a sum not exceeding twenty guineas to the planting of trees on the walls. In May 1782, the Corporation directed that the sum granted in August 1776 for planting the trees be paid to Sheriff Lennox for the purpose of building steps and making other improvements to the walls.

In his book, *The Walls of Derry: Their Building, Defending and Preserving*, Cecil Davis Milligan remarks: 'If some of the trees were cut down as a result of the 1752 resolution others survived for much more than another century and one for almost two more centuries.' The book was published in 1950, and the author related there were then 'twenty-five trees on the Wall between the Double Bastion and Butcher's Gate. They are all sycamores.'

Another of the memorial trees was blown down during a gale on 26 December 1862. The *Sentinel*, reporting this, said it was one of the sycamore trees 'planted on the Walls between Butcher's Gate and New Gate [Castle Gate]', adding 'some years ago two of the trees, which numbered fourteen, shared the same fate'.

Although the last surviving tree had been opposite the spot marked 'Site of Hangman's Bastion' it had no connection with that bastion; nor had the Hangman's Bastion any association with the incident relating to the driving of Protestants from the surrounding countryside under the walls by order of Marshal de Rosen in July 1689, and the defenders' threat to hang prisoners as a reprisal. The gallows for this purpose was erected on the Double Bastion.

Hangman's Bastion was named after an incident in which an escapee from the town had employed friends to let him down from the walls by a cord; they, by some erroneous means, got it about his neck and held him so long like that that they almost despatched him.

27 DECEMBER 1924

The few days after Christmas in 1924 saw a hurricane accompanied by heavy rain and resulting floods badly affect Great Britain and Ireland. Derry, on the western fringes, bore the full force of the typhoon that caused serious damage to the contents of shops in the lower part of Great James Street, Foyle Street and William Street, peaking on the morning of Saturday, 27 December. The Foyle overflowed its banks, drowning the quays and the adjacent thoroughfares. A particularly frightening element was the rapidity with which the waters rose and the depth they attained. Many people were trapped in their houses, the lower levels containing several feet of water.

In shops boxes of valuable goods could be seen floating about and businessmen were forced to wade with trousers rolled-up to get to their premises. The Great Northern Railway that ran from Foyle Road along the river as far as St Johnston was under three or four feet of water. William Hamilton, the harbourmaster, said that in thirty years of service he had seen nothing to equal it, while a member of his staff with fifty-three years' service said that it was much the worst he had seen. The foot of William Street, that had been built on the flood-plane, on land originally dredged from the river, was the worst hit. Water from the torrential downpour gathered at the foot of High Street, Harvey Street and Waterloo Street, meeting the tidal surge from the fast-flowing Foyle. The effect was to flood the ground floors of houses and shops to a depth of five feet. Residents forced to move to top floors could be seen waving handkerchiefs from upper-storey windows and offering words of sympathy to neighbours on the other side of the street.

Sackville Street was completely submerged and, though the inhabitants worked ceaselessly with brushes, there was little they could do until the ebb tide would allow the flood to wash back again into the river. One businessman who needed to leave his house to go to work was observed using a box and chair, stepping from one to the other in a tedious but ultimately effective process that finally got him out of the waters.

Not all the population were depressed at the catastrophe. Some children braving the December cold waded about the lesser-flooded streets, helping themselves to the apples, oranges and other fruits that were washed out of shops by the torrent. One grisly aspect of the flooding seized upon by the local press was the appearance of large numbers of rats which, dislodged from their usual nests, raced along the riverside streets looking for drier lodgings. The reporter covering the story for the *Derry Journal* summed up the reaction of older people in the oddly formal journalese of the time: 'The universally expressed opinion among aged citizens and businessmen of long standing was that such a visitation had never in their memory occurred in the city before.'

28 DECEMBER 1898

On Wednesday, 28 December 1898, evening strollers on Strand Road were alarmed to see flames under the archway that led into Rock Mills. In these days of instant communication it is odd to think how slowly things moved all those years ago. Wilson, the mill manager, was able to telephone the offices of the *Londonderry Sentinel* and ask the editor William Colhoun to go to the hundred yards to the fire station in Hawkins Street and give the alarm. No one thought it odd that the station did not have a telephone of its own and the local press congratulated the brigade in being at the scene within a quarter of an hour.

As happened on a later occasion when the Guildhall went on fire they had difficulty with water pressure. The jets could not reach beyond the first floor and the main source of what was now 'a seething mass of flame', as one reporter put it. It lit up the whole stretch of the river, brightening the dark December evening. The conflagration was clearly visible in the Waterside, and so significant did it seem from Ebrington Barracks that Captain Tisdall and Lieutenant Martyn mobilised a company of fifty soldiers and brought them 'at the double', carrying their own fire-fighting equipment. Tisdall considered the emergency so urgent that he did not follow the cumbersome protocol that the military might only be required to assist on receipt of a signed request from a magistrate.

In the best tradition of farce it was soon discovered that the army hose couplings did not fit the local hydrants, but the soldiers compensated by pumping water from the river, near at hand and with an inexhaustible supply. In spite of all the efforts of soldiers and fire-fighters it became clear to those in command that the old mill was beyond saving, and they decided that the local brigade should concentrate their hose-play on the expensive new engine that had been constructed in a separate building beside the mill and accessible to them from the Strand Road. The soldiers were given the task of saving the boiler located on the river's side. This entailed a certain amount of danger, and the word spread among the great crowd of spectators, that had pushed its way closer to the action, that there was a serious risk of the building exploding.

In this matter Robert Gilliland, a member of the family that owned Rock Mills, showed his mettle. In spite of the heat and the danger of wild fire, he entered the building and, opening the valves, removed the likelihood of blast. When it was seen that the boiler and the engine housings were safe the combined fire-fighting forces, military and civilian, turned their attention to a store facing the road and a roller mill at the other side. There were no personal injuries and the local press announced that the damage was at least partly covered by insurance.

29 DECEMBER 1891

On 15 December 1891, a barque, the *Countess of Dufferin*, under a Captain Doble, departed from St John's, the capital and seaport of Newfoundland, for Derry with a cargo of timber. For ten days she met with variable winds and weather but on Christmas Day a gale struck the barque with hurricane force. All that day the *Dufferin* attempted to hold her own, but it was only a matter of time before the ship would crumple in the turmoil. So passed the succeeding days of 26, 27, 28 and 29 December, with no sign of rescue.

That same December the *Arlington*, a barque whose master was Captain Samuel Davis, had brought a cargo across the Western Ocean and was homeward bound to New York. During the night of 28 December, Captain

Davis had a remarkable dream. He heard someone calling from a ship in distress. So vivid was the vision that he sprang from his berth and ran on deck to see if all was well. There was no sign of a ship, so Davis went below again. But his vivid dream would not disappear. Two items seemed to stand before his eyes and to ring in his ears: 'Latitude 52 North; Longitude 21 West.'

He got out his chart and fixed his position. It was a day's sail away to the northward, far out of the track of steamers and sailing ships. To search for a derelict there or thereabouts would mean a wide deviation from his course and serious loss of time. It might be a wild goose chase. Nonetheless, the cry for help was so real that the captain altered his course two points to make the *Arlington* cross the spot in the ocean where his dream told him the derelict was lying.

At breakfast he related his dream to the mate, James L. Hemeon, and though he did not, of course, protest, secretly he thought his captain had lost his wits. Nevertheless, he followed the orders, and all that day the *Arlington* ran on farther and farther north. Suddenly, about three o'clock in the darkness on 29 December, the lookout spied a darker mass upon the sea and sang out just in time: 'Something on the lee bow. No lights up. Cannot make it out.' Captain Davis pulled up, indignant, for running at night without lights was a crime, and shouted through the speaking trumpet: 'What ship is that? Why haven't you your lights on?'

Out of the dark came the answer: 'Barque *Countess of Dufferin*—water-logged—sinking—we have nothing to put up light with—please stand by till morning and take us off.' Davis shouted back: 'I'll stand by.' Five hours passed, the *Arlington* keeping her eyes on the derelict. By eight o'clock it was just light enough for the sailors to see what they were doing. Two trips were essential to take off the eleven men from the *Dufferin*. The operation took an hour-and-a-half but all the crew were rescued, having given up hope of ever seeing their native city again.

30 DECEMBER 1870

William Alexander Goligher, a native of Derry, was born on 30 December 1870, the third son of Mr and Mrs John Goligher. The following tribute, written by 'K.C.B.', appeared in the *Irish Times* shortly after his death, which occurred on 15 August 1941:

> Trinity College men and women who had the good fortune to be pupils of Dr
> Goligher twenty or thirty years ago will find it hard to believe that he is dead—so

active and energetic was he, so large a place did he fill in the life of the College. His small, squarely-built figure, crossing and re-crossing the Front Square, gave such an impression of power and energy that a cartoon of the period in which he was represented as a locomotive seemed to those who knew him to be happily inspired.

He entered Trinity College from the Academical Institution, Londonderry, in 1888. His undergraduate distinctions were many, including the Henry Hutchinson Literary Scholarship in 1891, and the Vice-Chancellor's Prize for English verse for a poem on 'The Tercentenary of Trinity College' in 1892. That year he graduated with Senior Moderatorships in classics and modern literature, winning a large gold medal in the latter, and, though in later life he was a classics man first and foremost, he retained his affection for German and Spanish to the end, and possessed a profound knowledge of these languages. He had also studied law with much success, and his legal knowledge was often of service to his university.

Shortly after his degree, Goligher set himself to work for Fellowship, and won Fellowship prizes in 1894 and in several succeeding years. He changed his plans, however, and for some time appeared to have given up the idea. He was induced to offer himself once more as a candidate in 1902, and was promptly elected. Shortly afterwards (1904) he was appointed to the Chair of Ancient History, a Chair already made famous by Mahaffy and Tyrrell. The appointment gave him much pleasure, for there was no savant for whom he had a greater admiration than Mahaffy, to whose memory he'd paid a brilliant tribute not long before on the occasion of the centenary of Mahaffy's birth.

In 1909 the scope of the chair was widened, and he remained Professor of Ancient History and Classical Archaeology until 1934, when he became Regius Professor of Greek. A most accomplished tutor, he was feared as well as respected by his pupils, for he did not suffer fools gladly. Most of them learned in time that great kindness dwelt behind a somewhat fierce exterior, and that this man who rebuked them so sternly for ignorance or neglect, would fight like a lion for them if they were in trouble.

After a long apprenticeship as representative of the Junior Fellows on the board, Goligher was Registrar between 1930 and '37, during which period he possessed a capacity for taking trouble over every detail which is both rare and valuable. With advancing years, too, he became less terrifying, and many a junior lecturer found himself put at ease by Goligher, who was never too busy to listen and help. When Dr Thrift was elevated to the Provostship in 1937 Goligher was chosen as natural successor in the Vice Provostship, and in that capacity retained all his interest, and much of his influence, in college affairs to the last.

The newspapers of the beginning of the twentieth century looked and felt notably different from the hot press of today. There were no screaming headlines, no print of greater size than 10-point and the default size for ordinary use was 8-point. The sentences and the paragraphs were longer and the standard of English much higher. Provincial papers had rarely more than four pages, but the print was so small and the pages so covered that there was plenty of reading material available. Most elderly people owned magnifying glasses to supplement their spectacles that were often bought across the counter in the forerunners of Boots. Headlines were printed in capitals and larger lettering reserved for advertisements, which were becoming a necessary source of income.

EPPS'S COCOA was given up to 30-point as were the many advertisements for undergarments, like corsets and camisoles, all terribly decorous and without illustrations. The word 'brassiere', though not unknown, was not current for at least a decade. Advertisements for patent medicines were in a majority, with 'lung' tonics, having a high content of alcohol and ether, beating the others in popularity, even with teetotallers. Other favourites were laxative products, especially Beecham's Pills, which led the others in a race to the water-closets, as lavatories were called at the time. Mention should be made, too, of pills to restore 'vitality' in men.

The *Derry Journal*, then published on Wednesdays and Saturdays, was facing stiff opposition from the first popular paper of the modern era, the *Daily Mail*, launched in 1896, which carried world news as well as the doings in Derry, Donegal and Tyrone. Its coverage of local stories was comprehensive but unsensational. A typical local account appeared in the edition of 1 January 1904. In a piece almost six inches by two and a quarter it gave an account of the inquest on a dead sailor.

With the headline 'River Foyle Drowning Fatality', it reported that the coroner Mr Lindsay held an inquest in Mr Conner's licensed premises in Strand Road on 31 December 1903 'touching the death of a young seaman whose body was recovered from the river Foyle the previous evening'. John McCarron, a twenty-year-old sailor from the steamer SS *Burtonport* had been missing since 21 November until his body was discovered 'at 3.30 p.m. on the evening of 30 December by Sergeant John Ferguson of the Harbour Police. Closer examination showed witness that the body was that of seaman John McCarron whom he knew. He had the remains removed to the morgue.'

Several witnesses, including McCarron's father, testified that he was of strictly sober habits. He had been last seen on Foyle Street by Detective George Taylor at 5 a.m. on 21 November heading for his boat berthed at the Liverpool shed, just behind the Northern Bank. It was just another human tragedy and the only verdict available to the jury was 'Found Drowned'.